Public Management and Administration

Also by Owen E. Hughes

BUSINESS, GOVERNMENT AND GLOBALIZATION (*with Deirdre O'Neill*)
AUSTRALIAN POLITICS
AUSTRALIAN POLITICS: Realities in Conflict (*with Hugh V. Emy*)

Public Management and Administration

An Introduction

Fourth Edition

Owen E. Hughes

palgrave
macmillan

Published by
PALGRAVE MACMILLAN

Palgrave Macmillan in the UK is an imprint of Macmillan Publishers Limited, registered in England, company number 785998, of Houndmills, Basingstoke, Hampshire RG21 6XS.

Palgrave Macmillan in the US is a division of St Martin's Press LLC, 175 Fifth Avenue, New York, NY 10010.

Palgrave Macmillan is the global academic imprint of the above companies and has companies and representatives throughout the world.

Palgrave® and Macmillan® are registered trademarks in the United States, the United Kingdom, Europe and other countries

ISBN 978-0-230-23125-2 hardback
ISBN 978-0-230-23126-9 paperback

This book is printed on paper suitable for recycling and made from fully managed and sustained forest sources. Logging, pulping and manufacturing processes are expected to conform to the environmental regulations of the country of origin.

A catalogue record for this book is available from the British Library.

A catalog record for this book is available from the Library of Congress.

Contents

List of Tables and Boxes		vi
Preface		vii

1	An Era of Change	1
2	The Role of Government	19
3	The Traditional Model of Public Administration	43
4	Public Management	74
5	Public Policy	103
6	Governance	123
7	Regulation, Contracting and Public Ownership	144
8	Stakeholders and External Constituencies	166
9	Accountability	185
10	Strategic Management	208
11	Leadership and Managing People	228
12	Financial and Performance Management	250
13	E-government	273
14	Public Management in Developing Countries	295
15	Conclusion: Paradigms in Public Management	315

References	338
Index	360

List of Tables and Boxes

Tables

2.1 General government total outlays as percentage of GDP, selected OECD countries, 1994–2010   38

2.2 Government spending, selected OECD countries, 2008   39

Boxes

1.1 The seven verities of traditional public administration   5

3.1 Weber's principles of bureaucracy   49

3.2 Weber and the position of the official   51

4.1 Functions of general management   77

10.1 The Bryson model of strategic planning   215

11.1 A typical career service personnel model   231

12.1 Public financial management reform   259

Preface

Since the 1980s, the public sectors of most Western countries have undertaken major changes. Many developing countries have also instituted reforms. To have such widespread reform is uncommon; in normal circumstances, reform may occur in one country or another more-or-less sporadically. On looking back, what does seem clear is that, from the mid-1970s, many governments had become dissatisfied with their own public sectors, and in particular with the methods of bureaucracy and a lack of managerial competence. The time-honoured processes, procedures and theories of public administration seemed ill-equipped to deal with rapid change, and with public administrators often being regarded by political leaders as obstructive and unresponsive. Reforms were instituted in many jurisdictions. And, once change began, it became apparent that many of the old ways were not universal, were not needed and could be supplanted by other forms of management. It is argued here that this period of change represents a paradigm shift from the traditional model of public administration, dominant for most of the twentieth century, to public management.

This fourth edition is a major rewrite of earlier editions. The first edition in 1994 was somewhat speculative in arguing that there was now a new approach to organizing government, and that the old model of bureaucracy was being replaced. By 2012 and the fourth edition, many of the changes have not only taken effect, but the corporate memory that there ever was an earlier theory has largely gone from actual practice. There may be some historical interest in the traditional model of public administration but its direct relevance has faded away. There are many opinions as to what constitutes public management, and various views are discussed in what follows. The fundamental point of difference between the two models, as discussed in Chapter 1, is that administration means following instructions, and management means control or taking in hand. A public manager is required to achieve results and is, moreover, personally responsible for doing so. From this change, much else follows. If the manager is to achieve results, the ways and means of doing so will draw on other disciplines to assist in the primary task.

The change to public management does not mean the automatic embrace of the reform movement known as 'new public management', often abbreviated to NPM. There were many reforms, and a range of approaches in different countries, so it was rather simplistic to classify them all as NPM. NPM has either been superseded or perhaps it never existed other than in the eyes of critics. 'Public management' is the term in general use now, being descriptive of what practitioners actually do.

The content and order of chapters has changed from the Third Edition. The first part (Chapters 1 and 2) are essentially introductory. Chapter 1 is still titled 'An Era of Change', as the era of public sector change that began in the 1980s shows no real sign of diminishing. Chapter 2 introduces the scope and scale of government, as anyone interested in public management needs to have some idea of the arguments about and theories of its roles in society and the economy.

The second part (Chapters 3–6) discusses different approaches to the study of the public sector, with chapters on public administration, public management, public policy, and governance. Chapter 3 is about the traditional model of public administration, argued here to be obsolete despite its long and distinguished history. Chapter 4 sets out the main changes involved in the adoption of public management and discusses why NPM is not a useful construct. Chapter 5 discusses public policy, and Chapter 6 is a new chapter on governance, an area of study seen by some as taking over from other kinds of management.

The third part (Chapters 7–9) looks at different ways of interacting with actors outside the agency, including stakeholders, business interests and the issues of accountability endemic in the public sector. An external focus is one of the key differences in a public management model compared to a public administration model. Public managers now have to interact with outsiders much more than before. It is normal to have to work with interest groups, to engage contractors and to work with business. The chapter in earlier editions on public enterprises has been subsumed into a new chapter, which now also looks at contracting and regulation.

The fourth part (Chapters 10–13) examines internal matters within agencies in the context of public sector change, discussing explicitly how these were run and organized in the traditional model and in public management. Major change has certainly occurred in all of these: financial systems have been transformed and personnel arrangements widely adopted that emulate practice in the private sector, rather than assuming that the old administrative ways were best. In all these cases, it is remarkable how far public management has now moved away from public administration. For example, the discussion of leadership (Chapter 11) is quite antithetical to a Weberian bureaucracy, as, in that theory, any kind of personality was strictly to be removed from any consideration. Chapter 14 looks at public management, with the key issue being whether developing countries need to be path-dependent by first following the traditional model of bureaucracy before adopting public management.

Finally, Chapter 15 considers the issue common across the whole work: whether public administration and public management can be considered paradigms, and in addition looks at some of the criticisms of managerial reform as a whole. Criticisms have been made by other writers regarding whether there is a new paradigm (or even an old one), whether there is a global movement of public sector reform, and even whether anything has in fact changed at all. The argument in this book is that there has been a major change and it deserves the appellation of a paradigm. Anyone working in public services can see that something has happened. Public management is different from traditional public administration and, regardless of critiques, it is here and here to stay. However, change does not occur without cost. There are perennial issues of accountability; and perhaps some managerial changes will result in little, if any, benefit. There is, however, no reason to assume that public management will be dropped and the traditional model re-adopted; indeed, more recent developments in the field, such as leadership, collaboration, co-production, even governance, are all even further away from the traditional model of public administration.

There are a number of people to thank. First, I wish to thank my publisher, Steven Kennedy, of Palgrave Macmillan – the publisher since the first edition back in 1994. I also wish to thank others who have helped me with this book and its predecessors. In the fields of public management and public administration these include, in no particular order, Peter deLeon and Linda deLeon, Delmer Dunn, Colin Campbell, Christoph Reichard, Neil Carter, Gordon Clark, Ferrell Heady, Stephen Osborne, Erik-Hans Klijn, Ignacio Criado, Dong Keyong, Zhang Chengfu, Li Bing, and Jean Hartley. At Monash, I must point to colleagues including Deirdre O'Neill, Linda McGuire, Rob Brooks, David Watson and Julian Teicher, and former Deans, Gill Palmer and Stephen King; and at the Australia and New Zealand School of Government, colleagues John Alford and Allan Fels. I must also mention Colin Reaney and Karee Dahl, whose house in France I stayed in while writing the first edition. Most of all I wish to thank Cathy Woodward and our three daughters Caitlin, Sophie and Lucy, now aged fifteen, twelve and nine.

OWEN E. HUGHES

Chapter 1

An Era of Change

Chapter Contents

- Introduction
- Administration and management
- Public sector reform
- Imperatives of public sector change
- Public management as a field of study
- Conclusion

Introduction

The internal operations of government have always been vitally important to the working of society, even though, most of the time, they barely capture the attention of the public mind. Only rarely have the organizational structures behind the more overt world of politics become notably controversial; only rarely have the more arcane debates held within those parts of academia dealing with public management and administration spilled over into wider arguments across society. It is argued here that the transition from what was once known as public administration to public management, starting in the latter years of the twentieth century, has been a time of change with quite wide ramifications in the governance of many societies around the world. For a time, at least, the management of government was actually noticed.

We contend that the traditional model of public administration, though time-honoured as a result of its tenure over most of the twentieth century, has been discredited both theoretically and practically. There were, in many countries, quite dramatic changes in how the public sector operated; indeed, it has been argued that the end of the twentieth century saw 'a revolution in public administration that is every bit as profound as that which occurred at the turn of the nineteenth century, when Weberian bureaucratic principles began to influence many governments around the world' (Kamarck, 2000, p. 251). A further ten years on, there has been no reduction in the demand for further reform as many countries face financial and societal issues of a

1

kind not seen for at least half a century. There seems to be a universal, though never-ending, demand for better management in government; but quite how to achieve this is less clear.

If an observer could compare an agency in, say, 1980, with the same one thirty years later, undoubtedly much would have changed. Here it is argued that this broad change can be characterized as the transition from traditional public administration to public management. What cannot be done is to nominate a single date, place, or even theorist or theory, that sets out precisely where the transition occurred; indeed, despite much having changed, the transformation is still not complete.

The adoption of new forms of public management has meant the emergence of what can be argued to be a new paradigm for the organization, management and governance of the public sector. After the first decade or so of reform, attention shifted to changes other than narrow managerial reform, including leadership, governance, collaboration and co-production, networks, sophisticated financial changes and much else. These are discussed in later chapters, but what they reinforce collectively is just how far public management has moved away from the precepts of traditional public administration. In a formal bureaucracy, for example, leadership is simply not needed; indeed, it should be avoided. Any kind of personality in administration – 'patrimonialism' in Max Weber's terminology – is irrational. Also, the traditional model of administration paid scant attention to the outside at all, where one of the more enduring themes of more recent managerial reform is active engagement with the community in various ways. A traditional bureaucrat would be against this, as, in his/her view, any solution derived from public engagement or participation by external stakeholders would be inferior to that derived from the internal logic of the rational/legal principles of formal bureaucracy.

In what follows it is argued that public management is quite different from public administration. A public administrator is someone who follows the rules to the letter, who carries out instructions given by someone else, in theory the political leadership. Socialized into the primacy of process and procedure, a public administrator is responsible only indirectly for the delivery of results. On the other hand, a public manager is personally responsible for the achievement of results, and from this fundamental change much else follows. If results are to be delivered, a way needs to be found to show that results have occurred. If a public manager is personally responsible for the delivery of results, he or she will draw on any kind of theory – management, economic, behavioural or sociological – that will help in carrying out the task.

While there has been a remarkable shift in many countries, public management, and most notably its market-based variants, has not taken over completely. It has been challenged in many ways, with virtually every aspect picked over by a legion of critics, many of them appearing to prefer the old ways. Particular reforms have not worked well. For example, the laudable idea of performance monitoring led to an often absurd regime of management to arbitrary targets with no obvious means of reaching them. Paying bonuses to good performers has also not worked; even modest bonuses led to resentment among those who did not receive them. Cutting government expenditure has also largely failed, as the notions of cuts were overcome by the reality of ever-increasing health and other social costs in ageing societies.

Public management has evolved from the somewhat extremist days of the 1980s and early 1990s. It has moved on into newer areas, with ideas such as governance, leadership, collaboration and co-production (to name but a few) coming to the fore, but there has been no perceptible reduction in the earlier preoccupation with economics. Compared to the days of public administration somnolence, there is a lively, if incomplete, debate about public management as a still-developing field. Even if the precise shape of newer approaches is not fully settled, the traditional public administration paradigm has been overturned and will not return.

Administration and management

Whether the words 'management' and 'administration' are different from each other is an obvious but important part of the present argument (but see also Hood, 2005). The words are close in meaning, but a brief foray into semantics allows a case to be made that the terms 'management' and 'administration' are significantly different, and that a manager performs a different role from an administrator.

The *Oxford English Dictionary* defines *administration* as: 'an act of administering', which is then 'to manage the affairs of' or 'to direct or superintend the execution, use or conduct of'; while *management* is: 'to conduct, to control the course of affairs by one's own action, to take charge of'. The Latin origins of the two words also show significant differences. Administration comes from *minor* then *ministrare,* meaning 'to serve, and hence later, to govern'. Management comes from *manes,* meaning 'to control by hand'. The essential difference in meaning is between 'to serve' and 'to control or gain results'.

From these various definitions it appears that administration essentially involves following instructions and service, while management involves, first, the achievement of results, and second, personal responsibility by the manager for results being achieved. Public administration is an activity that involves serving the public. It is concerned with procedures, with translating policies derived from others into action and with office management. Management does include administration (Mullins, 1996, pp. 398–400), but also involves organization to achieve objectives with maximum efficiency, as well as genuine responsibility for results. These two elements were not necessarily present in the traditional administrative system. Public administration focuses on *process*, on procedures and propriety, while public management involves much more. Instead of merely following instructions, a public manager focuses on achieving *results* and taking responsibility for doing so.

Closely related words may change by usage. As part of this general process, 'public administration' has clearly lost favour as a description of the work carried out within government; the term 'manager' is more common, where once 'administrator' was used. As Pollitt (1993) notes: 'formerly they were called "administrators", "principal officers", "finance officers" or "assistant directors". Now they are "managers"' (p. vii). This may simply be a 'fad' or 'fashion' (Spann, 1981), but it might also reflect a real change in expectations regarding the person occupying the position, pointing to the significant differences between administration and management.

These changes of title are not superficial. In the narrow sense, the words 'administration' and 'management' are shorthand descriptions of an activity or a function. It does not matter what a person or a function is called, so long as the work gets done. But in a broader sense, words have power. If changing a position description from 'administrator' to 'manager' changes the way the incumbent sees or carries out the position, or the expectations from superiors, the words used to describe it are far from trivial. The term 'manager' may be used more often, simply because it is a better description of the work now done.

Administration and management are argued here to have conceptual differences, and adding the word 'public' to them should reflect these differences. But there is more involved than merely a change of name. If a public manager is personally responsible for the achievement of results, there then need to be systemic changes to measure the performance of agencies and individuals alike. Conditions of employment and accountability arrangements also change as a consequence of public management; political leaders can no longer be regarded as the source of all policy, but nor are they irrelevant. The apparently simple acquisition of responsibility for results by public managers leads to much else.

The end of public administration

The traditional model of public administration was established by the end of the nineteenth century, though its antecedents had been in place much earlier (see Chapter 3). It was the dominant approach for most of the twentieth century. A set of precepts – what can be termed the seven verities of public administration – can be recognized as establishing the model.

Box 1.1   The seven verities of traditional public administration

1. Organization by the principles of *bureaucracy*. Governments should organize themselves according to the hierarchical, bureaucratic principles most clearly enunciated in the classic analysis of bureaucracy by the German sociologist Max Weber (Gerth and Mills, 1970). Although adopted by business and other institutions, these precepts were carried out far more diligently and for longer in the public sector.
2. There should be *one best way* of working, and strict adherence to scientific management principles (Taylor, 1911) would provide the single best way of operating an organization – with detailed procedures set out in comprehensive manuals for administrators to follow.
3. The principle of *bureaucratic delivery*. Once a government had involved itself in a policy area, it also became the direct provider of goods and services through the bureaucracy.
4. General belief among administrators in the *politics/administration dichotomy*; that is, where political and administrative matters could be strictly separated. The administration would be an instrument merely to carry out instructions, while any matters of policy or strategy were the preserve of the political leadership (Wilson, 1941).
5. The motivation of the individual public servant was assumed to be *the public interest*, in that service to the public was to be provided selflessly.
6. Public administration was considered to be a special kind of activity and therefore required *a professional bureaucracy* that was neutral, anonymous, employed for life (and under quite special employment conditions in many countries), with the ability to serve any political master equally.
7. The tasks involved in public service were indeed *administrative* in the dictionary sense; that is, following the instructions provided by others without having personal responsibility for results.

These points reinforce each other. As an administrator only carried out instructions from political leaders, this meant that he or she had to be neutral and anonymous. 'One-best-way' thinking meant that delivery could only be by the bureaucracy itself, as that was axiomatically the best way. An administrator is not responsible for results, and this meant that results became secondary to issues of process. Over time, though, the principles became self-reinforcing myths.

The seven verities of public administration were eventually challenged by a series of public sector reforms, starting in the early 1980s. For a start, and contrary to the first verity, bureaucracy is indeed powerful but does not work well in all circumstances. Being bureaucratic is now more often seen as being difficult and obstructive rather than axiomatically efficient. Second, trying to find 'the one best way' is elusive in practice; there are likely to be many possible solutions rather than just one. One-best-way thinking leads to rigidity in operation; and more flexible management systems pioneered by the private sector have increasingly been adopted by governments. Third, direct delivery by bureaucracy is not the only way to provide public goods and services; governments can operate indirectly through subsidies, regulations or contracts. At the time of writing, governments provide more services indirectly and this presents a challenge to the old ways (Kettl, 2002, p. 46). Fourth, the politics/administration dichotomy was a myth; political and administrative matters were in reality always intertwined. Even though this had generally been recognized for a long time in public administration, the implications for management structures had not been followed through and the myth was perpetuated. Fifth, while there may be public servants motivated by the public interest, it is now incontrovertible that they are also political players in their own right, working for themselves and their own advancement as well as for their agency. Also, there can be many versions of the public interest, so relying on such a vague notion is futile. Sixth, the case for unusual employment conditions in the public services is now harder to justify, given the changes that have taken place in the private sector. Old-style public service conditions of service such as a job for life are now rare in the private sector. Finally, the tasks involved in running the public sector are now considered to be more managerial and not merely administrative; that is, they require someone – a manager – to take responsibility for the achievement of results, and to be a leader.

We maintain that the seven verities constitute a paradigm of their own – the traditional model of public administration – but that a paradigm shift to public management began as a result of the theoretical and practical problems of the traditional model (see Chapter 3).

Public sector reform

In the early 1980s, governments in many parts of the world began to reassess their bureaucracies and to make fundamental changes. This process may have started following the severe economic problems in the United Kingdom, New Zealand and Australia, but a number of other countries followed. As Caiden (1991) argued, 'All blamed the dead hand of bureaucracy, especially the poor performance of public bureaucracies and the daily annoyances of irksome restrictions, cumbrous red-tape, unpleasant officials, poor service and corrupt practices' (p. 74). A radical change in organizational culture began. For those inside the system, the time of transition was difficult; it was a threat to their familiar way of life, and change was not achieved without cost. Newer managerial approaches had problems, not least of them the disruption to standard operating procedures, and poor morale. There seemed to be a long way to go before a new results-based management could emerge. It appeared that focusing on efficiency had led to public services becoming somewhat inhuman; trying to find measures for results led to questions about what the role of a government in society should be, and how it should be implemented.

By the 1990s, so many countries were undertaking reforms that the change could be seen as a global movement (see Kettl, 2005). In 1991, the term 'New Public Management' was coined (Hood, 1991), often abbreviated to 'NPM' to conceptualize in academic terms those changes that had occurred notably in the United Kingdom. NPM did become the most widely used term for the overall managerial pro-gramme. However, with hindsight, the term has not been useful or helpful in understanding managerial change. Instead of assisting in understanding the process, NPM eventually became little more than a convenient label used mainly by those opposed to managerial change in the public sector. Moreover, there were so many differing definitions and specifications of NPM that the concept itself had little utility.

Public management is a more useful term than NPM in accounting for and even describing the longer-run set of changes. Public manage-ment refers clearly to management in the public sector, but does not convey the sense of there being a single coherent programme or agenda. Public management simply means the management that is carried out in the public sector; it can and must vary over time and place, and in response to circumstance. Far more important in the longer run than the idea of a single managerial programme was the more gradual acceptance that the work of public servants was now about management in the sense of personal responsibility for the achievement of results.

Public and private management

One of the criticisms of public sector reform has been over its deriving theories and techniques from the private sector. However, in itself this is neither novel nor significant as a general criticism of reform, though particular aspects may not necessarily work in a different setting without due care being taken. Historically, the private and public sectors have borrowed from each other; from the emulation of military models of bureaucracy by the private sector, to explicit copying by governments of the ways of organizing private railway companies in the nineteenth century. Still, there are several reasons why the two sectors are not alike, and can never be so.

First, in a way that is not characteristic of the private sector, public sector decisions may be *coercive*. Citizens can be forced to comply with decisions, pay taxes, have their property compulsorily acquired, and be subject to sanctions deriving ultimately from the coercive powers of the state. Not all public activities are coercive, but those that are need to be performed carefully. Private enterprises have more freedom to be *arbitrary*. They can charge different customers varying prices; they can refuse to deal with them; they can ignore normal procedures. The public sector needs to be seen to be fair, to operate only through due processes, and not to misuse its undoubted coercive power.

Second, the public sector has different forms of *accountability* compared to the private sector. While company management is theoretically accountable to its board and shareholders, the public employee is accountable to the political leadership, parliaments, the public, and to various parts of the judicial system, often with differing views as to what the particular organization should do. Accountability can be problematic in the private sector (Chapter 9), but it is argued to be less certain and more uneven in its application in the public sector.

Third, the public service manager must cope with an *outside agenda* largely set by the political leadership. This is quite different from an organization where the shared motivation at all levels of the hierarchy is to make money. The presence of political authority 'is more than simply an influence on public strategic management; it is a defining characteristic' (Bozeman and Straussman, 1990, p. 214). Politicians may require action that detracts from good management practice, can change their minds frequently, and require administrative action to be taken for quite blatant political reasons. Having a large part of the agenda imposed by politicians reduces the scope of action of a manager, even as managerial change requires the public manager to be responsible for results.

Fourth, the public sector has inherent *difficulties in measuring output* or efficiency in production. It lacks 'bottom-line' criteria analogous to profit in the private sector. In government there is rarely agreement on goals or ways of measuring them, nor can it be assumed that every person in the organization will abide by them either. The difficulty of measuring performance in the public sector, whether of individuals, groups or whole organizations, permeates management as a whole. That there is a difficulty can be taken too far. Measurement and evaluation are possible in the public sector, but they may be less precise and perhaps less meaningful. Some assessment of performance still needs to take place, however, otherwise there might be a part of the public sector serving no useful function and evading scrutiny.

Finally, the public sector's sheer *size and diversity* make any control or co-ordination difficult. Governments and their advisers struggle to co-ordinate the very different activities for which they are responsible. Spending money on building a road can mean, at the margin, that a hospital or a school are not built. Co-ordination across portfolios must ultimately be a matter of political choice and there are limits as to how far choices can be informed technically. This too is unlike operations in the private sector.

It is clear that there are major differences between the private and the public sectors (see also Boyne, 2002). The question is whether these differences between them are, first, enough to need a specific form of management; and, second, to require the use of the traditional administrative model rather than any kind of managerial model. On the first point, it must be argued that the public sector is sufficiently different to need its own form of management. Flynn (1997), for example, suggests that managing public services is different from managing services in the private sector (p. 12). Allison (1982) also observes that 'public and private management are at least as different as they are similar, and ... the differences are more important than the similarities'; further, 'the notion that there is any sufficient body of private management practices and skills that can be transferred directly to public management tasks in a way that produces significant improvements is wrong' (p. 29). Boyne (2002) argues that management techniques 'cannot be exported successfully from one sector to another because of differences in organizational environments, goals, structures and managerial values' (p. 118). There may be advantages in adapting and using some practices pioneered in the private sector, but the basic task is different in each sector.

However, the second point does not necessarily follow. Even if it is argued that the sectors are different, this does not mean that the traditional administrative model is the only valid way of managing in the public sector. The development of public management as a discipline should be seen as due recognition that the task of public servants is now managerial and not administrative, and that a form of management can be developed bearing in mind the differences between the sectors.

Imperatives of public sector change

The wave of public sector reform that started in the 1980s was in response to several interrelated imperatives: first, the very weight of the public sector in society; second, changes in economic theory; third, the impact of changes in the private sector; and, fourth, changes in technology. Since the early 1990s, reform emphases have also changed. In the earlier period, there was more concern with reductions in the role of government than there was later, but all four imperatives have had lasting impacts.

The size and scale of the public sector

In the 1970s and early 1980s, there were wide-ranging attacks on the size and capability of the public sector (Friedman and Friedman,

1980). Governments themselves, and particularly their bureaucracy, had become a source of some unease in parts of the community – at the same time, paradoxically, as more services were demanded of them. Major reforms in the operation of the public sector followed the election of Margaret Thatcher as the British prime minister in 1979 and Ronald Reagan as the US president in 1980 (Ranson and Stewart, 1994; Farnham and Horton, 1996; Flynn, 1997). These were not, however, simply reforms; rather, the whole conception of the role of the public sector within society was challenged. These two governments were expressly, if paradoxically, anti-government, and they set about changing attitudes to government and the way it was carried out.

There were three main aspects to the attack on government. First, it was suggested that the *scale* of the public sector was simply too large; and that government consumed too much of the resources of the economy. To some extent, the reform of public sector management was 'a reaction to the perceived excesses of the welfare state, both in the macro sense, as reflected in the growing size of government and associated fiscal deficits, and in the micro sense, in the perceived recognition of limits to government's ability to solve all of our problems' (Holmes and Shand, 1995, p. 552). Cuts to government spending followed even in those European countries – Spain, Italy, Germany, Sweden – where the public services had traditionally been extensive.

Second, there were governmental responses to arguments about the *scope* of government. It was argued that governments were involved in too many activities, and that alternative means of provision existed for many of these. In response to these criticisms, many formerly governmental activities were returned to the private sector. While privatization of formerly public enterprise was contentious in the United Kingdom during the 1980s, it became a widely accepted strategy, including in developing countries. In some jurisdictions, any service that could conceivably be provided by the private sector was likely to be turned over to private providers, either by contract or direct sale.

Third, there was a sustained attack on the *methods* of government, with bureaucracy in particular becoming highly unpopular. Provision by bureaucratic means was regarded increasingly as guaranteeing mediocrity and inefficiency. If activities were to stay in government hands, other means of organization than bureaucracy needed to be found.

The ideological fervour of attacks on the role of government, and efforts to reduce its size, had faded somewhat by the late 1990s, and there was a greater appreciation of the positive role of government. Even international agencies, such as the World Bank and the IMF, which had earlier encouraged developing countries to reduce government input, changed their tune to focus on good governance (World

Bank, 1997). However, there is no doubt that trying actively to reduce government participation was a major reason for moving away from traditional bureaucracy in the early days of the reform movement.

The global financial crisis (GFC) that began in mid-2008 did seem for a time to have reinvigorated the scope of government. As an institution, governments did step in to save the financial sector from itself and in ways that seemed like a throwback to a more socialistic era, with nationalization of some banks and even, for a time, the large and iconic American car-maker General Motors (GM). However, it soon became clear that there was no ideological shift here; it was rather that nothing other than government involvement could stop the crisis getting worse. For the most part, enterprises were quite quickly returned to private hands, but what was left in most developed countries, notably the United Kingdom and the United States, was massive government debt. This debt burden would, in turn, lead to even greater pressure for the public sector to become more efficient, and for there to be a high probability of a further and even deeper round of public sector reform.

Economic theory

In the 1970s, some conservative economists (Stigler, 1975; Friedman and Friedman, 1980) argued that governments were *the* economic problem restricting economic growth and freedom. Theorists claimed that evidence backed up their arguments that less government interference would improve aggregate welfare by improving economic efficiency. Instead of governments forcing people to do things through the bureaucracy, markets were regarded as superior in every respect, with words such as 'freedom' or 'choice' (Friedman and Friedman, 1980) replacing what had been described as the 'serfdom' of government (Hayek, 1944). A harder-edged form of economics became prominent in the economics profession at this time, usually called 'neo-classical economics' or sometimes 'economic rationalism' (Pusey, 1991). This paralleled the decline of Keynesian economic thought, and the major role it gave to governments, as countries tried to cope with stagflation and other serious economic problems following the oil price shocks of the 1970s. Within governments, policy advisers and even politicians and the bureaucracy embraced neo-classical economics and its advocacy of making more use of markets inside and outside government for policy-making and the delivery of services (Kettl, 2002).

The change in economic thinking profoundly affected the public bureaucracy (Boston, 1995; Boston *et al.*, 1996). Government economists, influenced by outside groups and think-tanks, arrived equipped with theories that seemed to offer more precision, more utility and more consistency than the vague, fuzzy notions of traditional public administration. Economic theories, such as public choice theory, principal–agent theory and transaction cost theory (Walsh, 1995; Boston *et al.*, 1996; Kettl, 2002), seemed to offer more rigour and be more policy-relevant than vague notions such as 'the public interest' that were used in traditional administration.

Public choice theory

The sub-category of economics known as public choice theory gave theorists a plausible weapon to support their views that governments were too big and inefficient, and offered a sharp contrast to the traditional model of public administration. Public choice is concerned with the application of microeconomics to political and social areas (Mueller, 1989; see also Chapter 3 in this book). From standard economic assumptions of rationality, predictions can be made and evidence sought to check whether those predictions are borne out. For example, instead of being regarded as motivated only by the public interest, individual bureaucrats and politicians should be looked on as trying to maximize their own utility and enhance their own welfare, rather than focusing on furthering the public interest.

Making an economic assumption about behaviour does have its uses. It can be assumed that the consumption of a good supplied by the public sector follows standard supply and demand curves. It follows that, to reduce consumption by clients, the agency can set a higher price for it through user charges, or limit its supply by taking away eligibility to, say, high-income earners. Such strategies have become more common and tend to support at least this part of the theory. The difference compared to other policy or administrative models is that behaviour can be *assumed*, and models built on the assumption can be tested empirically. Public choice theorists do generally conclude that the 'best' outcome will involve a maximum role for market forces and a minimum role for governments. These views found a ready governmental audience.

However, at the time of writing, after more than thirty years of public choice theory and attempts to apply it to government, results have been mixed (Dunleavy, 1991; Self, 1993; Walsh, 1995, pp. 16–20). Markets do not work better than bureaucracy under all circumstances. It could be said that the assumption of individual rationality is too sweeping and ignores any public-spirited behaviour by public servants. On the other hand, an assumption of utility-maximizing behaviour is more able to account for behaviours such as office politics, agency politics and the ever-present drive for promotion, than can be explained by regarding public servants as selfless and motivated only by the public interest.

Principal–agent theory

The economic theory of principal and agent has also been applied to the public sector. The theory was developed for the private sector to explain the divergence often found between the goals of managers (agents) in private firms and shareholders (principals), and how to structure systems of accountability (Jensen and Meckling, 1976; Jensen, 2000). In the private sector, shareholders seek maximum profits, while managers – the shareholders' agents – might want long-term growth and higher salaries for themselves. Principal–agent theory attempts to find incentive schemes for agents to act in the interests of principals. The activities of agents (managers) need to be monitored by shareholders, through the possibility of takeovers or bankruptcy, while the presence of a non-executive board may help in 'attenuating the discretion of management' (Vickers and Yarrow, 1988, p. 13). In addition, to ensure that their behaviour complies with the wishes of the principals, agents should have contracts that specify their obligations and rights.

The application of principal–agent theory to the public sector leads to disturbing comparisons in accountability compared to the private sector. In the public context, it is difficult to determine who the principals are, or to find out what they really want. The principal – the owners – of the public service may be the public as a whole, but its interests are so diffuse that effective control of the agents – politicians and public managers – is unlikely to be effective. In the public sector, there is no influence, as there would be in the private sector, from the profit motive, the market in shares and bankruptcy or trading while insolvent. If principals have no adequate means of making sure that agents carry out their wishes, agents are less likely to perform. If there is an agency problem in the private sector, it is likely to be worse in the public sector.

Agency theory gives some backing to those arguing for contracting-out as much of the public sector as possible. In this way, the agency relationships would become those of the private sector, which are most often assumed to work better. Contracts could be used for employees and for organizations, and those arrangements would have incentives, both positive and negative, in an attempt to ensure accountability.

Transaction cost theory

The other key economic theory underlying the managerial changes has been that of transaction costs. As set out by Williamson (1986, 1996), this challenges the notion that transactions are without cost, and specifies the circumstances in which a firm might prefer market-testing or contracting to in-house provision. The same may apply to the public sector. There are some transactions that would be less costly if contracted out, to reduce administrative costs and provide some competition. However, following Williamson's argument further, there are some public sector transactions for which market testing has been made mandatory, where in-house provision would actually be better. A case-by-case approach is likely to be better than an ideological one.

The theories of the 'new institutional economics', particularly public choice theory and principal–agent theory, combined with an ideological predilection among many economists for market solutions, have provided some intellectual coherence to cutting public services, as well as restructuring their management. In addition, several public administration precepts – lifetime employment, promotion by seniority, the terms and conditions of public employment, traditional accountability, even the theory of bureaucracy – have been challenged for being based on poor theory and providing inadequate incentives for good performance.

Private sector change

A further imperative for public sector change has been rapid changes in the private sector, and the realization that the management and efficiency of the public sector affects the private economy. The desire to seek out and retain international business has led countries to try to reform their governments 'in order to create a better investment and business climate' (Kamarck, 2000, p. 232). The private sector in most countries has faced enormous changes in recent years, in an adjustment process that has generally been difficult. It would be defying the credibility of governments if they did not also change the public sector.

The moves towards privatization in its various forms – such as contracting-out and reducing government spending – could be considered as shedding aspects of government that are no longer parts of its 'core business'. Globalization adds an extra imperative to the reform of administrative structures within government (Hughes and O'Neill, 2008). In a number of policy areas it is important for governments to tailor their policies to stay competitive with other nations. Instead of an era of change in government, or an era of change in the private sector, it is now an era of similar changes in both sectors, an era claimed to be transformational (see Held *et al.*, 1999; Giddens, 2002).

Technological change

Technology should be regarded as another driving force both towards new forms of public management and away from traditional bureaucracy. Technological change affects management, including the management of government; indeed, technology 'may reshape organizations and institutions to better conform to its logic' (Fountain,

2001, p. 12). It could be argued that the theory of bureaucracy did fit
very well with the then-available technology of a single document that
is then passed up or down a hierarchical structure. What newer technology can do is to compress the levels of a hierarchy so that information is readily available to senior managers at the same time as at lower
levels. With the adoption of forms of e-government, technologically
driven change has accelerated. The use of information and communication technologies (ICTs) such as distributed computer systems, internet
linkages and relational databases has led to a reconceptualization of
the very way that bureaucracies work. There are those who believe that
ICT changes lead to a need to reconceptualize government completely
into something called 'digital-era governance' (DEG) which 'holds out
the promise of a potential transition to a more genuinely integrated,
agile, and holistic government' (Dunleavy *et al.*, 2005). The e-government movement may do this, or may also be seen in the longer run
merely as governments using the best tools available at the time, as
they always have. However, it is inarguable that management of the
public sector changes with the kinds of information technology currently available. The potential for e-government is discussed later in the
book (see Chapter 13).

Public management as a field of study

Public policy, public administration and public management are all
terms that refer essentially to the same thing, which is how the administrative parts of government are organized, and how they process
information and produce outputs in policies, laws or goods and services. It is notable, however, how little contact public administration,
public policy and public management academics have with each other
(Lynn, 1996; Kettl, 2002). Despite these approaches being innately
related to each other and to politics and political science, there are
often quite distinct academic followers of each approach, with their
own conferences and journals. There are differing views on the
primacy of these terms.

Rosenbloom (1986) argues that 'public administration is the use of
managerial, political, and legal theories and processes to fulfil legislative, executive and judicial governmental mandates for the provision of
regulatory and service functions for the society as a whole or for some
segments of it'. This is a comprehensive, overarching definition, putting
within public administration every conceivable part of the public
sector.

A narrower view is taken here. 'Public administration' refers to the
earlier form of both management and the academic study of the public
sector. The theory dominant for most of the twentieth century is

usually called the 'traditional model of public administration' in contrast to 'public management' or 'managerialism'. 'Public policy' refers to an output of government, as well as to the public policy or policy analysis school that places emphasis on rationality and empirical methods. Other terms such as 'the administration' or 'bureaucracy' are unavoidable and should be taken as having ordinary, rather than value-laden meanings. NPM is avoided as far as possible, because of its lack of specificity and because it is much more value-laden than other terms.

Another term is 'governance'. The notion of governance as something separate or different from public administration and public management, or even as the next grand theory, has re-emerged in recent years. This may be governance as an overarching concept, as what was once called public administration (Frederickson, 2005) or 'digital era governance' (Dunleavy *et al.*, 2005) or even 'New Public Governance' (Osborne, 2006) as the successor to NPM. Governance is hard to specify clearly, and the idea that governance is a completely new model or movement may well be overstated. It is, however, important to note the distinction made between government as the apparatus of coercive power and governance as a broader concept describing forms of governing that are not necessarily in the hands of the formal government (Pierre and Peters, 2000). The concept of governance can be useful for public management as opposed to the narrower concept of government. The best way of managing a particular policy issue may be to work with the private sector, or privatize a function or by use of regulation. Direct provision by government and the bureaucracy is not precluded; it rather depends on the circumstances where the best form of governance might be found.

The utility of any theory of public management, like public administration before it, should depend on how it helps practical public managers to understand and solve real problems. Public managers do set out to solve problems, and to achieve results, drawing on whatever skills, theories and practices they can muster. This is one reason why many governments turned away from the vague traditional notions and used economic models that seemed to offer more precision. Perhaps there is a new pragmatism where the ideological preconceptions and battles of the past are subsumed into simply obtaining results by using 'whatever works', and where practical managers attempt to solve problems in the best way they can (Alford and Hughes, 2008).

On the ground within agencies, the work of the public sector continues. Staff are employed, and functions carried out for, and on behalf of, the public. Much of what is done, particularly in service delivery, can be characterized as being largely that of public management. The generation that was familiar with the rigid bureaucratic model is rapidly disappearing, and younger public servants just get on with their work, wondering what all the fuss was about. It does seem clear that the reforms found greater acceptance within the public services than critics might have wished.

Conclusion

It is argued here that the traditional model of administration has been replaced by public management as the culmination of a reform process that started in the 1980s. The main reason for this change is simply that the old model no longer worked very well. Political leaders and the community alike regarded the service they received earlier from the public service as poor in quality, unaccountable, tied up in process and out of touch with reality. Governments responded to criticisms of their management by instituting a series of reforms. These have taken place in every conceivable area of public life: the machinery of government, personnel practices – recruitment, promotion, tenure, policy-making processes, financial management, relations with outside groups and all kinds of other procedures. There is greater use of empirical methods, sophisticated statistics, and, in particular, the theories and methods of economics and management.

The changes have not been free from tension. The early phases of public sector reform were often quite destabilizing for those working within the system. Old verities were replaced by uncertainty. Jobs that were once considered to be for a lifetime were replaced by systems of personal performance management, restructuring and redundancy, often for no apparent reason. Service-delivery agencies, which did not need to include government employees, could undertake the bulk of the day-to-day work under contract, with a small policy department. Governments still needed a public service, but tried to reduce its size.

Reform is undertaken with the aim of improvement, but it could also be argued that there has been so much reform, so much change, that management capability has not improved very much. In some jurisdictions, government agencies were hollowed-out so far that policy capability and corporate memory were lost. Any process of change involves winners and losers, and among the losses might have been some valued parts of the traditional model of administration. There remain serious questions to be addressed regarding ethics, accountability, the theoretical basis of the new model, and larger questions concerning the role and organization of public services. However, even if public management is not a settled model, even if some changes may work better than others, the likelihood is for even more change in the managerial direction. There would be no return to the traditional model of administration in place for most of the twentieth century.

Changes to the public sector have led to a fundamental questioning of its role and place in society. The main point to be made here, and in successive chapters, is that a new paradigm for the management of the public sector has emerged; one that has moved the public services inexorably away from traditional bureaucracy. Public administration is no longer a useful descriptor for the organizations and operations of the public sector; public management is now firmly in place. Despite criticisms of managerial reform, some of them justified, governments did not go back to the older model. Public management has changed significantly since the early days of reform. But public management it remains, and not public administration.

Chapter 2

The Role of Government

Chapter Contents

- Introduction
- The need for a public sector
- Instruments of government
- Market failure as the basis for public policy
- Phases of government intervention
- The size of government
- Conclusion

Introduction

The role of government in society should be of great interest to public managers. In mixed economies there must be some demarcation between, and a rationale for, those activities that fall into either the public or the private sector. The dividing line changes in different nations at various times: in some periods, government scope and scale increases; in others it decreases. In recent decades, the line has moved away from the public towards the private sector. This transfer of resources and functions to the private sector has affected those who work in the public sector or rely on it in some way. If a public activity is less valued by the community, if activities historically provided by governments are being marketized, the rationales for doing these things are of obvious interest to public managers.

Starting in the early 1980s, many OECD nations undertook a reassessment of the role of their public sectors. Those who believed in the model of the free market as the basis for a more dynamic economy asserted that governments were involved in inappropriate activities, and that their size and roles should be cut back drastically. Should governments provide the goods and services they do, or should some be handed to the private sector? Should governments subsidize or regulate to the extent they do? Such questions also raise the very political matter of how various members of the community perceive and value the things that governments do, as well as draw from and inform their ideological views as to the appropriate role of governments in society.

The extent of government in the economy – its scale and scope – has traditionally been the fundamental dividing line between the Right and the Left in ideological terms. In very broad terms, the Left favours greater government spending and control of economic activity, while the Right favours less of both. Unsurprisingly, the 1980s debate over the public sector became, at times, an intense ideological struggle in some countries, one in which the last vestiges of socialism were to be rooted out by new Right governments (Isaac-Henry *et al.*, 1997). Opposition to change was no less intense as public sector workers, unions and supporters tried to maintain government activities at their previous levels. Initially, public sector reform was seen as part of this great ideological debate about the role of governments. Certainly, the Reagan and Thatcher Governments led sustained theoretical and practical attacks on the *command* or bureaucratic part of society in favour of the *market* principle. In the early stages, the trend towards a market-based public sector reflected concerns about the role of government, as well as worries about the efficiency and effectiveness of the bureaucratic model. However, as the reforms continued through changes of government, it became clear that party-political considerations, even fairly ideological ones, were only a minor part of public sector reform.

In the first decade of the twenty-first century, the idea of government did make something of a comeback. In the wake of the terrorist attack on New York in September 2001, the prestige of the United States government rose, as it was the only institution that could deal with such a crisis. Corporate failures such as Worldcom or Enron reduced confidence in the private sector and increased demands for government regulation of the activities of business. The global financial crisis which began in 2008 showed what could happen when regulation of the financial sector was inadequate, and again, governments were turned to for a solution. In a return to Keynesian theory, seemingly discredited in the 1970s, stimulus packages of government spending attempted to ameliorate the effects of the crisis. And, despite a 25-year history of privatization, the British government found itself the owner of financial institutions, while the United States government became the effective owner of GM, once the world's biggest car maker and a bastion of the free enterprise system. But, even as governments regained more of a role, there seemed to be little thought about this being a fundamental turn to socialism, rather it was seen as a temporary expedient to cope with an immediate problem.

Attacks on the scale, scope and methods of the public sector in the 1980s did give credence to measures to reduce government operations and change its management. Governments wishing to cut the public sector found little impediment in a community seemingly disillusioned with bureaucracy, even if it wanted no cuts in services. Moreover, the lack of support for bureaucracies and public servants meant that these became useful and defenceless scapegoats for governmental problems. It does seem paradoxical that the main reason for the increase in the size of government is public demand for more services, such as health care and welfare for ageing populations, but at the same time there is great hostility to the levels of taxation required to pay for them.

Societies do need to better appreciate the positive roles of what are their own governments. It is no exaggeration to say the public sector affects the entire economy and society. Without a legal framework to enforce contracts, private business activity would not work. Regulations, taxes, permits, infrastructure, standards, and conditions of employment all affect decisions made in private markets. The public sector is a large purchaser of goods and services from the private sector. Government redistributes income from better-off members of the society to those less wealthy. The public sector has a crucial role to play in determining real living standards, which depend for most people on government services – the quality of schools, hospitals, community care, the environment, public transport, law and order, town planning and welfare services – at least as much as the quality of consumer goods and services.

As will be seen, there are various theories put forward to decide which functions should be provided by governments. Some argue that only goods or services that cannot be provided by markets should be provided by governments. Others contend, however, that as government is the embodiment of the will of the people expressed through the political process, there should be no limits to its scope.

The need for a public sector

By convention, the economy is divided between the private and public sectors. The public sector is defined by one author as 'engaged in providing services (and in some cases goods) whose scope and variety are determined not by the direct wishes of the consumers, but by the decision of government bodies, that is, in a democracy, by the representatives of the citizens' (Hicks, 1958, p. 1). This definition does not capture the full scope of public sector activity, but it does contain the key point that the public sector is the result of public, political decision-making, rather than involving market processes. Another view is that the prevalence of government 'may reflect the presence of political and social ideologies which depart from the premises of consumer choice and decentralised decision making' (Musgrave and Musgrave, 1989, pp. 5–6). If the normal mechanism of exchange is through the market, what are the possible functions of government?

Governments are command-based – they can force people to comply – whereas markets are voluntary. Also, every person in a society is subject to the state. Both these points – universal membership and compulsion – make governments fundamentally different from the private sector. Membership of a state is not usually a matter of choice, and 'the fact that membership is compulsory gives the State a power of compulsion which other organizations do not have' (Stiglitz, 1989, p. 21). Other transactions are voluntary. The private sector does have ways of forcing compliance – with contracts, for example – but in legal activities the only allowable force to compel compliance is through the system of laws provided by government and backed, ultimately, by the police and the army. Even privately provided mediation or arbitration relies, in the end, on the legal system provided by government.

Though the private and public sectors are usually seen as being quite separate, the division of the economy into two mutually exclusive sectors may be artificial (McCraw, 1986). There is so much interaction between the two that setting up a strict dichotomy is rather misleading. It could be argued that the modern capitalist economy is a 'thoroughly mixed system in which public and private sector forces interact in an integral fashion' and the economic system is 'neither public nor private, but involves a mix of both sectors' (Musgrave and Musgrave, 1989, p. 4). The private sector relies on governments for infrastructure and the system of laws, notably the key requirements of property rights and the enforcement of laws, both being necessary for markets to work (Stiglitz, 2001). Governments rely on the private sector for the production and supply of goods and services, and for tax revenue. The interaction between sectors is more subtle than simply seeing them as separate and necessarily antagonistic.

There are some things governments should or should not do; some that it does well and some that it does badly. Even during the time of *laissez-faire* economics, in the nineteenth century, there was some role for government. The most fervent market economist today still sees some use for government even beyond Adam Smith's three roles for the sovereign discussed later in this chapter.

The World Bank has stated that there are five fundamental tasks that lie at the core of every government's mission. These are: (i) establishing a foundation of law; (ii) maintaining a non-distortionary policy environment, including macroeconomic stability; (iii) investing in basic social services and infrastructure; (iv) protecting the vulnerable; and (v) protecting the environment (World Bank, 1997, p. 42).

Anderson (1989, pp. 19–22), lists seven basic functions of government, which he claims are generally applicable:

- *Providing economic infrastructure.* Governments provide the basic institutions, rules and arrangements necessary for the satisfactory operation of a modern capitalist system. These include the definition and protection of property rights, the enforcement of contracts, the provision of a standard currency, weights and measures, corporate charters, bankruptcy, patents, copyright, the maintenance of law and order, and the tariff system. Modern economic societies are also political; it would not be possible for the economic system to operate without the rules of the game and the framework for economic life being provided by the political system. Contracts are legally binding because of the laws established by the state and backed, in the last resort, by state sanctions.

- *Provision of various collective goods and services.* There are some public goods which, while being valuable to the whole society, are difficult for individuals to pay for according to the amount of good used. Once they have been provided for one person, they are available for all. These include such items as national defence, roads and bridges, aids to navigation, flood control, sewage disposal, traffic control systems and other infrastructure. Many are characterized by their broad use, indivisibility and non-excludability and are, therefore, public goods.

- *The resolution and adjustment of group conflicts.* A basic reason for the existence of government is the need to resolve or ameliorate conflict in a society in pursuance of justice, order and stability. This may include actions to protect the economically weak against the economically strong. Governments may seek to replace exploitation with equity through child labour laws, minimum wage legislation, or workers' compensation programmes.

- *The maintenance of competition.* Competition does not always maintain itself in the private sector, and government action is often required to ensure that businesses do compete. Without government monitoring, the benefits of the free enterprise system would not necessarily be apparent. In the absence of suitable regulation, companies would be able to form cartels, restrict access to their products and fix prices.

- *Protection of natural resources.* Competitive forces cannot be relied on to prevent the wasteful use of natural resources, to protect against degradation of the natural environment, or to care for the interests of future generations. Damage to the environment from market activity is a textbook example of externality and market failure. Action by governments is the main way to alleviate environmental damage.

- *Minimum access by individuals to the goods and services of the economy.* The operation of the market sometimes produces results that are cruel or socially unacceptable in their impact on people – causing poverty, unemployment or malnutrition, for example. Others, because of illness, old age, illiteracy or whatever, may

simply exist outside the market economy. There is often disagreement over the level of assistance needed, the aggregate cost, and particular programmes that might have some social costs.
• *Stabilization of the economy.* There have always been fluctuations in the business cycle of the economy, with boom conditions being followed by recessions. Government action may be able to alleviate these through the budget, monetary policy, or control over wages or prices. While government action is often imperfect and sometimes wrong, the community regards its government as being responsible for the state of the economy, and there is a public expectation that governments should act to try to solve any problem.

Anderson (1989, pp. 22–3) points out that the functions outlined here are pretty much universal and are, in fact, a fairly standard set of government functions applicable to most countries. Some are market failures – the provision of public goods, or environmental damage, for example – but others are not. Rather than reflecting any particular theory, the list reflects how things are in reality. What is missing, however, is exactly how the government is to act in a given case. Even if the government is justifiably concerned with, for example, the water supply for public health reasons this does not necessarily mean it should be the sole supplier. It could allow for private suppliers with government regulation. The precise instrument to be used and the design of public policy are not trivial matters even where intervention is justified.

Instruments of government

An instrument is the method that a government uses to intervene; the mechanism used when government action is justified in some way. Most government intervention in the economy can occur through four available instruments: (i) *provision,* where the government provides goods or services through its budget; (ii) *subsidy,* a sub-category of provision, where the government assists a company or organization in the private economy to provide government-required goods or services; (iii) *production,* where governments produce goods and services for sale in the market; and (iv) *regulation,* which involves using the coercive powers of the state to allow or prohibit certain activities in the private economy. The use of these has varied over time and according to the particular government function.

Government provision

Direct provision by a government through its budget forms the major part of its operations. The budget sector includes those areas of government funded by taxation rather than user charges: that is, those that provide non-market goods and services – such as roads, defence, education, health and some social welfare schemes. The budget sector includes transfer payments where the government does not ultimately spend money, but redistributes it from one class of taxpayer to another. Most government activities occur through direct provision and are set out in the budget (see Chapter 12). While there have been attempts to reduce government provision, this has proved difficult to do. There is obvious and understandable resistance to cuts in pro-grammes that benefit individuals or groups, particularly those of polit-ical importance.

Subsidy

Subsidies are where the private sector provides a particular good or service, but with some assistance from government. Subsidies vary widely: they can include subsidies to farmers or industry, or to private bus companies or private schools, trains, airlines or health insurance; indeed, there is no real limit to scope. While part of the funding is public, the detailed administration takes place in the private sector, with govern-ments mainly involved in monitoring activities to ensure their money is being spent in approved ways. In practice, it is hard to separate the cate-gory of government subsidy from government provision. The amount of subsidy appears in the budget in the same way as provision.

Production

Unlike provision or subsidy, government production takes place outside the government budget, and users are charged in the same way as if the items had been provided by the private sector. The govern-ment, usually though not always through a public enterprise, sells a private good (or service) – for example, electricity supply – to con-sumers and use is precluded if consumers are unwilling to pay. Some countries maintain large public enterprise sectors – for example, in China and in some countries in Europe – but the United States has always had very little public enterprise beyond the US Post Office. As might be expected, there is rather more controversy over the role of the public enterprise part of the public sector, and the process of privatiza-tion in the 1980s and 1990s greatly reduced examples of it (see Chapter 7).

Regulation

Regulation is where a government uses its power to make laws to allow or prohibit activities, usually in reference to the economy, though they may involve other parts of society. Regulations can include setting tariffs on imports, granting licences or permits to allow particular activities, and regulating the labour market. These rules can vary from the minor and non-intrusive – the collection of statistics, for example – to a blanket prohibition of specific economic activities with very high penalties for non-compliance, such as for the smuggling of illegal drugs.

Regulations can be either economic or social, with the former being aimed at encouraging business and other economic actors to undertake certain activities and avoid others. Social regulation is usually seen as an attempt to protect the interests of citizens and consumers, especially with regard to quality standards, safety levels and pollution controls. Regulation of the business sector is widespread, including financial regulation, often price regulation, quantity regulation, quality regulation and various product or packaging standards. Particular professions may be licensed by a government agency, and businesses must comply with government-mandated occupational health, safety and environmental standards. Also, most countries have some kind of competition policy or antitrust legislation to enforce competition within private markets and to restrain any tendency to collusion and monopoly by businesses.

Changes to regulations and the regulatory system have been a major part of public sector reform. Much economic regulation – that is, regulation explicitly intended to affect entry, supply or pricing decisions in the private sector – has already been eliminated or revised in a number of countries. At the same time as there are demands to reduce regulation, however, there are other demands to increase it. In the United States, the passing of the Sarbanes–Oxley Act in 2002, requiring enhanced accountability for companies, followed a period of corporate scandal widely held to be the result of inadequate regulation of business. Similar regulatory failure of financial institutions has been blamed for the global financial crisis (GFC) that began in 2008. Calls for deregulation and so-called 'cutting red-tape' continue, but it is likely that there will be more regulation rather than less in the future.

Choice of instruments has been further classified by Salamon (2002) who argues for what he calls 'tools' – a wider range than those discussed here as instruments. He argues that 'whereas earlier government activity was largely restricted to the direct delivery of goods or services by government bureaucrats, it now embraces a dizzying array of loans, loan guarantees, grants, contracts, social regulation, economic regulation, insurance, tax expenditures, vouchers, and more' (p. 2). Bardach (2009) also lists eleven things that governments do: taxation, regulation, subsidies and grants, service provision, agency budgets, information, the structure of private rights, the framework of economic activities, education and consultation, financing, and contracting and bureaucratic and political reforms (pp. 127–35). It is correct that there is a 'dizzying array' of possible government actions, but they all fall into the four instruments discussed here. Tax expenditures, for example, are best seen as subsidies, as are loan guarantees and insurance. Social and economic regulation are sub-categories of regulation. Provision, subsidy, production and regulation encompass the economic instruments available to government, though governments do have other ways of acting – mediation, exhortation, information, and non-economic laws, to mention but a few – that are hard to fit into neat economic categories.

Which instrument to use?

There is no simple answer as to which instrument of government policy is preferable. Different instruments have been invoked by particular theories and at different times. Countries without a history of government production, notably the United States, do have a long history of government regulation. Depending on how tight regulation is in practice, a government could be almost as intrusive as if it were providing the good or service itself. Also, the instruments of public policy need not be mutually exclusive. Combinations are possible, with the precise mix varying between nations.

There have been attempts to reduce government provision and subsidy through the government budget, although even famed budget-cutters such as Mrs Thatcher in the United Kingdom found this very difficult to carry out in practice. Still, there was what turned out to be only a short-term reduction in the seemingly inexorable increase in the share of government in the economy. There is also a difference in the way that government services are provided, with these occurring less often through public services and more often through the private or voluntary sector, via contracts. The shift to contracts should not be seen as a reduction in provision. Rather, it is a change from final delivery by public services to delivery by the private sector of a government service with the taxpayer still bearing the cost through the government budget.

Government production has declined markedly with the extensive privatization of public enterprise. As an instrument of government policy, the idea of production certainly lost favour in the 1980s. It is unlikely to return other than as a temporary policy response to the failure of a private company deemed worthy of a government bail-out. Such a case was the rescue by the United States government of GM, in mid-2009, during the GFC. Within two years it was returned to majority private ownership, so its 'nationalization' was only temporary and expedient rather than an ideological preference for government ownership. The preferred instrument of government does appear to be towards regulation rather than direct provision, subsidy or production, though with a shift in its character from the restrictive role of regulation, which was often anti-competitive, towards pro-competitive and more responsive regulation.

Market failure as the basis for public policy

While the sale of goods and services is the very basis of a capitalist society, there are some circumstances where markets may not provide all the goods and services that are desired, or may do so in ways that have an adverse effect on the society as a whole. The market mechanism alone cannot perform all economic functions; public policy is needed 'to guide, correct, and supplement it in certain respects' (Musgrave and Musgrave, 1989, p. 5). Theories and models can be developed which state that government action should occur where markets fail, provided that governments would do a better job in those particular circumstances. Some of the goods or services which markets may not provide optimally include: education, law and order, environmental values, national defence, roads and bridges, hospitals and health care, welfare services, public transport and the like. Even if markets can provide these there may be socially undesirable effects. Markets are undoubtedly powerful and can provide a system of allocation and distribution for many goods and services, and do so without the intervention of governments. But markets cannot do everything and there are several kinds of market failure.

Public goods

There is a reasonably clear distinction to be made between public and private goods. A private good is enjoyed by whoever paid for it, and other potential users can be excluded. Once someone pays the asking price – for example, to buy a car – the property is owned by that person through the process of exchange and no one else can use it unless the owner gives permission. Public goods are quite different as they benefit all users whether or not they have paid the purchase price. They are 'non-excludable'; that is, if provided to one, the goods are available to all. A lighthouse cannot be reserved for the use of only those ships that have paid for the service. It is not possible for citizens to decide what level of national defence they individually want and then pay precisely that amount in their taxes. Some citizens may object to paying anything for national defence and there are obvious issues of 'free-riders' opting out of paying. Also, there are roads and bridges that benefit a particular community, but for which tolls or some other way of charging individual users are not feasible or too costly.

There seems to be no way except through government of providing such public goods, though the dividing line between public and private goods is often rather blurred. There are now fewer undisputed public goods than once was thought to be the case. Some roads or bridges may be directly charged for, or there may be other payment methods such as an annual fee for bridge or motorway use. Road usage could be calculated and charged through satellite tracking. Defence remains the classic public good, however, one which, in practice, can only be paid for by taxation of the whole society, not merely by those who value being defended by the armed forces. This is normally funded as a part of the government budget, though in Chile, starting in the late 1950s, a large proportion of the nation's defence spending came directly from royalties on copper production. This kind of hypothecated funding is most unusual.

The literature also points to *merit goods*. These are services, such as education and health care, that are socially desirable, but which markets may not provide optimally. The market could provide them in a technical sense – they can be excludable – but there may be benefits to the whole society that can justify some government involvement. An educated workforce is economically desirable because an educated worker is able to perform more complex tasks; government provision or assistance may improve overall educational outcomes for the benefit of society as a whole. But how education is funded is a general problem. If education is regarded as a purely private good, there are obvious equity problems between individuals as well as efficiency problems if those with innate ability are not educated. Some level of government funding could assist in overall societal outcomes.

Health care funding is another difficult merit good issue. While the delivery of health services by doctors and hospitals is broadly consistent across developed countries, there are varying mechanisms of financing it, with some countries seeing health care essentially as a private good (USA), others as a public good (UK), and others as a mix of both (Canada, France and Australia). Private health insurance markets may not provide adequate cover when individuals assess their risk of illness or accident as being lower than it actually is. Also, private providers have incentives to deny health insurance to individuals from at-risk groups or those who are already sick. As a result, there tends to be under-insurance and eventual demands for government involvement. Many countries have an uneasy mix of private and public provision of these merit goods, without there being any definitive answer as to the most desirable point on the public–private continuum.

Externalities

Market transactions often have effects on third parties, or on the environment, that only government action can alleviate. As noted earlier, it is possible to buy a car and its fuel through the market, as private goods, but the externality or 'spill-over' effects on air quality or vehicle accidents are not captured by the price paid for the items causing the problem. Environmental effects are usually seen as requiring some kind of government action. There are market approaches to government action, such as tradable pollution permits, even an emissions trading scheme, but these still take place firmly within a framework of government regulation. A carbon tax is an even more direct approach by government to address an externality issue.

Natural monopoly

There are some goods or services that are characterized by declining marginal cost; that is, when supplied to one customer, it becomes cheaper to provide it to the next. Such a circumstance is referred to as a natural monopoly, as the characteristics of the market are such that there is a tendency to be only a single provider. The problem happens most often in utilities with networks, such as telephones, electricity, gas and water. The existence of a natural monopoly has been used as a rationale for some form of government involvement or even ownership, though there are fewer industries or parts of industries now universally regarded as natural monopolies. In any case, there are examples, particularly in the United States, where such utilities are privately owned but regulated by the government. In other words, government involvement need not mean direct government provision or ownership; these can be effectively replaced by some form of government regulation attached to their private ownership.

Imperfect information

A case can be made that poor information, or 'asymmetric information' (Kay and Vickers, 1990), can be considered as an example of market failure. Market theory does assume perfect information for both buyer and seller. To the extent that information is not obtained, especially by the buyer, markets can be less than optimal. Consumer protection or packaging information might be examples where, through government action, information can be provided so that markets function better. Regulations imposed on blatantly unsafe products may be seen as providing information to those unable or unwilling to gather it for themselves.

Other kinds of imperfect information may arise with respect to 'adverse selection', where, for example, the unhealthy are more likely to be buyers of health insurance, and 'moral hazard' where the self-assessment of risk – for example, by cigarette smokers or motorcycle riders – is far less than their actual risk. Both of these can cause market failures as a result of failures of information.

Limitations of market failure

The theory of market failure can provide some signposts to government action, but particular aspects may be problematic if used as a complete guide to what governments should or should not do. On the one hand, some market economists, notably Stigler (1975) and Friedman and Friedman (1980), disagree with the notion that market failures provide a justification for government action, as they result in too much government involvement. Stigler (1975) argues that governmental action for consumer protection is unnecessary and inferior to the 'doctrine of *caveat emptor*' – 'let the buyer beware' – and 'the great engine of competition'. Stigler claims that 'public regulation weakens the defences the consumer has in the market and often imposes new burdens upon him, without conferring corresponding protections'. But even though competition and 'buyer beware' are undoubtedly strong, it is unlikely that the public finds the relatively small cost of consumer protection to be burdensome, compared to the cost involved in the sale of unsafe children's toys or clothing, or unlicensed drugs, or of trying to gain any redress through the legal system.

On the other hand, the concept of market failure could be argued to reduce the scope of government action artificially. The theory de-politicizes economic problems by treating them as technicalities when strong political conflicts may be present. It assumes that efficiency is the only value that should guide government intervention. Other important values – equity, equality of opportunity, democratic accountability, and freedom – are neglected. Also, the theory does little to explain why the set of government policies active at the time of writing was adopted. Many market failures will exist, but the precise point at which government intervention is justified is unclear. Markets may fail, but government action to alleviate a problem may also fail. The concept of market failure provides some signposts to those things that governments may involve themselves in, but it does not establish a complete answer to the 'allowable' activities of government (see also Walsh, 1995, pp. 4–12).

Phases of government intervention

'What should governments do?' forms perhaps the oldest continuous

debate in political philosophy. The extent of government involvement
in the economy is, in many ways, the most fundamental of ideological
divisions. A continuum can be visualized between those on the far
Right, who, other things being equal, favour the absolute minimum of
government involvement; and the far Left, who favour total government involvement in the economy (Downs, 1957). The Right argues
that individuals should be left to make economic decisions for themselves, while the Left believes that only collective action and ownership
or intervention by the state can solve the social problems and inequalities thought to be inherent in capitalism. It is generally the case that
Leftist regimes have favoured greater government involvement in production while Rightist regimes have favoured less. Political debate
usually takes place some distance from each end of the continuum;
however, at different times in Western societies since the 1800s, the
pendulum of state involvement has oscillated between different points
on it. During that time there have been several main phases of government involvement in society.

The laissez-faire society

For our present purposes, the late eighteenth century is a good starting
point for discussing the role of government in mixed economies. This
was the final stage of mercantilism, a time in which governments were
intimately involved in the minutiae of the economy. Regulations were
focused on developing the wealth and power of the nation by
restricting external trade, but also entailed internal regulations for
national purposes. The general aim was to use the government to
further the economic ends of the nation, but by a set of *ad hoc* decisions rather than a clear, consistent programme. The mercantilist's role
for government was large and intrusive; in other words, the political
part of society dominated the economic.

As a reaction against this kind of society, Adam Smith wrote *The
Wealth of Nations* in 1776, in which he argued, in addition to advocating free trade among nations, for a greatly reduced role for government. According to Smith (1976, pp. 208–9), the 'duties of the
sovereign' – in other words, the role of government – were as follows:

> First, the duty of protecting the society from the violence and invasion of other
> independent societies; secondly, the duty of protecting, as far as possible, every
> member of the society from the injustice or oppression of every other member
> of it, or the duty of establishing an exact administration of justice; and thirdly,
> the duty of erecting and maintaining certain public works and certain public
> institutions, which it can never be for the interest of any individual, or small
> number of individuals, to erect and maintain; because the profit could never
> repay the expense to any individual or small number of individuals, though it
> may frequently do much more than repay it to a great society.

There are several key ideas here about the role of the public sector, including the beginnings of the theory of public goods.

Smith envisaged a smaller role for government than that in place at the time he was writing. The first duty – that of defence – has always been a government role, perhaps even the main reason why governments came into existence at all. The second duty – to provide a system of laws – has two main aspects. It is an extension of the defence role within the country – a society needs to protect itself from those unwilling to abide by its rules. It also has a market role. The free market system Smith advocated needs a system of laws to enforce contracts and to safeguard property. The third duty is rather more complex. There are certain goods that a government can provide for the benefit of society as a whole, but for which it is difficult to devise any way of making the direct beneficiaries pay. These goods, such as roads and bridges, later called 'public goods', are best provided by the government. It is not easy to specify exactly which activities fall within the third point, but much of what we would now call 'infrastructure' was clearly meant to be included, as was education, in Smith's view, of at least a basic kind.

Other than these rather minimal functions, the desirable role for the government in Smith's view was simply to stay out of economic life as far as possible. Market processes would, by themselves, lead to better overall outcomes than those that could be achieved by the government. This theory is the reverse of mercantilism. Politics and government institutions were simply less important than the drive to self-betterment through the economic system. Governments should be facilitators for the market and should step in reluctantly and only as a last resort. The importance of Smith's writing is that his views have enjoyed substantial acceptance to the present day. The neo-classical or libertarian economists of the late twentieth century (Friedman and Friedman, 1980) certainly saw Smith as the key influence on their ideas.

The rise of the welfare state

In the nineteenth century, especially in Britain, there was a serious attempt to establish the kind of minimal state advocated by Smith and his followers. However, while overall living standards greatly increased in Victorian Britain, there were unfortunate side-effects, including the exploitation of child labour, inadequate housing and poor public health. It was in part as a reaction to the excesses of *laissez-faire* capitalism that Marx and others asserted in the mid-nineteenth century that there were contradictions within capitalism that led irrevocably to the exploitation of workers. Towards the end of the nineteenth century, what later became known as 'the welfare state' arose to alleviate some of the worst excesses of capitalism by re-establishing the state's responsibility for the well-being of its citizens.

The welfare state is usually considered to have begun in Germany in the 1880s, when Chancellor Otto von Bismarck, despite being an arch-conservative, saw some electoral advantage in expanding welfare. The main impetus in Germany was to counter the danger to the political and social order from a socialist workers' movement, which was regarded by some contemporaries as a revolutionary threat (Ritter, 1983, p. 131). As Bismarck said, 'Whoever has a pension to look forward to in his old age is much more contented and more easily taken care of than the man who has no prospect of any.' On another occasion, he remarked that such pensions would teach 'even the common man' to look upon 'the Empire as a benevolent institution' (Ritter, 1983, pp. 33–4).

There were undoubted electoral advantages attached to adopting such programmes, with such adoption perhaps being related to the extension of the franchise in the second half of the nineteenth century. The promise and delivery of services to the public became a major part of party competition and, from the 1930s, the economic theories of J. M. Keynes appeared to allow a major role for government in stabilizing the economy and ameliorating social ills.

Many European countries had substantial welfare programmes by the beginning of the twentieth century. But, because of the greater persistence of *laissez-faire* thought, the first programmes in the United Kingdom were adopted only just prior to the First World War, and in the United States not until the Roosevelt years of the 1930s. This period and the immediate post-war period were the high points of what Friedman and Friedman (1980) call 'Fabian socialism and New Deal liberalism'. In the United Kingdom and Europe, but not the United States, there was also a related programme of industrial nationalization where it was felt that the commanding heights of the economy – coal, steel, railways, and telecommunications – should remain in public hands. In the period after the Second World War, most European countries adopted ever more elaborate welfare programmes to safeguard their citizens 'from the cradle to the grave'. They provided generous unemployment benefits, universal health schemes, educational assistance and social aid programmes aimed at the disadvantaged.

Ordinary members of society do benefit from welfare programmes. In response to electoral pressure, Western governments have provided greater opportunities in education at all levels, health care, and income support for retirement or for the unemployed, all of which meant a steady increase in the size and scope of governments at least until the 1970s or early 1980s. However, the welfare state was never uncontroversial. It was an attempt to reassert the political over the economic, and was therefore diametrically opposed to the *laissez-faire* system. There were three problems. First, there was an aggregate problem of financing, as the welfare state 'increasingly brought countries face-to-face with the issue of affordability' (Holmes and Shand, 1995, p. 559). Someone had to find the money to pay for welfare programmes, which, in the end, must derive from taxes on the wealth generated by the economic system. Second, and related to the first point, a political programme of this kind relies on broad-based political support, which in the later 1970s and 1980s was no longer given as freely as once it had been. The Reagan and Thatcher Governments are long gone, but they did cause some resentment in the community about the size and scope of government and concomitant levels of taxation in the welfare state period. Third, the economic and political theories behind the welfare state became less fashionable. Within the economics profession, the neo-classical school came to enjoy a new ascendancy and provoked a reaction against the welfare state. Neo-classicists advocated a return to a more dynamic economic society based once again on the ideas of Adam Smith.

Neo-classicism

Starting in the mid-1970s, there was a movement away from the larger, implicitly collectivist role of government that had been present for most of the century. Though the extent of change did vary between countries, there certainly was a 'turning of the tide' (Friedman and Friedman, 1980). Within the ranks of government, among policy advisers, and in key parts of the bureaucracy, there was a dominance of neo-classical economics and what was sometimes called 'economic rationalism' (Pusey, 1991). There are four aspects to this theory:

- *The assumption of individual rationality.* Individuals can be assumed to prefer more of something rather than less and will act rationally in pursuit of goals, at least in the aggregate. Individuals are assumed to be the best judges of their own (economic) interests. They should be given as much freedom as possible to develop their own strategies for achieving these. They are capable of deciding how much of any particular good or service they want, and how much they are prepared to pay for it.
- *The elaboration of models from this assumption.* From the first assumption, quite elaborate empirical models can be constructed, especially by using techniques developed in rational choice and/or game theory. The application to politics is also called public choice theory.
- A *maximum role for market forces.* Economic rationalism includes the view, derived from models, that private markets are both efficient and self-regulating. Services or goods able to be provided by markets should be provided by markets.

- *A minimum role for government.* Government interference with the self-regulating mechanism of the market will be inherently inefficient. It should therefore be minimized. This is the obvious corollary to providing for a maximum role for market forces.

Such views captured the economics profession from the mid-1970s and, soon afterwards, governments and the bureaucracy as well. The election of the Thatcher Government in Britain in 1979 and the Reagan Government in the United States in 1980 saw attempts to introduce many 'small government' policies. This was followed by other countries. The early managerial reform of the 1980s should be seen as an expression of governmental desire actively to reduce the scope of governments.

Governments make a comeback

The election of the Clinton Administration in the United States in 1992 may have signalled a partial return to governmentalism after twelve years of virulent anti-governmentalism. Also, prime ministers John Major and Tony Blair in the United Kingdom were less extremist and confrontationist with regard to the public sector than was Mrs Thatcher. David Cameron's coalition Government, too, despite rhetoric about cuts, has found the actuality of reducing government input rather more difficult to bring about than the prime minister might have thought before being elected in 2010. It is notable that Leftist parties in government in France, New Zealand and Australia have been just as eager to reduce government involvement as were Reagan and Thatcher. A corollary is that under George W. Bush – a notionally Right-wing figure – the size of government in the United States increased substantially.

Governments may no longer be seen as the all-purpose villains responsible for society's ills. Following the terrorist attack on the World Trade Centre in New York in 2001, approval ratings of government institutions rose to high levels. Shortly after that, the collapse of large businesses in the United States led to calls for more government involvement to keep the private sector in order. The eight years of the Bush presidency, from the year 2000, were something of a paradox. Despite his conservative credentials, Mr Bush presided over a big increase in government spending and seemed to be more interested in social conservatism than in winding back the role of government in the economy at all. In 2000, US government spending was 34.2 per cent of GDP and this increased to 38.6 per cent by 2008, at a time when most other similar governments were reducing their spending.

Several issues around the role of government came to a head with the GFC in 2008. A decline in house prices in the United States, evident by 2007, led to a banking and financial crisis affecting the USA and a number of other countries. In some American states, half of all mortgagees had negative equity in their homes. Only the government was able to do anything to resolve the situation, but stimulus packages, and rescues of banks and some other companies led to very large government budget deficits and an ongoing risk of sovereign debt defaults, most notably in Europe. During the earlier era of deregulation, markets were assumed to be able to look after themselves. That this view was shown to be inadequate during the GFC is an understatement. That involvement of the government was needed to support the private sector was a massive shift from the economic approaches dominant over the previous 30 years. Governments not only stepped in with stimulus packages but actively investigated ways of setting up regulatory systems for the future to prevent such problems arising again.

Societies where the citizenry had been comfortable with governmental involvement, notably in Europe, seemed better able to deal with the enhanced role for governments that arose from the GFC, even if it was only temporary. The United States is somewhat exceptional here. Even if other countries have seen that governments can indeed be part of the solution to economic problems, in the USA debate on the issue has become far more polarized. On the Right, arguments are still put forward that it is the government that is the problem and only by 'starving the beast' (see Krugman, *New York Times*, 22 February 2010) can it be reduced to a more manageable size. A somewhat irrational populist movement, arguing against government, has gained adherents. It does appear that other countries are more able to sustain a conversation about government and its positive and negative aspects than the United States is able to do. Dealing with the consequences of the GFC has become a major issue for many governments. Government debt re-emerged as a critical problem, especially for those countries that already had high levels of debt before the crisis struck. High debt levels inevitably place pressure on government budgets, and even more demands for greater efficiency in governmental management.

The role of government has waxed and waned over the past 250 years in Western societies. The method of government involvement has also varied. In the mercantilist era, the main instrument used was government regulation, as budgets were very small and there was little government production. The era of the welfare state relied heavily on government provision of goods and services through higher general taxation and, in some countries, government ownership of major industries such as steel, coal and utilities. While there are adherents to different ideological perspectives, one sign of a new pragmatism about government is that there seems to be less heat generated in the debate over its economic role than there has been in recent decades. There is currently little argument in favour of further extending the reach of the public sector, and only rather muted voices in favour of further wide-spread cuts.

The size of government

There was a debate in the 1970s over the size and growth of governments, with fears being expressed that governments would become bankrupt (Rose and Peters, 1978). The proportion of government spending seemed to be on an ever-increasing path. It was not unusual, particularly in Europe, for the government budgets of some countries to exceed 50 per cent of GDP. In such circumstances, there were real fears that the private sector would be marginalized. Though the sizes of governments do vary over time and between countries, the concern over their scale and efficiency led to some questioning of the effects of governmental size on the economy as a whole. In its most extreme forms, it was argued that countries with high levels of government activity and/or high rates of increase in the levels of government activity would have lower growth rates. There are still legitimate arguments about the proper size of governments, but the debate has now moved on to what governments do.

The most common measure of government size is to look at the total amount of government outlay as a percentage of the total economy. Table 2.1 shows that some control over spending was regained by 2002, but if the overall goal was to cut spending, only partial success had been achieved, as there was only a short-term decline followed by a further rise.

In 1980, government spending across the OECD as a whole was 36.5 per cent of GDP, rising to 42 per cent in 1994. While there was a

Table 2.1   *General government total outlays as percentage of GDP, selected OECD countries, 1994–2010*

	1994	1998	2002	2006	2010
Australia	37.1	34.4	34.7	33.5	35.0
Canada	49.7	44.8	41.2	39.4	43.5
Germany	47.9	48.1	48.0	45.3	46.8
Japan	35.0	42.5	38.8	36.2	40.6
New Zealand	42.7	41.0	37.3	39.9	44.2
Sweden	69.6	58.8	55.6	52.7	54.5
United Kingdom	44.6	39.5	40.9	44.3	51.0
United States	37.1	34.6	34.2	36.0	42.2
OECD	42.0	40.8	40.4	39.9	44.6

Source: *OECD Economic Outlook*, 88 (Paris: OECD, 2010).

Table 2.2   *Government spending, selected OECD countries, 2008*

	General government revenue	General government expenditure	Final government expenditure	Social security transfers
Australia	35.8	34.9	18.3	7.9
Canada	40.4	39.3	19.3	9.9
Germany	43.9	43.9	18.0	17.3
Japan	34.6	36.0	17.7	11.4
New Zealand	44.4	39.9	18.3	9.4
Sweden	56.0	52.6	25.9	15.3
United Kingdom	41.8	44.6	21.6	12.8
United States	34.2	36.6	16.0	17.1

Source: OECD, *National Accounts of OECD Countries* (Paris: OECD, 2008).

slight decline after that, the extent of decline was not large and by 2010 the level had risen again. It does appear that attempts to rein in spending largely failed; even if there was no great ideological move to increase spending, health and welfare spending increased along with the ageing of populations. New Zealand, supposedly the most managerial state, did reduce government spending, but only for a time before it began to rise again, most notably with the GFC. It did appear that there was more convergence between countries. For example, Sweden showed government spending of 69.6 per cent of GDP in 1994 and this fell to 52.7 per cent in 2006; while being still above the OECD average, it was much closer to it.

Government spending as a proportion of GDP may be the commonest measure, but this does not measure what the government actually consumes. Government final expenditure measures the amounts that a government actually spends on its own operations. In other words, transfer payments are taken out on the grounds that they are finally spent by someone other than the government. For example, the recipient of a government pension has money transferred through the government budget but then spends it him/herself. It is not direct government expenditure, it is a transfer. Table 2.2 shows that there is some variation in spending levels between different countries in the OECD.

Column 2 in Table 2.2 provides a comparison of taxation levels, ranging from the United States at 34.2 per cent to Sweden with 56 per cent of GDP. Column 3 sets out current budget (general government) outlays. Column 4 – final government expenditure – is how much the government consumes – that is, actually spends itself rather than passing money to someone else to do the ultimate spending. Except for some extremes, government expenditure on goods and services varies less between countries than the other figures; the main reason for the marked differences in total outlays is the wide variation in the amount of transfers.

In the 1970s, it was easy to extrapolate a future in which the size of a government would overwhelm the society as a whole. At times, since then, there has been an intense ideological debate over the size of governments and their role in society. However, the optimal scale and scope of governments remains an unresolvable question. There is no optimal level for the sizes of governments or of what governments do. Some people will feel their freedom threatened even by a relatively small government. Others may be willing to give up more personal freedom if this makes their material circumstances more tolerable. Even when government spending is high, there are those who benefit. The very high government spending in Sweden, for example, is not necessarily wasted. It goes on social services, on assisting the disadvantaged, and on education, health and child care of a very high standard. For generations, its citizens were willing to trade-off high taxes for high levels of government-provided services, but even there the levels of spending became economically unsustainable in the 1990s and were reduced.

Early public sector reform did aim to cut the size of government, but this aspect of reform largely failed. Despite the extensive arguments put forward about reducing government input, and despite the theoretical arguments for a greater role for the private sector, the size of governments did not diminish significantly. There may have been a slowing in the rate of growth, but that was all. Entitlement programmes, combined with an ageing of the population in Western societies, along with resultant big increases in health care spending, generally increased faster than the cuts in other areas. Even if there were managerial efficiencies as part of the reform process, the amounts saved were dwarfed by increased programme spending. Contracting out of service delivery may save money in some situations, but the amount saved is only the difference between public service delivery and final delivery by a contractor. This would usually be only a small percentage of the programme cost itself.

The GFC did lead to an immediate increase in government spending in many countries. However, without that, there is little doubt that the crisis would have been deeper, and more ordinary people would have been made much worse off. This increase in spending has led to renewed arguments that governments were now too big. For example, as *The Economist* (19 March 2011) remarked in a special survey:

> States exist not only to lead society towards common goals; they must also provide people with the liberty to live their own lives. Over the past century government has moved too far towards the former. Now is the time to turn the

dial back. Nothing would add more to the sum of human happiness in the West than a smaller, better state.

Such comments are being made increasingly frequently and it seems inevitable that there will be a further round of public sector cuts. The Conservative–Social Democrat Coalition in the United Kingdom, elected in 2010, avowed its intention to reduce government in many ways, though without setting a specific target in terms of percentage of GDP. And in the United States, a far-Right movement, under the general banner of the Tea Party, aimed to cut government involvement drastically, but without saying quite how or what they were going to cut. The size of governments and their scope in society do remain matters of legitimate public debate, but populism is no answer.

Conclusion

Public sector reforms have led to an array of changes in the role of government, including attempts at cutbacks in expenditure, the drive for efficiency, and various forms of privatization. Some questioning of the role of the public sector is healthy in a democratic society; however, governments have a positive role to play in the community and this has been developed over a long period of time in response to the political wishes of the electorate. Following some experimentation with a minimalist state, it did appear that a new age of pragmatism about the role of government was emerging. Rather than the best government being one that was reduced to the barest minimum, governments were seen as important and powerful institutions that could facilitate the role of the private sector instead of being its axiomatic competitor.

The question of size needs to become a question of what governments do. There simply is no independent, objective way to establish the ideal size of a government, or to decide which activities should be located in the public sector. The public sector in a society is a construct of its citizens. There may be fairly general agreement that government is not very good at running companies selling private goods; also that the private sector is not very good at running the welfare sector or some other core parts of the public sector. There is a change in the role of a government, with it becoming 'less of a producer and more of an enabler' and there is 'a better appreciation of the limits of government power to achieve outcomes without broad-based citizen support and/or in opposition to market forces' (OECD, 1998a, p. 61). This new role for government attempts to draw on the strengths of both sectors in the economy.

Public managers need to understand their place in the overall system of government and in relation to theories about the desirable scope of government. Those working in the public sector therefore need to have some idea of the history of the public sector and some knowledge of the arguments put forward by those who wish to cut the role of government even further.

The Traditional Model of Public Administration

Chapter Contents

- Introduction
- Early administration
- The reforms of the nineteenth century
- Weber's theory of bureaucracy
- Wilson and political control
- Taylor and public administration
- Problems with the traditional model
- Conclusion

Introduction

What is here called the traditional model of public administration was once a major reform movement in its own right. Prior to the embedding of the traditional model into the public sectors of many countries, starting in the latter part of the nineteenth century, public administration was carried out largely by amateurs bound by personal loyalties to their leaders, sovereigns and politicians. With the advent of the traditional model, the task of administration became a professional occupation carried out by a distinct merit-based public service. Serving the public became a high calling, one that required the best people available to form a distinct administrative elite within the society, and that would always act according to the law and established precedents. Politicians might come and go, but while the apparatus of government was in the hands of permanent officials, the transition between regimes could be handled smoothly. Public administration as both theory and practice lasted in most Western countries with remarkably little theoretical change until around the last quarter of the twentieth century. Change did occur – public administration was not entirely static – but it did not threaten the established paradigm.

The traditional model paradigm can be characterized as: an administration in the strict dictionary sense, under the formal control of the political leadership, based on a rigidly hierarchical model of bureaucracy, staffed by permanent, neutral and anonymous officials motivated only by the public interest, serving any governing party equally, and not contributing to policy but merely administering those policies decided by the politicians. The traditional model does remain the longest-standing and most successful theory of management in the public sector. It did not disappear overnight and elements of it still exist, but its theories and practices are now considered to be old-fashioned and no longer relevant to the needs of a rapidly changing society.

Early administration

Public administration has a long history, one paralleling the very notion of government. As Gladden (1972) notes, some form of administration has existed ever since there have been governments: 'First comes the initiator or leader to render society possible, then the organiser or administrator to give it permanence. Administration, or the management of affairs, is the middle factor in all social activity, unspectacular but essential to its continuance' (p. 1).

Administrative systems existed in ancient Egypt to administer irrigation from the annual flood of the Nile and to build the pyramids. China in the Han dynasty (206 BC to AD 220) adopted the Confucian precept that government should be handled by men chosen, not by birth, but by virtue and ability, and that its main aim was the happiness of the people. In Europe, the various empires – Greek, Roman, Holy Roman, Spanish and so on – were, above all, administrative empires, controlled from the centre by rules and procedures. The growth of 'modern' states in the Middle Ages is argued by Weber to have 'developed concomitantly with bureaucratic structures' (Gerth and Mills, 1970, p. 210). Though some kinds of administration existed earlier, the traditional model of public administration dates from late in the nineteenth century.

Earlier systems of administration shared one important characteristic. They were 'personal' – that is, based on loyalty to a particular individual such as a king or a minister – rather than being 'impersonal', based on legality and loyalty to the organization and the state. The practice of administration often resulted in corruption or misuse of office for personal gain, though the idea that these are undesirable features of administration only derives from the traditional model. Practices that now seem alien were commonplace ways of carrying out government functions under earlier administrative arrangements. It was once common for those aspiring to employment by the state to resort to patronage or nepotism, or by purchasing offices – that is, to pay for the right to be a customs or tax collector, and then to charge fees to clients, both to repay the initial sum invested and to make a profit. Key administrative positions were often not full-time but were only one of the many activities of someone in business. The normal way for a young man to secure government employment (and only men were employed) was to apply to some relative or family friend who was in a position to help. There was no guarantee that people employed by the system would be competent in any way.

In the United States, for most of the nineteenth century there existed what was termed the 'spoils system' of administration, derived from the saying 'to the victor belong the spoils'. After an election in which a new party was elected – and this applied to elections from the local level to the presidency – every administrative job from the top to the bottom could be filled by an appointee from the winning party. This system reached its nadir in the 1830s during the presidency of Andrew Jackson, who once said (White, 1953, p. 318):

> The duties of all public offices are, or at least admit of being made, so plain and simple that men of intelligence may readily qualify themselves for their performance. Offices were not established to give support to particular men at the public expense. No individual wrong is, therefore, done by removal, since neither appointment to, nor continuance in office is a matter of right. He who is removed has the same means of obtaining a living that are enjoyed by the millions who never held office.

In other words, there is no specific expertise involved in public administration, nor is there any reason that the administration of government should persist when the political leadership changes. The benefits of public office – patronage, direct financial benefits – rightly belong to the successful party in an election and these can and should be distributed to its members and supporters after winning an election.

Jackson thought there were advantages in making the administration more egalitarian and democratic: 'I cannot but believe that more is lost by the long continuance of men in office than is generally gained by their experience.' Presumably, by changing officeholders whose loyalties were clearly to the party, much could be gained, perhaps even reduced corruption. It could even be argued that political accountability was enhanced in 'reaction to a sense that government had not been sufficiently responsive to changes in the electoral will' (Romzek, 1998, p. 196). This egalitarian philosophy did fit well with the American distrust of government, but had major drawbacks (Mosher, 1982, p. 65):

> Among the consequences of the spoils system run rampant, were: the periodic chaos which attended changes of administration during most of the nineteenth century; the popular association of public administration with politics and incompetence; the growing conflicts between executive and legislature over appointments, which led in 1868 to the impeachment trial of an American

president; and the almost unbelievable demands upon presidents – and upon executives of state and local governments as well – by office-seekers, particularly following elections. Such a system was neither efficient nor effective. Citizens did not know where they stood when government administration was, in effect, a private business in which government decisions, money and votes were negotiable commodities.

Eventually, the inherent problems of the spoils system led to changes in the latter part of the nineteenth century and to the Progressive Era reforms (see Kettl, 2002) associated with the traditional model of administration. Vestiges of the spoils system do remain in the United States with what is called the 'Plum Book', listing close to 1,500 appointments that can be made by an incoming president, with or without Senate confirmation, plus another 2,800 non-competitive appointments (United States, 2008, pp. 197–9). Political appointees to administrative posts remain even more common in some US states. Such non-competitive appointments may not be large in number compared to the total number of civil servants, but it does mean that positions at the apex of the US system are still subject to political whim, for good or ill.

What Weber termed pre-modern bureaucracies were 'personal, traditional, diffuse, ascriptive and particularistic' where modern bureaucracies, as exemplified by Weber, were to become 'impersonal, rational, specific, achievement-oriented and universalistic' (Kamenka, 1989, p. 83). Earlier practices now seem strange because of the very success of the traditional model of administration. Professional, non-partisan administration is so familiar to us that it is hard to imagine that any other system could exist.

The reforms of the nineteenth century

The traditional model of administration is often regarded as starting in mid-nineteenth-century Britain. Following several years of investigations into departmental efficiencies (Greenaway, 2004), the Northcote–Trevelyan Report was set up to look more widely into the administration of government. It recommended that 'the public service should be carried out by the admission into its lower ranks of a carefully selected body of young men' through 'the establishment of a proper system of examination before appointment'. It also recommended the abolition of patronage and the substitution of recruitment by open competitive examinations under the supervision of a central examining board; the reorganization of office staffs of central departments into broad classes to deal with intellectual and mechanical work, respectively; and filling higher posts by promotion from inside based on merit. Northcote–Trevelyan signals the start of merit-based appointments to the public service and the gradual decline of patronage, though it was many years before these changes were widely adopted. The Report emphasizes personnel matters, and its recommendations were implemented only slowly, but it does represent a beginning to the traditional model of public administration. As Greenaway (2004) states, 'If one takes a long perspective, Northcote–Trevelyan seems important because it was able to dovetail, and to some extent influence, various historical developments that shaped the next half century or more. It laid [*sic*] a seed which later germinated' (pp. 10–11).

The United Kingdom reforms of the mid-nineteenth century influenced opinion in the United States. The evils of the spoils system were all too evident in the corruption endemic in government, particularly in the cities and notably in the presidential administrations following the Civil War. In 1881, President Garfield was assassinated by a disappointed spoils seeker – someone who thought he had been promised a civil service position – and this event gave further impetus to the movement for reform that was already in existence. As a result, in 1883, the Civil Service Act (the Pendleton Act) was passed, which established a bipartisan Civil Service Commission and contained four key points: (i) the holding of competitive examinations for all applicants to the classified service; (ii) the making of appointments to the classified service from those graded highest in the examinations; (iii) the interposition of an effective probationary period before absolute appointment; and (iv) the apportionment of appointments at Washington according to the population of the several states and other major areas (Gladden, 1972, p. 318). The Pendleton Act was inspired by the British civil service reforms, though the United States did not adopt the rigid four-class system or the requirement that entrance be only at the base grade (Mosher, 1982, p. 68).

In terms of theory, the traditional model was influenced greatly by Woodrow Wilson in the United States – one of the key activists in the United States reform movement, and Max Weber in Europe. Wilson put forward the view that politicians should be responsible for making policy, while the administration would be responsible for carrying it out. Weber set out the theory of bureaucracy, the idea of a distinct, professional public service, recruited and appointed by merit, and politically neutral, which would remain in office throughout changes in government. From both is derived the notion that administration could be instrumental and technical, removed from the political sphere. Still later, the principles of scientific management developed by Frederick Taylor were adopted for the public sector (see also Kettl, 2002).

Wilson, Weber and Taylor, who were contemporaries, are considered to be the main influences on the traditional model of public administration. Only Taylor had immediate influence in the United States, with Wilson's and Weber's work not being well known until some years after their original publication. This delay in dissemination is sometimes used as an argument for there being no paradigm of traditional administration (see Lynn, 2001b). However, indirect dissemination of the ideas may have occurred; also, bureaucracy as a practice was well established before Weber set it out as a theory. Similarly, Wilson's views were well known and used even if the original article was not. Each key theorist will now be considered in turn.

Weber's theory of bureaucracy

The most important theoretical principle of the traditional model of administration is Weber's theory of bureaucracy. There may be arguments about its direct influence on theory or practice, but, as Ostrom (1974) remarks, Weber's theory of bureaucracy 'was fully congruent with the traditional theory of public administration in both form and method' (p. 9). Throughout its long history, the traditional model followed Weber's work virtually to the letter, either implicitly or explicitly.

Weber argued there were three types of authority – 'legitimations of dominance': the *traditional* – such as the authority of a tribal chief; the *charismatic* – the appeal of an extraordinary leader; and *rational/legal* authority (Gerth and Mills, 1970, pp. 78–80). The latter was the authority of legal statute and 'rationally created rules' and this kind of domination is to be 'exercised by the modern "servant of the state" and by all those bearers of power who in this respect resemble him' (Gerth and Mills, 1970, p. 80). Rational/legal authority is contrasted with the other forms of authority, which were essentially irrational and extra-legal, because of its modernity and efficiency. Weber maintained that a capitalist market economy 'demands that the official business of the administration be discharged precisely, unambiguously, continuously, and with as much speed as possible' (Gerth and Mills, 1970, p. 215). Only bureaucratization could offer all this.

Weber set out six principles for modern systems of bureaucracy, deriving from the idea of rational/legal authority (Gerth and Mills, 1970, pp. 196–8) as set out in Box 3.1.

The first of Weber's principles means that authority derives from the law and from rules made according to the law. No other form of authority is to be followed. Following from this, the second principle is that of hierarchy, perhaps the most familiar of Weber's ideas. Strict hierarchy means that rational/legal authority and its innate power are maintained organizationally, not by any individual but by the position he or she holds in the hierarchy. Particular functions could be delegated to lower levels, as the hierarchical structure meant that any official could act with the authority of the whole organization. The third point adds to this. The organization has an existence separate from the

---

Box 3.1   Weber's principles of bureaucracy

1. The principle of fixed and official jurisdictional areas, which are generally ordered by rules, that is by laws or administrative regulations.
2. The principles of office hierarchy and of levels of graded authority mean a firmly ordered system of super- and subordination in which there is a supervision of the lower offices by the higher ones.
3. The management of the modern office is based upon written documents ('the files') which are preserved. The body of officials actively engaged in 'public' office, along with the respective apparatus of material implements and the files, make up a 'bureau' ... In general, bureaucracy segregates official activity as something distinct from the sphere of private life ... Public monies and equipment are divorced from the private property of the official.
4. Office management, at least all specialized office management – and such management is distinctly modern – usually presupposes thorough and expert training.
5. When the office is fully developed, official activity demands the full working capacity of the official ... Formerly, in all cases, the normal state of affairs was reversed: official business was discharged as a secondary activity.
6. The management of the office follows general rules, which are more or less stable, more or less exhaustive, and which can be learned. Knowledge of these rules represents a special technical learning which the officials possess. It involves jurisprudence, or administrative or business management.

private lives of its employees; it is quite impersonal. Written documents are preserved in files – something that is essential, as previous cases become precedents when similar events occur. Only through the existence of files can the organization be consistent in its application of the rules. The fourth point is that administration is a specialist occupation, one deserving of thorough training; it is not something that can be done by just anyone. Fifth, working for the bureaucracy is a full-time occupation, not the secondary activity it once was. Finally, office management is an activity that can be learnt, as it follows general rules. These rules would presumably be carried out in the same way by whoever occupied a particular office.

These principles of bureaucracy seem obvious, but only because they have now become ingrained in society. The main differences and advances of the Weberian system are best understood by comparison with earlier models of administration. The key contrast, the most important difference between Weber and previous models, is the replacement of personal administration by an impersonal system based on rules.

An organization and its rules are more important than any individual within it. The bureaucratic system must be impersonal in its own operations and in how it interacts with its clients. As Weber stated (in Gerth and Mills, 1970, p. 198):

> The reduction of modern office management to rules is deeply embedded in its very nature. The theory of modern public administration ... assumes that the authority to order certain matters by decree – which has been legally granted to public authorities – does not entitle the bureau to regulate the matter by commands given for each case, but only to regulate the matter abstractly. This stands in extreme contrast to the regulation of all relationships through individual privileges and bestowals of favour, which is absolutely dominant in patrimonialism, at least in so far as such relationships are not fixed by sacred tradition.

This is a very important point. Earlier administration was based on personal relationships – loyalty to a relative, patron, leader or party – and not to the system itself. It could be argued that the earlier personal model may have been responsive politically, in that the administration was more clearly an arm of the politicians or the dominant classes favoured by appointments. But it was also often arbitrary, and arbitrary administration can be unjust, especially to those unable or unwilling to indulge in political games. An impersonal system based on Weber's principles removes arbitrariness completely – at least it does so in the ideal case. The existence of the files, the belief in precedent and the basis in law mean that identical decisions are always made in identical circumstances. Not only is this more efficient, but citizens, and those in the bureaucratic hierarchy, know where they stand. As a result, they have more confidence in the system as a whole.

Other differences follow. A rigid system of hierarchy follows naturally from the arrangement's basis in rules and impersonality. The system and its rules persist despite individuals leaving the organization. Though Weber's emphasis is on the system as a whole, he did pay attention to the terms and conditions of those working in the bureaucracy.

The position of the official

The individual official occupies a key place in Weber's theory. Office-holding is considered to be a vocation, following examinations and a rigorous course of training. Unlike earlier forms of administration, office-holding is not considered a resource to be 'exploited for rents or emoluments'. Neither does it 'establish a relationship to a person ... modern loyalty is devoted to impersonal and functional purposes'. According to Weber, 'entrance into an office is considered an acceptance of a specific obligation of faithful management in return for a secure existence'. He specified the position of the official in the following way (Gerth and Mills, 1970, pp. 199–203):

Box 3.2   Weber and the position of the official

1. The modern official always strives for and usually enjoys a distinct social esteem as compared with the governed.
2. The pure type of bureaucratic official is appointed by a superior authority. An official elected by the governed is not a purely bureaucratic figure.
3. Normally, the position of the official is held for life, at least in public bureaucracies.
4. Where legal guarantees against arbitrary dismissal or transfer are developed, they merely serve to guarantee a strictly objective discharge of specific office duties free from all personal considerations.
5. The official receives the regular pecuniary compensation of a normally fixed salary and the old age security provided by a pension. The salary is not measured like a wage in terms of work done, but according to 'status', that is, according to the function (the 'rank') and, in addition, possibly, according to the length of service.
6. The official is set for a 'career' within the hierarchical order of the public service. He moves from the lower, less important, and lower paid to the higher positions.

Weber's six points on the position of the official follow logically from the six principles of bureaucracy. The official is to be part of an elite with a status higher than that of ordinary citizens. As Northcote–Trevelyan had also noted, Weber's theory required recruitment by merit, not by election or by patronage, into a position normally held for life in exchange for impartial service. Part of the lifetime and full-time career of the public servant is the principle of fixed salary and the prospect of advancement through the hierarchical structure.

The two principles – the model of bureaucracy and the position of the official – had specific purposes. A formal, impersonal system offers 'the optimum possibility for carrying through the principle of specialising functions according to purely objective considerations'. Decisions would and should be made according to 'calculable rules' and 'without regard for persons' (Gerth and Mills, 1970, p. 215). To Weber, the specific nature of bureaucracy develops more perfectly the more it is dehumanized; 'the more completely it succeeds in eliminating from official business love, hatred, and all purely personal, irrational, and emotional elements which escape calculation' (Gerth and Mills, 1970, pp. 215–16). The general aims were certainty, impersonality and efficiency. The principle of specialization of function is meant to increase productivity; the hierarchy of authority and the system of rules make for certainty in decision; and the impersonality of the system implies that a previous decision can be repeated in identical circumstances. Decisions are not made arbitrarily.

The idea was to create a system that was at the highest possible level of technical efficiency. As Weber argued (in Gerth and Mills, 1970, p. 214):

> The decisive reason for the advance of bureaucratic organisation has always been its purely technical superiority over any other form of organisation. The fully developed bureaucratic mechanism compares with other organisations exactly as does the machine with non-mechanical modes of production. Precision, speed, unambiguity, knowledge of the files, continuity, discretion, unity, strict subordination, reduction of friction and personal costs – these are raised to the optimum point in the strictly bureaucratic organisation.

Weber's claim that bureaucracy was the most efficient form of organization applies to both the private and the public sector, but there is little doubt it was embraced more readily and for longer in public administration.

Wilson and political control

In the traditional model of public administration, the rules linking the political leadership with the bureaucracy are clear, at least in theory. Woodrow Wilson – a Professor at Princeton University for many years before becoming president of the United States – argued that there should be a strict separation of politics from the administration; and of policy from the strictly administrative task of carrying it out. As he stated in 1886 (1941, pp. 197–222):

> Administration lies outside the proper sphere of politics. Administrative questions are not political questions. Although politics sets the tasks for administration, it should not be suffered to manipulate its offices ... Public administration is detailed and systematic execution of public law. Every particular application of general law is an act of administration. The assessment and raising of taxes, for instance, the hanging of a criminal, the transportation and delivery of the mails, the equipment and recruiting of the army and navy, etc., are all obviously acts of administration, but the general laws which direct these things to be done are as obviously outside of and above administration. The broad plans of governmental action are not administrative; the detailed execution of such plans is administrative.

Wilson believed that the evils of the spoils system resulted from the linking of administrative questions with political ones. If administrators act in an overtly political manner, whether through the process by which they were appointed, or their continuing role within the party organization, corruption is likely to result and arbitrary decisions are almost certain to occur. Separation of the political sphere (from which policy derives) from the administrative sphere (where policies are administered) could address many evils of the spoils system. Wilson was 'a great admirer' of the Northcote–Trevelyan Report and, while he had hoped to administer through a merit-based system, 'the US spoils system was too strong for him' (Foster, 2001, p. 427).

Weber too maintained that civil servants do not exercise leadership, and it is only at the political level that there is any personal responsibility. As he argued (in Gerth and Mills, 1970, p. 95):

> To take a stand, to be passionate ... is the politician's element, and above all the element of the political 'leader'. His conduct is subject to quite a different, indeed, exactly the opposite, principle of responsibility from that of the civil servant. The honor of the civil servant is vested in his ability to execute conscientiously the order of the superior authorities, exactly as if the order agreed with his own conviction. This holds even if the order appears wrong to him and if, despite the civil servant's remonstrances, the authority insists on the order. Without this moral discipline and self-denial, in the highest sense, the whole apparatus would fall to pieces. The honor of the political leader, of the leading statesman, however, lies precisely in an exclusive 'personal' responsibility for what he does, a responsibility he cannot and must not reject or transfer.

Here Weber sets out a division between politics and administration that could well derive from Woodrow Wilson. Not only is leadership reserved for the politician; it is explicitly ruled out for the administrator.

Traditional public administration elevated the distinction between administrative and political matters to one of its guiding principles – that of the politics/administration dichotomy. Politicians would decide policy and administrators carry it out. Neither would venture into the territory of the other. The dichotomy became an all-encompassing myth, a justification that the work of public servants would be that of administration, and only following instruction. Even if there were few immediate effects of Wilson's views in the United States, the idea that administration could be a separate, non-political instrument was influential on the discipline for many years.

There are three main facets to political control in the traditional model of administration. First, there is a clear relationship of accountability and responsibility. A department or agency has two basic roles: to advise the political leadership on the development, review and implementation of policy, and to manage its own resources so that policy may be implemented. Each public servant is technically accountable, through the hierarchical structure of the department, to the Cabinet, and eventually to the people of the country. Second, there is intended to be a strict separation between matters of policy, which are formally the province of politicians, and matters of administration, which are left to the public service. Third, the administration is presumed to be anonymous and neutral; that is, not associated personally with any decisions or policies that are carried out only in the name of the minister; and non-partisan in the party-political sense, being able to serve any political leader equally. In the United Kingdom, the Westminster-derived parliamentary systems added the formal system of ministerial responsibility. If ministers accept personal responsibility for all the activities of their departments, public servants can remain anonymous and not be identified publicly with the advice they give to these ministers. In return for serving ministers from whatever party to the best of their ability – that is, for acting impersonally and objectively – public servants receive certain benefits in their conditions of service, such as security of employment, despite changes of government, and at the end of their working life, a decent pension.

While the theory of separation – of dichotomy – between politics and administration was a major part of the traditional model of administration, it was for many years widely regarded as a myth, especially useful for the evasion of responsibility. In reality, the two functions are effectively 'fused with politicians performing administrative duties and administrators assuming political responsibilities' (Caiden, 1982, p. 82). It was a fantasy to assume that politicians and administrators could be separate, but bureaucratic structures were constructed as though the myth was reality.

Taylor and public administration

The theoretical foundations of bureaucracy and political control were established firmly through Weber and Wilson. All that was needed for a complete theory was a way of working, of organizing, to be added to the bureaucratic model of Weber, the political control of Wilson and the merit appointments and political neutrality of Northcote–Trevelyan. This was found by adopting into the public sector the scientific management principles put forward for the private sector by Frederick Winslow Taylor (1911), the American management writer usually credited with formulating the theory of scientific management (Kettl, 2002). As Dunsire (1973) contended, the addition of scientific management ideas led to a complete model of administration and 'the twin ideas of the politics/administration dichotomy and Scientific Management, gave a form and purpose, a self-confidence to both the practice and the study of administration in the 1920s and 1930s' (p. 94).

Scientific management

Taylor's scientific management involved standardizing work, which meant finding the 'one best way of working' and 'controlling so extensively and intensively as to provide for the maintenance of all these standards' (Kakar, 1970, p. 3). Scientific management included (i) time-and-motion studies to decide a standard for working; (ii) a wage-incentive system that was a modification of the piecework method already in existence; and (iii) changing the functional organization. Taylor did not invent time-and-motion studies, but he did carry them out more thoroughly than had his predecessors. There were the famous experiments with shovel size, bringing the work closer to the worker, reducing the number of movements, all carried out with the ever-present stopwatch. How to carry out a particular task was to be decided by management; procedures were set out and workers chosen to fit the tasks. Taylor advocated paying workers by a modified piece-work method, so that someone who produced above the measured standard for a day's work would be paid more for the entire output, while performance below the standard would attract the normal rate (Kanigel, 1997, pp. 210–11). Scientific management became an evangelical force in the early years of the twentieth century (Copley, 1923). What Taylor sought was a fundamental change, as efficiency and science replaced *ad hoc* decision-making; even a societal change as, through scientific management, the interests of employees and employers could be shown to be the same.

The factory assembly line was the main area influenced by Taylor's ideas, but it was not long before enthusiasts applied scientific management to governments. Taylor too thought that scientific management could be useful in government, since, 'in his judgment, the average public employee did little more than one-third to one-half of a good day's work' (Fry, 1989, p. 47). As it turned out, scientific management did fit very well with the theory of bureaucracy: the skills of the administrator, the compilation of manuals to cover every contingency, the advance of rationality, and impersonality, are aspects of both theories. The ideas of 'one best way' and systematic control were a perfect fit with rigid hierarchy, process and precedent. They also appealed to Weber, as he commented (in Gerth and Mills, 1970, p. 261):

> With the help of appropriate methods of measurement, the optimum profitability of the individual worker is calculated like that of any material means of production. On the basis of this calculation, the American system of 'scientific management' enjoys the greatest triumphs in the rational conditioning and training of work performances.

Standardization of tasks and fitting workers to them was perfect for the traditional model of administration. Even the measurement of performance by stop-watch was common in the organization and methods (O&M) branch of large public bureaucracies.

As far as the operations of government were concerned, scientific management 'did not waste away in textbooks; it was highly influential in the practice of public administration and in government research' (Bozeman, 1979, pp. 33–4). Taylor was important in government management at least as early as the 1920s. He remains important for public administration, as his theory of scientific management became a key influence on what followed in the management of both public and private sectors (Schachter, 1989). While particular points could be disputed – the crude theory of personal motivation, time-and-motion studies – the idea that management could be systematic, and that efficiency should be aimed for, remained important in the public sector and clearly fitted very well with the traditional model of administration. As Stillman (1991) argues, 'it all fits neatly together: a strong, effective administrative system could flourish if politics was restricted to its proper sphere, if scientific methods were applied, and if economy and efficiency were societal goals' (p. 110).

Human relations

Another theory – human relations – is often contrasted with scientific management. The focus of human relations is more on the social context at work rather than regarding the worker as an automaton responsive only to financial incentives, as Taylor is sometimes portrayed. The human relations school had its roots in social psychology, and while quite different in some respects, it became as much of a continuing tradition in public administration, as did scientific management.

The human relations idea has many theorists, but the real founder was Elton Mayo (1933). Following a series of experiments during the 1930s, Mayo contended that the social context of the work group was the most important factor in management. Conflict was regarded as pathological and to be avoided, and there was no necessary antagonism between management and workers. In what became known as the 'Hawthorne experiments', referring to the Hawthorne plant of the Western Electric Company, Mayo claimed that productivity increased most where management took an interest in the workers; and other factors, including financial incentives, were much less important.

Mayo and his followers had a substantial impact on the management of the public sector, even if more recent work has cast doubt on the value of interpretations of the original Hawthorne data, showing most particularly that financial incentives were important after all (Schachter, 1989, pp. 16–17; Gillespie, 1991). Consideration of the psychological context of the organization was responsible for schools of thought based on organizational behaviour and organizational psychology. The idea that individuals responded to other than financial motives led to an improvement in working conditions.

Mayo influenced those who thought management should be kinder to their workers and provide some kind of social interaction. While the motivation of workers remains an open question, human relations theory has been important in the public context, and its influence continues in the debate over managerialism. As Pollitt (1993, p. 17) states:

> The significance of this work for managerialist ideologies today is that it established the idea that informal relations within and without the organisation are of considerable importance. It is not only the formal organisation chart, distribution of functions and systems of work measurement which are important, but also the feelings, values, informal group norms and family and social backgrounds of workers which help determine organisational performance ... Subsequently this general message has been developed in many and various detailed applications – modern techniques of job enrichment, participative management styles and self-actualisation are part of the intellectual heritage of the human relations school.

It could be argued that human relations theory was applied to a greater extent in the public rather than in the private sector. Public organizations had fewer competitive constraints, and arguably went further in introducing human relations, particularly in the 1960s and 1970s.

A continuing debate

The debate between scientific management and human relations still continues. It may be tempting to regard the theories of Taylor and Mayo as being mutually exclusive – at one time one of the theories is pre-eminent while at other times the other is the most popular – but it would be 'a mistake to see classical theory and human relations as antithetical' (Bozeman, 1979, p. 96). The overall goals of Taylor and Mayo were not that different; the Hawthorne studies 'left the old goals of hierarchy, cost efficiency, and managerial supremacy intact, changing only the means of achieving the goals' (Bozeman, 1979, p. 100). Like Taylor, Mayo did not favour unions or industrial democracy (Fry, 1989, p. 131). Like Mayo, Taylor suggested the importance of co-operation in the workplace (Fry, 1989, p. 68). The goal of both – increased productivity – was the same, and both continue to influence management in the public sector.

Some of the more recent arguments about management in the public sector are continuations of a longer debate over scientific management and its alleged counterpart (Pollitt, 1993). According to Schachter (1989, p. 1):

> Taylor's ghost hovers over the modern study of public administration. Although he has been dead for over seventy years, discussion of his work quickly degenerates into polemics. Much of the modern literature depicts him as authoritarian, equating motivation with pay incentives. This denigration, however, focuses on a narrow range of quotations or confuses his own ideas with their purported application by people he specifically repudiated.

Schachter traces the influence of Taylor in public administration texts over the century and argues that the dichotomy between scientific management on the one hand and human relations on the other is a false one. A thorough reading of Taylor shows anticipation of many points the human relations theorists claimed as their own.

Some reinterpretation is needed, though the tradition of there being two opposing theories is likely to continue. It was stated earlier that, for most of the twentieth century, Taylorism was a major influence on the public sector, as it was on the private sector. Taylor undoubtedly influenced job design in both sectors. His model was rigid, bureaucratic and hierarchical, and quite obviously suited to the public sector in the heyday of the traditional model of administration. Much could be gained by treating workers humanely, but Taylor also favoured that, and at least was prepared to give increased pay to workers who achieved above the norm. Similarly, both the public and private sectors used the human relations school to some extent; if it helped productivity to see the workers as social beings, there was something to be gained by counselling, improving working conditions, funding a social club, or anything that could increase the attachment of the worker to the organization.

The Golden Age of public administration

Public administration in its Golden Age, from around 1920 to the early 1970s, was a worthy and satisfying enterprise, with government and public service offering the hope of improving society. Public administration was responsible for some major achievements during this time, ranging from administering the New Deal, to building dams and running the nascent welfare systems of developed countries as well as entire economies during the Second World War.

It seemed that all that was needed was to establish a set of nostrums, follow them exactly and the outcome would be all that could be desired. One variant was the 'POSDCORB' set of functions, which stood for (Gulick and Urwick, 1937; Stillman, 1987, p. 175):

- *Planning*: goal setting techniques/methods applied by executives as a means of preparing future courses of organizational action.
- *Organizing*: arranging the organizational structure and processes in an appropriate manner essential to achieving these ends.
- *Staffing*: recruiting and hiring personnel to carry out the essential agency work.
- *Directing*: supervising the actual processes of doing the assignments.
- *Co-ordinating*: integrating the various detailed elements of these tasks in co-operation with other units and people in government.

- *Reporting*: tracking and communicating the progress of the work within the organization.
- *Budgeting*: fiscal and financial activities necessary to support the completion of these programmes, services, or activities economically.

An administrator would simply follow these for an organizational outcome. But, as early as the 1940s, POSDCORB was attacked as being counter to the human relations movement. POSDCORB and other classical approaches 'were viewed as attempts to exploit, control, and manipulate workers' (Graham and Hays, 1991, p. 22).

A strict administrative system has some advantages and, for most of its history, there was little criticism of its principles and effectiveness. The hierarchical system meant that everyone knew his or her place and extent of authority. Someone was always technically accountable for all actions, from the lowest level to the highest. For the career public servant there was a steady, stable and secure (if unspectacular) progress through the hierarchy. The system was also reasonably efficient and effective in a narrow sense. As Behn (2001, pp. 40–1) stated:

> Wilson, Taylor and Weber all strove to improve efficiency. And, although efficiency is a value in itself, it has another advantage. This efficiency is impersonal. By separating administration from politics, by applying science to the design of its administrative processes, and by employing bureaucratic organizations to implement these processes, government would ensure not only that its policies were fair but also that their implementation was fair.

Administration meant that instructions were carried out, especially when they were given clearly. It was also reasonably free from the temptation to divert public funds for the personal use of bureaucrats. When tasks were administrative and relatively simple, when the environment was stable, the system worked well.

However, the traditional model of administration was rigid and bureaucratic, narrowly focused and preoccupied with structure and process, despite being better than what existed previously. Merit-based appointment, formal bureaucracy and the notion that politics and administration could and should be separated were adequate principles for an administrative system, particularly one operating in a time of stability. However, there are major criticisms of the traditional model; while it was a good model for a long time, its time has now passed.

Problems with the traditional model

The inadequacies of bureaucratic administration became apparent in the 1970s and 1980s. Hierarchical structures are not necessarily the most efficient of organizations if one is comparing outputs with inputs. Bureaucracy may be ideal for control but not necessarily for management; it allows for certainty but is usually slow in moving. Work may be standardized, but at the cost of innovation. Also, the model of political control was always problematic in assuring genuine accountability.

From the 1970s onwards, the public services encountered increasing criticism in most developed countries. There were four main problems. First, the model of political control was inadequate and illogical. Second, 'one best way' thinking was problematic. Third, the theory of bureaucracy was no longer universally considered to provide the technical efficiency that Weber thought it provided, as well as tending to be undemocratic. Fourth, there was criticism from the Right (here termed the 'public choice critique') of the whole idea of bureaucracy as taking away freedom as well as being axiomatically inefficient compared to the market.

The problem of political control

The separation between policy and administration advocated by Wilson in the 1880s was designed to counter the spoils system, then still rife in the United States. However, a strict separation between politicians and administrators, between policy and administration, was never realistic even in its original home. The reform movement in the United States was not able to separate policy from administration, or politicians from administrators. It was only able to clarify the precise point at which political appointments to the public service were to be separated from career appointments. In Westminster-derived parliamentary systems, the precept was actually followed to a large extent, but became more of a justifying myth than a formal way of ordering the roles of either ministers or officials.

In reality, the relationship between government and administration is not as simple as the Wilson model suggests, and probably never was. Relationships between the political leadership and bureaucrats are complex and fluid: they do not reflect the formal, linear logic of the Wilson model. Politics cannot be separated from administration; political acts cannot be completely divorced from how they are implemented; and administrative procedures can and do have political consequences. The traditional form simply does not reflect the extensive, managerial and policy-making role performed by the modem public service. It imposes a negative form of control, which seeks to avoid embarrassing mistakes rather than to provide any positive incentive to improve efficiency or effectiveness. The attempt to be 'non-political' meant a reluctance to recognize the policy and political significance of public service work. Public servants also have an important managerial role, something more important than merely administering or following instructions.

The model of political control in the traditional model was unrealistic in that politics and administration are necessarily intertwined. The work of public servants needs to be regarded as fundamentally political, although not necessarily party political. Some practitioners may still argue that they are only implementing policy and not making it, but this is a matter of 'ideological advocacy' (Peters, 1996, p. 5) rather than a recognition of empirical reality. Though this theory was long considered to be unrealistic, it did form a major underpinning of the traditional model of administration. However, relying on a theory that does not work, and which has been widely regarded as not working for a long time, suggests that something is wrong with the whole model.

The problem of 'one best way'

Implicit in the traditional model was that, through the theories of bureaucracy and scientific management, the single 'one best way' of dealing with a given problem could be found. Gulick's POSDCORB and Taylor's scientific management were 'popular manifestations of this one best way theorising' (Stillman, 1991, p. 9).

Following on from Taylor, the one best way was to be determined by examining all the steps involved in a task, measuring processes to determine the most efficient one and, most important, setting out this method as a set of procedures. In the public services, the procedure manuals became ever larger, with the prescribed way of dealing with every conceivable contingency spelt out in great detail. Once this was done, the task of the public official was purely administrative, merely involving consultation of the manual and following the procedures laid down. In principle, there needed to be little thought and no creativity other than finding the right page of the manual. Administrators, by definition, have no responsibility for results; and one best way thinking allowed them to evade responsibility completely, provided there was no deviation from the letter of the manuals covering every contingency.

It was only later, as managers became responsible for results, that there was any real thought that different methods could lead to differing results, or that methods and actions should be tailored to circumstances. In reality there is no 'one best way'; there are many possible answers (Behn, 1998a, p. 140). As will be argued (see Chapter 4), public management does aim for results, but makes no assumption that there will be only one way to reach an outcome. In the abstract, responsibility is to be given to a manager without any prescription as to how results are achieved. One of the manager's roles is to decide a way of working, and he or she is then personally responsible if results are, or are not, forthcoming.

The problem of bureaucracy

A further problem with the traditional model was its reliance on the Weberian model of bureaucracy. Critics argued that the structure and management of the traditional model were obsolete and in need of drastic reform, because of problems with the concepts of bureaucracy and bureaucratic organization. Formal bureaucracy may have its advantages, but, it is asserted, it also breeds time-servers rather than innovators. It encourages administrators to be risk-averse rather than risk-takers, and to waste scarce resources instead of using them efficiently. Weber regarded bureaucracy as the highest form of organization, but it is also criticized for producing inertia, lack of enterprise, red tape, mediocrity and inefficiency, all conditions thought to be endemic in public sector bodies. Indeed, the word 'bureaucracy' is today more usually regarded as a synonym for inefficiency (Behn, 1998a, p. 140). There are two particular problems with the theory of bureaucracy. These are, first, the problematic relationship between bureaucracy and democracy; and, second, that formal bureaucracy is no longer considered to be a particularly efficient form of organization, or, more correctly, the circumstances where formal bureaucracy is the best theory to use are quite limited, rather than being universal in application.

With its formal rationality, secrecy, rigidity and hierarchy, it seems inevitable that there would be some conflict between bureaucracy and democracy. Even Weber saw this. It was inevitable that bureaucracy would become universal as it 'inevitably accompanies modern mass democracy' (Gerth and Mills, 1970, p. 224), but equally, democracy 'inevitably comes into conflict with bureaucratic tendencies' (p. 226). Those who are ruled, for their part, cannot dispense with or replace the bureaucratic apparatus of authority once it exists (p. 229). While Weber regarded bureaucracy as inevitable with the modernization of society, there were clearly aspects that worried him. There was and is some conflict between bureaucracy and democracy; it did not make sense for a democracy to have a distinct elite acting secretively. Moreover, the individual bureaucrat, to Weber, hardly had an ideal life (Gerth and Mills, 1970, p. 228):

> The professional bureaucrat is chained to his activity by his entire material and ideal existence ... In the great majority of cases, he is only a single cog in an ever-moving mechanism, which prescribes to him an essentially fixed route of march. The official is entrusted with specialised tasks and normally the mechanism cannot be put into motion or arrested by him, but only from the very top. The individual bureaucrat is thus forged to the community of all the functionaries who are integrated into the mechanism. They have a common interest in seeing that the mechanism continues its functions and that societally exercised authority carries on.

As Weber noted: 'every bureaucracy seeks to increase the superiority of the professionally informed by keeping their knowledge and intentions secret', adding that 'the concept of the official secret is the specific invention of bureaucracy' (p. 233). This concern still exists today. Bureaucracy is regarded by some as abrogating the power of the citizen or the politician and thereby making political accountability problematic. This poses a problem to some in society, as they see unelected officials having wide powers over their lives.

The early 1990s saw the fall of the communist regimes in Eastern Europe, regimes where bureaucracy was carried out to a far greater extent than in the West. Detailed bureaucratic control over markets and individuals did not appear to provide the goods and services wanted by citizens in the former Eastern bloc, and it is likely that this apparent failure may be a failure of the theory of bureaucracy itself. According to Jacoby (1973, p. 156):

> Wherever bureaucratic control becomes all-encompassing it also creates an obsession with power which overshadows rational tendencies as has been shown by the Russian example. But what developed to its fullest extent under special historical conditions is everywhere inherent in the bureaucratic mind.

Though writing many years before the fall of the communist regimes, Jacoby did point to a general problem with bureaucracies unconstrained by a suitable system of accountability.

The second problem of bureaucracy was one Weber did not foresee. This is the questioning of the supposed technical superiority of the bureaucratic model that Weber saw as being greater than any other conceivable process. Such confidence in the technical superiority of bureaucracy is no longer generally accepted, for two reasons. First, there were always some extreme interpretations of Weberian principles, particularly in the personnel system, which was made more rigid, more formal and less elitist than Weber had imagined, and this tended to reduce its efficiency. The principle of hierarchy was implemented to a ridiculous extent in some countries, with dozens of levels, each with several sub-levels and with barriers established to restrict progress beyond certain points. The principle of employment for life came to mean that it was practically impossible to dismiss anyone, even for manifest incompetence. The idea of a separate pension scheme for old age also had deleterious side effects. Generous government pension schemes attracted complaints from private sector managers, who felt that governments were more generous with their pensions than they could afford for their private sector employees. Bureaucracy also led to the problem of the 'time-server', the person who did not work effectively, but who was impossible to dismiss, and merely waited in post for retirement day.

The seniority principle was commonplace, where promotions were decided purely on length of service. This too survives in some areas, but it could hardly be said to conform to Weber's aim for technical efficiency. If promotion to higher positions results purely from length of service, then leadership will often tend to be incompetent, and talented workers will leave early in frustration. The idea that recruitment should be at the base grade, with recruits coming direct from school, was sometimes distorted to mean that all recruitment should be at that level, with active discrimination against those with higher qualifications.

The laudable principle of political neutrality led in some instances to the idea of 'service to the nation', above and beyond that of advising and carrying out the wishes of the elected government. This produced problems of accountability; unelected officials acted as a kind of mandarin class, doing what they wanted rather than what the politicians wanted them to do. Weber expected the bureaucracy to be a distinct elite within society, but, as the century progressed, more societies began to reject this model. Apart from a few countries where elite training for public service continued – for example, in Japan and France – the best and brightest no longer considered public service to be an occupation attracting high status. The general low esteem in which public service was held also meant that it became an easy target for cuts.

Second, new theories of organizational behaviour indicate that formal bureaucratic models are no longer particularly efficient or effective in any sense, when compared to more flexible forms of management. Rigid, hierarchical structures are now more often regarded as imposing costs as well as benefits, and may stifle creativity and innovation. Informal networks spring up alongside the formal ones; 'there is a complex set of informal behaviours in every organization, and these may or may not be consistent with what is depicted in the organization chart' (Bozeman and Straussman, 1990, p. 139). Political behaviour by individuals aiming to advance in the organization reduces overall efficiency, as more time and effort is often spent in seeking advancement than in doing the assigned task. When officials offer greater loyalty to their office than to the elected government; when they actively compete with other branches or agencies, management is likely to fall well short of the optimum. Intrigue and empire-building are rife in bureaucracy and probably always were. Individual bureaucrats are not automatons impersonally following rules as assumed by Weber's model. A more realistic theory of bureaucracy than Weber's, with its emphasis on precision and reliability in administration, on its rule-bound character, needs 'to be supplemented by a recognition that human attitudes and relationships are involved' (Kamenka, 1989, p. 161).

Behavioural theories of organizations illustrate that what really happens in bureaucracies is considerably different from what the rational/legal authority model predicts. The bureaucratic organization adopts fixed operating procedures but, in consequence, the achievement of results may become less important than maintaining the processes and rules. Robert Merton (1968, p. 260) commented that rigid adherence to rules could have unanticipated consequences, including a reduction in efficiency:

> Adherence to rules, originally conceived as a means, becomes transformed into an end-in-itself, there occurs the familiar process of displacement of goals whereby 'an instrumental value becomes a terminal value'. Discipline, readily interpreted as conformance with regulations, whatever the situation, is seen not as a measure designed for specific purposes but becomes an immediate value in the life-organization of the bureaucrat.

In other words, the rules themselves become what organizational effort is directed at achieving, rather than fulfilling the organization's purpose.

Michel Crozier goes further. He asserts that bureaucratic organizations are axiomatically inefficient, even that 'a bureaucratic organization is an organization that cannot correct its behaviour by learning from its errors' (Crozier, 1964, p. 187). Instead of bureaucracy being axiomatically efficient, as Weber argued, it is more often now regarded as the reverse. Caiden (1981, p. 181) too claims that the price to be paid for bureaucratic 'efficiency' is:

> A narrow sameness, restrictions on individual enterprise and creativity, an intolerant conformity, competent but not excellent performance and an indifferent complacency. Providing one accepts things as they are, then all is well and the future looks after itself ... When bureaucratism is overdone, its vices may replace its virtues. Instead of careful planning, there may be hasty improvisation, and panicky manipulation, neither well thought out, and both turning order into chaos. Instead of high productivity, there may be low productivity as work may become a boring ritual and the rewards for good performance may not be much different from those for poor performance.

Even when formal bureaucracies work well, they tend to do so in times of stasis and find it difficult to cope with changed circumstances. Fixed procedures and orderly working patterns do not function when the environment is constantly changing. Perhaps in the Golden Age of public administration, change was slow enough to allow the luxury of operating in a fixed environment, but this is a societal situation that rarely exists now. The only constant in public services more recently is change, and the traditional, hierarchical model of government 'simply does not meet the demands of this complex, rapidly changing age' (Goldsmith and Eggers, 2004, p. 7).

Traditional bureaucracy is input dominated, with output being only incidental. It was thought, as far as results were considered at all, that they would follow naturally from organization and structure. Of course, the organization had some purpose, but once set up it was assumed that establishing the hierarchy, the personnel system and so on would of themselves lead to satisfactory outputs. Measuring achievement was arbitrary, *ad hoc* and often regarded as too difficult to do in the public sector. Even evaluation of whether an agency or a programme was doing anything worthwhile was rare and unsystematic. That the seniority system was resorted to is an acknowledgement of failure to establish any real measure of personnel competence.

Lack of leadership

It may have been a laudatory idea to aim for a completely impersonal system, but this also creates a major problem. It is simply impractical to completely discard personal interactions and motivations in organizations that are constructed by humans and serve human purposes. As Behn (1998b) states, 'if organizations could function as machines, leadership by individuals would not be necessary' and, because organizations are not machines and individuals do not behave as part of a machine, 'public managers have to lead' (p. 212) and then adds:

> If human organizations are machines, they don't need motivation, and they don't need inspiration, and they don't need leadership. But if human organizations are composed of real humans – not a cloned collection of 'normal' interchangeable people but diverse individuals with different competencies – then getting such people within these organizations to actually do their jobs requires motivation and inspiration. It requires leadership.

Leadership becomes necessary, then, as the machine model of bureaucracy breaks down. In the real world of organizations there are all kinds of personal political games, jealousies, varying levels of competence, personal foibles and personality conflicts. A Weberian view would be that such matters of personality are innately inefficient and should be sublimated for the greater good or removed altogether. But they are simply unavoidable and to construct a model of management around a pretence that they do not exist is unrealistic. And an absence of leadership also means an avoidance of personal responsibility.

Bureaucracy as a power structure

A major problem for the public sector is that it persisted with the habits and practice of administration, which were being modified elsewhere. Newer theories of organizational behaviour recognize that formal bureaucracy has its strengths, but that alternative structures are possible (Volberda, 1999; Vecchio, 2006). Bureaucracy is not appropriate for non-routine activities that involve creativity and innovation. Once dominated by its own unwieldy bureaucracy, the private sector has moved away from formal bureaucratic structures and rigid hierarchical structures towards decentralization and devolution of real authority to lower levels as profit centres, as well as to greater flexibility in structure and staffing, and an increased emphasis on performance and speedy response. However, to change the existing public system into one that is speedy, risk-taking, output-oriented, innovative and efficient requires a total change in organizational culture. The focus of subsequent reforms in the public service has been to move away from the idea of a rigid and bureaucratized career service towards a more fluid structure. While there may be a need for order and precision in management, there is now a greater need for speed, flexibility and results. In short, the formal bureaucratic model is really more suited to administration, or carrying out instructions, than management, or achieving results.

It remains an open question in organizational behaviour whether more recent changes to Weber's model are evolutionary or revolutionary: whether there are so many alterations that bureaucracy is no longer really Weberian. In one view, organization theorists are constantly 'grappling with alternatives to the hierarchical image of bureaucracy, but the Weberian closed bureaucracy has staying power' (Bozeman and Straussman, 1990, p. 142). Meier and Hill (2005, p. 67) contend that:

> Bureaucracy will continue to flourish in the twenty-first century for many of the same reasons that ... [it] flourished in the last century, it facilitates the governance process in ways that other organizational forms do not. Challenges to bureaucracy will always be challenges at the margin, moving tasks from a public sector bureaucracy to a private sector one, for example. Underneath these cosmetic responses to reforms, however, one will still see Weberian bureaucracies continue to perform a myriad of tasks.

Meier and Hill argue that the six principles set out for Weberian bureaucracy still apply, with the possible exception of the 'written files'. They claim that bureaucracy as set out a hundred years ago is still the prevailing theory.

There are problems with this view. As a system of power, bureaucracy is certainly not dead, but as a practice – as a system of management – there are profound differences from Weber. Public servants are not employed at the base grade and for life. In many jurisdictions they do not have the distinct social status for which Weber argued, nor the special pensions. Promotion is no longer generally gained by seniority alone, even though some vestiges of this practice remain. Strict hierarchy has broken down, and rightly so. There are undoubtedly circumstances where managers may use strict bureaucratic methods, but only as one of a number of possible choices of methods. This is the same as in the private sector, where bureaucracy was once the method of choice, but is no longer. The key feature of formal bureaucracy is that outcomes or results are not mentioned and it is presumed that merely organizing bureaucratically is all that is needed. Ideally, a manager should be able to determine how best to achieve an outcome.

Blau and Meyer (1987, p. 162) also argue that changes have modified the bureaucratic model as outlined by Weber, but 'his model has not been abandoned'. They draw three conclusions: first, that bureaucratic principles do achieve co-ordination and control in administration, but:

> Whether bureaucratic principles always affect efficiency remains open to question. Compared to traditional forms of administration, bureaucracy is undoubtedly superior. Compared to the new organizing principles that substitute financial controls for command hierarchies in large corporations, bureaucracy may be at a disadvantage. But the applicability of these new organizing principles is restricted to business settings, and even in business their superior efficiency has not been demonstrated conclusively. A second conclusion, therefore, is that bureaucratic principles may achieve efficiency in administration, but even where they do not, alternative forms of administration may prove even less desirable. (p. 186)

Their third conclusion is that 'bureaucratic organizing principles can effectively serve many purposes, which may be in opposition to one another' (p. 187). While their main point is that these make the relationship between bureaucracy and democracy problematic, it is hard to escape the conclusion that the bureaucratic model has so many contradictions that it is understandable why governments now look to other forms of organization derived from business.

It is sometimes stated that even if business or private administration is moving away from formal bureaucracy, public administration should remain in the Weberian style. Blau and Meyer's conclusions suggest this. In this way, the important values in Weber – impersonality, consistency – would remain, as would the important social and ethical questions that are lacking in private sector management. On the other hand, at least some parts of the public sector are analogous to business. They produce products, goods and services that are amenable to better management and have quite similar production functions as the private sector.

For some tasks, a model of authority without hierarchy may be more efficient, as may personal relations and individual leadership rather than the impersonality outlined by Weber. In Weber's time, the scope of bureaucracy was far less than it is now. The bureaucratic task was then one where a small elite could carry out the functions of state, but now the state is involved in a vast array of service delivery functions and some of these do not have to be delivered bureaucratically at all. Newer forms of management focus on achievement of results as the prime goal with organizational form being of secondary importance.

However, despite its problems with efficiency, the system of *power* within the public sector remains that of bureaucracy. To Olsen (2005), bureaucracy signifies three things: first, 'a distinct organizational setting, the bureau or office'; second, 'a professional, fulltime administrative staff'; and third, 'a larger organizational and normative structure where government is founded on authority, that is, the belief in a legitimate, rational-legal political order and the right of the state to define and enforce the legal order' (pp. 2–3). This is a useful distinction. The critique of bureaucracy is focused mainly on the first two of these rather than the third.

Above all, bureaucracy can be seen as a system of power, of authority, of force if necessary, and only secondarily as a set of ideal-type prescriptions set out by Weber. Instead of a new form of rational/legal authority needing to be found for public management (Lynn, 1997), the different aspects of Weber in terms of bureaucracy need to be considered anew. Where the bureaucratic state maintains its strength is in its legal framework. The legal specification of the state as set out by Weber is not altered by adopting a managerial framework, even if the detailed points he set out for the personnel system are no longer necessary. Perhaps public sector reform simply means a new way of organizing within government, but without altering the legal structure of a bureaucratic state. It remains a bureaucracy in the power sense, it still operates according to Weberian rational/legal principles, and it still operates in a democratic polity, but many of the detailed principles of the traditional bureaucratic model can be discarded.

The public choice critique

Public choice theory argues for the maximization of choice by individuals for reasons of individual freedom and efficiency. It is, in essence, the application of microeconomic principles to political and social areas. Analysis of government processes through this lens did point to theoretical and practical flaws in the old model of administration.

Following standard principles of rational behaviour (see Chapter 1), the assumption is that bureaucrats will attempt to maximize their own utility; that is, they aim to increase their own power, prestige, security and income by using the hierarchical structure for their own ends instead of advancing the goals of the organization. Weber's model relies on bureaucrats being essentially disinterested and motivated by higher ideals, such as service to the state. From a public choice assumption of behaviour, this kind of motive is illogical. Public choice theorists argue that individual ambition can lead to outcomes that are not necessarily in the best interests of the organization.

Niskanen (1971, 1973) argued that individual ambition leads to budget maximization by the agency; bureaucrats will benefit personally if they obtain a larger budget, as this means they will have more staff and, conceivably, more power and a higher status in the organization. This perspective does help to explain the pervasive feature of 'office politics' found in any bureaucracy, and the argument that individual bureaucrats work for themselves, rather than the public interest, cannot be totally discounted. Individuals do seek personal advancement, and bureaucrats in a position to do so tend to press for more resources for their agencies. An education department would have impeccable reasons for spending more each year; while the navy wants more ships. This may not always be related to personal motives, but personal and organizational motives may coincide. A successful bureaucrat is often the one who can defend or increase the agency's budget. The traditional model of administration has no satisfactory explanation for office politics of this kind.

Ostrom (1974) also noted that the work of contemporary political economists – public choice theorists – based on a paradigm derived from economic theory, 'challenges many of the basic assumptions in the traditional theory of public administration' (p. 73). And he argues that bureaucracies are inefficient (p. 64):

> The very large bureaucracy will (i) become increasingly indiscriminating in its response to diverse demands; (ii) impose increasingly high social costs upon those who are presumed to be the beneficiaries; (iii) fail to proportion supply to demand; (iv) allow public goods to erode by failing to take actions to prevent one use from impairing other uses; (v) become increasingly error prone and uncontrollable to the point where public actions deviate radically from rhetoric about public purposes and objectives; and (vi) eventually lead to a circumstance where remedial actions exacerbate rather than ameliorate problems.

Bureaucratic organization and markets are therefore opposing types of organization, and Ostrom sees the former as being less efficient or effective than by allowing choice through markets. Markets generally provide a more efficient form of allocation in that they allow for individual ambitions to lead to optimal outcomes following the insights of Adam Smith (1976). Competition, consumer sovereignty and choice provide incentives to lower costs, which are arguably absent in the bureaucratic model of administration.

Public choice arguments are directed overwhelmingly towards lowering government input and reducing bureaucracy. The alternative usually put forward, regardless of the specifics of a given case, is to rely more on market structures. One result of public choice work has been to push back the barriers between public sector and private sector, attempting to define those circumstances where public provision is justified. Ostrom (1974) advocates following the theory of public goods (see Chapter 2), which leads to a much-reduced role for the public sector, as does other work inspired by public choice. As Niskanen

(1973) argues, 'if the structure and incentives in a bureaucracy have to be changed so much to improve its performance, why not rely more on private markets, where this structure and incentive system now exist' and 'a wide range of services financed by government are also marketed, or are potentially marketable in the private sector' (p. 54). From this perspective, public service should be reduced to the bare minimum, with many current functions being returned to the private sector or simply abolished.

Public choice arguments about bureaucracy, while being plausible, are hardly proven and have been challenged, even from within their own framework (Dunleavy, 1991). The question about bureaucrats maximizing budgets to achieve their personal ends suffers from a marked lack of evidence or empirical examination (Lane, 1995, pp. 64–5). Niskanen (1994) later commented that his initial formulation was inadequate, and that bureaucrats aim to maximize their discretionary budgets rather than the total budget (p. 281). It is also possible that the theory may be more applicable to the United States, where agencies build their own separate political relationships with Congress, and where fiscal responsibility is hard to locate.

The public choice approach has some value because it enables generalizations to arise from quite simple assumptions. However, there is an increasing recognition even among economists that their notion of 'rational economic man' (or woman) is too often 'introduced furtively and left under-specified' (Dunleavy, 1991, p. 4; see also Monroe, 1991). Even if there is only a need for these assumptions to apply in the average or aggregate, there are greater problems when the area of application is further away from strict market behaviour. One of the strongest areas in economics more recently is behavioural economics, which includes psychology and is where assumptions of individual rationality can be relaxed. Policy prescriptions can be drawn from this research (see Thaler and Sunstein, 2009).

Another point is that, in this kind of criticism, bureaucracy is seen as somewhat sinister, as an all-purpose societal villain, as a 'traditional bête noire' or 'some kind of alien force' (Goodsell, 1983, p. 149). This view exaggerates the power of bureaucracy and disregards its public purpose. The case against bureaucracy at some points is extrapolated into a case against all government or all non-market entities, in all circumstances, instead of pointing to more realistic problems in one kind of organization, or places where it might or might not work.

There are those, such as Meier and Hill (2005) who argue that bureaucracy is enduring, and that it will continue to thrive in the twenty-first century. Olsen, too, comments that perhaps it is time 'to rediscover bureaucracy' (2005) and makes a strong case for doing so. But, in the end, this is not entirely persuasive. Bureaucracy is undoubtedly an instrument of power, and its use within those parts of government that exercise authority is undiminished. But, in those areas that interact with citizens, that involve service delivery where process and procedure derogate from responsiveness, bureaucracy has been rightly criticized. Even if the greatest attacks on public bureaucracy have occurred in those countries with a strong ideological motivation – the United Kingdom in the Thatcher era, and the United States in the Reagan era – there have also been effects in other countries. Whether this is a result of the influence of the Right, or of public choice economic theory, is an open question. Perhaps more important has been the realization that the traditional theories of public administration were no longer effective and were, accordingly, no longer relevant to the governing of society.

Conclusion

The traditional model of administration was an outstanding success and was widely emulated by governments around the world. As both theory and practice, it had its good points. Compared to earlier forms of administration that were rife with corruption, it was more efficient, and the idea of a professional service was a great improvement on a personal or amateur one. It is argued here, however, that the problems of the model are now such that it can be regarded as obsolescent if not obsolete.

Traditional bureaucracy developed at a particular point of industrial development; its systems and technology were suited to an earlier age. If public servants are considered to be no more than automatons responding to simple stimuli, who cannot be trusted with the scope or responsibility of making decisions, and for whom every conceivable contingency must be set out in operating manuals, then the traditional model of administration may be appropriate. However, formal systems of hierarchy are no longer regarded as working very well in the private or public sectors. The traditional model was a great reform in its day, but the world has moved on.

The theoretical pillars of public administration are no longer seen as being adequate to analyse the reality of government. The theory of political control was always problematic. Administration means following the instructions of others, and therefore necessitates an orderly method of giving and receiving instructions, including a clear separation between those who give instructions and those who carry them out. This was never realistic, and became less so with the increase in scale and scope of public services. The other main pillar – the theory of bureaucracy – is no longer considered to be a particularly efficient or effective form of organization. Bureaucratic organization may not be the single best way of organizing, and its undesirable aspects – concentration of power, reduction of freedom, usurpation of political will – may be thought worse than its desirable features. The traditional model of public administration has been superseded; there is now a greater focus on results rather than on process, on personal responsibility rather than its evasion, and on management rather than administration.

Chapter 4

Public Management

Chapter Contents

- Introduction
- The meaning of management
- The beginnings of a management approach
- Theoretical bases of management
- The problem of New Public Management
- Public sector reform
- Criticisms of managerialism
- Conclusion

Introduction

The 1980s and 1990s saw the emergence of a new approach to management in the public sector, as a direct response to what many had regarded as the inadequacies of the traditional model of administration. In the earliest stages of reform, quite radical change occurred. Far greater attention was paid to the achievement of results and the personal responsibility of managers. There was an expressed intention to move away from classic bureaucracy to make organizations, personnel, and employment terms and conditions more flexible. Organizational and personal objectives would be set clearly, to enable measurement of their achievement through performance indicators. Similarly, systematic evaluation of programmes became commonplace, more rigorously than before, to find out whether government programmes were achieving their goals. Government functions were more likely to face market tests; in separating the purchaser of government services from the provider, in other words the separation of 'steering from rowing' (Savas, 1987). It was argued that government involvement in an area need not always mean government provision through bureaucratic means. There was a parallel trend towards reducing government functions through privatization and other forms of market testing and contracting, in some cases quite radically. All these points were linked and all were derived from the overall change from process to results.

Managerial reform has been controversial. Critics regard managerialism as simply an unquestioning adoption of the worst features of private management with no regard being paid to the fundamental differences of the public sector environment. Managerialism is seen by the critics as in some way being against the traditions of public service, inimical to service delivery, and undemocratic, even with dubious theoretical backing. Some writers, particularly from a public administration tradition, argue that the good parts of the old model – high ethical standards, service to the state, time-honoured processes, regarding all public servants as a special kind of worker deserving novel terms and conditions of work – are being cast aside in the headlong rush to adopt some new approach that is untested and unlikely to work. Practising public managers have been caught between, on the one hand, their government wanting tasks to be carried out with even greater efficiency, and on the other, those who criticize the managers' actions.

One emerging problem in coming to terms with the change from public administration to public management has been the invention of the term New Public Management (NPM). Starting with Hood (1991), the main use of NPM has been by critics, in explicitly or implicitly criticizing public sector reform in general. Even if the argument is mainly about the market-based reforms often identified as being characteristic of NPM, the lack of specificity as to what is actually involved in NPM raises major problems. There is no agreement as to what NPM actually is; different theorists put forward quite different lists of characteristics. Not only is there no agreed content in NPM, it is also hard to find any kind of advocate. NPM is fairly universally an epithet, a term of criticism, and this has led to a widening gap between public management practitioners and public management academics. Practitioners may feel that all they are trying to do is to perform their jobs satisfactorily, but they face criticism from academics about what they do.

The argument here is that public management is indeed different from public administration, sufficiently so to be regarded as a new paradigm in its own right (see also Chapter 15). But this does not mean that the replacement for public administration is a single, unvarying entity called 'New Public Management' – a programme that is simply rolled out in all circumstances and all countries. The key difference between public administration and public management is that a public manager is personally responsible for the delivery of results. And once this expectation is made clear, a public manager will then act according to his or her perspective as to how results are to be achieved. This is, on the surface, quite a simple change, but it has major ramifications in practice. Other points noticed by critics – the adoption of private management ideas and practices, the use of economic theory and models, and the obsession with performance management – are all subsidiary to the notion that a public manager is now personally responsible for delivering results.

Public management has now effectively supplanted the traditional model of public administration. The public sector in the future is likely to move even further away from traditional public administration, in both theory and practice; indeed, more recent changes to public management – leadership, governance, collaboration and co-production – are even further removed from the traditional bureaucratic model. Public management need not mean the widespread and uncritical adoption of practices from the private sector. What it should mean is that a distinctive public management needs to be utilized. This takes into account differences between the sectors, but still recognizes that the work being done by public servants is now managerial rather than administrative.

The meaning of management

It was stated earlier (Chapter 1) that management is different from administration in meaning. Essentially, administration means following instructions, whereas management means the achievement of results and taking personal responsibility for doing so. Management is a much more active word than administration; it does imply taking charge, and having responsibility for results. How management is different from administration can be considered by looking at what Allison (1982) refers to as 'functions of general management' (see Box 4.1).

Allison's model captures the main points about management. In addition, while this was not his purpose in the original article, Allison's framework can be used to compare a model of management with a model of administration in the public sector.

The first main function of general management set out by Allison is that of *strategy* (see also Chapter 10). This involves deciding the future of the organization, establishing objectives and priorities, and making plans to achieve these. The earlier model of public administration required little conception of strategy. Public servants 'administered' in the dictionary sense, simply carrying out the instructions of the politicians who were presumed to develop and be responsible for all policy and strategy. Traditional public administration tended to consider short-term goals within the organization, but public management aims at the longer term and at the relationship between the organization and the external environment. Successful public management 'inevitably requires a feel for strategy'; it is 'broader, more integrative, and less defined by functional expertise than is public administration' (Bozeman and Straussman, 1990, p. 214). Agencies themselves are required to

---

Box 4.1   Functions of general management

STRATEGY

1.   Establishing objectives and priorities for the organization (on the basis of forecasts of the external environment and the organization's capacities).
2.   Devising operational plans to achieve these objectives.

MANAGING INTERNAL COMPONENTS

3.   Organizing and staffing: in organizing, the manager establishes structure (units and positions with assigned authority and responsibilities) and procedures for co-ordinating activity and taking action. In staffing, he tries to fit the right persons in the key jobs.
4.   Directing personnel and the personnel management system: the capacity of the organization is embodied primarily in its members and their skills and knowledge. The personnel management system recruits, selects, socializes, trains, rewards, punishes and exits the organization's human capital, which constitutes the organization's capacity to act to achieve its goals and to respond to specific directions from management.
5.   Controlling performance: various management information systems – including operating and capital budgets, accounts, reports, statistical systems, performance appraisals and product evaluation – assist management in making decisions and in measuring progress towards objectives.

MANAGING EXTERNAL CONSTITUENCIES

6.   Dealing with 'external' units of the organization subject to some common authority: most general managers must deal with general managers of other units within the larger organization above, laterally and below to achieve their unit's objectives.
7.   Dealing with independent organizations: agencies from other branches or levels of government, interest groups, and private enterprises that can affect the organization's ability to achieve its objectives.
8.   Dealing with the press and public, whose action or approval or acquiescence is required.

Source: Allison (1982, p. 17).

---

develop objectives and priorities rather than assuming that policy derives from politicians.

The second main function is *managing internal components*. This involves staffing and the setting up of structures and systems that help to achieve the objectives identified by strategy. Traditional public administration did require the expenditure of effort on the 'managing internal components' function of general management, though there are some significant ways in which this was not carried out to its fullest. Certainly, public administrators had to organize the bureau, hire staff, train and promote them, and deal with all the other aspects of the personnel system, but the controlling of performance was always rather weak. This has also changed substantially with managerial reform; measurement of the performance of agencies and individuals has now become a routine part of financial reform.

The third function looks at the organization in its external context. Within the traditional model, any dealings with outside organizations, the press or the public were not matters involving administrators. This has changed markedly. Public servants are now much freer to speak out in public, to appear at professional forums, to write articles for journals, and generally to be visible and public figures. Public management, as it developed, especially after the mid-1990s, has expressly concerned itself with developing better relationships with external stakeholders and collaborators, again very different from the insularity of the traditional model.

Since the implementation of various reforms that began in the 1980s, all three of Allison's groups of functions of general management are now routinely carried out by public servants, which suggests that the actual work done is now more managerial than administrative. Outlining the functions of general management as they apply to the public sector does not necessarily mean that management is generic – a criticism often made of public management, or that there is no difference between public and private management. It is rather that there are certain functions which characterize a *general* management function.

The beginnings of a management approach

For much of the twentieth century there was little difference in management structures or styles between the private and public sectors; large companies in the private sector were as hierarchical and Weberian as any government department. It was only from the 1950s or 1960s that the problems of bureaucratic rigidity became evident in the private sector. The rise of the manager in the private sector coincides with the realization that the division of tasks and the writing of manuals to cover every contingency had limitations. Someone needed to take charge and to take personal responsibility for the achievement of results.

It is hard to delineate exactly when management began to take over from administration in the public sector. The apparent success of managers in the private sector led to concerns being expressed, including by governments themselves, that the public sector had fallen behind in terms of good practice. A starting point was the Fulton Report (1968) in the United Kingdom, which noted concerns with the management capability of the UK's Civil Service. It recommended that the system be opened up, that outsiders be employed at all levels, and that the rigid hierarchical structure in which barriers were placed at several points be removed. It was not completely clear what Fulton actually meant by management. At one point the report noted that management 'consists of the formulation and operation of the policy of the enterprise' (Keeling, 1972, p. 22). Here, the Fulton Report expresses a modern, results-based view of management similar to the dictionary meanings discussed earlier. However, in other parts of the Report, management seems to be defined as what the Civil Service does, which is not particularly helpful (Keeling, 1972, p. 23). Fulton could be described as a start, rather than as a thorough attempt to infuse management principles into an administrative system. Moreover, Fulton's recommendations were not implemented at the time; they were deferred until a more conducive time. As Flynn commented, 'no government had much enthusiasm for the task until the Thatcher administration' (1997, p. 31). However, it is interesting that even in 1972 Keeling saw management – defined as 'the search for the best use of resources in pursuit of objectives subject to change'– as the coming thing (Keeling, 1972; Pollitt, 1993).

In the United States there was also a demand for improved management in the public sector, at least from the Carter Administration onwards. The Civil Service Reform Act of 1978 aimed at giving managers greater responsibility for results. It included merit pay for middle management and the establishment of a Senior Executive Service to form an elite group at the top. Though focused on personnel, it was an attempt to improve management in the public sector, which was perceived as lagging behind the private sector.

On setting up the Reid Inquiry into the Australian public service in 1982, the then prime minister, Malcolm Fraser, noted: 'the government believes there is a question whether the public service, as presently organized, has the management tools, the flexibility and the capacities to meet the challenges that presently exist and that lie ahead' (Reid, 1983, p. 131). A number of recommendations were made by the inquiry and many were implemented by the incoming Hawke Labor Government (Hughes, 1998). Despite being from the other end of the political spectrum, its views on the managerial capacities of the public service were largely the same as its predecessor. Even more radical managerial changes occurred at the same time in New Zealand, again following a change of government. The late 1970s and early 1980s can now be seen as the beginning of a more managerial approach to government in what could be called the Anglo-American democracies. Changes in other countries came later.

There were several reasons for this seeming disenchantment with the skills and capabilities of public services as they had operated up till then. From the mid-1970s, governments experienced severe resource constraints as tax revenues declined in a relative sense. Practical politics dictated that no cuts were to be made in actual service delivery to the public. This in turn meant a squeeze on the public service in an attempt to manage the same – or even increased – functions, with less money and fewer staff. Changes of government brought with them quite detailed ideas on how to change the management of the public service. It is noteworthy that the impetus for managerial change came largely from the political leadership and not the public service itself. It also crossed the party divide rather than being confined to a particular ideology. The reform imperative was similar with parties of the Right and Left. At the same time, there was an intellectual climate conducive to reducing the public sector or, at the very least, making it work harder (see Chapter 2).

The main reason for the eclipse of the old traditional model of administration was simply that it no longer worked very well, and was widely perceived not to be working. Governments realized this first and began to challenge some of the most basic beliefs of the traditional model. They began to hire economists or people trained in management in preference to generalist administrators, borrowed management techniques from the private sector, pushed back the dividing line between public and private sector activity with the aim of cutting costs, and set out to change working conditions accordingly. As governments were faced with declining real revenue, but with political demands to maintain services at the same levels, the only alternative was to improve productivity in some way. When theories suggested that bureaucratic provision is inherently inefficient, when economic studies showed the same thing, and when the public made constant complaints about red tape and inefficiency, it was little wonder that politicians began to ask awkward questions. Why should public servants have permanent lifetime employment when no one else did; and why should they not be hired by contract? If someone is employed to do a job, what is wrong in seeing that it is being done efficiently? The public services lost public support to such an extent that governments found little resistance to changes that would once have been regarded as destroying the very notion of a public service. And, once change began, the various aspects – the old verities – of the traditional model of administration were dismantled.

By the beginning of the 1990s, a new model of public management was under way in most advanced countries and in many developing ones. Initially, the new model had several names, including: 'managerialism' (Pollitt, 1993); 'New Public Management' (Hood, 1991); 'market-based public administration' (Lan and Rosenbloom, 1992); the 'post-bureaucratic paradigm' (Barzelay, 1992); or 'entrepreneurial government' (Osborne and Gaebler, 1992). The literature more-or-less settled on New Public Management (NPM), even though the term lacked precision and an agreed meaning. In addition, 'public management' became more widely accepted as a description of the overall disciplinary area than 'public administration'.

Public management change began in the United Kingdom in the early 1980s with the widespread privatization, government cuts and load shedding that started during the early years of the Thatcher Government. Before too long, some theorists began to see the trend as a more general phenomenon. Hood (1991) and Rhodes (1991), drawing on Hood, were the first to refer to NPM. By the end of the 1990s, Horton (1999) noted that 'during the 1980s and 1990s the civil service moved from an administered to a managed bureaucracy and from a system of public administration to one of new public management (NPM)' (p. 145). The early public service reforms were quite contentious in the UK, perhaps not so much from their seeking greater efficiency in government, but because, to some, they attacked the very fabric of civil society. Public sector reform was seen as applied Thatcherism.

The New Zealand reforms of the 1980s came out of a serious economic crisis. Traditional export industries had collapsed and the internal systems of industry protection and government-owned enterprises covering much of the economy had become unsustainable. By the late 1980s the crisis culminated in actions aimed at transforming the public sector. As Scott (2001, p. 365) – a senior practitioner at the time – observed:

> The 1987 Labour government was seeking from the public sector greater efficiency, better information, increased fiscal control, tighter accountability for delivering on the government's objectives, the ability to shift resources from low- to high-priority areas, and an end to the employment protections peculiar to the public service. There were significant gains made by the government in respect of every objective. Many critics might wish that these had not been the objectives but that is another debate.

The public sector reform that occurred in New Zealand was extensive but was much more about trying to respond to economic crisis than it was to set up a new kind of public management. The people involved were clearly trying to solve practical problems; significantly, they did not regard standard public administration approaches highly and quite consciously drew from other theoretical frameworks, including economics (Boston *et al.*, 1996).

In the United States, a key event was the publication of *Reinventing Government* by Osborne and Gaebler (1992). Even if somewhat simplistic at times with its use of anecdotal examples and its similarity to other works looking at the private sector (Peters and Waterman,

1982), *Reinventing Government* became a runaway best-seller. The book cover included an endorsement by then presidential candidate Governor Bill Clinton. It was no surprise that, after his election, the new president took an avid interest in reforming government.

After his inauguration as president, Mr Clinton gave the task of conducting the National Performance Review to Vice-President Al Gore (Gore, 1993). This review was clearly influenced by Osborne and Gaebler, in its diagnosis of the problem as being too much bureaucracy, the solutions advanced, and the language of reinvention used. The Gore Report set out to change the culture of American federal government through four key principles: (i) cutting red tape: 'shifting from systems in which people are accountable for following rules to systems in which they are accountable for achieving results'; (ii) putting customers first; (iii) empowering employees to get results; and (iv) cutting back to basics and 'producing better government for less' (Gore, 1993, pp. 6–7). The Gore Report also cited innovative practices in Britain, New Zealand and Australia, perhaps suggesting that the United States saw itself as lagging behind somewhat in developing this new management.

International organizations, notably the Paris-based Organisation for Economic Co-operation and Development (OECD) and, to a lesser extent, the World Bank and the International Monetary Fund (IMF) also became interested in improving the public management of their member and client nations. In 1991, the OECD stated that most countries were following 'two broad avenues' to improve production and delivery of publicly provided goods and services (OECD, 1991a, p. 11). The first was to 'raise the production performance of public organizations' including relaxing administrative controls while imposing strict performance targets, and the second to 'make greater use of the private sector' in a number of areas including 'contracting out production of publicly provided goods and services and contracting in intermediate goods and services' (OECD, 1991a, p. 11). A later OECD paper argued that improving efficiency and effectiveness of the public sector itself 'involves a major cultural shift as the old management paradigm, which was largely process- and rules-driven, is replaced by a new paradigm which attempts to combine modern management practices with the logic of economics, while still retaining the core public service values' (OECD, 1998a, p. 5). For a time, international organizations led management reform in government, even though they generally stopped short of advocating NPM.

The underlying theories of the traditional model of public administration were, as discussed earlier, bureaucracy, 'one best way', the public interest and a separation of politics from administration. All had their problems; indeed, the management paradigm was 'a direct response to the inadequacies of traditional public administration – particularly to the inadequacies of public bureaucracies' (Behn, 2001, p. 30). Public sector reform has been driven by totally different underlying theories: that economic insights have a major role in government; that private management flexibility provides lessons for government; and that there can be no separation of politics and administration. But the biggest change and the biggest difference from public administration was the requirement for public managers to accept personal responsibility for the achievement of results. This is, in the long run, far more significant than any other change.

Theoretical bases of management

It was noted in Chapter 3 that traditional public administration was based on two theories: the theory of bureaucracy; and the theory of separation between politicians and administrators. The main theoretical bases of public management reform are to be found in economics and private management.

That these are the two main theoretical bases for new public management is not really a matter of controversy. Pollitt (1993), for example, states that management is 'clearly an activity which is intimately concerned with directing flows of resources so as to achieve defined objectives', and these objectives 'are defined predominantly in the language of economics – "output" and "value for money"' (p. 5). The OECD notes that the old paradigm of public sector management 'is replaced by a new paradigm which attempts to combine modern management practices with the logic of economics, while still retaining core public service values' (OECD, 1998a, p. 5).

The economic basis to managerialism allows it to draw on what can be argued to be the most powerful of social science theories. Predictive models can be derived provided that people can be assumed, in aggregate, to act as if they were rational. Economics aims to be *deductive*, something that sets it apart from other social science theories, which usually draw their scientific basis from inductive work. Economists and economic thinking became more influential in government from the 1960s and 1970s (Carter *et al.*, 1992). It is easy to see why. Compared with the rather vague public interest theories of public administration, economics seemed to offer precision, prediction and empiricism, backed by a motivational theory of how people acted. Economics also had direct relevance to governing. The public sector does things: it provides goods and services, and should do so in the most efficient way possible. The focus of management models on results, efficiency and measurement owes much to economics.

A key early theorist of an economic approach to public administration was Ostrom (1974, 1989). In the early 1970s, he argued that there were two opposing forms of organization: bureaucracy and markets, and that bureaucracy had major problems compared to markets. Bureaucratic organization was to Ostrom less efficient or effective than allowing choice through markets; competition, consumer sovereignty and choice provide incentives to lower costs, which are argued to be absent in the bureaucratic model of administration. He argued that 'alternative forms of organization may be available for the performance of those functions apart from an extension and perfection of bureaucratic structures' (Ostrom, 1989, p. 16), and that the work of contemporary political economists, based on a paradigm derived from economic theory, 'challenges many of the basic assumptions in the traditional theory of public administration' (1989, p. 64). The way that public administration changed bears out much of what Ostrom advocated, even if the ideas took some time to be adopted. Public management does draw on economics – using such theories as public choice, principal–agent theory and transaction cost theory (Walsh, 1995; Boston *et al.*, 1996; Kaboolian, 1998, p. 190); and, second, it aims to move away from bureaucracy as an organizing principle, just as Ostrom had argued.

The second theoretical basis for public management can be found in private management. There are several managerial changes with antecedents in the private sector. In the private setting, there is greater flexibility in tailoring the organization to circumstance, instead of necessarily following a rigid Weberian model. While the private sector was once as bureaucratic as any government, it moved earlier towards more flexible forms of management, and the managerial changes in the public sector follow these. The focus on results could be said to derive from economics, but is also present in private management, because without achieving results a company would be out of business. The greater attention now paid to strategic planning and management in the public sector also derives, in its most recent incarnation, from the private sector (see Chapter 10). Private sector personnel practices have been adopted to some degree in government, including the greater use of incentives and disincentives throughout the organization. The adoption of more formal means of evaluation has private sector roots, as does the improvement in information systems to provide accounting or other data. These could all be said to derive from the private sector, but none could be seen as being exclusively a private sector technique.

Where private management is particularly helpful for managerialism is in deconstructing parts of the public system once considered to be fundamental. Of course, the public sector must be fair and impartial in dealing with clients, but this does not mean that public servants need be politically neutral or have a job for life. It may be difficult to measure performance in the public sector, but this does not mean that no attempt should be made. The political nature of the public sector does make it different from the private sector, but this does not mean that *all* acts are political, or that *all* policy actions need to be undertaken by politicians. This is particularly the case with the input factors identified earlier, such as the generous staffing conditions once thought necessary for public servants. It is hard to see how service delivery is necessarily damaged by employment by contract or on a part-time basis, or if staff are initially hired at higher levels than the base grade. However, all these are against what was once thought necessary for all public employment. If much of the actual work in the public sector is the same as the private sector, other than at the highest levels, it is hard to justify unusual employment practices or pension schemes that are far more generous than in the private sector.

Perhaps the most important point imported from the private sector is the focus on objectives. Making the achievement of results the primary aim, with everything else being secondary, is a major change of mind-set. Also, bureaucratic organizations are not axiomatically efficient, as discussed earlier. The private sector has experimented with other organizational frameworks – profit centres, decentralization, staffing flexibility, all of which have public sector parallels. The movement in the private sector towards flexibility is now also being emulated by the public sector. However, the borrowing from the private sector can be overstated. It is unhelpful merely to argue that, as a particular point derives from private management, it cannot work in the public sector.

The problem of New Public Management

As noted earlier (Chapter 1), the managerial changes largely became referred to as 'New Public Management' or NPM. NPM became a kind of shorthand used to describe the economistic, managerial changes in public management. It has not been helpful in terms of any kind of precision around the reform process as a whole. As will be argued, the understanding of public management reform has not been assisted by the invention of the term NPM.

In what appears to be the first use of the term, Hood (1991) declared that the managerial programme, or what he named 'New Public Management', comprises seven main points (pp. 4–5):

- *Hands-on professional management* in the public sector. This means letting the managers manage, or, as Hood puts it, 'active, visible, discretionary control of organizations from named persons at the top'. The typical justification for this is that 'accountability requires clear assignment of responsibility for action'.
- *Explicit standards and measures of performance*. This requires goals to be defined and performance targets to be set, and is justified by

proponents as 'accountability requires [a] clear statement of goals; efficiency requires a "hard look" at objectives'.

- Greater emphasis on *output controls*. Resources are directed to areas according to measured performance, because of the 'need to stress *results* rather than *procedures*'.

- A shift towards *disaggregation* of units in the public sector. This involves the breaking up of large entities into 'corporatized units around products', funded separately and 'dealing with one another on an "arm's-length" basis'. This is justified by the need to create manageable units and 'to gain the efficiency advantages of franchise arrangements *inside* as well as outside the public sector'.

- A shift to greater *competition* in the public sector. This involves 'the move to term contracts and public tendering procedures' and is justified as using 'rivalry as the key to lower costs and better standards'.

- *A stress on private sector styles of management practice.* This involves a 'move away from military-style "public service ethic"' and 'flexibility in hiring and rewards', and is justified by the 'need to use "proven" private sector management tools in the public sector'.

- A stress on greater *discipline* and *parsimony* in resource use. Hood sees this as 'cutting direct costs, raising labour discipline, resisting union demands, limiting "compliance costs" to business' and typically is justified by the 'need to check resource demands of public sector and "do more with less"'.

In setting out these points, Hood (1991) was not putting NPM forward as a programme to be followed, nor should he be seen as an advocate of any kind. What Hood did was to aggregate a set of disparate changes, most notably from the UK, as if they were sub-categories of a wider movement of change, and then give it a title – 'new public management'. However, the term has not been very useful for several reasons: it regards disparate changes as part of a unified whole; it has a usage really only among critics of public sector reform; it is a diversion from the real changes that have taken place; it has led to an unhelpful gap between actual public management practice and academic discussion of it; and, finally, there is neither an agreed set of points constituting NPM, nor is there a theorist who can be identified as an advocate. These points are elaborated later (see Chapter 15). A *programme* it never was; and an *agenda* it never was, other than in retrospect. No one, even in the UK, put the parts together as a coherent programme to be followed step-by-step. NPM was, at most, a convenient label for disparate changes.

Many of Hood's detailed points have a much longer history than being part of something new, which would in the future deserve the title 'NPM'. The last point, on greater discipline and parsimony in resource use, is a long-standing public administration concept around safeguarding the public purse. Private sector styles of management – the penultimate point above – also have a long history in public administration; indeed, the history of management thought is replete with any number of borrowings from private to public and vice versa. Contracting out is hardly new, either. Contracting and tendering have a history within government, including in Britain, of literally hundreds of years. Moreover, governments everywhere contract for supplies from the private sector; the precise point at which goods or services are delivered in-house or bought in from outside might change over time, but the principle is unexceptional and not novel at all. The second and third points above are essentially the same as each other, about measuring performance and directing resources to areas where results have occurred. The extent of this may indeed have been enhanced in recent decades, but only gradually and not as a part of a consistent NPM programme. Performance management is also linked with the old public administration value of value for money; it 'both pre-dates and persists strongly beyond NPM' and exists in countries without NPM-like reforms (Halligan, 2007, p. 43). In the United Kingdom, using performance management to enhance productivity dates back to the beginning of the twentieth century (Bouckaert and Halligan, 2008, pp. 71–3). During the time of the traditional model, performance decisions were still made, but were more *ad hoc* and often arbitrary. Performance management systems may now be more formalized than before, but the principle is not new at all.

Two points remain from Hood's list – 'hands-on professional management' and 'disaggregation'. The first of these does mark a major shift, but was hardly new. It is probably not possible to determine the precise point where public servants began to be regarded as responsible for the achievement of results, but it was much earlier than 1991. The second – disaggregation – was never a requirement of managerial reform generally even though it was used in the UK and New Zealand in the early days.

Hood states that 'there is no single accepted explanation or interpretation of why NPM coalesced and why it "caught on"' (1991, pp. 6–8). He does mention four possibilities: first, as a 'whim of fashion'; second, as a 'cargo cult' – the endless rebirth, in spite of repeated failures, of the idea that substantive success ('cargo') can be gained by the practice of particular kinds of (managerial) ritual; third, as 'an attraction of opposites'; and fourth, as 'a response to a set of special social conditions' which itself includes 'changes in income and distribution, post-industrialism, post-Fordism, new machine politics and a shift to a more white-collar population'. A further point, but not mentioned by Hood, was that there was a widespread perception that the old model simply did not work.

By the early 1980s, governments in key countries seemed to be convinced that there were managerial inadequacies in their public services and there was, as a result, a general aim to improve their operations. Once reform started, other governments copied what had been implemented by other jurisdictions, but with the exception of a predilection, as in New Zealand, towards economics, the reforms were not particularly theoretical. Following a review of the reforms many years later, Hood and Peters noted (2004, p. 268) that there was no definitive treatise on NPM (see Chapter 15). Other than mentions of the early involvement of practitioners such as the New Zealand Treasury and that the apparent coherence of the ideas attracted debate and attention, they argued that NPM was 'somewhat mystical' with different authors listing different features that characterized NPM.

There was no theoretical treatise that emerged because there was no theoretical treatise to emerge. Hood and Peters are also quite correct in pointing out that no two authors list exactly the same points for NPM; what this does is damage the very notion that there ever was a new public management. All this is not to deny that there has been real and substantial change in the public sector. It is just that the change becomes a *tendency* rather than a clear programme that marks a major discontinuity from past practice.

That NPM was only a tendency can be shown by looking at what Pollitt (2001) considered to be a number of general elements of the new model accepted by most commentators (pp. 473–4):

- A shift in the focus of management systems and management effort from inputs and processes to outputs and outcomes.
- A shift towards more measurement, manifesting itself in the appearance of batteries of performance indicators and standards.
- A preference for more specialized, 'lean', 'flat' and autonomous organizational forms rather than large, multi-purpose, hierarchical bureaucracies.
- A widespread substitution of contract or contract-like relationships for hierarchical relationships.
- A much wider than hitherto use of market or market-like mechanisms for the delivery of public services (including privatization, contracting out, the development of internal markets, etc.).
- A broadening and blurring of the 'frontier' between the public and private sectors (characterized by the growth of public/private partnerships of various kinds and the apparent proliferation of 'hybrid' organizations).
- A shift in value priorities away from universalism, equity, security and resilience and towards efficiency and individualism.

There are three points to make about Pollitt's listing of elements of the new model. First, there is no sense that added together there is a consistent programme at all, or at least one that is truly novel. Some of Pollitt's points about NPM are related to Hood's list, and some are new. Again there is mention of measurement; again there is a preference for contracts; again there is the shift from inputs and processes to outputs and outcomes. 'Sort of new' is the wider use of market mechanisms and the shift in value priorities. A quibble could be made about the validity of a shift in value priorities both before and after reform, but, in general, Pollitt's list of elements does provide a good summation of the overall reform programme.

Second, the very language used by Pollitt in his list of elements is enlightening. There are various 'shifts', a 'preference', a 'much wider use of market mechanisms', a 'broadening and blurring of the frontier between public and private' and the like. Rather than sharp change, these can all be considered to point to incremental shifts and changes of emphasis. Therefore the new model can be argued to be a *tendency* towards change, an exaggeration of past practice, rather than something completely novel. The reform process has been real. It has been substantial. But what it has done most of all is indicate a shift in direction, not a revolution, certainly not one that deserves the special appellation of 'New Public Management'.

Another complication is that there are a number of formulations of NPM, indeed almost as many as there are theorists. The arguments as to what NPM is, or what it has done, or is doing, have been unproductive. What has often been missed, however, in the fruitless arguments about management consultants, economics, private management practice, performance management, accrual accounting and so on is that actual reform has taken place. The reform has occurred regardless of the critics and their comments. The changes in a managerial direction were significant, but they also showed considerable continuity with previous reform (Rugge, 2003). That there have been reforms is undoubted; where there is a problem is in the argument that is often put forward, that there is a single programme or agenda to which all reform can be attached.

Public sector reform

The argument about NPM should not become a diversion from the much broader set of changes that have resulted in the replacement of public administration by public management. The reforms that have occurred are rather more likely to be tailored to country and to circumstance. A useful characterization is in what Kettl terms the core components of public sector reform. These are: *productivity* – more services for less of an outlay; *marketization* – using market-style incentives to 'root out the pathologies' of bureaucracy; *service orientation* – more responsive service delivery; *decentralization* – devolving responsibility for delivery to lower levels of government, notably in federal systems; *policy* – improving the capacity to devise and track policy, including a separation of purchasing services from provision; and *accountability* – a focus on outputs and outcomes rather than on processes and structures (Kettl, 2005, pp. 1–3). These are all commonly found, as Kettl points out, in countries around the world where the reforms 'sought to replace traditional rule-based authority-driven processes with market-based, competition-driven tactics' (p. 3). Note that Kettl is not stating that there is a single programme of reform delivered unvaried around the world. It is a more general trend rather than following a specific programme. The following nine sub-sections set out some of the changes that have been typical in public sector reform.

Management not administration

The key change in the public sector is from public administration to public management. A public manager is now required to achieve results and take personal responsibility for their achievement. Public organizations do things. Governments now want to know what they do; how well they do it; who is in charge; and who is taking responsibility for results. There are subsequent changes: managers are now involved in matters of policy; they may also be involved in matters of strict politics; they take charge of delivery, all as a consequence of being responsible for achieving results. High-profile managers are often appointed on short-term contracts, have management backgrounds and are employed to get results. They may also be public figures in a way not previously considered normal for a public servant, and may prefer working for one side of politics. Another change in senior management is the move away from specialist heads – such as engineers or scientists in technical areas, or doctors in health departments – to managerial heads of agencies. Management is seen more as a function requiring its own skills rather than something that specialists from technical areas can simply 'pick up'.

Leadership

A managerial model requires leadership; indeed, this is another of the key aspects of the change from the traditional administrative model. A strictly bureaucratic model has no place for leadership or any other personality-driven behaviour from anyone in the system. A managerial model not only recognizes that informal, personal behaviour will exist in reality, but sets out to capture it and use it for organizational benefit. As Behn (1998b, p. 211) states:

Leaders exercise initiative by articulating and clarifying purposes; by setting and pursuing performance targets; by educating, persuading, and motivating people; by choosing among alternatives; and by experimenting with strategies and tactics. It is all very public. And it is all very personal.

Instead of decisions being made by impersonal application of the rules, they are to be made in order to achieve results, to solve problems, and, crucially, a manager is required to do this as a *person*, as an individual.

A focus on results

With the manager being responsible for the achievement of results, the organization must as a consequence have some focus on results and their measurement. Traditional public administration looked more to processes rather than results, or at least assuming that the processes themselves would lead to results. Agencies are now expected to develop some way of measuring the progress made towards achieving declared objectives. A formal performance appraisal system is now commonplace for individual staff. This replaces the informal methods that always existed but which would more often now be considered to be ineffective and leading to inferior organizational outcomes. Performance monitoring includes more than performance indicators. A performance orientation requires 'changing the incentives in the institutional framework – the budget and personnel systems, the approach to control and risk management, etc. so that performance is encouraged, rewarded and required' (Holmes and Shand, 1995, p. 563). A performance and results orientation has been one of the most controversial aspects of managerial reform, but if scarce public money is to be allocated to a task, there should be some way of being able to tell if the desired results have been achieved.

A more strategic approach

Strategic planning and strategic management (Bryson, 2004) can be used to provide a longer-term perspective on what governments and agencies aim to achieve (see Chapter 10). Only by knowing what government organizations do, what they aim to do in the future, and how they have progressed towards declared objectives, can the political leadership decide which programmes or even agencies or departments are worth retaining. Strategy is one of those so-called private sector techniques that is often criticized, but any means of moving away from the short-termism endemic in government should not be dismissed out of hand.

Improved financial management

Better ways of accounting for government activity follow directly from the requirements for the achievement and measurement of results. Financial management has been one of the more successful of the public sector reforms, in particular the performance and programme budgeting systems that have largely replaced the older line-item budget and accounting systems. The focus was formerly on inputs rather than outputs, or on what the agency actually does. To take into account changes in the value of assets and to be more like private sector practice, accrual accounting has replaced cash accounting in some countries. This is hard to implement but potentially much more accurate than traditional budgeting practices. It is more common now for budget responsibility to be devolved to lower levels, where it is part of the management task.

Flexibility in staffing

Again, the requirement for managers to take personal responsibility for results leads to changes. Traditional public administration staffing practices, such as only hiring at the base grade, promotion by seniority, inability to terminate the contracts of poorly performing staff, and inadequate performance appraisal often led to mediocrity. A general set of staffing changes has led to much more flexibility, with the aim of improving overall efficiency by developing the service's management capability. There has been a general recognition that good staff need to be paid much higher salaries. At the same time, inefficient staff can now be dismissed more quickly, though with retention of some protection against arbitrary or politically motivated dismissal.

Competition and contractualism

The contracting out of government services on the grounds of competition has often been considered one of the big changes in the reform process (Davis, 1997; Greve, 2007). The significance of this has been overstated, given that governments have always contracted out to some extent. Still, because there has been a re-emphasis on contracts and competition it has meant that internal provision has faced some challenges. It is argued by proponents that if services are 'contestable' they should be put out to tender. Widespread privatization is part of this shift, but is not the only means of reducing governmental scope. Competition for provision through contracting, sometimes within government, is seen as reducing costs compared to bureaucratic provision.

Under what has been called 'contractualism' (Davis, 1997), any conceivable government service can be provided by contract, either externally through private or voluntary sector providers, or internally with other parts of government. Compulsory competitive tendering was adopted in local government in the UK in the early 1980s and in other parts of the government later (Walsh, 1995, pp. 110–37; Flynn, 1997, pp. 114–15), though its utility was questionable and its actual success doubtful. Far more important than compulsory tendering has been the realization that tendering for a particular good or service is one of the possible ways for public managers to attain the results they are required to achieve.

Relationships with politicians

When managers take responsibility for the achievement of results, their relationship with politicians and the public must alter. In the traditional model, the relationship with the political leadership was narrow and technical, of master and servant, of those giving the orders and those carrying them out. Under the public management model, the relationship between politician and manager is more fluid. It is not a narrow and technocratic form of management, as political authority still exists. In other words, there is not an unrealistic formula for the relationship between politician and manager, there is interaction.

The major skill needed of a public manager is how to be a bureaucratic politician in a way, to be able to interact with politicians and with the outside world. The behaviour required is not party-political, rather it is politics in terms of being able to work with people. The traditional model tried to de-personalize and de-politicize what was essentially political. Public management recognizes the essential political character of government; public servants work with politicians in an interactive process. Of course, politicians have the final say, but the unrealistic separation of policy-making from administration has finally been discarded.

Relationships with the public

There is more recognition of the need for direct accountability between managers and the public, as the result of demands for a 'client focus' and for greater responsiveness to outside groups and individuals. This is another big difference from the traditional model of administration, where there was little contact with the outside world, even with clients. Public management is now much more open to active participation from the citizenry, from clients, and from stakeholders. Rather than there being a single one-best-way solution there are many possibilities. In addition to active participation, public managers realize that much of what they do relies on collaboration with the public (see Alford, 2009).

These nine points of reform do not constitute a single unvarying model or programme. There could be other points added; also, in some countries, particular ones may be emphasized more than others. To reiterate, the single key change is that a public manager is personally responsible for the achievement of results. From this simple change, most of the others naturally follow. The nine points cited are tendencies; changes of emphasis from prior practice. Added together, they sum to real and substantial differences between what is termed here the traditional model of administration and public management.

Criticisms of managerialism

There have been sustained criticisms of reform from its beginnings in the 1980s. In some countries, particularly the United Kingdom, there has been quite overt hostility about any kind of managerial reform. There are some aspects of public sector reform where the criticisms have been justified; and there are other aspects that have not been justified. Some particular points will be examined briefly here, while some key criticisms of the entire public sector reform era will be considered later (see Chapter 15).

The economic basis of managerialism

One of the criticisms of managerialist thinking derives from its foundation in economics. Of course, no theory is immune from criticism. Economics is often attacked for its supposed ideological bias and unrealistic assumptions. In the real world, all individuals do not behave rationally all the time, and not all governmental problems will be amenable to economic techniques. Perhaps there are limitations to the use of economic methods in the essentially political environment of the public sector.

There are two main criticisms of the economic basis of managerialism. The first is that economics is a flawed social science and its application to government is similarly flawed. This is not a new criticism and has been made ever since economics and the capitalist system matured. More to the point in a general criticism of economics is that neo-classical economics is only one strand and, if dominant at the present time, there are other economic theories that allow a greater role for government, and a consideration of economics where individual psychology is taken into account, including behavioural theories (see Thaler and Sunstein, 2009).

The second, and more common, criticism is that, while economics has some validity as the basis for the economic system and the private sector, its application to government is ill-conceived. Pollitt (1993) comments that public services are more distinctive than any generic model of the consumer would allow, for two reasons. First, the 'provider/consumer transactions in the public services tend to be notably more complex' than those faced by the consumer in a normal market; and, second, public service consumers 'are never merely "consumers", they are always citizens too, and this has a set of unique implications for the transaction' (Pollitt, 1993, pp. 125–6). Both points have some validity. Public service transactions are indeed more complex, and the consumer being a citizen does make for some complications. It has always been paradoxical that particular citizens could, on the one hand, demand more government services and, on the other, complain about taxation levels.

However, it is then necessary to explain why the supply and demand of particular governmental goods or services do *not* behave in the same way as in other markets. In most circumstances the laws of supply and demand work for government services in a similar way to the private sector. If governments wish to reduce the consumption of oil among the population, the easiest way is to increase its price through increasing its level of taxation. Increasing farm subsidies will increase the supply of farm produce, as the European Union's agricultural policy demonstrates. Where there may be difficulties is at the edges of market behaviour. Does increasing the monetary support for sole parents increase their numbers, as some conservatives might claim? Along with other policy issues this would have to be studied, but where economics, even public choice economics, can be helpful is in giving a framework for that study. It should be seen as a tool rather than a programme.

It does seem odd that traditional public administration eschewed the use of economics, given that government operates in an environment of resource scarcity where there are many competing demands. Rather than criticizing public management for incorporating economic ideas and methods, the question should be why traditional public administration avoided them.

The basis in private management

The derivation of managerialism from a private business model is a source of some criticism. It might be argued that the public sector is so different that generic or private sector models of management become irrelevant to its operations. For example, altering the focus of organizations from inputs to outputs has several linked steps – determining strategy and setting objectives, devising programmes to meet objectives, setting structure and funding by programme, measuring performance, and evaluating achievements. The steps follow each other in a logical progression; once objectives and results can be specified, the other points also become necessary. However, this means that, if objectives are difficult to set in practice, the other points become irrelevant as they rely on the existence of clear objectives.

Staffing changes are sometimes seen as being derived from the private sector. This could include fitting staff for their positions, appraising their performance, and rewarding them accordingly with merit pay. The emphasis on performance also leads to short-term appointments by contract, and being able to terminate staff who are not performing. Such changes may have derived from the private sector, where staffing and budgeting flexibility had long been a source of some envy for managers in the public sector. However, it should not be seen as something 'necessarily derived from the private sector' (Holmes and Shand, 1995, p. 560). Even if it is harder to determine objectives or to measure results in the public sector, surely some attempt needs to be made because, without objectives or some idea as to what has been done, how can a particular agency or government function at all?

Perhaps there are some inherent differences between the sectors that impose limitations on which reform is adopted and its eventual success. Of course, the uncritical acceptance of particular private sector practices may well fail in the public sector, but that does not mean that the public sector should be managed by traditional, time-honoured means. It is odd that there is so much criticism of private sector management techniques being imported into the public sector. More important is, for a start, how they are translated and, second, if they work. Any technique needs to be modified to fit its new environment. But the comparison needs to be made with what went before, instead of simply arguing that because it came from the private sector it will not work.

'Neo-Taylorism'

A particular theoretical criticism put forward by Pollitt is that managerialism represents a revival of the scientific management ideas of Frederick Taylor (1911) discussed earlier (see Chapter 3). Pollitt (1993) describes the managerial reforms as 'neo-Taylorian' as 'the central thrust, endlessly reiterated in official documents, is to set clear targets, to develop performance indicators to measure the achievement of those targets, and to single out, by means of merit awards, promotion or other rewards, those individuals who get "results"' (p. 56). However, it is misleading, and an odd reading of management history, to see public sector reform as being Taylorian. In fact, there is far greater commonality between Taylor and the traditional model of administration, which adopted Taylor's scientific management enthusiastically in the 1920s, than with public sector reform.

Taylor (1911) did believe in picking people for particular jobs, rewarding them according to performance, and measuring what they did. According to Pollitt (1993), the chief features of Taylorism and managerialism were that 'they were, above all, concerned with *control* and that this control was to be achieved through an essentially *administrative* approach – the fixing of effort levels that were to be expressed in quantitative terms' (p. 188). Some forms of managerialism, notably in the early days, did do those things. Management by arbitrary target was also used. However, while it is certainly the case that measurement is emphasized in managerialism, it is used in a quite different way than in Taylorism. Taylorism did use measurement but to set processes and procedures; the one best way to carry out a task was measured and then subsequent users of a machine or process would follow that method exactly. Performance measurement is, or should be, about how to provide information on *results,* not to establish procedures to be followed in every case. In its expressed aim to be more flexible, public management should be rather *less* Taylorian than traditional public administration was previously; indeed, Taylorism was a much closer fit with the traditional theory of bureaucracy, which happily adopted it into public administration by the 1920s.

Politicization

Changes to public sector management are said to involve 'politicizing' it – involving it directly in matters of party politics (Pollitt and Bouckaert, 2004). It is the case that political leaders are now more likely to select their agency head, and to require some sympathy with their political goals. This does cut across the traditional model's emphasis on neutrality and non-partisan administration; to the extent that these are valued, management does mean a derogation of time-honoured precepts. What is not clear is how much difference it makes in practice. There are two sides to the question of politicization.

On the one hand, it could be said that those putting forward arguments about 'politicization' ignore the fact that public service is fundamentally a political instrument. What is happening now is that a problematic feature of the traditional model of administration – that public servants were not supposed to be 'political' – is being viewed in a more realistic way. As in the American system, even overtly political appointments may be of general benefit, provided they are recognized as such and do not go too far down the hierarchy.

On the other hand, politicization could lead to problems of the kind that Woodrow Wilson and the reform movement in the 1880s tried to repair. Wilson argued that separation between politics and administration would reform the spoils system and reduce the corruption that the system engendered. If managers are to be made responsible for their own results, and the system becomes more political and personal as a result, the same kinds of problems could recur. If this happened because public servants were too political, there might be demands to reinstate the notion of neutrality.

One of the supposed strengths of the traditional model of administration was its refusal to acknowledge or be involved in politics. This was always naïve and unrealistic, given that the administration of government is inevitably a political process in its own right. Public managers do involve themselves in politics, though not necessarily party politics, and this fact should be openly acknowledged. Instead of hiding behind a false neutrality, public managers should be clearer about the political costs and benefits of alternative courses of action.

Reduced accountability

There is some concern as to whether the new managerial concepts and procedures fit in with the system of accountability (see Chapter 9). If public servants are to be managerially accountable, this could be seen as detracting from the accountability of a political leader. And how can a citizen call a public servant to account? Accountability may become a real problem, though the old system was unrealistic and a very poor guarantor of accountability in any case. In addition, the managerial changes do promise greater transparency, so that the achievements of particular programmes can be seen. This may actually improve accountability, in that the public should have a better idea of what governments are doing, while the greater involvement of external stakeholders means that their interests are taken into consideration more than before.

Difficulties with contracting-out

While it is easy to argue that private markets are superior and efficiencies will result from privatizing government activities, implementation is not simple. To make contracting-out actually work is very different from thinking it is a good idea; there are awkward details to be worked through. It takes a lot of effort and experience for public servants to become skilled at contract management. And following from Williamson (1986, 1996), the transaction costs may be greater for some tasks in contracting-out than in keeping them in-house. Contracting-out should be seen as another tool for public managers, which may or may not be more efficient, depending on the particular case.

Disaggregation

Disaggregation means splitting up large departments by setting up agencies to deliver services for small policy departments. The extent that this was ever required from public sector reform is a real point of contention. It has been argued that disaggregation was a requirement of NPM (Hood, 1991; Dunleavy *et al.*, 2005). Disaggregation was used in the UK, starting with the 'Next Steps' initiative in 1988, and in New Zealand in its early reforms, but it makes no sense to regard disaggregation as being fundamental to public sector reform.

The basic model specified in the 'Next Steps' report was to set up a separate agency responsible for the delivery of services, which it did on a contractual or quasi-contractual basis with the relevant policy department. To some extent this was not new; the practice of dividing large departments into smaller segments was accepted in a number of countries such as the United Kingdom, New Zealand and the Netherlands and has been established in the Scandinavian countries for decades (Peters, 1996, p. 31). However, despite appearing in Hood's NPM list, disaggregation is not a logical requirement of public sector reform. In other countries than the United Kingdom, such organizations 'have been established on a case-by-case basis reflecting some focus on disentangling service provision, funding and regulation' (Holmes and Shand, 1995, p. 569). Given the overall policy goal of flexibility and allowing managers to design their own organization, within limits, the requirement for 'Next Steps' agencies in the United Kingdom goes against these goals.

Holmes and Shand are critical of the UK structural reforms, arguing that there needs to be a system-wide assessment of the policies themselves and whether they are working. Structural changes, 'such as imposing service-delivery agencies separate from policy departments, or even the compulsory tendering of local government services, do not do this by themselves' (Holmes and Shand, 1995, p. 566). Early reforms did set up a plethora of agencies in New Zealand, but many were swept away later following a review as they were considered not to be assisting managerial reform. Disaggregation was not a fundamental requirement for managerial reform even though it was considered important in some countries.

Ethical issues

There are concerns expressed about ethical behaviour in public services following reform. Hood (1991) remarks that the new public management 'assumes a culture of public service honesty as given' and 'its recipes to some degree removed devices instituted to ensure honesty and neutrality in the public service in the past (fixed salaries, rules of procedure, permanence of tenure, restraints on the power of line management, clear lines of division between public and private sectors)' and the extent to which the change 'is likely to induce corrosion in terms of such traditional values remains to be tested' (p. 16). On the other hand, deLeon and Green (2004) state there are several constructs from managerial reform that would be useful in combating the excesses of political corruption, including 'community-owned government, competitive government, mission-driven government, and results-oriented government that is enterprising, anticipatory, and decentralized' as well as 'modern accounting and management information systems' (deLeon and Green, 2004, p. 240).

There may be some tension between a requirement to improve management and system design as a strategy to reduce corruption on the one hand, and active discouragement from using better management in order to do so, on the other. There may well be opportunities for the unscrupulous in the greater use of contracting, but there were already avenues for enrichment in the traditional model of administration, as developing countries have shown, in such areas as the allocation of licences and permits, as well as government purchasing. Whether greater ethical problems do occur as a result of managerialism is not clear. The benefit of the old system was its high standards of behaviour, but its weakness was that results were only incidental. Greater transparency and freer availability of information may be sufficient incentive devices for the maintenance of high ethical behaviour by managers.

Are there ways of improving or maintaining ethical standards while gaining the benefits of a managerial approach? Perhaps managerialism offers greater transparency so that unethical or corrupt behaviour can be detected more easily; the greater stress on measurable performance may impose its own kind of behavioural standard. Perhaps managers can be inculcated with the ethical standards common in the old model. Further, as there is supposed to be no change to political accountability, politicians will remain responsible for ethical lapses in agencies under their control. The fact that ethical problems are unsolved in the private sector should be a caution to public managers.

Implementation and morale problems

Managerial changes were usually instigated from the top and with insufficient attention paid to implementation as well as the negative effects on staff. This has been a real problem, although in some countries where time and resources have been devoted to the reform process, it has been carried out well. Better training should occur as part of the overall package, particularly management training for senior staff, but, when resources are cut, such activities are seen as expensive luxuries. In fact, following through with the details may make the eventual difference between the success or failure of reform.

Perhaps the reform process was carried out at such a pace that people in the system did not know where they stood. Morale suffered, particularly in the early stages. Even where change was widely seen to be necessary, questions arose as to whether it might have been handled better. But, as the reform process continued and as new staff were employed with no direct knowledge of the old system, expectations changed. The terms and conditions of employment may now be much more like those prevailing in the private sector, but newer staff appear to accept this, even if the cost is perhaps a reduced willingness to regard their job as one for life.

The critique in sum

In the final analysis, the critique of the transition to public management has some valid points but is unconvincing, or at least unproven. Further criticisms of it will be addressed in subsequent chapters. However, the real test is the performance of a managerial model as *compared* with the old model. Governments provide scarce resources to public programmes and would like to know that public ends are being served in an efficient and effective manner. Strategic planning techniques can specify what departments are to do; programme budgeting and accrual accounting mean that scarce funds can be better targeted; performance indicators allow some measure of how well targets are being achieved; and personnel changes increase flexibility so that the most able are rewarded and the inadequate can be removed. While no theory can be expected to apply perfectly, the important point is that the old system performed poorly on all these points.

Conclusion

The public services of many developed countries and some developing countries could now be regarded as following the precepts of public management. There are still elements of the traditional model of administration around in an uneasy coexistence with public management. The formal power structure of bureaucracy remains, but conditions of employment and delivery of services have been reformed. The logic has been established and fits what governments actually want, which is the maximum of service delivery at the lowest administrative cost, and with the designated public manager taking responsibility for results.

Public management does not mean usurpation of government by technocrats, a reduction in accountability or a diminution of democracy. All the managerial changes do is to allow for public actions to be carried out in a more efficient, cost-effective way, by providing more and better information to those making decisions. In the final analysis, these decision-makers are politicians working with the public service in an interactive process justifiably called management.

What we are witnessing may be a new theory of management, but so far it has been a theory of public management rather than generic management. Public management will not be developed further merely by transferring private management techniques to the public sector, but rather by a consideration of what the general management function entails; understanding what the peculiar features of management in the public sector are; and the derivation of a new system of management to suit that sector.

Despite criticisms, changes of government and misgivings from parts of the citizenry, public management is now firmly established. Who now mentions public administration or describes their job as a 'public administrator'? Public managers are responsible for the achievement of results; they have to develop innovative ways of supplying goods and services; and they will manage risk instead of avoiding it, which was a characteristic of administration. Once change is accepted, it is hard to stop. But what remains to be seen is if the best parts of the old model – professionalism, impartiality, high ethical standards and the absence of corruption – can be maintained, along with the improved performance a managerial model promises.

Chapter 5

Public Policy

Chapter Contents

- Introduction
- Public policy, administration and management
- Policy analysis
- Economic public policy
- Political public policy
- Evidence-based policy
- Limitations of policy analysis
- Conclusion

Introduction

In the early 1970s, public policy arose as a separate field within the broader area of public administration. Adherents distanced themselves consciously and deliberately from the older discipline; their movement derived from 'an assumption that orthodox public administration had reached a dead end' (Kettl, 2002, p. 13). Most public policy practitioners at the time saw it as being about decisions, and in particular with the application of formal, mathematical methods to solve public sector problems. Public policy is important in its own right and as an influence on public management, but there is a question as to whether it is truly different from other approaches to the public sector, and whether there is any advantage in maintaining it as a separate discipline.

Public policy could be seen either as a reaction to and a critique of the public administration tradition, or as the long-overdue adoption of formal techniques by the public sector. Another usage of the term 'public policy' is that by applied economists, meaning the application of economic methods and models to governmental issues. Despite both groups using the same name, their approaches are very different. To confuse the issue even further, one of the biggest differences between public management and public administration is the former's openness to the use of economics. The economic versions of public policy appear to have become predominant in government.

103

The meaning of public policy is unclear. A recent survey of the field (Moran *et al.*, 2006) sheds little light; indeed, a practitioner would find its vagueness, lack of coherence about fundamentals, and absence of lessons of practical utility to be good reasons to avoid completely debates about public policy. And yet, public policy is important. At its most simplistic, public policy is what governments do in terms of aiming at a result of some kind; and public management is how to reach that point. Practically, though, this is not a great advance, as it could be regarded as a new version of the discredited policy/administration dichotomy. In the United Kingdom, after the 'Next Steps' initiative of 1988, there was a structural separation of policy, provided through a small policy agency, from its delivery through a larger agency set up for that purpose with the relationship governed by a quasi-contractual agreement. This did not work well. The idea that an individual, or group or office, devotes the whole working day to devising policy flies in the face of reality. Policy and its management are necessarily integrated; and perhaps there is no need for public policy to be seen as theoretically or analytically distinct from either public administration or public management.

The argument here is that there are several quite different public policy approaches, each with its own concerns and emphases. The first is termed 'policy analysis'; the second is 'economic public policy'; and the third is 'political public policy'. A possible fourth approach is 'evidence-based policy' (Nutley *et al.*, 2002; Nutley *et al.*, 2007), though it could be argued that a requirement for an evidence base should inform all public policy. The policy analysis people are those who have continued to develop the field in the way it began; that is, by the use of sometimes highly abstract statistics and mathematical models, with the focus on decision-making and policy formation. Political public policy theorists are more interested in the results or outcomes of public policy, the political interactions determining a particular event, and in policy areas – health, education, welfare and the environment, for example – rather than concentrating on the use of statistical methods. Economic public policy could be argued to be part of policy analysis in the first sense; however, it makes more sense to regard it as a completely different view as it uses assumptions and deductive methods, whereas policy analysis is more inductive.

Taken together, these views of public policy did point to some dissatisfaction or impatience with public administration, notably the traditional model, where a concern either for numbers or for outcomes was subsumed by a concern with process. As a comprehensive survey on the discipline of public policy noted, it was during the period roughly from the 1950s to the 1970s that 'public policy really began to take off, and public administration began to move into a state of decline which was to accelerate in the 1980s' (Parsons, 1995, p. 7).

Public policy in the policy analysis sense could then be considered either as a separate paradigm competing with public administration and public management, or as a set of analytical methods applicable to both. It is argued here that the public policy movement is really part of the traditional model of public administration, with its implicit acceptance of the bureaucratic model and its 'one best way' thinking. The extent of its critique of the traditional model was to argue for more usage of empirical methodology to assist or even supplant decision-making, rather than more fundamental questioning.

The public policy movement is important to the study of the public sector even though it might have lost some impetus in recent years. Its methods have been criticized for being too narrow and its conclusions are seen as being of dubious relevance to the task of governing. However, public policy and policy analysis remain useful in drawing attention to what governments do, as opposed to the public administration concern with how they operate, and in using empirical methods to analyse policy.

Public policy, administration and management

Students of government have long struggled over what is meant by 'policy' and 'policy-making'. Definitions of public policy found in the literature range from 'declarations of intent, a programme of goals, and general rules covering future behaviour to important government decisions, a selected line or course of action, the consequences of action or inaction, and even all government action' (Lynn, 1987, p. 28). The word 'policy' could refer to: the intentions declared by parties in an election; a rather more precise programme than an intention; general rules such as 'foreign policy'; government decisions in a policy document; and to even larger areas, such as everything the government does. One work (Hogwood and Gunn, 1984) finds ten separate meanings.

There are differences in definition between the policy analysis and political public policy schools. From a policy analysis perspective, Putt and Springer (1989) stated: 'The function of policy research is to facilitate public policy processes through providing accurate and useful decision-related information. The skills required to produce information that is technically sound and useful lie at the heart of the policy research process, regardless of the specific methodology employed' (p. 10). This definition emphasizes methods, as does Quade (1982, p. 5), who defined the area as:

> A form of applied research carried out to acquire a deeper understanding of socio-technical issues and to bring about better solutions. Attempting to bring

modern science and technology to bear on society's problems, policy analysis searches for feasible courses of action, generating information and marshalling evidence of the benefits and other consequences that would follow their adoption and implementation, in order to help the policy-maker choose the most advantageous action.

These points set out what the more formal, policy analysis, approach aims to do. Quade (1982) draws on a rich tradition of the application of science and statistics to government (deLeon, 1988). The focus is on methods and science, in using such procedures to find or even make decisions.

The approach taken by Lynn (1987) is quite different and emphasizes the political interaction from which policy derives. In Lynn's definition (p. 239):

> Public policy can be characterized as the output of a diffuse process made up of individuals who interact with each other in small groups in a framework dominated by formal organizations. Those organizations function in a system of political institutions, rules and practices, all subject to societal and cultural influences.

Key features of this definition are, first, that public policy is the *output* of government. This neatly avoids some of the problems associated with attempts at more precise meanings, or needing to specify the exact kind of output for particular circumstances. Governments provide goods and services, and most often do this following policy announcements. Even a term as vague as foreign policy has some meaning as the output of views, statements or actions affecting relations outside a nation. Second, the process is described as being diffuse; the formulation of public policy is an elusive process. This is far more realistic than regarding policy-making as either to be carried out by politicians under the traditional model of administration, or through some other idealized process, which can be modelled. No one really knows from where policies are derived, other than through the internal political processes of governments, in which the bureaucracy is as much a political actor as are outside interest groups or politicians. Nor is there any reason to assume that the process will be the same for all policies. Third, Lynn (1987) expresses the idea of constraints quite precisely. Public policy-making does not occur in a vacuum; there are constraints of organization, institutions, interest groups and even 'societal and cultural influences'. It is easy to find more complex definitions, but public policy is to be regarded here as the *output* of government, and policy analysis as the more formal, empirical approach to deriving and explaining policy arising from the 1970s critique of public administration.

There are real problems in delineating a public policy approach from public administration, politics or public management. All are concerned with the operations of government and the public sector. There are some rather obvious differences between public policy and public administration. The traditional model had little interest in policy, as policy was assumed to derive from political leaders. From its beginnings, public policy analysts were a rather different set of people, more concerned with analytical methods and numbers compared to what they regarded as the generalist approaches of public administration. Public administration was considered to be the domain of the gifted amateur, where governing wisely and well had little to do with any kinds of methods or statistics. Public policy is expressly more 'political' than public administration and has also emphasized more technical approaches to decision-making. Public policy may be a little more realistic than public administration in that it does allow the bureaucracy to have decision-making and political roles, and to pay some attention to what is actually produced by it.

It is more difficult to separate public policy from political science. Sometimes it would be hard to decide whether a particular study was one of public policy or politics. Political science during the behavioural era was not much interested in matters of policy (John, 1998, p. 3) so perhaps early public policy was something of a reaction to that. Public policy could be considered to be an attempt to apply the methods of political science to actual policy areas such as urban renewal, health policy, welfare, housing, the environment and so on.

The relationship that public policy has with public management is also difficult to pin down. It is argued here that public management has superseded traditional public administration and is a more realistic description of what actually happens in the public sector. However, the relationship between public management and public policy is not as simple as supersession. Public managers may also use empirical models, but these are more often those of economics. Policy analysis might have used economics, but as only one of many possible methodologies. Both would probably claim their own perspective to be a strength, though governments have certainly shown their preference for using economic methodology over other kinds in recent years.

Policy analysis

Public policy began with the systematic analysis of data for governmental purposes. The word 'statistics' even derives from 'state'. Despite this, policy was not greatly informed by systematic data until after 1960, with the implementation of large-scale government programmes in the United States by the Kennedy and Johnson Administrations (deLeon, 1988, 2006). Mathematical techniques deriving from Rand or the United States Defense Department under Robert McNamara could be applied to the public sector. It was an age of science; an age in which any problem was seen as having a possible solution that could be discovered through the proper application of the scientific method. Related to the belief in solutions was the availability within government of large-scale computers and suitable software for processing statistical data. In these earlier stages, public policy analysts seemed to regard decision-making as a rational process leading to an ideal outcome.

After 1980, Putt and Springer (1989) perceived what they termed a 'third stage' of public policy, in which policy analysis is seen as 'facilitating policy decisions, not displacing them' (p. 16). As they explain:

> Third-stage analysts decreasingly serve as producers of solutions guiding decision makers to the one best way of resolving complex policy concerns. Policy research in the third stage is not expected to produce solutions, but to provide information and analysis at multiple points in a complex web of interconnected decisions which shape public policy. Policy research does not operate separated and aloof from decision makers; it permeates the policy process itself.

Instead of providing an answer themselves, empirical methods were to be used to aid decision-making and not be a replacement for politics. The availability of data allows all participants in the policy process to use statistics to reinforce their arguments, but the data by itself is not necessarily conclusive. Statistics are contested and contestable rather than definitive, providing information for the policy debate but not supplanting political argument.

Empirical methods

Much has been said in passing of the empirical methods and skills needed by policy analysis and policy analysts. In one view, two sets of skills are needed. First, 'scientific skills', which have three categories: information-structuring skills that 'sharpen the analyst's ability to clarify policy-related ideas and to examine their correspondence to real world events'; information-collection skills that 'provide the analyst with approaches and tools for making accurate observations of persons, objects, or events'; and information-analysis skills that 'guide the analyst in drawing conclusions from empirical evidence' (Putt and Springer, 1989, p. 24). These scientific skills are not independent but rather interrelated; they are also related to what the authors call 'facilitative skills' (p. 25) such as policy, planning and managerial skills.

So, while empirical skills are needed, there are other, less tangible, ones that are also needed. Both sets of skills point to the emphasis on training found in policy analysis. If analysts inside the bureaucracy can be trained in scientific and facilitative skills, it should be possible to improve policy-making and its outcomes.

Some of the empirical methods used in policy analysis include: (i) cost–benefit analysis (optimum choice among discrete alternatives without probabilities); (ii) decision theory (optimum choice with contingent probabilities); (iii) optimum-level analysis (finding an optimum policy where doing too much or too little is undesirable); (iv) allocation theory (optimum-mix analysis); and (v) time-optimization models (decision-making systems designed to minimize time consumption) (Nagel, 1990). In their section on options analysis – which they regard as the heart of policy models – Hogwood and Gunn (1984) point to various operations research and decision analysis techniques, including linear programming; dynamic programming; pay-off matrix; decision trees; risk analysis; queuing theory; and inventory models.

As probably the key person involved in developing mathematical approaches to policy issues, Nagel is naturally enthusiastic about their benefits, arguing that policy evaluation based on management science methods 'seems capable of improving decision-making processes' (Nagel, 1990, p. 433). One can admire the idea that societal improvement can result from empirical decision-making methods. There are undoubtedly some areas in which these techniques can be very useful, and, even in matters of complex policy, information may be able to be acquired when it could not be found by normal means. For example, monitoring or controlling road traffic is a governmental function everywhere. Traffic studies have always been done at the relatively low level of counting cars. When this is extended through decision analysis, by taking numbers to a higher level, or building scenarios into computer-based models, it becomes possible to predict future traffic patterns, to decide where to place traffic signals, or to use cost–benefit analysis to decide between two sites for a traffic interchange. In this kind of example, empirical methods undoubtedly improve the making of policy and are widely used by governments; however, other kinds of public policy may be less amenable to thorough statistical analysis.

Policy process models

There are almost as many models of the policy process as there are public policy theorists, all deriving to some extent from Lasswell (1971). Anderson's (1984) model of the policy process has five stages: problem identification and agenda formation; formulation; adoption; implementation; and evaluation (p. 19). Quade (1982) also sees five elements: problem formulation; searching for alternatives; forecasting the future environment; modelling the impacts of alternatives; and evaluating the alternatives. Stokey and Zeckhauser (1978) also set out a five-step process in which the analyst is required to determine the underlying problem and objectives to be pursued; set out possible alternatives; predict the consequences of each alternative; determine the criteria for measuring the achievement of alternatives; and indicate the preferred choice of action.

The Patton and Sawicki (1986) model has the basic aim of assisting an analyst who is required to assess a given situation and to derive a policy to deal with it. This model is fairly representative of its ilk, with six steps: define the problem; establish evaluation criteria; identify alternative policies; evaluate alternative policies; display and select among alternative policies; and monitor policy outcomes.

Bardach's eightfold path

Another model is that of Bardach (2009) who sets out what he terms the 'eightfold path', referring to what he regards as the eight steps of practical policy analysis. Bardach observes that policy analysis is 'a social and political activity' and 'more art than science' (2009, pp. xv–xvi). This quite neatly sets up a more realistic approach to policy-making than the ones that propose analysis alone.

Bardach's schema is similar to the others described above, though it has the advantage of allowing for political interaction where other theorists might not include that possibility. The first step is to define the problem. It is often hard to do this for the public sector, where policy objectives may not be clear, or aim to do several things at once. Public agencies often have several missions at the same time, and need to respond to different interest groups. It is particularly difficult to define problems in large areas of policy such as health or welfare. But without being able to define the problem it becomes impossible to design a policy. The second step is to 'assemble some evidence'. This is nicely framed in already setting up the point that no evidence is likely to be definitive; indeed, evidence is more often than not contested and contestable. The third step is to 'construct the alternatives'. These are 'policy options or alternative courses of action or alternative strategies of intervention to solve or mitigate the problem' (Bardach, 2009, p. 15). The fourth step is to 'select the criteria' for evaluation. These may vary but could include efficiency, cost-effectiveness, social justice or political acceptability. Step five is to 'project the outcomes'; in other words, to extrapolate what is likely to occur from the alternatives chosen in Step three, using the criteria established in Step four. Bardach refers to an 'outcomes matrix' where alternatives are listed together with the evaluation criteria (2009, pp. 49–51). Step four is then to 'confront the trade-offs'. Some alternatives may have outcomes that work better than others, but none of them is likely to be superior in all aspects. This means that judgement must be made as to which alternative is, on balance, better. Step seven is to 'decide'; and the final step, Step eight, is to 'tell your story'.

Bardach's model is a sensible and practical schema for designing public policy, one of undoubted value for public managers when faced with a policy problem. The use of this model or the Patton and Sawicki (1986) (or any similar) model can bring benefits in analysing a matter of public policy. As with any set of headings, it can guide or suggest things to look at when someone in government is faced with a particular policy problem. It is likely that the results of the analysis might be better than without any such list, or without any specific framework.

In general, though, there are some difficulties with the policy process approach. In some circumstances a model like this could be helpful to making public policy; but in other circumstances it would not. As John (1998) comments, 'Just a casual experience of the messiness of policy-making, the twists and turns of decisions, the reverses, the quixotic failures and the surprises is enough to alert the researcher that, even as an ideal type, the sequential model has its problems' (p. 25). Policy is not often made in a linear way. It is often made in response to crisis, as the result of a half-baked idea, or to meet a perceived ideological need rather than resulting from any logical process or evidence at all.

At the end of the process, what we have is a *framework* rather than a *method*: a set of headings rather than a concrete approach. The fact is that a person could follow the headings perfectly and derive a disastrous policy, while someone else could follow none of the rules and derive a better one. There are problems in using any model, not the least of which would be the temptation to simply follow a menu rather than to really *analyse* what is happening. A fundamental question of policy analysis is whether it is art or science, or whether it is an attempt to quantify the unquantifiable or rationalize the quasi-rational. Models may help, but provide no guarantee of making better policy. Policy models do not deal very effectively with policy change or with the prediction of future action

Economic public policy

Public policy can also be formulated using the tools of economics; indeed, public policy is often seen as a school within the discipline of economics. However, the public policy approach used by economics is very different from the policy analysis approach outlined above. Economic models and evidence might have been acknowledged by policy analysis theorists as one of the possible approaches that can be used, but the basic parameters of the two disciplines are worlds apart. It is interesting that, if there is a contest between analytical models, governments in general have increasingly opted for economic policy models to inform what they do. It is worth considering why this might be so, and what economic models have to offer that may be more robust than those coming from public policy in its policy analysis variant.

Economics can be used in many areas of policy, from identifying governmental goals in welfare economics; 'the allocation of resources across competing claims (the domain of cost-effectiveness analysis)'; and for analysing how policies can be implemented (Donahue and Zeckhauser, 2006, p. 496). It has become a matter of routine for governments considering policy change to commission economic modelling as to its effects. Also, many of the major policy changes since the 1980s have been ones that originated in the economic literature – free trade, for example, by lowering tariffs, cutting taxes to improve choice, acknowledging levels of debt, and many more. Economics does seem to offer more to governments – at least, governments have been more willing to consider economic advice, and in a way that would be likely to cause envy among other varieties of policy analyst. It could be argued that one of the reasons that traditional public administration has faded away is that it eschewed the use of economics. As mentioned earlier (see Chapter 4), the key theoretical cornerstones of public management reform are private management and economics, particularly economics of the microeconomic or public choice kind. This goes a stage further than the rational models of policy analysis, by declaring that the good to be maximized by those involved is economic utility, and deriving policy from there.

A fundamental difference between the two approaches is that public policy analysis is based on the empirical methods of political science dating from the 1960s and 1970s. A clue to the problem this engenders may be gained from one of the scientific skills noted earlier: 'information-analysis skills guide the analyst in drawing conclusions from empirical evidence' (Putt and Springer, 1989, p. 24). This comment points to a key problem, not only in policy analysis, but also in behavioural political science, from which policy analysis theories derive. Most social science, from the beginnings of collection of data or sample surveys, has been expressly inductive; that is, based on the idea that, from gathering masses of information, inferences can be made. A large part of the philosophy of science in the second half of the twentieth century was concerned with showing that data does not lead to conclusions, and that such inductive science is inherently flawed (Popper, 1965).

Despite criticism (see, for example, deLeon, 1997) a major part of the success of economic public policy in recent years is that it is expressly deductive – that is, based on theory leading to predictions. If evidence for those predictions can be found, the theory is supported. A theory is not proven, but can stand if it is not disproved. As an example of the difference, consider the traffic problem mentioned earlier. An inductive approach to traffic congestion would involve gathering data about traffic conditions, making sense of it and drawing conclusions from the data. A deductive or public choice approach would assume there was a scarce good being maximized by people; in this case, probably commuter time, so predictions could be made about what the behaviour of people might be in trying to minimize the time taken in traffic. Instead of trying to *derive* explanations of behaviour from evidence, a rational behavioural response can be *assumed* and then tested.

It is arguable whether the increased use of economics in public policy-making is part of formal policy analysis. Given that public policy analysts were drawn from political science, it may be quite separate and belong to a quite different intellectual history. An interesting synthesis is that of Weimer and Vining (2011); they offer due acknowledgement to the other kinds of policy analysis, and to motivation other than economic, but their work is very much an application of economic concepts to policy.

Political public policy

A far less rigid approach to looking at policy is put forward by other writers, such as Lynn (1987), deLeon (1997) and John (1998). Policy-making is viewed by them as a political process rather than a narrowly technical one. Lynn (1987) sees public policy as the output of people in organizations and 'to understand policy-making it is necessary to understand the behaviour of and interactions among these structures: individuals holding particular positions, groups, organizations, the political system, and the wider society of which they are all a part' (p. 17). Therefore, instead of involving particular methodologies, policy-making is a matter of adapting to and learning to influence political and organizational environments.

The focus for Lynn is understanding how particular policies were formed, developed and work in practice; these are concerns broader than a focus on decision-making or mathematical models. Lynn argues that policy-making 'encompasses not only goal setting, decision making, and formulation of political strategies, but also supervision of policy planning, resource allocation, operations management, programme evaluation, and efforts at communication, argument, and persuasion' (p. 45). Public policy in this perspective is a process, but one that is political above all other considerations; one in which those Lynn calls 'managers of public policy' – an interesting amalgam of terms – use any means to achieve their goals. Instead of being a formal process, they are strictly limited, as 'public executives pursue their goals within three kinds of limits: those imposed by their external political environments; those imposed by their organizations; and those imposed by their own personalities and cognitive styles' (p. 42). Rather than being technical experts, effective managers of public policy (p. 271):

- establish understandable premises for their organization's activities;
- attain an intellectual grasp of strategically important issues; identify and focus attention on those activities that give meaning to the organization's employees;
- remain alert to and exploit all opportunities, whether deliberately created or fortuitous, to further their purposes;
- consciously employ the strong features of their personalities as instruments of leadership and influence; and
- manage within the framework of an economy of personal resources to govern how much they attempt to accomplish and how they go about it.

Managers work in this way because their own positions are on the line; they must achieve results or their job will be at risk, so any means of being successful must be considered.

Public policy-making viewed from this perspective becomes much more a political process. Hogwood and Gunn (1984), who cross public policy perspectives, argue that analysis is seen as 'supplementing the more overtly political aspects of the policy process rather than replacing them' and 'to treat politics as a residual is to doom analysis, not politics, to irrelevance' (p. 267). They put forward a nine-step approach to the policy process, which they say is 'mixed'; that is, it can be used for both description and prescription. Their model is: (i) deciding to decide (issue search or agenda-setting); (ii) deciding how to decide; (iii) issue definition; (iv) forecasting; (v) setting objectives and priorities; (vi) options analysis; (vii) policy implementation, monitoring and control; (viii) evaluation and review; and (ix) policy maintenance, succession, or termination.

This model is atypical in that it incorporates both the policy analysis and political perspectives. Hogwood and Gunn (1984) maintain that their approach is concerned both with the application of techniques and with political process; and they argue for a 'process-focused rather than a technique-oriented approach to policy analysis' (p. 6). Analysis is primarily about 'determining the characteristics of the issue being analysed and the organisational and political setting of the issue, with the actual mechanics of particular techniques being secondary and consequential' (p. 263). It is seen as 'supplementing the more overtly political aspects of the policy process rather than replacing them' (p. 267). Their model may be more realistic and more useful as a result.

Policy analysis looks for the best answer from a set of alternatives, and has a battery of statistical weapons at its disposal to do so. Political public policy sees information in an *advocacy* role; that is, it realizes that cogent cases will be made from many perspectives, which then feed into the political process. Simon goes somewhat further (Simon, 1983, p. 97; also quoted in Hogwood and Gunn, 1984, p. 266):

> When an issue becomes highly controversial – when it is surrounded by uncertainties and conflicting values – then expertness is very hard to come by, and it is no longer easy to legitimate the experts. In the circumstances, we find that there are experts for the affirmative and experts for the negative. We cannot settle such issues by turning them over to particular groups of experts. At best we may convert the controversy into an adversary proceeding in which we, the laymen, listen to the experts but have to judge between them.

There is, then, no single best answer, there is only an answer that survives the political process in what is often a contest between policy experts on all sides of a public policy issue.

Other analysis of the policy process takes the political aspect somewhat further. John (1998) maintains that there is a 'new policy analysis' (p. 157):

> Moving from the modest claims of ideas-based empiricism, the new policy analysis makes claims about the primacy of ideas and the indeterminacy of knowledge. Rather than rational actors following their interests, it is the interplay of values and norms and different forms of knowledge which characterise the policy process.

This view is less rigid than the sequential view of policy and more open to political interplay, and includes a much wider set of influences than earlier policy analysis. It offers an interesting view for future policy work.

Governments or the bureaucracy may try to persuade participants in the policy process of the advantages of maximizing benefits. By including those from the outside they are raising the possibility of compromise and political action. Public policy-making, as distinct from its study, now seems to be an interesting amalgam of several perspectives, and public management may be able to combine them. Net benefit maximization may be the express aim of governments, but the methodology of government is now much more that of microeconomics rather than of old-style policy analysis. At the same time, groups have been brought into policy-making to a greater extent than before. But rather than mediating between groups, public managers – or managers of public policy, to use Lynn's (1987) phrase – try to persuade groups that there are advantages for them in net benefit maximization. All parties involved in the process realize that politics defines the nature of the policy game. The only problem with this rather sensible and realistic approach is how to classify it. It could be viewed as political public policy, managing public policy, or as public management.

Evidence-based policy

Another movement in recent years advocates evidence-based policy (Nutley *et al.*, 2007). On the surface it does seem odd to have to advocate the use of evidence in policy; indeed, there are immediate questions as to how policy could be made in the absence of evidence. Policy analysis in general has always wished to operate with an evidence base; policy analysis and economic public policy as well as political public policy approaches have pointed to the need to gather data. Why, then, is a movement for evidence-based policy needed? In the real world of policy-making, policy can be made for all kinds of other reasons, some of them not based on evidence of any kind.

The evidence-based policy movement began in health policy, most notably health policy in the United Kingdom. One account (Black, 2001) suggests that there are six reasons why evidence is not used in this area of policy: (i) some policy-makers 'have goals other than maximising clinical effectiveness' – the goal may be social or financial, or be shaped by electoral considerations, so local policy-makers are therefore 'under a myriad of often competing pressures, of which scientific evidence is but one'; (ii) research evidence 'may be dismissed as irrelevant if it comes from a different sector or specialty'; (iii) there may be 'a lack of consensus about the research evidence' because of its complexity, scientific controversy or different interpretations; (iv) policy-makers 'may value other types of evidence' such as personal experience, local information on services, eminent colleagues' opinions; (v) the social environment 'may not be conducive to policy change'; and (vi) 'the quality of the "knowledge purveyors" may be inadequate'. Given that the medical profession itself relies perhaps more than any other on the use of statistics, it is hardly surprising that there would be some demand to make health policy subject itself to similar rigour.

There are calls for a greater use of evidence in the making of public policy. The OECD (2009, p. 21), for example, comments that:

> Evidence-based policy making can help governments chart their return to a sustainable growth path. Coherent policies and, *de facto*, more effective policies and regulations require governments to take account of all pertinent information for more informed decisions. In particular, this implies that governments assess the benefits of policy proposals in relation to the future costs, and the interactions among structural reform policies. Through a coherent design, the return of each specific reform can be maximised.

This comment is doubtless well-meaning, but only points to the innate problems of public policy-making in general. The OECD paper suggests a counsel of perfection; if policy-makers did collect information and act according to it, then the quality of policy probably would be better. But in a political system there are competing pressures that act against creating public policy always based on sound data. The evidence-based policy movement could be seen as an implicit attack on governments for acting in ways that are against good policy by whatever measure can be found.

Limitations of policy analysis

The policy analysis approach is, to some extent, an advance on the traditional model of public administration, even though it clearly derives from it and shares many of its intellectual preconceptions. Governments do collect all kinds of data, much of which should be amenable to mathematical approaches. But the approach falls short in a number of ways.

Over-emphasis on decisions

In practice, a relatively small proportion of a manager's time is taken up by making decisions amenable to analytical processes. Even someone with a title of 'policy analyst' is much more likely to be occupied by issues of management, supervision of others or day-to-day problem-solving, rather than sitting down to design a policy. Successful managers are less analysts than organizers, less technocrats than politicians. Rather than there being one single outcome that is optimal, as is assumed through much policy analysis, there is a range of possible answers, each of which has its own costs and benefits in terms of acceptance. In addition, the absence of *personality* is a problem for public policy models. Political and interpersonal factors may be better able to be considered from a public management perspective.

Despite numerous books on policy analysis and a variety of approaches, there is little evidence that formal methods are actually followed in a practical situation. Or, if they were followed at one time, they are now not followed as much. The fact is that 'many studies of public policy determination are quite general and abstract and distant from the operating reality of government' (Lynn, 1987, p. 13). Day-to-day management activities involve many things other than making decisions and 'a high proportion of the activities in which public managers engage are not amenable to the application of analytic techniques; a small proportion are' (Elmore, 1986). There are no 'correct' answers in practice, and trying to find a single answer is akin to embracing the old 'one best way' thinking of public administration. Within the bureaucracy, policy analysis does not seem to have passed the test of relevance.

Quantitative methods

Numbers are useful and provide information to decision-makers, but public policy placed too much emphasis on them. It is very easy to decry formal mathematical approaches as being unrealistic if applied to the world of policy and politics, and to argue that politics is not necessarily rational in a strict numbers sense. However, the problem is not in the use of numbers, but rather in levels of abstraction leading far beyond any conceivable policy relevance. Even the same numbers can attract different perspectives as to what they really mean. It is more often than not the case that statistical information is contested by the various participants in policy debates, rather than being accepted as facts. There has also been little attempt to delineate the areas in which policy analysis can work very well from ones in which the political and societal problems are far more contentious. Being sold, or rather over-sold, as a set of techniques for all areas has probably reduced its use in those areas where it might be more meaningful.

The rational model

In what Putt and Springer (1989) termed the first and second stages of policy research, the rational model was expressly followed, even though complete rationality is not likely to be found in practice. As is well-known following from the work of Simon (1957), a completely rational decision-making process demands too much of those making decisions. Instead of making an ideal decision, individuals will break large and complex problems into small, more understandable parts; choose the first alternative that is satisfactory; avoid unnecessary uncertainty; and behave in accordance with repertoires of appropriate and useful behaviour. This means that 'although individuals are intendedly rational, their rationality is bounded by limited cognitive and emotional capacities' (Lynn, 1987, p. 84).

Policy analysis in the 'third stage' always warns against placing too much reliance on the rational model. For example, Patton and Sawicki (1986, p. 25) point out that:

> If the rational model were to be followed, many rational decisions would have to be compromised because they were not politically feasible. A rational, logical, and technically desirable policy may not be adopted because the political system will not accept it. The figures don't always speak for themselves, and good ideas do not always win out. Analysts and decision makers are constantly faced with the conflict between technically superior and politically feasible alternatives.

There are two problems with this. First, the Patton and Sawicki model is quite definitely a rational model as described by Lindblom (1968), despite their protestations. The steps in their process are quite rational: deciding on the valued good; setting out alternatives and choosing the alternative with the highest utility weight. They do allow for the good to be maximized to be any valued good, but so does the formal rational model. It is the logic of the steps to be followed that determines rationality, rather than the assumptions. Second, policy analysis has declined as a framework by being overtaken by an even more rigorously rational model of economics.

Following the rational model by analysis of the facts and deriving the best possible outcome could be undemocratic unless the solution happened to agree with what the target audience or the wider political system wanted. This would only occur by chance. Denhardt (1981) contends that policy analysts typically apply technical solutions to the solution of immediate problems and 'under such circumstances, technical concerns would displace political and ethical concerns as the basis for public decision making, thereby transforming normative issues into technical problems' (p. 631). Even a small-scale issue such as the location of a local road can rarely be decided technically as there are likely to be people involved who will not accept a technical solution. Politics, as required by a democracy, may intervene unless a technical answer is imposed, which would often be undemocratic. As deLeon notes (1997, p. 100), 'the analytic priesthood is doing little to discourage the ebbing of ... faith in government and, by extension, the democratic system, as it carries out its personal preferences, in procedure if not in specific programs'.

A separate public policy discipline

As is natural for enthusiasts, the beginnings of a public policy discipline lay in its explicit separation from the discipline of public administration, from where it really came. Adherents developed separate professional journals, separate conferences and, though they shared antecedents, had very little in common at times with public administration. This was unrealistic and unnecessary. No sharp line can be drawn between making policy and implementing it, nor can one be drawn between policy and administration, once the unrealistic Wilsonian separation thesis was discarded. But the disciplinary separation had other effects in that it created distinct professional groups within the bureaucracy that had little in common with the rest of the workplace. In some agencies the people with public policy training emerged ahead, while in others those with public administration training did so. Without this apparent split, public policy and public administration might have had more influence. In the event, both groups tended to be marginalized by those with training in economics.

Criticisms have been made about policy analysis for some years. In a defence of the approach, Nagel (1990, p. 429) argued that policy analysis can incorporate values other than those for which it is criticized, and move away from earlier criticism. He refers to the traditional goals under the 'three Es' of effectiveness, efficiency and equity. According to Nagel, effectiveness refers to the benefits achieved by alternative public policies; and efficiency refers to keeping costs down when achieving benefits, as measured by benefits minus costs, or a maximum level of costs across individuals, groups or places. He says that these should also be balanced with the 'three Ps' as high-level goals, meaning public participation, predictability and procedural due process. Public participation refers to decision-making by the target group, the general public or other relevant interest groups; predictability refers to making decisions so that a similar decision would be arrived at by others following the same criteria; and procedural due process, or procedural fairness, means that those who have been unfairly treated are entitled to have recourse to other avenues of appeal (Nagel, 1990, p. 429).

If implemented, these provisions would go some distance towards countering the criticisms of those who argue that policy analysis, even the whole public policy school, has no interest in the political consequences of its analyses or the fact that there are people involved in their abstract decision-making. In Nagel's (1990) response, the more mechanistic aspects have been modified, and more traditional public administration virtues such as participation are superimposed. But the attempt to do this seems forced and unconvincing. The strength of the policy analysis approach is in its treatment of statistics and its rational approach, even given their limitations. To include all the other features would take away its power by making it attempt to be all things to all people. Too much is being claimed for the field in which Nagel has probably been the largest contributor. Certainly, the empirical work is useful; and certainly it may be more useful than what existed before. But there is an endemic problem with empirical work in the public sector when it goes further than occupying an information role.

If data, no matter how it is gathered, can be presented to policy-makers, this must be useful in improving the quality of decisions made. But if data or methods alone are considered a sufficient basis on which to make decisions, this approach will inevitably fail. A good point is raised by deLeon (2006, p. 49), who asks 'what value added does the study of public policy and the policy sciences bring to a political policy-making process that is often and decidedly unanalytic?' A partial answer is that policy analysis of the formal kind can provide good information in some circumstances, but that may be all.

Referring specifically to regulation, Sparrow (2000) refers to the need to 'pick important problems and fix them' (p. 9). This simple perspective may have a wider use. Policy analysis and public policy more generally can be enlisted to assist in the solving of problems. Even if the very choice of a problem is contested and contingent, and even if the methods, evidence and solutions are similarly contested, a purposive policy approach can still be useful. Often the information used will be irrelevant, and often it will have to confront conflicting information from other sources, so often it will be rejected. If policy analysts could accept a role in which they may provide useful information for policy-makers, that role could be valuable; the trouble is, they did tend to claim a far grander role in the heyday of the policy analysis school.

Conclusion

Public policy and policy analysis formed a distinctive approach to the management of the public sector, one that caused a fundamental rethinking of public administration in the 1970s and early 1980s. Adding more sophisticated forms of empirical analysis meant that public administration moved some distance away from amateurism and towards professionalism. According to one admirer, policy analysis, as a field and a movement, has come 'a long way in reshaping the discipline' of public administration (Goodsell, 1990, p. 500). This may once have been the case, and the introduction of empirical techniques must count as an advance on the traditional model. But public policy and policy analysis have to a great extent been bypassed by the debate over managerialism. It could be argued that public management incorporates analytical techniques, rather than the two requiring a separate existence and separate disciplines.

The public policy literature has been 'too concerned with policy decisions and the broad process of policy formulation and implementation with too little attention to the roles and practices of managers of organizational entities within those processes' (Rainey, 1990, p. 159). Confronted by a decision to build a dam, say, any government or government agency would gain by commissioning empirical studies. These could be cost–benefit studies, path analyses, demographic or other social studies, but what these studies cannot do is to make actual decisions. Regardless of the quality of information, politicians and other policy-makers must make such decisions based on the shifting sands of political opinion. Even if the decision eventually made goes against the most rigid and empirically rigorous analyses that is not to deny its rationality in some other sense.

One way in which public policy and policy analysis have been enduring successes is that they paved the way for other empirical kinds of analysis, particularly those of economics. But the difference between them is marked. Public policy in the policy analysis sense belongs to the value-free and inductive social science of the 1960s and 1970s. Economics has come to have greater influence and be used more because it can promise outcomes more like those that governments want, such as more output for less money. Public policy analysis was always concerned with decisions rather than results, and with procedure rather than outcomes in a management sense. So, in the end, a part of policy analysis – that analysis could be valuable – was absorbed into public management. Public policy did represent a substantial advance on the traditional model of public administration, but its intellectual home was still there, with its methods being those of its close relative in political science. As such it has become less relevant as governments and their bureaucracies have found another approach. To an increasing extent public policy and policy analysis are being replaced by economics, allied with modern management, as applied to the public sector.

Chapter 6

Governance

Chapter Contents

- Introduction
- The meaning of governance
- Corporate governance
- Governance as the New Public Management
- Governance and networks
- Conclusion: the usefulness of governance

Introduction

Since the mid-1990s, there has been something of a re-emergence of concepts of governance in public management. Though the word 'governance' is far from new, with its meaning dating back several centuries in English and even further back in French, the recent revival of its usage has been most useful in those circumstances where 'government' is too narrow and too specific to capture all interactions. Perhaps 'government' has inadequate explanatory power when societal institutions in the very broadest sense can organize and provide a social benefit without direct involvement from any governmental authority.

Governance does have a wide ambit. In the private sector, issues of corporate governance have become far more important as company boards and regulators look for better ways to organize companies for the benefit of their shareholders and the wider society. Scholars of international relations have used theoretical ideas of governance at the level of the nation state and relationships between states (Rosenau, 1992, 1997; Keohane and Nye, 2000). Governance has become important within the public sector; in one view, it would be 'only a slight exaggeration to say governance has become the subject formerly known as public administration' (Frederickson, 2005, p. 284).

The concept of governance does assist in illuminating a long-standing preoccupation in public management regarding drawing a boundary for the exercise of authority. This is a valuable, if perennial, area of thought. In the search for a clear line, it has become apparent that government and governance are not the same. Government is about the exercise of authority, while governance is more about inclusion; governance can occur without government (Rosenau, 1992; Rhodes, 1996). The original, standard meanings of governance are about running organizations, and about setting up structures or institutional arrangements to enable an organization to be run. These standard meanings of 'governance' have resonance, utility and acceptability, and can provide valuable insights into the theories and operations of management in the public sector.

The fact that various discussions about governance have emerged points to how far public management has moved away from the precepts of the traditional theory of public administration. In the traditional model it was far simpler. There is a government comprised of political leaders and administrators, and members of the latter group merely administer policy for the former. Both sets of actors are supreme within their sphere. Any idea that governance could occur without government, and any idea that outside groups could assist government officials in carrying out their functions, would be quite antithetical to the traditional model. It is argued here that, while governance is a useful word, it has become over-used. Some of the definitions, meanings and usages of governance lead to greater obscurity rather than clarity. But used in accordance with its original meanings, governance can be both interesting and useful when applied to public management.

The meaning of governance

Governance is hard to define. Pierre and Peters (2000) assert that 'the concept of governance is notoriously slippery; it is frequently used among both social scientists and practitioners without a definition which all agree on' (p. 7). For some reason, 'governance' has become a word where, despite the innate slipperiness of the concept, there are attempts – often wildly different – at precision in definition or ascription of uses. It is argued here that some of these attempts do not add much to understanding; the major reason being that alongside the more abstruse recent usages, there are standard meanings that are clear, generally used and well understood.

Fairly obviously, 'governance' derives from the verb 'to govern' which comes from the Latin *gubernare*, meaning 'to steer, direct, rule' and this, in turn, derives from the Greek *kubernan*, meaning 'to steer'. 'Governance' is but one of many nouns deriving from 'govern'; others include 'government', 'governor' and 'governability'. The *New Shorter Oxford Dictionary* has three related meanings for governance: the first is 'the action, manner, or fact of governing; government' and includes 'controlling or regulating influence, control, mastery' and 'the state of being governed; good order'. The second meaning is 'the function or power of governing; authority to govern' and 'a governing person or body'; and the third is 'conduct of life or business, behaviour'. None of these are new, with the first meaning being from Middle English; the second is later Middle English to the late sixteenth century; and the third is late Middle English to the mid-seventeenth century.

Despite there being three meanings listed by the dictionary, they are not inconsistent with one other, or with other dictionaries. From these, governance is essentially about devising institutional arrangements, about steering (as in the original derivation), how to organize, and how to set procedures for the running of an organization. This can be regarded as the standard meaning. It makes perfect sense to refer to the governance of schools and golf clubs, corporations, universities, even entire societies or international institutions such as the World Bank or the United Nations. It is also quite in order to discuss the 'governance of contractual relations' (Williamson, 1996), governance of the courts or regulatory governance. Here, governance is taken in its broadest meaning, consistent with the standard dictionary definition and usage, and where governance is seen as 'the setting of rules, the application of rules, and the enforcement of rules' (Kjaer, 2004, p. 10). Thinking about governance means 'thinking about how to steer the economy and society, and how to reach collective goals' (Pierre and Peters, 2000, p. 1). Governance is about setting up structures, institutions, and ways of providing some kind of accountability. As Donahue (2002) comments, 'one broad model of accountability is governance – the rules and institutions for the authoritative organization of collective life' (p. 1).

After this start, though, there is little agreement about governance, particularly in public management and administration. Its definitions and usages have become controversial, perhaps even more than the other nouns deriving from 'govern'. That there is a noun 'governance' is without doubt; but precisely what it means is contested, so contested that the word loses much of its utility. Frederickson (2005) has noted 'because governance is a power word, a dominant descriptor, and the current preference of academic tastemakers, there has been a rush to affix to it all of the other fashions of the day' (p. 285).

Some definitions are too narrow. For example, Newbold and Terry (2008, p. 34) define governance as 'the historical, political, institutional, legal, and constitutional foundations that enable government to exist and function within the boundaries established by the U.S. Constitution'. This is not useful. Governance does not need to be constitutional, least of all only applying to the American constitution. Neither can governance be reserved to be about any single state, or even states in general. Another view of governance is that it is about 'relationships between state and society' (Pierre and Peters, 2000, p. 12). This too is inadequate, though it would work if it was referring to a sub-category such as public governance or political governance, or social-political governance (Kooiman, 1999, 2003). There is nothing in the definition that reserves the idea of governance to be only about state and society. Indeed, much of the recent action around governance has not involved direct relationships with the state.

It needs to be agreed that governance is not only about government, but is also about setting up mechanisms to run any kind of organization. As Keohane and Nye state (2000, p. 12):

> By governance, we mean the processes and institutions, both formal and informal, that guide and restrain the collective activities of a group. Government is the subset that acts with authority and creates formal obligations. Governance need not necessarily be conducted exclusively by governments. Private firms, associations of firms, nongovernmental organizations (NGOs), and associations of NGOs all engage in it, often in association with governmental bodies, to create governance; sometimes without governmental authority.

Keohane and Nye's definition is a particularly useful one, especially in terms of its broad ambit. It is just as relevant to speak of the governance arrangements of a company, a voluntary association, a non-governmental organization or an international organization as it is for the governance of an entire society.

Kooiman (2003) argues that 'governance can be seen as the totality of theoretical conceptions on governing' (p. 4). While this does provide an additional layer of abstraction, Kooiman's work draws quite explicitly on the 'steering' meaning of governance through the Dutch *besturen*, which means steering. What Kooiman (1999) terms 'social-political governance' is defined as 'all those interactive arrangements in which public as well as private actors participate aimed at solving societal problems, or creating societal opportunities, and attending to the institutions within which these governing activities take place' (p. 70). Social-political governance is, then, about the sub-category of governance that refers to society and politics – a useful distinction to make – and presumably does not rule out the possibility of there being other sub-categories. Kooiman (1999) also distinguishes between governance and governability: governance 'can be seen as the total effort of a system to govern itself; governability is the outcome of this process – not an "end state" but a stock-taking at a particular moment in times of complex, diverse and especially dynamic processes' (p. 87). Regarding governance as being about 'interactive arrangements', and 'as the total effort of a system to govern itself', is entirely consistent with the standard meaning.

Government and governance

There is general agreement now that 'government' and 'governance' have different meanings. As Rhodes (1996) notes, 'current use does not treat governance as a synonym for government' (p. 652). Pierre and Peters (2000) also comment that government and governance may have the same derivation, but 'they need not, and indeed, should not, be taken to mean the same thing' (p. 29). Often, though, government and governance are put together in not entirely helpful ways.

An OECD paper on governance defines it as 'the formal and informal arrangements that determine how public decisions are made and how public actions are carried out, from the perspective of maintaining a country's constitutional values in the face of changing problems, actors and environments' (OECD, 2005, p. 16). As this definition is really only about *public* governance, it is less than satisfactory. Moreover, the same paper states:

> The 30 member countries of the OECD share core governance elements. These have emerged with the evolution of the modern state and include: democracy and citizenship; representation; a constitution; the rule of law; competitive party and electoral systems; a permanent civil service; separation of powers between the executive, the legislature and the judiciary; and secularity. (p. 15)

A footnote at this point says 'drawn from Finer (1997)'. Finer does in fact mention all these things, but he is referring quite clearly to *government* – the focus of his magisterial work. Finer's work is explicitly about the state, the authoritative forces of the police and the military, about the apparatus of the government, but not about governance in its wider sense. The features listed by OECD (2005) could be considered as aspects of social-political governance, but not governance in its widest sense.

If it can be agreed that government and governance are different in current usage, there does appear to be some clearer understanding at present attached to the word 'government'. A government can impose its will on the society and its people through the state-sanctioned use of force. Both government and governance 'refer to purposive behavior, to goal-oriented activities, to systems of rule' but, as Rosenau argues (1992, p. 4):

> Government suggests activities that are backed by formal authority, by police powers to insure the implementation of duly constituted policies, whereas governance refers to activities backed by shared goals that may or may not derive from legal and formally prescribed responsibilities and that do not necessarily rely on police powers to overcome defiance and attain compliance.

Governments have force at their disposal; they can require compliance through laws, and the coercion implied by such laws can be applied (see Chapter 2). In societies with some pretence of democracy, the use of force may be muted – the army and the police are not large enough to maintain the regime through force alone – and the legitimacy of government is maintained by some kind of popular sovereignty. But the key point about government is that force is ultimately behind it; no other lawful authority than government can compel people to act in the ways that it prescribes.

Governments, though, along with other institutions, have been seen increasingly as having lost power. Michalski *et al.* (2001, p. 9) contend that:

> Looking at governance as the general exercise of authority, it seems that over the long run there has been a clear reduction in the absolute or unconstrained power of those in positions of power. This has been a marked trend both at the macro-political level, where the state attempts to effect society-wide governance, and at the micro-level, where firms and families have experienced important changes in the exercise of authority.

In the international relations sphere there are similar arguments made that governments themselves have less of a role, and that there are other players than nation states. Keohane and Nye (2000) make a case that, with globalization, governance is becoming more diffuse, and that instead of governments having a monopoly over issues of governance there are now many players involved. As they argue (p. 37):

> Rulemaking and rule interpretation in global governance have become pluralised. Rules are no longer a matter simply for states or intergovernmental organizations. Private firms, NGOs, subunits of governments, and the transnational and transgovernmental networks that result, all play a role, typically with central state authorities and intergovernmental organizations. As a result, any emerging pattern of governance will have to be networked rather than hierarchical and must have minimal rather than highly ambitious objectives.

Even if governments maintain their sovereignty, the actual scope they can exercise is much more constrained than it once was. By making agreements with other governments, national governments do give up some of their freedom. Increasingly, too, NGOs and other non-state actors are involved in matters that were once within the scope of nation states.

The traditional model of public administration and early managerialism do share a taste for the exercise of authority. As public management has developed since the start of the 2000s – with leadership models, governance, collaboration and co-production – so too has the apparent exercise of authority been reduced. The change poses fairly major problems for public managers. How could government, or governance even, operate without recourse to the kind of authority it always had? As Kettl (2002, p. 46) contends:

How could its hierarchically structured, authority-managed agencies effectively manage increasingly non-hierarchical, non-authority-based administrative systems? Hierarchy and authority worked, more or less well, in an era in which the government produced most of its goods and services itself. As government employed more indirect tools, however, the management strains grew.

The state is still important but no longer controls everything. As Pierre and Peters (2000, p. 68) state:

> The state no longer has a monopoly over the expertise nor over the economic or institutional resources necessary to govern. However, the state remains the key vehicle for the pursuit of the collective interest in society and what we are witnessing is a transformation of the state to fit the society of the late twentieth and early twenty-first century ... The new governance ... does not mean the end or decline of the state but the transformation and adaptation of the state to the society it is currently embedded in.

So far, then, the argument is that there has been more interest in ideas of governance in recent years; governance is wider in scope than government; and that governments have, with other institutions, lost power to an extent. After this, though, the governance story gets more complicated.

More definitions of governance

One of the most widely cited formulations of governance, drawing on Rhodes (1996), is that of Bevir and Rhodes (2003, pp. 45–53) who list seven definitions: (i) governance as corporate governance; (ii) governance as the new public management; (iii) governance as 'good governance'; (iv) governance as a socio-cybernetic system; (v) governance as international interdependence; (vi) 'governance as the new political economy'; and (vii) governance as self-organizing networks. Some of these are interesting and novel, and will be addressed later; others, though, are not definitions at all, merely quite ordinary usages of the standard meanings of governance discussed earlier.

For example, one of the Bevir and Rhodes (2003) definitions of governance is 'governance as good governance'. They argue that good governance refers to international agencies such as the IMF and the World Bank, and their promoting of better governing. It is the case that these agencies have set out to improve governance in developing countries and have made recommendations as to what good governance should look like (World Bank, 1997). But surely all that these international agencies are doing is trying to assist developing countries to be better run? Bevir and Rhodes (2003) assert that 'good governance tries to marry NPM to the advocacy of liberal democracy' (p. 47). Presumably this means that good governance is about international agencies packaging up NPM with liberal democracy and selling it to developing nations under the guise of good governance. It is an odd claim, given that there has been great caution in the application of NPM in such contexts, and that building institutional capacity in general has been the main emphasis (Minogue *et al.*, 1998) rather than advocacy of NPM. More applicable here is Kettl's (2005) argument that the management reform movement 'builds on the notion that good governance – a sorting out of mission, role, capacity, and relationships – is a necessary (if insufficient) condition of economic prosperity and social stability' (p. 6).

In all of this, however, there is no new meaning of governance in the phrase 'good governance'. Certainly, the World Bank and other international institutions have become more interested in how countries, particularly countries receiving aid, organize and administer themselves. They have indeed become interested in good governance; that is, that societies are well run. But this does not require any new definition beyond the ordinary meanings of governance.

Governance 'as international interdependence' is similarly not a meaning and even less a definition. For Bevir and Rhodes (2003), this involves the weakening of the nation state's capacities for governance, through hollowing out of the state and multi-level governance (p. 47). While there is extensive discussion of governance issues by international relations scholars – indeed, the recent revival of such issues arguably began with these – there is no need for a special usage or meaning to be attached to the use of governance in such a context. 'International interdependence' is not necessary as a definition of governance for international relations. Rosenau (1997), for example, observes that governance refers to 'mechanisms for steering social organizations toward their goals' (p. 40); also that 'the process of governance is the process whereby an organization or society steers itself' (p. 146). Both points use the ordinary 'steering' definition of governance and apply it to the running of entire societies and nation states. Governance as 'international interdependence' is also not a definition.

A further 'definition' of governance in Bevir and Rhodes (2003) is 'as a socio-cybernetic system'. In this definition, 'there is no longer a single sovereign authority and blurred boundaries between public, private and voluntary sectors', and examples cited include 'self-regulation and co-regulation, public–private partnerships, co-operative management, and joint entrepreneurial ventures' (p. 48). This point does have some validity, but is not a definition as such; rather it is a recognition that governance needs to be looked at in its wider (and original) sense of 'steering' rather than as a synonym for government. There is utility in looking at the diffusion of authority; 'governance' is a better way of considering this than 'government' but, again, no new meaning is involved. Also, it is an unhelpful term that Bevir and Rhodes have invented for the purpose. Given that 'cybernetics' derives from the same Greek and Latin root as does 'governance' (Rosenau, 1997; Pierre and Peters, 2000), calling governance 'a socio-cybernetic system' is a tautology. It is also unhelpful to define governance in relation to another term – cybernetics – that similarly evades an agreed definition.

It is also difficult to see a distinction between this definition and that of governance 'as the new political economy' which 're-examines both the government of the economy and the boundaries between civil society, state and the market economy as they become increasingly blurred' (Bevir and Rhodes, 2003, pp. 48–9). With blurred boundaries, the main point in this definition, and the socio-cybernetic one, is surely that there is no separate meaning either. In both of these, the site for governance – an interesting area for investigation – cannot be located with certainty. As Kennett (2008) argues, 'with the change from government to governance the governing administration is now only one player amongst many others in the policy arena' (p. 4). This is a useful point to make, but it is not a *definition* of governance; it is at most a usage. Other actors may exercise governance functions, but such activities can co-exist within the normal meaning of governance as laying down a set of rules with which to run organizations.

In all of the 'definitions' from Bevir and Rhodes examined thus far, there is no real novelty as far as the concept of governance is concerned. While they do point to some items of interest, they are in no sense *definitions* of governance; rather, they are standard uses of the standard meaning. There are three more of the Bevir and Rhodes (2003) definitions of governance that do warrant further discussion, however: governance as corporate governance; governance as the new public management (NPM); and governance as networks.

Corporate governance

Even if corporate structure and mechanisms of accountability in companies have been persistent issues in the private sector, it is undoubted that, from the late 1990s, they became even more important. In examining the rules around companies, both inside them and in terms of their regulation, the most common term has become 'corporate governance'. Bevir and Rhodes (2003, pp. 45–6) regard 'corporate governance' as another definition of governance.

There is a large and important literature about the running of corporations, in particular their accountability structures, principal–agent issues and so on (Jensen, 2000; Keasey *et al.*, 2005). There may well have been more action, and more serious theorizing about corporate governance in the private sector than about public sector governance in recent years. The quest for better corporate governance was heightened in the years after a series of financial crises – the Asian banking crisis of 1997, the 'dot com' bubble of 2000, the collapse of Enron and WorldCom in 2001 and 2002, respectively, and the global financial crisis that began in 2008. These may have been caused by regulatory failures, but inadequate corporate governance was also a major issue. Corporate governance looks at issues such as the responsibility of directors, how to ensure that management acts to further the interests of shareholders, and how to set up accountability mechanisms more generally.

The Sarbanes–Oxley Act, passed by the United States Congress in 2002, set out much more stringent requirements for companies, including clarifying corporate responsibilities, financial disclosures, auditor independence, an advisory board for accounting practice with powers to inspect, investigate and discipline accounting firms, and with enhanced penalties. Despite the increased costs of compliance, there were still issues of corporate governance persisting up to the time of the global financial crisis; indeed, they were the likely causes of it. Even more stringent corporate laws were to follow.

It is not surprising that issues of corporate governance have preoccupied management in the private sector in recent years. Of course, there may be some government involvement in that a corporation's legal environment as set out by government is a key consideration in issues of corporate governance. But it is not the only consideration, and nor is it necessarily the most important. More recent concerns about corporate governance have been mainly about designing structures of internal accountability that lead to good managerial performance. The motivation has mainly been to maintain and enhance shareholder and investor confidence rather than to satisfy any direct requirements from governments.

However, despite all the action, and despite the prominence of the related issues in the private sector, there is no sense that 'corporate governance' has any meaning other than that fitting within the standard definition. For example, the Cadbury Report in the UK in 1991 defined corporate governance as 'the system by which companies are directed and controlled' (Keasey *et al.*, 2005, p. 21). It is about finding mechanisms for the internal, and presumably external, steering of corporations. 'Corporate governance' is, then, similar to 'social-political governance' in the sense that it looks at governance issues within a specific sector. It is not a definition of governance.

Governance as the New Public Management

Another odd definition by Bevir and Rhodes is 'governance as the New Public Management' (Rhodes, 1996, 2000; Bevir and Rhodes, 2003). Presumably this means that the reform programme referred to as New

Public Management (NPM) was about governance to such an extent that it requires a new definition for governance itself. For this to be workable, it would have to be established that (i) NPM was primarily or at least significantly about governance; and (ii) that the usage of 'governance' in NPM has been so unusual or extensive as to justify it as another definition of the word itself.

In formulating the definition, Rhodes (2000) points out that initially NPM had two meanings: corporate management, and marketization. As he contends (p. 56):

> Corporate management refers to introducing private sector management methods to the public sector through performance measures, managing by results, value for money, and closeness to the customer. Marketization refers to introducing incentive structures into public service provision through contracting-out, quasi-markets, and consumer choice. NPM is relevant to the discussion of governance because steering is central to the analysis of public management and steering is a synonym for governance.

It is the case that governance involves steering, by definition, but the argument that, therefore, NPM is a definition of governance does not follow.

Bevir and Rhodes argue that Osborne and Gaebler (1992) were NPM theorists, and that their use of governance is in some way different and could presumably then warrant yet another definition of the word governance. As they (Bevir and Rhodes, 2003, p. 46) assert:

> Osborne and Gaebler distinguish between 'policy decisions (steering) and service delivery (rowing)'. They argue bureaucracy is a bankrupt tool for rowing. In place of bureaucracy, they propose 'entrepreneurial government' which will stress competition, markets, customers and measuring outcomes. This transformation of the public sector involves less government (or less rowing) but more governance (or more steering).

In similar fashion, Peters and Pierre (1998) discuss the similarities between NPM and governance, and like Bevir and Rhodes, draw on Osborne and Gaebler in referring to the idea of steering in both NPM and governance. Peters and Pierre (1998, p. 231) maintain that:

> Osborne and Gaebler (1992) coined the seductive slogan that governments should focus more on steering and less on rowing, and this managerial perspective plays a prominent role in both governance and NPM. Much of this steering refers to organizations cutting back while they simultaneously face increasing expectations on diversified and customer-driven services. Governance, to a much greater extent than NPM, is concerned with enhancing government's capacity to act by forging strategic inter-organizational coalitions with actors in the external environment. Steering, in this perspective, is largely about setting priorities and defining goals. In the NPM, steering is primarily an intra-organizational strategy aimed at unleashing productive elements of the public service.

However, there are some problems with both these views.

For a start, it is quite misleading to claim that Osborne and Gaebler coined the phrase 'steering not rowing'. The distinction between steering and rowing was in fact made by Savas (1987) and is duly attributed by Osborne and Gaebler (1992) when they use the expression. Second, it is also rather misleading to characterize Osborne and Gaebler as being about steering and rowing, or even of having much focus on governance. Their book is about entrepreneurial government, with most of the examples being drawn from innovations in local government. Third, at no point in their book do Osborne and Gaebler (1992) even mention NPM. Their ten principles of 'entrepreneurial government' are quoted by Rhodes (1996) who then states that 'clearly, NPM and entrepreneurial government share a concern with competition, markets, customers and outcomes' (p. 46). While this has some validity, it is arguable whether Osborne and Gaebler can be associated so easily with NPM. Neither governance nor steering is greatly emphasized by Osborne and Gaebler, though both are mentioned.

Moreover, when Osborne and Gaebler (1992) do use the term 'governance' it is done in a standard way. For example, they argue (with original emphases) (pp. 23–4):

> Our fundamental problem is that we have *the wrong kind of government*. We do not need more government or less government, we need *better* government. To be more precise, we need better governance. Governance is the process by which we collectively solve our problems and meet our society's needs. Government is the instrument we use. The instrument is outdated, and the process of reinvention has begun.

At another point, Osborne and Gaebler assert that governance cannot be contracted out (1992, p. 45):

> Services can be contracted out or turned over to the private sector. But *governance* cannot. We can privatize discrete steering functions, but not the overall process of governance. If we did, we would have no mechanism by which to make collective decisions, no way to set the rules of the marketplace, no means to enforce rules of behavior.

There is no new use of the word 'governance' here, no novelty, only the use of the word in its standard dictionary sense. Governance is indeed about steering; and Osborne and Gaebler are doing nothing more than using the term quite correctly. It is not logical to say, as Bevir and Rhodes seem to suggest, that as governance is about steering, then NPM must be a definition for governance.

In addition, as is argued elsewhere (see Chapters 4 and 15), NPM is insufficiently precise to be a useful framework in public management. Even with some allowance being made for the vagueness that surrounds NPM, its system design aspects in terms of societal governance were never as substantial as the concerns about managing within government. Societal or political governance issues were not greatly affected by NPM-style reforms, particularly the early ones. Kettl (2005) points out that 'the global public management movement is part of a fundamental debate about governance' (p. 6). But debates about governance were only a relatively minor part of public sector reform. Its governance aspects were incidental rather than central.

Two other uses of 'governance' in the context of public management need to be mentioned, one from Dunleavy *et al.* (2005) and the other from Osborne (2006). Dunleavy *et al.* (2005) argue that NPM is dead and has been overtaken by what they term 'digital era governance' (DEG). They assert that (p. 468):

> The intellectually and practically dominant set of managerial and governance ideas of the last two decades, new public management (NPM), has essentially died in the water. This cognitive and reform schema is still afloat, and a minority of its elements are still actively developing. But key parts of the NPM reform message have been reversed because they lead to policy disasters, and other large parts are stalled.

There is, however, no real explanation by Dunleavy *et al.* as to how digital era *governance* is different from digital era *government*; indeed, their argument appears to be more about enhancing the role of government through technology rather than anything related to governance in its wider meaning. The argument seems to be that by using large-scale computer systems, governance can again be centralized through a rediscovery of the benefits of bureaucracy. It is quite possible that IT infrastructure will lead to reintegration and bureaucratic control, though the alternative of further contracting to outside computer firms may be even more likely given the expertise asymmetry between public and private sectors. Moreover, not only do governments have a poor record when it comes to contracting for IT provision (Heeks, 1999, 2006), a strong case could be made that the technology will continue to move away from large, centralized computer solutions towards distributed expert systems using free or freely available software from the internet. This would appear to fit more within a managerial framework than a bureaucratic one. Also, Dunleavy *et al.* criticize NPM for its focus on economic efficiency, and yet the large-scale adoption of DEG is most likely to occur for this very reason.

Osborne (2006) remarks that the time of NPM was 'a relatively brief and transitory one between the statist and bureaucratic tradition' of public administration and 'the embryonic plural and pluralist tradition' (p. 377) of what is termed New Public Governance (NPG). NPG posits 'both a plural state, where multiple inter-dependent actors contribute to the delivery of public services and a pluralist state, where multiple processes inform the policy making system' and as a 'consequence of these two forms of plurality, its focus is very much upon inter-organizational relationships and the governance of processes, and it stresses service effectiveness and outcomes' (p. 384). There may be something in this idea even if NPG has so far been diffuse and ill-defined. In the same way that failure ever to establish what the NPM programme was doomed it as a movement, a similar fate may well occur for NPG. But a governance related to NPG that is not too pretentious; a governance that looks to reform; and a governance that relies on ordinary meanings for an ordinary word, is a governance with a future.

Governance and networks

One particularly contentious use and 'definition' of governance is as it is applied to networks (Klijn and Koppenjan, 2000). Rhodes (1996) argues that 'governance has too many meanings to be useful, but the concept can be rescued by stipulating one meaning … So, governance refers to self-organizing, inter-organizational networks' (p. 660). The argument about an increased role for networks is an interesting one, and has some basis in the incorporation of the outside world into processes formerly carried out only within government. But Rhodes is stressing rather more than this. The only meaning now stipulated by him for the word 'governance' is that governance means networks. Such a definition must be all-encompassing and sufficiently robust to capture all governance behaviours. And if there is to be only one meaning, then there is a presumption that all others need to be discarded, including the standard dictionary definitions discussed earlier, as well as the usage outside the social-political arena in such areas as corporate governance.

In their definition, Bevir and Rhodes (2003) assert that 'governance consists of self-organizing, inter-organizational networks' and, further, (p. 53) that:

> These networks are characterized, first, by interdependence between organizations. Changes in the role of the state mean the boundaries between the public, private and voluntary sectors are shifting and opaque. Second, there are continuing interactions between network members, caused by the need to exchange resources and to negotiate purposes. Third, these interactions resemble a game with actors' behavior rooted in trust and regulated by rules that are negotiated and agreed by network participants. Finally, the networks have a significant degree of autonomy from the state. Networks are not accountable to the state; they are self-organizing.

The self-organizing aspect, and with a significant degree of autonomy from the state, involves a considerable step further than mere consultation with government or the inclusion of interest groups in decision-making. Real power is to be held by non-state actors.

There is a perennial debate in social science between the merits and costs of two contrasting forms of organization – markets and bureaucracies. The argument put forward by Bevir and Rhodes is that the network concept is a third alternative. Donahue (2002) compares governance with markets and contends (p. 1) that:

> Another broad model of accountability is the market – cooperation arising out of voluntary exchange based on individual assessments of value. Each of these generic models has taken on countless different forms through human history ranging from primitive to intricate in their construction, from crude to sophisticated in their operation, and from triumphant to calamitous in their consequences.

Donahue sets up two forms of organization here; one is governance, which can include the authority of government, and the other is markets. This is similar to Ostrom's (1974) argument, that 'bureaucratic organization is an alternative decision-making arrangement to that of individualistic choice' (p. 58). In other words, for Ostrom too there are two forms of organization: bureaucracy and markets, with bureaucracy being based on compulsion and markets based on choice. Bureaucratic organization is based on authority – the government's ability to employ force – where markets are voluntary, in that a buyer and a seller have to agree before a transaction can occur.

Networks are argued to be a means for co-ordinating and allocating resources, a new form of organization, a third way of organizing, and 'to markets and hierarchies, we can now add networks' (Rhodes, 1996, p. 653). In effect, public policy is to be made by networks, and these networks exist independently of government, as they are self-organizing by definition. Rather than there being any idea that network actors are consulted by governments or included by governments, it is networks themselves that make policy. This is an important claim, and part of an ongoing discussion of the relative importance and interactions of governance, networks and markets. Even if the government then makes some kind of enactment of what has been agreed in the network, the real power lies with the network rather than the government. The governmental role is merely to bring into being the result of the action that has taken place within the network.

Kamarck (2002) also sees three models, with the market as the third one alongside government and networks. As she points out (pp. 249–50):

> In entrepreneurial government the public's work is done by people who work for the government; in networked government the public's work is paid for by

the government even though it is performed by people who do not work for the government. In the third emerging model of government – market government – the work of government involves no public employees and no public money. In market government, the government uses its power to create a market that fulfils a public purpose.

It is a big claim to regard networks as a third force alongside the more familiar bureaucracy and market divide. There are only two societal mechanisms backed by the sanctions of the state: the bureaucratic edict and the contract. A government can either issue an edict, law or rule, or engage the private sector by using a contract. The exercise of governmental power requires one or the other. Where the network model is of some utility is in describing the political machinations, the interest group involvement, the individuals and the interactions that lead to either an edict or a contract. It is open to question as to where the locus of government – the decision point – actually is. Depending on point of view, it could be in the politicking before a decision point is reached, or the exercise of power by government itself. In other words, is the crucial part of the policy story in the action leading up to a decision or with the decision itself?

Bevir and Rhodes (2003) also argue that 'although the state does not occupy a privileged, sovereign position, it can directly and imperfectly steer networks' and the 'key problem confronting government is, therefore, its reduced ability to steer' (p. 53). The reduced ability to steer may be somewhat overstated. It is the case that 'government action depends increasingly on nongovernmental partners, from nongovernmental organizations that deliver public services to private contractors who supply important goods' (Kettl, 2005, p. 6). But this does not mean any necessary decline in the power of government; rather, an increased realization that the formal, rational bureaucratic model is no longer appropriate and that it actually suits governments to involve a wide range of actors in what they do. Once the Taylorian 'one best way' is discarded, the range of possibilities opens up opportunities for outside actors to put their views forward.

Take, for example, a tax office as a governmental organization that has substantial, real power to force citizens to comply with rulings. Once, during the apogee of the traditional bureaucratic model, such an organization operated with little regard for the outside. It would just pass a law and enforce it, based on information and the assumption that the single best answer is to be found by a dispassionate and rational process. More recently, it has become evident that agencies which act in a high-handed manner can lose public support even though their actions are entirely within their legal powers. And an agency that loses support may lose its 'authorizing environment' (Moore, 1995) and have its status and standing decline in the public mind.

Perhaps all that is happening with networks is that governments are exercising their undiminished powers in a smarter way. Those in charge of the tax office now realize that the views of clients, accountants and other players are quite valid inputs and, without changing their powers one iota, actively solicit opinions from stakeholders. There may be what looks like a network operating here, but the point is that, far from the network being in a position of governing, it is rather that the exercise of power by government can be better directed with active outside involvement. On a contentious issue such as accounting standards, the outside professional body has substantial input into legislation, but rather than the government conceding power it is rather exercising its unchanged power more judiciously. And as networks have become more important, 'government officials have increasingly reached out to sweep them into the reform movement as well' (Kettl, 2005, p. 6).

It is no concession of power to a network to involve it in decision-making. Perhaps other organizations are merely assisting the government in doing what it wants done and 'despite the view of some who persist in seeing networks as a weakening of the state, networked government can also be looked at as a different way of implementing the goals of the state' (Kamarck, 2002, p. 246). Pierre and Peters (2000) make a similar point (p. 49):

> The creation of a more participatory style of governing does not mean that government is in reality less powerful. It does mean, however, that state and society are bonded together in the process of creating governance. If anything that state actually may be strengthened through its interactions with society. The state may have to abdicate some aspects of its nominal control over policy, especially at the formulation state of the process. On the other hand, it tends to gain substantial control at the implementation stage by having in essence co-opted social interests that might otherwise oppose its actions. The ultimate effect may be to create a government that understands better the limits of its actions and which can work effectively within those parameters.

It is quite obvious that there is a lot of political bargaining at all levels in governments and societies. Networks exist and do have influence; they are 'by no means novel features of contemporary political life' (Pierre and Peters, 2000, p. 20). But there is some distance from seeing the existence of bargaining to say that networks *are* effectively the government. What is novel is that networks are said 'to challenge state powers; they are essentially self-regulatory structures within their policy sector' (Pierre and Peters, 2000, p. 20). Networks and governments may find mutual advantage by working together. Networks want something from government; governments want to use networks for their own ends. The outcome will be a law or an edict or perhaps a tender for contract; but only government can execute any of those things. There may be action by networks before this decision point, but that could be described as ordinary politicking with the power of government unaffected.

The argument that the only allowable definition for governance is self-organized networks lacks coherence. One obvious critique for the self-organizing approach to governance 'is that governments establish the basic parameters within which markets, and even social groups, function' (Pierre and Peters, 2000, p. 39). Indeed, the whole idea of networks is also somewhat problematic. Political science has for a long time examined interest groups, with 'iron triangles', policy communities and other characterizations to find out where policy derives. It is not immediately obvious what the concept of networks adds to this. Precisely what they are is far from clear; 'among academics there is no consensus about whether networks are a theory, an approach, a phenomenon, a pattern, or a relationship' (Kettl, 2009, pp. 2–3).

Pollitt (2003) is not overly impressed by the network approach, finding it 'unsatisfying, indeed, at times, frustrating' (p. 65). He does not like the 'ahistorical assumption' that networks are new; nor the assertion that there are now more networks or that these are in some way more democratic; and the methodological and theoretical weaknesses (pp. 65–6). As he notes, the biggest disappointment for the public manager is 'the paucity of interesting and tested propositions for action coming from network theory' (p. 66). This is a particularly important point. If networks are to be a form of governance, more needs to be demonstrated than that there is a lot of interaction going on between interests and governments. As Pollitt contends (p. 67):

> This is not to say that network theory has nothing to offer. Rather, I see it as just somewhat overblown. At its worst it offers a romantic vision of a whole new way of governing, pivoted on a disparate bunch of case studies, usually drawn from a limited number of sectors. At its best, though, it reminds us of the (longstanding) importance of informal relationships *between* organizations and groups, and how these organizational dynamics can set the context for more formal and specific processes of decision-making.

Mintzberg (2000) too argues that reliance on the network model 'can be overdone' and refers to France, where 'both public and private sectors have long been dominated by a powerful and interconnected élite that moves around with a freedom and influence that is proving increasingly stifling to the nation' (pp. 78–9). The same general point could be made for other European countries.

Pierre and Peters (2000) observe that the self-organizing power of networks 'is especially self-evident in societies such as the Netherlands that have a very rich organizational universe and a government that has a history of accommodation to social interests' (p. 39). This could be stated in another way. In societies such as the Netherlands, where the political system is usually characterized by shifting coalitions of political interests, it may be necessary to resort to other means – networks or the bureaucracy, for example – in order to get anything done. In the Anglo-American countries the political part of government is most often much stronger, though the existence of a coalition government in the United Kingdom after the 2010 election has changed this verity as well.

An additional point to consider is whether the case has been made for discarding all the other definitions of governance apart from the definition of governance as networks. Even with due allowance being made for hyperbole, the network model is not sufficiently robust to have moved the English language away from what has been established over several centuries as the standard dictionary meanings of governance. To regard networks as governance or governance as networks, in other words as synonyms, is bold but cannot be substantiated. Rhodes (1996) argues that only one meaning of governance is to be accepted – that is, governance as self-organizing, inter-organizational networks. This means that he considers all other usages need to be discarded. There is some utility to the network approach either as an organizing principle or as one approach to governing, but to say that there is only one meaning of governance and that is as networks is, indeed, overblown.

Conclusion: the usefulness of governance

The consideration of issues of governance can add to the understanding of public management. Despite some issues with the idea of governance, especially in some usages of the term, it does remain a concept that has real value. Its original meaning of steering is very useful when applied to a range of societal situations, as is the idea that there can be varieties of governance without government, and its usage as an overarching concept that can include, for example, the institutional arrangements whereby government can be derived, such as the electoral system, as well as the way government then operates.

Tarschys (2001) makes a useful distinction between tight and loose governance, with tight governance standing for 'a variety of steering methods based on clearly determined objectives, rigorous instructions and meticulous follow-up' and offers 'military organisations, totalitarian political systems, and industries organised along the principles of Taylorism and scientific management' as archetypes of tight governance. He adds (pp. 37–8):

> Many elements of this strategy recur in the wave of proposals and reforms entitled 'new public management', in which imitation of the private sector is an

important trend ... In these approaches, a strong goal orientation is combined with a relatively pessimistic or sceptical assessment of human nature. Individuals, if left to themselves, will pursue their own ends and disregard those of the organisation – hence a need for firm frameworks, active efforts to strengthen motivation, and vigilant supervision.

This argument would suggest that old-style government and old-style public administration as well as managerialism of the NPM kind, can be considered as examples of tight governance. Tarschys continues (2001, p. 38):

> Loose governance, by contrast, is built on a less suspicious view of human behaviour and is linked with more agnostic or empiricist ideas about the choice of organisational means and goals ... Loose governance relies on confidence, subtle signals and co-operative environments. It tends to resort to recommendations and 'soft law' rather than commands and strict regimes. Key concepts are innovation, adaptability, and learning capacity. Organisations should preferably be flat if not altogether replaced by networks of independent actors.

As governance becomes less 'tight', as the outside is included through collaboration and co-production and the like; the more does loose governance seem appropriate. However, both tight and loose governance may have their problems. Tight governance 'generates complaints about overregulation, red tape, government failure and intrusive bureaucracies'; and, with loose governance, 'there is always a risk that trust turns into gullibility and that flexible arrangements give room to laxity, waste and corruption' (Tarschys, 2001, p. 38). The assumption that the world is heading towards forms of loose governance may not necessarily work. In times of crisis, government returns to the fore along with its core assets of force and authority.

Kettl (2002) maintains that 'as authority has become a less effective tool with which to solve problems, managers have struggled to determine what can best replace it' (p. 59). There have been various suggestions put forward in recent years, not much different from each other – all rather variations on a theme of greater involvement of the citizenry, and the perceived reduction in the power of government. Public managers are central to the processes even if they do not have the untrammelled scope for action and exercise of authority that they had during the traditional model of administration.

Governance can be a useful approach provided it is not overblown, as noted earlier. As Frederickson argues (2005, p. 292):

> Although the critique of governance is a serious challenge, does it render the concept useless? The answer is no. There are powerful forces at work in the world, forces that the traditional study of politics, government, and public administration do not explain. The state and its sub-jurisdictions are losing important elements of their sovereignty; borders have less and less meaning. Social and economic problems and challenges are seldom contained within

jurisdictional boundaries, and systems of communication pay little attention to them. Business is increasingly regional or global. Business elites have multiple residences and operate extended networks that are highly multi-jurisdictional. States and jurisdictions are hollowing-out their organization and administrative capacities, exporting to contractors much of the work of public administration. Governance, even with its weakness, is the most useful available concept for describing and explaining these forces.

Clearly, the idea that there can be societal benefit from actors other than governments does have some utility. Clearly, too, the idea that governments have lost some aspects of their sovereignty, and that a broader perspective can be useful, is also pertinent. But governments are not going away, and the actual reduction in their power may be somewhat exaggerated; it just does not need to be invoked quite as readily as it once did.

Governance is a good word, one with many uses, but it is a word in need of rescue. It risks being so burdened with meaning that its ordinary standard dictionary definitions – entirely appropriate for many current uses – become lost. The more esoteric definitions of governance do not add to our understanding. Governance is about running organizations, public and private; it is about steering, as in the original derivation; it is about solving societal problems; and it can be about structures and institutions that have nothing to do with the political system.

Governance cannot be confined to a public sector context. Some definitions of governance pay insufficient attention to its usage and meaning in other contexts. The concept of governance needs to be able to include how to run any organization. In addition, the discussion about governance also points to just how far the transition from public administration has progressed. Many of the ideas around governance are worlds away from the ideas of authority, bureaucracy and process that were characteristic of the traditional model of public administration.

Chapter 7

Regulation, Contracting and Public Ownership

Chapter Contents

- Introduction
- Regulation
- Contracting out
- Public enterprise: government as producer
- The privatization debate
- Conclusion

Introduction

Governments obviously interact with businesses in many ways; through regulation, through taxation, through purchasing, and through provision of goods and services, to mention but a few. Both government and business are interested in the creation of a buoyant economy, and interact in a number of ways to this end. Some private companies owe their very existence to government contracts; and lobbying activity can be directed at achieving commercial advantage from governments. Rather than examining the broad relationship of government and business (see Hughes and O'Neill, 2008), this chapter focuses on three aspects of it, each of which has featured as part of recent public sector reform. First, through *regulation*, governments set the rules within which the private sector has to operate; second, through *contracting out*, governments purchase goods and, increasingly, services from the private sector, and may even deliver some of its own work through such means; and, third, through *public enterprise*, governments may sell goods or (more likely) services to the public in the same way as though they were companies (see Chapter 2).

Each of these – regulation, contracting out and public enterprise – has undergone major change in recent decades, as part of the ongoing process of public sector reform. There has been a general shift away from public enterprise through the process of privatization. But contracting out and regulation have increased in importance even as they have changed

144

how they work. Old-style regulation was where governments would further the interests of particular favoured groups or individuals, through licences or other restrictions on possible competitors. Regulation is now more likely to be pro-competitive and to be focused on outcomes rather than merely prosecuting transgressors. And while the contracting out of the provision of goods and services is hardly new, there has been much more recourse to contracting by government in one form or another with the private or not-for-profit sectors.

The three points are related to one other. Regulation can be an alternative to public enterprise; that is, governments can regulate rather than owning enterprises that have natural monopoly characteristics that were once seen as a reason for government ownership. Contracting with the private sector is a strategy used more often to reduce government final delivery of goods and services, and is a form of privatization. An important sub-category of contracting out is that of public–private partnerships (PPPs), where the private sector provides the infrastructure – most often, though not exclusively – through a long-term contract with the government. Despite three decades of privatization, public enterprise still remains important in some countries. The ability of governments to intervene in the private sector by taking a stake in – or even total ownership of – companies returned to the fore during the global financial crisis (GFC) of the late 2000s.

What regulation, contracting and public enterprise have in common is that all are at the intersection of the public and private sectors. Since the early 1980s, many governments have systematically sold or shut down public enterprises, contracted out more of the provision of government services, and aimed expressly at deregulation. Privatization has been successful, at least in the narrow sense that there is now less government ownership of enterprises. However, deregulation has not proceeded all that far if one looks at the total amount of regulation in society. Certain kinds of deregulation have appeared – airline deregulation, for example – but in general there is now *more* regulation than before. With the size of governments ranging from a third to a half of the GDP in most developed economies, it is not surprising that there is much interaction between the public and private sectors – with the government as producer, as contractor and as a commercial partner with the private sector. These relationships are of interest not least because of real issues about management and accountability in government.

Regulation

Governments have the undoubted power to make laws or regulations over any activity in society. Regulations can be economic or social, though social regulations are often just called laws. Social regulations are aimed at protecting citizens and can include environmental rules, occupational safety and regulations on employment. Probably the most prominent usage of the term 'regulation' is in allowing or prohibiting activities in the economy, or in setting conditions to govern how economic relations are accomplished. Economic regulation is not very different from laws affecting social behaviour; for example, the rules setting out employment conditions could be considered both social and economic. Also, all regulations, all laws, have at their origin the government's monopoly of compulsion and force in exactly the same way as any restriction on criminal activity.

Through their regulations, governments set out the rules for markets to work optimally. As Stiglitz (2001, pp. 346–7) argues:

> If markets are to work effectively, there must be well-established and clearly defined property rights; there must be effective competition, which requires antitrust enforcement; and there must be confidence in the markets, which means that contracts must be enforced and that antifraud laws must be effective, reflecting widely accepted codes of behaviour.

There are several points to consider here. In the absence of competition policy, companies would collude; laws must not only be enacted, but they must also be obeyed. But the two key points are, first, enforcing contracts, and second, establishing property rights. Much of regulation concerns these two matters.

The private sector relies on contracts and these must be able to be enforced. Without enforcement, contracting parties would be able to renege on the deal and, if this behaviour became widespread, there would quickly be a complete lack of confidence in the system of exchange. The legal system provided by government is one of the greatest assets for a market system, and in particular for the enforcement of contracts. It is important to note that having suitable institutional support is essential before government activities can be contracted out. Contracting cannot work if there is insufficient institutional support in a society to enforce contracts; it can fail as a result of inadequate institutions.

Markets can exist without secure property rights, but it could be argued that markets are not likely to work well in the absence of such rights. With further economic development there follows a demand for the protection of intellectual property and other intangibles. A firm's real assets are increasingly likely to be in the skills of its workforce, its value-added in terms of design and innovation – in intellectual property, in other words – rather than in being a price taker from what it produces. As a result, institutions that can protect information and property rights attached to information become more important. Establishing property rights can be a rationale for privatization. When an enterprise is held in government hands, its ownership is quite diffuse; but transferring an enterprise to private hands is assumed to improve both efficiency and accountability, as an owner takes more care of an asset in which it has a property right.

Other institutions can enhance the operations of markets. Grindle (2000) adds 'independent central banks and tax agencies, stock markets, and regulatory bodies for privatized industries and financial institutions' (pp. 180–1) to contracts and property rights. These most often rely on the instrument of regulation. Businesses must comply with government-mandated occupational health, safety and environmental standards. Also, most countries have some kind of competition policy or antitrust legislation to enforce competition within private markets and restrain any tendency to collusion and monopoly among businesses.

Despite the undoubted asset that the legal system provides, there is some controversy over the role of regulation in the economy and its burden on the private sector. There are regular complaints that there are too many regulations and that they have become too intrusive, stifling business and affecting competitiveness. Changes to regulation and the regulatory system have been a major part of public sector reform. Much economic regulation – that is, regulation explicitly intended to affect entry, supply or pricing decisions in the private sector – has already been eliminated or revised in a number of countries. There are some specific kinds of regulation.

Financial regulation

This part of the regulatory system includes interest rates, supervision of the banking and financial sector in general, exchange rates, foreign investment and requirements regarding the registration of companies and their directors. Financial market regulation requires market participants to set out specified information so that investors can make informed decisions – information must be set out in a prospectus in a prescribed form – as well as prohibitions on some activities, including conflicts of interest. Directors must be named and have clear duties. Accounting standards set out how the accounts are to be organized, and specific rules as to how activities such as borrowings are to be accounted for in the accounts. There are rules for tax treatment and for auditors.

Whenever a financial crisis hits there inevitably follows a demand for better regulation. The passing of the Sarbanes–Oxley Act in the United States in 2002, requiring enhanced accountability for companies, followed a period of corporate scandals. A few years later, with the GFC, other apparent failures of financial regulation led to further demands to deal with even greater failures. Safeguarding the public interest requires the regulation of private markets. Inadequate regulation, it appeared, had led directly not only to banks failing and companies being dragged down with them, but also to governments having to bail them out, with taxpayers ultimately footing the bill. The GFC showed that existing financial regulation, while adequate for day-to-day events, could not cope with the systemic risk posed by what was a near collapse of international finance.

Restrictions on supply of goods and services

Governments often use regulations to allow or prohibit activities in the private sector. There can be regulation on price, quantity and quality, plus various product or packaging standards. It is common for transport industries to be regulated: the taxi industry is in most countries, along with railways; and there are domestic and international regulations covering airlines and shipping. Television and radio stations are licensed as a matter of course. Regulations surround the gambling industry. Imported goods may attract tariffs and quotas or non-tariff barriers. Much of this kind of regulation is demanded by the industry itself and for its benefit. Many governments have looked at this kind of regulation quite closely as part of wider public sector reform.

Occupational licensure

Particular professions, such as medical practitioners, dentists, lawyers, plumbers and electricians often require a government-issued licence in order to practise. This kind of regulation has been regarded by critics as a restriction on economic freedom; a bad lawyer or even a poor doctor should be sued if their work is not adequate (see Friedman and Friedman, 1980). This argument was always a bit too extreme to be taken seriously, especially for those professions where the public would prefer them to have some test of qualifications before they were engaged. However, the general point did have some effect for occupational regulations that appeared to have no real basis. In some jurisdictions, interior decorators require a licence, and there would seem to be no public interest in that. There is some tension in the relationship between safeguarding the public interest by requiring qualification standards and what can be a desire of professions to restrict their numbers to maintain or improve the incomes of their members.

Standards

Decisions to create a standard may be agreed within an industry or can be mandated by government. Not all standards are enforced by regulation, though many are. An economy has more standards than can easily be counted, ranging from building standards such as for concrete, fire control systems, electricity appliance regulations, to food standards. Standards may be international; for example, shipping containers come in either 20 ft or 40 ft lengths. It is hard to think of an industry anywhere in the world that can operate without agreed standards, and even if an industry agrees to their implementation, they are often enforced by the use of regulation.

Competition policy

This is a special category of regulation aimed at making firms in the private sector compete with one another. It can be defined as 'those policies and actions of the state intended to prevent certain restraints of trade by private firms' (Doern, 1995, p. xi). Without competition policy, its advocates argue, firms would collude; form cartels; restrict access to their products; fix prices; behave in a predatory manner; or merge with competitors – all with the aim of reducing competition and keeping prices and profits high.

National laws do differ, but there is general agreement as to the practices that are to be listed as illegal. Among the practices outlawed in the United States even before the First World War, and followed later by other countries, were resale price maintenance, price fixing by cartels, and mergers resulting in a substantial lessening of competition. These are still the main points followed by competition authorities now. In addition, some have taken on the role of the regulation of natural monopolies and consumer protection.

The regulation of competition has not been without opposition. Arguments against include (i) the existence of monopoly is relatively uncommon and does not justify government regulation; (ii) markets are resilient rather than fallible, and the distortions that result from monopolies or effective monopolies are rare and do not deserve the full weight of the law; and (iii) that intervention by government in the market is against the principles of liberty and justice. In general, though, competition policy has become stronger in recent decades. Competition authorities have found their actions supported by the courts and in the even more important court of public opinion. Competition policy provides a compromise. Governments can regulate markets at a relatively small cost to themselves, given that competition authorities are fairly small, and, by forcing competition to occur, the community at large can benefit.

Environmental regulation

As discussed earlier (see Chapter 2), there can be externality effects on the environment, most notably water and the atmosphere, that are not captured by an economic transaction that causes them. For example, it is possible to buy coal and to burn it, thus creating pollution, but the external effects on air, water or land are not paid for by the purchase of the coal. Only through government action can the public's interest in clean air and water be addressed, with the most common way of doing this being through the use of regulation. Since the 1960s, environmental regulation has grown. The problem of climate change felt to be aggravated by increases in greenhouse gases has led to proposals to deal with this through a market-based mechanism using tradable permits. However, both this approach and traditional environmental regulation exist firmly within the instrument of regulation using the coercive powers of the law.

Responsive regulation

As many of the economic reforms promoted by governments since the 1980s illustrate, the debate about regulation has largely been conducted between those who seek greater regulation of economic activity and those who would prefer to see less. To Sparrow (2000), deregulation represents 'yet another swing of a now familiar regulatory pendulum' between two apparently irreconcilable regulatory styles – one adversarial and punitive and the other more inclined to persuasion and negotiation (p. 34). However as Sparrow and others argue, the swinging of the pendulum is not necessarily inevitable.

One alternative to the conventional view of regulatory policy is that of 'responsive regulation' (Ayres and Braithwaite, 1992; Braithwaite, 2006). The traditional approach to regulation is to prosecute regulatory breaches as they are found, using the full force of the law. This is how and why laws were created. However, there is a movement within regulation towards responsive regulation and more of an outcomes focus rather than a punitive one.

For example, when the penalty for a regulatory breach is too extreme, such as the revocation of a licence, it is rarely invoked. Ayres and Braithwaite (1992) suggest that there needs to be a graduated set of responses – the regulatory pyramid – and the state can escalate according to the response of the transgressor to lower-level penalties. The highest penalty is argued to be a 'benign big gun' that is only brought out occasionally, but exists as a perpetual threat. This approach leads to regulation being regarded as an interaction, where the ultimate aim is to get a result rather than merely to prosecute. As another example, if there are two parties to a cartel, the first one to inform the regulator may escape penalty completely. The desired result is achieved, even though one admitted lawbreaker may go free.

Sparrow (2000) calls for agencies to 'pick important problems and fix them', emphasizing practical managerial responses to problems, notably in regulatory areas. Instead of a successful outcome in regulation being the prosecution of an offender, it becomes a more general change in behaviour in an industry and correcting the problem itself. To Sparrow, 'regulators face no shortage of strategies, methods, programs and ideas. Rather, they face the lack of structure of managing them all' (p. 49).

In many countries it is no longer accepted automatically that regulation is always in the public interest. As a consequence, there has been much deregulation of markets and privatization of economic activity that was undertaken previously by the state. However, it would be a mistake to interpret regulatory reform as evidence that governments are now undertaking less regulation. While it is probably true that regulation is greeted with more scepticism than was the case in the past, governments continue to regulate and do so 'in the public interest'. State intervention through public ownership has been largely discarded, and anti-competitive restrictions and industry-specific regulations have generally lost favour. With these changes, new forms of regulation have emerged. There has been a shift in character from the restrictive role of regulation, which was often anti-competitive, towards pro-competitive regulation to force the private sector to be more efficient through competition.

Contracting out

Arguments are sometimes put forward that the adoption of contracting out by various governments, starting in the 1980s, was a major change from previous practice and a defining characteristic of managerial reform (Smith, 2005, p. 591). For Hood (1991), as part of his specification of NPM, greater competition in the public sector includes 'the move to term contracts and public tendering procedures' and is justified as using 'rivalry as the key to lower costs and better standards' (pp. 4–5).

However, contracting was hardly new even in the 1980s or 1990s. Contracting and tendering have a history within government of literally hundreds of years (Bandy, 2011, p. 157). What was different was the extent of contracting by governments of service delivery. Increasingly, activities once provided directly by governments began to be provided by contracts with private firms or not-for-profit organizations. Contracting became the preferred way of market-testing government activities to separate the purchaser of government services from the provider; in other words, the separation of 'steering from rowing' (Savas, 1987). In some jurisdictions, contracting extended to any good or service for which there was an advertisement in the Yellow Pages (Hughes and O'Neill, 2001).

Governments everywhere contract for supplies from the private sector. The precise point at which goods or services are delivered in-house or bought in from outside might change over time, but the principle is unexceptional. As noted earlier (see Chapter 1), the theory of transaction costs (Williamson, 1986) has been used as part of the reason behind contracting out more government services. A firm in the private sector can be regarded as a series of contracts between different parts. These contracts inside a firm may become real contracts with outside suppliers, and the precise point at which this occurs depends on the transaction costs involved. There are some transactions that would be less costly if contracted out, to reduce administrative costs and provide some competition. However, there are some public sector transactions for which market testing has been made mandatory, where in-house provision would actually be better if it could be shown to have lower transaction costs.

The contracting out of government services can, in some senses, be considered a financial reform. It is usually assumed that cost savings will be made, perhaps of the order of 20 per cent (OECD, 1998a) or 15–30 per cent (Osborne and Gaebler, 1992, p. 89). Incontrovertible evidence is elusive, however. Contracting can be an extension of programme budgeting in that, by specifying the terms of a contract, it is necessary to spell out exactly what is to be achieved and the mechanisms of monitoring. The detailed delivery may then be in the hands of outsiders, but in principle there is little difference compared to what could occur within government, by setting out exactly what an agency or a section is to achieve and funding it accordingly. If the mechanisms are precise enough, there should be no great difference in internal or external provision, other than not having public servants carrying out the delivery.

Contracting for government services should not be regarded as a panacea for solving public management problems. A requirement to contract out or privatize may ultimately be more costly than in-house delivery. Private contractors need to add profit margins to the cost of provision, so if all other things are equal, their use would cost more. In most circumstances the efficiency gains of private provision might still be present, but this needs to be investigated and not merely assumed. As Donahue (1989) argues, 'Private firms in competitive markets *are* frequently more efficient than government bureaucracies, but it is romantic to infer from this that the mere fact of private organization, *without* competition and *without* market tests, leads to efficiency' (p. 222). The circumstances in which contracting out will work are spelt out by Donahue (p. 98):

> The more precisely a task can be *specified* in advance, and its performance *evaluated* after the fact, the more certainly contractors can be made to *compete*; the more readily disappointing contractors can be *replaced* (or otherwise penalized); and the more narrowly government cares about *ends* to the exclusion of *means,* the stronger the case for employing profit-seekers rather than civil servants. The fundamental distinction, however, is between competitive, output-based relationships and non-competitive, input-based relationships rather than between profit-seekers and civil servants *per se.*

There is considerable promise in privatizing or contracting out, but the approach needs to be pragmatic rather than ideological.

In theory, private contractors should work more efficiently, but there is an added burden for public managers above those of simply contracting out. This is to ensure *compliance* with the terms of the contract to make sure that contractors perform as expected. Compliance is not straightforward, as several questions, both political and technical, need to be dealt with. Administrative and technical questions involve such matters as 'drafting the contract, meeting legal requirements for bidding, creating adequate performance specifications, monitoring the contract properly, encouraging competition, and avoiding excessive dependence on contractors' and 'these administrative matters involving how to contract become more important than the basic policy question of whether to contract' (Rehfuss, 1989, p. 219). Contracting out may reduce the size of the bureaucracy, but ensuring compliance and monitoring contracts is likely to require a public service with higher skills. If there are no benefits to be gained by contracting out, then the provision should be in-house.

In 1988, a scheme of compulsory competitive tendering (CCT) was started in the United Kingdom. Local authorities were required to 'expose specific services to competitive tendering at fixed intervals and subject to national guidelines' (Szymanski, 1996, p. 1). There was some evidence that contracting was more cost-effective than in-house provision, most notably for services that were easy to specify such as refuse collection. Contracting out of such services was theoretically justified, as Szymanski asserts (1996, p. 4):

> The rationale behind CCT might be thought to accord with standard economic theory. Refuse collection constitutes a natural local monopoly because of 'economies of contiguity': it is cheaper for a single vehicle and operating team to collect waste from a given street than for several competing operators to do so. However, under monopoly conditions, an operator may be able to extract rents from a local authority because of asymmetric information problems such as the limited observability of effort or the inability of the authority to identify the operator's underlying efficiency.

However, CCT was contrary to the principle that managers should manage. Whether to contract or not should be decided by management, bearing in mind the need to be efficient and effective. But the national requirement – the compulsory part of CCT – took this away from local managers. CCT became highly unpopular, with arguments being made that the reductions in costs were not a result of greater private sector efficiency but by cutting staff and their conditions of service.

Privatization in the contracting out sense does offer benefits, but only in some circumstances at some times. When it works well there are benefits to privatization. However, when it works badly, 'privatization can muddy public finance, make public management more complex and awkward, strip away vital dimensions of the public purpose that are hard to pin down contractually, transfer money from public workers to contractors without any savings to the collective fisc, allow quality to decay, and *increase* costs' (Donahue, 1989, p. 217). Setting the conditions is not a simple task. However, it should be approached pragmatically rather than ideologically, and attention should be paid by public servants to the important task of monitoring.

There may be problems if contracting out goes too far. A public service operating under explicit contracts with the private sector, or explicit contracts between policy departments and service delivery agencies, would be a very different public service. There can be no thought of service to the public or even service to the government. If everyone is a contractor, no one has a longer time horizon than the end of their contract; if everyone is a contractor, there can be no such thing as the public interest, only what appears in the terms of a contract. Forcing public activities to be contracted out, through compulsory tendering, for example, takes away from management accountability. Simple ideological nostrums should be replaced by careful consideration of all the costs and benefits.

Public–private partnerships (PPPs)

A special sub-category of contracting used much more by governments in recent years has been the public–private partnership (PPP). There are differing views as to what constitutes a PPP. Skelcher (2005) notes that PPPs 'combine the resources of government with those of private agents in order to deliver societal goals' and that they include 'contracting out of services, business management of public utilities, and the design of hybrid organizations for risk sharing and co-production between government and private agents' (p. 347). This list is too wide in scope. Ordinary contracting is quite different from constructing a toll road with a PPP; and contracting with a non-profit organization for a short-term welfare contract is very different from a contract to manage a railway with an expiry date of more than 30 years.

However, providing a project through a PPP is really a form of contracting rather than something completely novel. PPPs are best seen as a special kind of contract involved in infrastructure provision, such as 'the building and equipping of schools, hospitals, transport systems, water and sewerage systems' (Erridge, 2009, p. 101). Hodge *et al.* (2010, pp. 5–6) state that there are five different families of possible partnerships for PPPs: institutional co-operation for joint production and risk sharing; long-term infrastructure contracts (LTICs); public policy networks; civil society and community development; and urban renewal and downtown economic development. Klijn *et al.* (2008) define a PPP as 'a cooperation between public and private actors in which actors develop mutual products and/or services and in which risk, costs and benefits are shared' (p. 253). This would appear to rule out contracting in the sense of supply of goods or services, but embraces the kinds of infrastructure project that PPPs usually include. Greve and Hodge (2007) comment that PPPs in their broadest sense are 'just about every type of interaction between public and private actors' but add that, in a narrower sense, 'PPPs are distinct institutional models mainly used for infrastructure development, such as build-own-operate-transfer (BOOT), build-own-operate (BOT) and lease-build-operate (LBO)', and that these economic and financial models 'tend to dominate' the public administration literature (p. 180). Some of the issues involved in PPPs of this kind are applicable to contracting in general, but PPPs of the economic and financial kind have more issues than more normal short-term contracts to provide goods or services.

For governments, PPPs offer a way of financing over a longer term than may be available through the regular budget process, especially where there is some kind of constraint on borrowing. Obtaining finance from the outside may mean that projects can be delivered earlier than they might be otherwise be able to be provided. For the private sector, a PPP offers some certainty as an investment and some reduction in risk by making a deal with government (Greve and Hodge, 2007, p. 181). Governments and the private sector may be able to find common ground for certain kinds of activities. For example, a toll road may solve a road congestion issue that the government does not have the resources immediately available to address, but providing a long-term revenue stream, backed by the regulatory powers of government, for the private investor.

PPPs came out of the Private Finance Initiative (PFI) in the United Kingdom in 1992 and were used extensively in Britain by both the Conservative and Labour Governments. Other jurisdictions also used them: for example, for toll roads in Sydney and Melbourne in Australia. One of the features of the PFI scheme was that the financing arrangement was in reality an artificial device to evade limits on government borrowing. Later changes to accounting standards meant that the full liability had to be included and this reduced the attractiveness of PPPs, as did the adoption of accrual accounting.

There are issues of accountability with PPPs in that a government is responsible for any use of government money and assets but then commits to a project not only itself but often also its successors. Duffield argues (2010, p. 212):

> PPPs are significantly different from other procurement approaches. PPPs involve the private sector taking the greatest responsibility for service delivery

over the life of the facility compared with the other contracting options considered. They also have the highest level of price certainty, but this comes at the cost of responsibility for day-to-day decisions relating to both assets and the way in which services will be delivered – the setting of service standards remains a governmental decision.

Skelcher (2005) contends that 'buying through a PPP predominates over making through a bureau as the preferred model of public service delivery in the early twenty-first century' (p. 362). This surely is an exaggeration, though there is no doubting the popularity of PPPs for large-scale infrastructure in some jurisdictions. But it is hardly the preferred model. In limited circumstances, a small number of PPPs might emerge, but much more infrastructure will continue to be delivered by the government itself or by regular contracting out. Duffield (2010) argues that 'PPPs can work in the right situation', however, they 'are complex and generally require a very large financial transaction, due caution and high levels of expertise' (p. 213).

Hodge *et al.* (2010) also argue that important as the trend towards PPPs has been, 'it is also important to remember that PPPs did not wipe out public investment, or indeed infrastructure projects handled either by the public sector alone or by the public sector contracting with the private sector in traditional ways' (p. 596). Even in the United Kingdom, which went further than other countries, the 'reality is that PPPs became a more accepted form of infrastructure project delivery, but not the dominant mode *per se* (p. 596). While there were a large number of such projects in the United Kingdom, the total value amounted to only about 11 per cent of government investment (Flynn, 2007, p. 253).

One of the biggest problems with PPPs, and one not shared with regular contracting, relates to the duration of some contracts signed. It is not unusual for contracts to be for 30 years or even longer. Contracts with such long terms are not that common in the private sector, for the obvious reason that conditions can change and one of the parties could be left at a disadvantage. Governments signing such long-term contracts also have a problem in being stuck with assets or deals they may no longer wish to have. There are issues of accountability in that even if a government is responsible for any use of government money and assets, by entering into a long-term contract it commits, not only itself, but also its successors for many years and through changes of government.

Contracts should not be regarded as the single best way for governments to be more efficient. Their use needs to be dependent on time and place. In some circumstances, costs can be reduced; in others, a contract gains no benefit. One of the tasks of public managers is now to be a manager of contracts, but, especially in the earlier period under question, drawing up and monitoring contracts was not done particularly well. Expertise has been gained only through substantial experience, and contractual problems have not entirely dissipated.

Public enterprise: government as producer

Governments can use their powers for many purposes, including setting up enterprises to sell goods or services to the public. Starting in the early 1980s, the widespread privatization of public enterprise in many countries greatly reduced the scale and scope of the sector. This was a marked change to the existing scope of government and an explicit rejection of the idea that governments themselves should own key industries. As public enterprises operate at the boundary of the public and private sectors, arguments about their role are often about the desirable role of government itself. In the 1980s, privatization was the subject of highly contentious and acrimonious debate in many countries. In the event, the answer in the debate was overwhelming, in developed and developing countries alike, that governments should dispose of their public enterprises. The most significant of the early programmes of privatization was in the United Kingdom. Between 1979 and 1993 nationalized industries in Britain fell from a share of 11 per cent of GDP to 2 per cent, and from 1.8 million employees in 1980 to less than 400,000 in 1994 (Kamarck, 2000, p. 240). The privatization movement spread to other countries, to the extent that, from the early 1980s to 1993, more than 7,000 enterprises had been privatized (Farazmand, 1996, p. 18).

Public enterprises are a noteworthy part of the public sector. They may shrink so far as to become nothing more than an interesting diversion in the history of governmental institutions. They may gain a new lease of life, as they did during the GFC from 2008, when governments in the United Kingdom and even the United States bailed out some key private enterprises by taking up equity or even outright ownership.

Reasons for establishing public enterprise

Governments have established public enterprises for a variety of reasons. Rees (1984) argues that there are four reasons for the existence of public enterprise: to correct market failure; to alter the structure of pay-offs in an economy; to facilitate centralized long-term economic planning; and to change the nature of the economy, from capitalist to socialist (p. 2).

The first point refers to goods or services, which are desired, but will not be provided adequately by the market. Market failure can occur for reasons of natural monopoly, restriction of competition in some other way, externalities or spill-over effects on to others, and where the goods produced are to some degree public goods (see Chapter 2). To have such industries in public hands may be 'a way of retaining the cost advantage of a sole seller while preventing the resource misallocation which would result from a profit-seeking monopoly' (Rees, 1984, p. 3). The second point – the structure of pay-offs – means altering the benefits received by particular individuals or groups. Beneficiaries could include the employees, consumers or government. Some critics argued that government ownership leads to 'featherbedding', providing terms and conditions for employees above those that could be obtained elsewhere, including the employment of more staff than might be needed.

The third point – centralized long-term planning – is a motivation used in some countries. Government ownership of electricity and the railways in France enabled the provision of services ahead of demand as part of the planning process for the nation, especially in regard to the government's attempts to decentralize the economy. In some sparsely settled countries such as Australia and Canada, utilities were established in government hands from the outset, because of the inability of private providers to make an economic return. The choice was either to have the government provide services, or for them not to be provided to consumers at all. The fourth point – to change the economy from capitalist to socialist – was a major factor in some countries. In the United Kingdom in the immediate post-war period, railways, steel and coal were nationalized, so that the commanding heights of the economy were in government hands. Public enterprise had been regarded as a form of 'soft' socialism, perhaps a transitionary stage on the way to full socialism and it was thought that if important industries were in government hands as public enterprises, this would facilitate the transition to a socialist state.

There has been no single consistent governmental aim for using public enterprise. There been a set of diverse reasons beyond mere profit-making. Public enterprises have always had objectives other than making a profit.

Kinds of public enterprise

A public enterprise is a particular kind of statutory authority: one that sells goods and services to the public on a large scale, with the financial returns accruing in the first instance to the authority itself (Uhrig, 2003). Public enterprises provide many services, including, in some countries, utilities such as telecommunications, electricity, gas supplies, water and sewerage; transport, such as rail, airlines, shipping services and urban public transport; financial services, notably banks and insurance companies; and agricultural marketing. Some countries have government-owned oil companies, motor vehicle companies, tobacco and alcohol companies. Indeed, it is hard to imagine a product or service that has not been government-owned in at least one country at some time. The only point in common among all of these is their government ownership.

The most important public enterprises have been public utilities, providing services such as water, sewerage, electricity, gas and telecommunications. All these are essential for the economy as a whole – hence the name utilities – but as they are services with connections to households by a network they have a real (or at least a tendency towards) 'natural monopoly' (see Chapter 2). A competitor would not appear, as its prices would need to start higher than those of the public utilities as it set up its own network. As public utilities are essential services they are politically sensitive, and there is great disruption to the private economy and households if supplies are interrupted. As a result of political sensitivity and the tendency to natural monopoly, historically many governments have favoured outright ownership of public utilities. Even if natural monopoly is no longer seen as existing for the full range of utilities, governments still generally maintain fairly tight control through regulation.

Another category is that of essential services that face competition. In many countries the postal service is publicly owned, even in the United States, but Germany privatized theirs in 1995, and Japan in 2005. The letter mail is an essential service, but while ordinary letter delivery may have tendencies towards natural monopoly, it faces competition from direct mail, courier services and telecommunication services, including fax and electronic mail. A postal service would still be seen as an essential service but whether it is government-controlled or not seems less important than it once did. Public freight transport is similar in that it faces competition from private operators, while public passenger trains and buses compete with private cars, airlines and private buses. Other forms of public enterprise are those that exist by using the government's legal powers, such as to compulsorily acquire commodities, particularly rural commodities for further sale, or to require the purchase of insurance for motor vehicles. The use of compulsory acquisition or compulsory purchase is what distinguishes this group of enterprises, as their main asset is the coercive power of government.

The other key public enterprises are government-owned corporations, which compete directly with private companies and in the same market. This category includes banks, insurance companies, airlines and oil companies, to name but a few. The list of public enterprises in competitive environments has been considerably reduced by privatization. The question is, if they are profitable and operate no differently from competitors, why should they be government-owned? On the other hand, if they are profitable and well managed, why shouldn't the government keep them and use the profits in some socially productive way? Governments have involved themselves with enterprises in competitive environments for many reasons; however, privatization in the

1980s and 1990s saw a clear expression around the world that this strategy was no longer in favour.

Some categories of public enterprise offered no great advantage to the public by being government-owned. Others where there was some kind of public interest might still have been better in private ownership and regulated by government rather than owned. Interestingly, years later there is little nostalgia for the great days of public enterprise, and no serious attempt to nationalize those industries that had been privatized. The public debate faded away too. The foray into public enterprise again with the GFC was only short-term in nature and did not mark a change of ideology.

The privatization debate

The election of the Thatcher Government in the United Kingdom in 1979 led to an intense debate over the question of privatization, and the 1980s saw an extensive and continuing programme of sale of public enterprises. The debate did not stop there, and the apparent success of the United Kingdom programme was followed by other countries – for example, New Zealand, which saw privatization as a way of concentrating on core activities as well as a handy means of raising revenue.

While selling public enterprises was the most visible form of privatization it was not the only kind. In the United States, where there was little public enterprise in any case, privatization included the contracting out of services formerly provided by the government. It makes sense to see privatization as the reduction of government involvement in general: as a reduction in production, but also a reduction in provision, subsidies or regulation. Even if much of the argument about public enterprise has been about selling enterprises – reducing production by de-nationalization – the other features are also crucial. Liberalization, by means of reducing regulation, is a critical part of privatization, while contracting out and charging are occurring right across the public sector.

Economic arguments for privatization

Economic arguments for privatization include exposing activities to market forces and competition; reducing both government spending and the government's share of the economic cake; and reducing taxes by using the proceeds from sales of public enterprises. In theory, competition provides powerful incentives to both produce and price efficiently. If competition is seen as desirable, the different instruments of privatization need to be compared. Competition could be introduced by selling assets or de-regulating to allow for the entry of competitors, or by calling for competitive contracts for particular activities. Selling assets only improves competition if an enterprise is already in a competitive environment; and selling a monopoly with its regulation intact does nothing for competition. As Stiglitz (2001, p. 350) argues:

> A regulatory structure can be created to ensure that some of the efficiency gains from privatization are shared by consumers and other users and that other social objectives, such as universal service, are enhanced. But the proposition that privatization can, in principle, increase the efficiency of the economy and achieve other social objectives should never be confused with the proposition that, in the absence of effective regulatory structures, privatization may do neither in practice.

Competition can provide benefits, but the best way of introducing competition is to de-regulate the industry, rather than necessarily sell assets, unless de-regulation occurs at the same time as assets are sold. Capturing the benefits of competition requires careful regulatory design. For example, franchising is more difficult in practice than in theory. The successful bidder has clear advantages when the contract comes up for renewal, and the system would still require substantial government regulation. Political bargaining may become more important in deciding who wins a franchise than genuine 'arm's-length' contracts. If privatization does not result in greater competition, there are unlikely to be major benefits for consumers.

Preventing monopoly exploitation was once regarded as one of the main reasons in favour of public ownership of enterprises, but it is now less significant. Advances in economic theory, particularly 'contestable market theory', suggest that monopolies are constrained from being predatory by the *potential* entry of competitors (Baumol *et al.*, 1982). They cannot charge too much above reasonable prices because then a competitor might appear. If a monopolist is being constrained in this way, there is no need for government intervention. In addition, even where there are genuine monopoly problems, as in electricity and telecommunications, these may only occur in part of an enterprise's operations.

A further economic argument for privatization has been to reduce cross-subsidies. This is where an enterprise varies its prices so that, within its overall functions, profitable activities subsidize unprofitable but desirable activities. Privatization is seen as a way of charging for services in accordance with their true costs. If the government desires the provision of specific services, it should provide the funds for the purpose through the budget.

Managerial efficiency and privatization

The efficiency argument for privatization claims that private management is inherently superior to public management. Clearly, the managements of private and public sector organizations do operate in quite different environments and often have quite different objectives. There are theoretical differences between them in the structure of incentives available to management and, because the public sector operates in a political environment, management there may be said to be less straightforward. Perhaps public service conditions are not conducive to excellence? But the managerial argument is more than this: it is that public management is *inherently* inferior. The private sector is assumed to have a time-tested set of incentives and accountabilities in place, and as these are not present in the public sector, there must be inefficiency. The only problem with this view is that evidence is hard to locate, and is far from persuasive when it is found (see Hodge, 2000).

For small-scale operations there is some evidence that private provision is more efficient. For example, a comparison of private and public refuse collection shows that private contractors tend to be cheaper than public ones (Savas, 1982). At such a local level, there may be a case for a greater use of contracting out in areas such as refuse collection or road construction. It is, however, only a minimal form of privatization. It is still a government service or asset, and the only saving is the difference between contractors and government day labour, which varies according to the activity itself. Often, the ease of gaining data at the lower level means that studies about refuse collection are used to substantiate the general case for private provision over public. But it is a far cry from this to the level of large enterprises.

The absence of systematic differences is surprising. Perhaps the proponents of privatization make the mistake of comparing actual public sector management practices with an idealized private management world. In this ideal, management is controlled by, and accountable to, its shareholders; workers feel part of their enterprise; the share price reflects the value of the company; and the final sanction for poor management is the threat of a takeover. In some cases, these views may be realistic, but private managers are often averse to taking risks, treat their shareholders with contempt, and takeovers may be concerned with making paper profits rather than improving management. The available evidence seems to suggest no measurable difference between the two sectors. The differences that do exist are more related to the regulatory environment than to ownership and some parts of the public enterprise sector may have greater inefficiencies than others.

Ideological arguments

Privatization is part of the more general debate about the respective merits of market and non-market systems of resource allocation. Ideological considerations have been important in the privatization debate. The early Thatcher Government privatization was largely driven by ideology, assisted by pro-market think tanks and changes in economic theory. The ideological fervour faded somewhat, even before the Conservative government was replaced by Labour in 1997. Privatization, in its various forms, began to be viewed pragmatically, as a device that could be used in some circumstances but was not a solution to every problem.

If there has been an ideological debate over privatization, it has certainly been won by those favouring privatization, judging by the policy outcome. This has happened even though the economic arguments for privatization are less than overwhelming; there is no incontrovertible evidence supporting the superior efficiency of private sector provision (though there is a similar lack of evidence of any public sector superiority); and the ideological arguments are unconvincing. The arguments and evidence for privatization were not strong but, in the final analysis, there was no serious and sustainable argument from those in favour of *retaining* activities in public hands. There now seems to be fairly general agreement that running public enterprises is no longer part of the core business of government, and that if other services can be contracted out the relative costs and benefits should at least be considered.

Accountability

A key issue shared by regulation, contracting out and public enterprise is that of accountability. Of these, regulation may be the least problematic, but even there the real political accountability of regulatory agencies with often highly complex rules and procedures can pose real questions. Some forms of contracting have real issues of accountability. Contracts are often secret, with commercial in-confidence provisions often being used. Not only is the legislature not aware of the precise details, but members of the government may not actually know them either. The longer contract terms are, the more that accountability becomes problematic. If a public–private partnership has a term of more than 30 years – which is not unusual – the government's accountability to the public for such a contract is most dubious. The government would change many times over such a long period; indeed, the contract – which any successive government would be bound to honour – would have tenure far longer than the government that signed it.

Public enterprises have always had particular management problems, including accountability, regulation, social and industrial policies, investment policy, and financial controls. Of these, control and accountability are particular problems for public enterprises, which are set up deliberately to be relatively independent of direct political control. If control is too tight, there is no advantage in having them set up as entities with a significant degree of independence. But on the other hand, if government control is too loose, an enterprise may not be accountable to its owners – the public – raising the question as to why it is in government hands at all.

The accountability problem of public enterprise can be seen from its three distinguishing characteristics: 'First ... they must be owned by the government. Second ... [they] must be engaged in the production of goods and service for sale ... Third, sales revenues ... should bear some relationship to cost' (Aharoni, 1986, p. 6). These characteristics can lead to confusion in accountability. Public enterprises are organizations designed to be a part of the government sector, but also to operate commercially. Despite operating commercially, however, they have no shareholders; and they are government-owned but are usually not funded by government. They have their own management and boards of directors, but are also responsible to a minister. A public enterprise is often required to meet other objectives, rather than simply trying to maximize profit as would a private company.

The questions of privatization and accountability are linked. One of the arguments for privatization is that public ownership means an absence of real accountability. In this view, the absence of the kind of accountability presumed to exist in the private sector implies that public enterprises have no place in society. Part of the early public sector reform process involved reasserting control over public enterprises, making them pay larger dividends, and devising better means of ensuring accountability. The success of these changes was mixed, and inevitably led to further privatization. If accountability is poor and improvements not possible, the case for privatization becomes much stronger.

Conclusion

Governments have a range of contact points with business. Taxation is a perennial interaction, but the three discussed here – regulation, contracting and public enterprise – are probably the most important in terms of public management reform.

The level of regulation has not been reduced, as was often talked about in the early years of managerial reform, but it has changed in character, with much less special regulation to benefit a small group and much more regulation aimed at making businesses actually compete with each other. But there is a long way to go before many of the more petty regulations are removed, even though many governments have regulation reviews and regulation review units. It is usually harder for a government to take away a regulation that benefits someone than it was to enact it in the first place. There has been a significant level of regulatory reform, but there is no real prospect of regulation being cut substantially. The contracting out of government services is often regarded as one of the key features of managerial reform. It has been argued here that there is indeed an increase, but that contracting out is by no means novel.

The great public enterprise experiment seems to be over. It is difficult to see any long-term future for the public enterprise sector in any advanced or even developing country, especially for those enterprises supplying goods or services on a large scale. Apart from small-scale activities, it is likely that public enterprise will eventually disappear as an acceptable way of delivering private goods and services. Even the revival during the GFC was expedient rather than a lasting return to the ideas of the 1950s.

Even if the precise dividing line between government and the private sector cannot be drawn with any great precision, there are major differences between them, notably in terms of accountability. All government organizations are assumed to be accountable in some way to the public through the political system. Private organizations are accountable to their direct owners, or their indirect owners – the shareholders. The accountability requirements are so different that there needs to be a warning for all governments that get too close to business. A government is not a business and should not behave as if it is one.

Chapter 8

Stakeholders and External Constituencies

> ## Chapter Contents
>
> - Introduction
> - The need for an external focus
> - External relations in the traditional model
> - External relations as a management function
> - Interest groups
> - Beyond the policy community
> - Issues regarding over-reliance on the outside
> - Conclusion

Introduction

One of the key parts of the transition from the traditional model of administration to public management has been the extra attention paid to matters affecting the organization which are outside its immediate control. Part of this renewed external focus, as noted earlier, has been to look at strategy, and at the threats and opportunities in the environment in which the organization finds itself. The other part is the need to deal directly with outside individuals and institutions, and how to manage these relationships. A key role for any manager is to attempt to control the organization's environment, or at least to influence as far as possible any factor that might impinge on its mission and objectives. External constituencies are important influences and any manager needs to take them into account in the management task.

The management of stakeholders and other external constituencies is now carried out quite differently from how it used to be under the traditional model of administration. There are two aspects to this. First, there is the real and perceived need inside the bureaucracy to manage external relations – something that, by itself, is quite different from the traditional model's narrow focus inside the organization. Second, interest groups – the most important of the external actors – are now regarded as having a far greater and generally positive role in the policy and administrative process. The relationship is now closer between bureaucracy and groups, even symbiotic, but this is both a more realistic and a positive development in public sector management when compared to the administrative system, where groups were regarded as essentially negative actors to be kept at arm's length.

As managerial reforms have been implemented, there have been greater opportunities to involve outside bodies in the achievement of joint goals. Where once the most that a traditional bureaucracy could cope with was some cursory consultation with stakeholders, after which it would make up its own mind, public managers now routinely set out to achieve real collaboration with the outside world. Early managerial reform also tended towards a way of thinking where outside actors had no role. More recently, co-production of various kinds is 'very much on the agenda of governments' (Alford, 2009). Once it is generally accepted that there is no 'one best way' to achieve an outcome, as was assumed in the traditional model or early managerialism, public managers can, with the assistance and active engagement of clients and citizens more generally, find a good, workable solution to public problems. Involving stakeholders is much more likely to lead to a lasting solution to problems than one imposed by bureaucratic rationality alone.

The need for an external focus

Any organization needs to pay some attention to the outside world, for that is where context, opportunities and threats may be found. This is especially true of public organizations as they are influenced by outside bodies to a greater extent than those in the private sector. Public programmes are more visible; they belong to all citizens and not just to immediate consumers. Users and taxpayers feel some ownership of all the activities of governments. For example, government assistance to the arts is of obvious and direct interest to the arts community, but it may also concern taxpayers who have no interest in the arts and might resent their money being used in this way. This wider interest means greater scrutiny of the public sector by the media and the public at large than is the case in the private sector.

The public sector does not even have control over its own resources or goals, as Wilson (1989, p. 115) argues:

> To a much greater extent than is true of private bureaucracies, government agencies (1) cannot lawfully retain and devote to the private benefit of their members the earnings of the organization, (2) cannot allocate the factors of production in accordance with the preferences of the organization's administrators,

and (3) must serve goals not of the organization's own choosing. Control over revenues, productive factors, and agency goals is all vested to an important degree in entities external to the organization – legislatures, courts, politicians, and interest groups.

The additional scrutiny should not be surprising, as public organizations were created at some stage by the political process and are therefore subject to public accountability. Public organizations are owned by the community, and are therefore always open to scrutiny from the public and the media. Having external political limits and high levels of accountability suggests a greater external focus by the public organization, in order to be aware of its environment and to manage its constraints.

Outside organizations do need to be dealt with. Procedures need to be developed and implemented; in short, the process of dealing with external components is a function of management. In Allison's model (1982, p. 17), the 'managing external constituencies' part of the general management function involves: (i) dealing with external units of the same organization or the co-ordination of parts of the organization; (ii) dealing with independent organizations such as other parts of government, business and interest groups; and (iii) dealing with the press and the public.

The first external constituency function is essentially co-ordinative; that is, it concerns the managerial procedures by which organizations subject to the same authority co-ordinate their activities. Different parts of the same organization need to deal with one another, even as they often regard each other as rivals. The second involves dealing with those organizations that are not controlled by the agency, but can influence its operations in some way. These organizations have a wide range and include other parts of government; other governments; other levels of government or even other nations; individuals; and interest groups. The third function, dealing with the press and the public, is a matter of public relations strictly defined. It is a normal organizational task, though the public sector environment may make it more difficult than most public relations tasks in the private sector.

All these functions pose challenges for public management. External constituency management now involves service delivery, the beginnings of consumer sovereignty and the 'empowerment' of clients. All these contrast with external relations in the traditional model of administration. Dealing with the outside has become far more important for public organizations with the decline of the traditional model. It could even be argued that the failure of the older model to consider external constituency relations adequately was a significant reason for its decline.

External relations in the traditional model

External relations were not considered to be particularly important in the traditional model of administration. The focus of attention was inside the organization – on structure and process. As part of the strict separation between matters of policy and matters of administration, the task of dealing with the outside world was reserved for the politician. Dealing with the press, the public, interest groups or other organizations was outside the remit of the public servant. When individual public servants are regarded as anonymous, they are neither able nor willing to appear on behalf of a department or its policy, let alone have any ownership of it in the public mind. Similarly, the concept of neutrality meant that a public official's external focus was limited by the fear of being 'political', and in these circumstances, the public servant was quite willing to defer to the politician.

In the United States, where the strict separation between policy and administration was not followed to the same extent as in parliamentary systems, there was still a similar division of labour between politicians and public servants. American agencies were always relatively open, with a major part of an agency's budgetary success being how well it could deal with outside groups such as Congress and its committees, the press and the public. However, most outside contacts were usually carried out by the political appointees to the bureaucracy, who came and went with a particular administration. In fact, that was their main purpose. Career administrators did not usually deal with outside bodies to the same extent as politicians, either outside or within the bureaucracy.

Looking again at Allison's (1982) points for managing external constituencies, it can be argued that all were either not handled at all or handled badly in the traditional model of administration. First, co-ordination was handled bureaucratically, if at all. Relationships between parts of the same agency were assumed to be as specified on organization charts, and co-ordination was managed hierarchically and only by their common authority. Any notion of bureaucratic politics was disregarded. There was little concern with the way that activities added up to some agreed general function of the whole organization. That was a 'political' function and not the concern of public servants who, by definition, would only perform administrative functions.

Second, the relationships with independent organizations were also presumed to be managed by the political leadership, including the relationship with other branches or levels of the government. Interest groups were barely tolerated by the public service and any contact with them was left to politicians. These groups might lobby for or against some things, particularly to have government money directed to them, but that was something for the politicians to worry about, and not public servants.

Allison's third point involves any dealing with the press and the public. Both of these were regarded rather negatively by the bureaucracy and were again parts of the external constituency function left for politicians to worry about. Any relations that did exist with the press and public were more often exercises in damage control than genuine attempts to inform or persuade the wider community in which the public organization existed. Another part of external relations in the traditional model was of a rather negative kind, where the public service jealously guarded every scrap of information. With this mentality being pervasive, it is little wonder that dealing with the outside world generally, and the press and the public in particular, was regarded unfavourably. In general, as expected in a bureaucratic organization, the outside world was regarded as being beyond the interest or knowledge of the public administrator. A strict bureaucracy is internally focused and does not need outside help. It is presumed to be self-sufficient and proceeding to the 'one best way' answer through deliberation, process and precedent, with the views of outsiders only detracting from this rational process.

Despite the discussion about public participation that began in the 1970s, the traditional model was not equipped to permit meaningful participation by outsiders. Political relations were to be carried out only by politicians. The primary attention of the public servant was directed inside the organization, with questions of how the organization existed in a larger context, or how relations with the outside were to be managed, being quite unimportant, other than through traditional accountability to the political leadership.

External relations as a management function

One of the biggest changes from the traditional model of administration to public management has been that external constituencies can and should be *managed* by the bureaucracy itself. The outside world need not be regarded as a threat, but as something of interest to the organization. It may even become an asset for the agency. Instead of the usual response being the bureaucratic one of denying information, or to otherwise restrict access or contact, public managers are required to engage actively with stakeholders. External constituencies of all kinds have become much more important and take up an increasing amount of any senior manager's time. Politicians now demand that agencies and public servants under their nominal control involve themselves in matters of strategy, rather than regard these as being reserved for the political leadership. Similarly, there are marked changes in the functions involved in dealing with the external environment, and it would now be regarded as normal practice for public managers to pay attention to wider stakeholders as well as to the agency's direct clientele.

There is now much greater attention being paid by public servants to all the external constituency areas mentioned by Allison (1982) – co-ordination within government, dealing with independent organizations, and dealing with the press and the public. Co-ordination should be improved by having a better idea of what the department or agency is supposed to do through the strategic management process, and by financial resources being directed towards areas of identified priority. Governments now often seek 'whole-of-government' solutions to problems that once stayed within agency silos. Also, co-ordinative activities can be described more accurately as a political process. Partisans for particular parts of the bureaucracy, or for particular policies, compete with others for resources and such bureaucratic politics needs to be managed through a process that involves both public managers and political leaders.

Second, dealings with independent organizations should also be characterized as a political process in which public servants are necessarily involved. What makes a good manager of the relationships with other parts of government and with organizations outside government is how well s/he manages the various interactions. The relationship with groups is important, both in its own right and for the way in which the outside can be used to win internal bureaucratic battles. There is a two-way relationship between groups and the system as a whole, as 'to survive as effective political institutions they must offer services needed by their host political system, receiving in return specific benefits for themselves and their members' (Pross, 1986, p. 88). Private enterprises, interest groups and other governments are all involved in the game of politics, in which bureaucratic politics is no less a form of the high art than is party politics. Increasingly, public managers are required to make deals, negotiate compromises, engage in diplomacy, and be involved in areas in which they do not exercise direct authority. Agencies on the ground often have to work with each other as actual problems often cross agency boundaries.

Third, public managers have to deal personally with the press and the public. These relations should now be seen as vital parts of the management function. As Allison (1982) notes, managers must deal with the press and public 'whose action or approval or acquiescence is required' (p. 17). This is a key point. Under the traditional model, the press and public were peripheral to the main function of the agency, which was merely administrative, so that the only outside person for insiders to talk to was the person who had given the instructions to an administrator. This was, and is, unrealistic. Agencies need the press and good managers realize this. Of course, they try to manage relations by putting a favourable slant on everything by having press offices and publicity machines, and even commissioning opinion polls and the like. The important point is that public officials have realized the importance of being in this kind of game. This was not the case under the traditional model.

Public service anonymity and neutrality have certainly declined along with acceptance of the manager's role in those functions once formally the preserve of the politician. The reality is that many public servants are well known for their views, are associated with the activities of their agencies in their own right and not simply as instruments of the politicians, and are sometimes even known for their personal or party political views. Public servants are now freer to speak out in public, to appear at professional forums, to write articles for journals, and generally to be visible and public figures.

Another part of the changed relationship with the outside is the extra effort put into relations with an organization's clients. This is an external constituency of a particular kind. There are demands to provide more of a client focus and for the administration to be responsive. Kettl (2005) argues that such demands have helped in driving the process of reform (p. 54):

> Customer service has played an important role in government reform. In many countries citizens have received a powerful signal that their government is interested in improving its service to and relationship with them. Customer service also has transformed the behaviour of government officials by shaking them out of their bureaucratic routine and making them focus on citizens' needs ... Unlike private companies, government agencies typically cannot choose their customers. In many government programs, especially those involving taxation and regulations, citizens cannot choose whether to deal with government; private sector comparisons therefore are suspect in these cases. The overall approach, however, has been useful in changing bureaucratic behaviour.

Responsive administration and a client focus challenge administrative cultures because the traditional bureaucracy is uncomfortable with external relations. A managerial approach is more open and better equipped to cope with the outside. There are obvious advantages for the quality of administrative processes if client views are considered at an early stage in the policy process.

Interest groups

Wilson (1990) defines interest groups as 'organizations, separate from government though often in close partnership with government, which attempt to influence public policy' and, as such, they 'provide the institutionalized linkage between government or the state and major sectors of society' (p. 1). Saying that groups are the institutionalized linkage between government and society is a long way from the largely nega-tive role they had for most of the twentieth century. Interest groups are now recognized as doing far more than simply exerting pressure on political parties or governments.

As recently as the 1960s, the general public 'treated pressure group participation in policy-making as illicit', with some 'guilt by associa-tion'. Lobbying was one reason for this, as well as the view that 'pres-sure group intervention in policy-making offended public perceptions of democratic government' (Pross, 1986, p. 53). The bureaucracy agreed with this view; all the relevant expertise was inside the depart-ment and there was simply no need to deal with the outside.

Dealing with interest groups is now seen as an important part of managing stakeholders and external constituencies. Interest groups are regarded increasingly as vital to the policy and management processes. Interest groups have a number of what Pross (1986, p. 84) terms 'sys-temic functions': they facilitate communications between members and the state; provide legitimation of the demands their members make on the state and the public policies they support; regulate their members; and sometimes assist the state in the administration of policies and pro-grammes. It could be argued that work carried out on interest groups in the late 1970s and 1980s (Richardson and Jordan, 1979; Pross, 1986) helped to point out the inadequacy of the traditional model in terms of its external relationships.

Managing in the public sector now has far more to do with working with interest groups than it did in the past. Instead of being regarded as something of a nuisance, such groups are being wooed increasingly. The bureaucracy relies on interest groups in making policy. The demands made by interest groups may be a *resource* to be used by the agency; they provide resources in the political games the agency is required to play and can be channelled into suitable directions.

Policy communities

From the late 1970s there was much more discussion around the idea of policy communities; particular agencies and the interest groups belonging to those areas were seen as effective partners in the policy process. This has implications for the political process, as Richardson and Jordan argue (1979, p. vii):

> The familiar framework for studying policies – examining legislative behaviour, political parties, elections – inadequately explains how key issues are managed. We see the current policy style as the balancing of group pressures. It may once have been legitimate to see the role of groups as simply articulating demands to be 'processed' in the legislative/governmental machine. Now the groups are inti-mately involved in decision and implementation processes. A symbiotic relation-ship has developed.

The bureaucracy could itself be seen as an interest group, in that official organizations and agencies behave 'in almost exactly the same way as more conventional external pressure groups' (Richardson and Jordan, 1979, p. 25). Groups can be allies of departments, and while there may be conflict between ministers and groups over details of policy, there is a generally shared desire for more resources for that policy area. Politicians do not necessarily make policy, nor is it made by politicians together with the bureaucracy, but by the interaction of the bureaucratic part of government and the relevant groups. As Richardson and Jordan observe (1979, pp. 73–4):

> In describing the tendency for boundaries between government and groups to become less distinct through a whole range of pragmatic developments, we see policies being made and administered between a myriad of interconnecting, interpenetrating organizations. It is the relationships involved in committees, the policy community of departments and groups, the practices of co-option and the consensual style that perhaps better account for policy outcomes than do examinations of party stances, of manifestoes or of parliamentary influence.

This theory provided a more realistic account of what actually happens in government, and could be regarded as the beginning of the idea of networks where policy is effectively made. It also fits the change from a bureaucratic focus to one in which internal politics is recognized. Particular parts of the bureaucracy develop their own interest groups to assist them in the real political battle; that is, the struggle for resources with other parts of the bureaucracy.

Pross (1986, 1992) commented that, in Canada, with the decline of mass parties in terms of membership, and with parties becoming oligarchies, the policy agenda increasingly passed to outside interests. Real competition in the political arena was that of policy communities, an entity defined as 'that part of a political system that by virtue of its functional responsibilities, its vested interests, and its specialized knowledge – acquires a dominant voice in determining government decisions in a specific field of public activity, and is generally permitted by society at large and the public authorities in particular to determine public policy in that field' (Pross, 1986, p. 98). A policy community is populated by government agencies, pressure groups, media people, and individuals, including academics, who have an interest in a particular policy field (p. 98).

The development of the policy community had implications for the operation of the bureaucracy deriving, according to Pross (1986), from the decline in the influence of the bureaucracy. Public officials now had to generate support in the policy community, 'winning the approval of the other government agencies, the pressure groups, corporations, institutions, and individuals with a vested interest or an explicit concern in the policy field' (p. 132). It was realized increasingly that agencies need their clients, and need them to be organized into groups. If relevant interest groups did not exist, agencies would be very likely to sponsor their formation. There are two aspects of this move towards policy communities that are most relevant for our present purposes.

First, the decline in prestige and influence of the bureaucracy and the bureaucratic model led to other initiatives in the relationships between government and interest groups. The decline in bureaucracy is consistent with the decline of the traditional model of administration. If the power and influence of the bureaucracy had indeed declined, then legitimacy needed to be derived from somewhere else. The relevant interest groups could be argued to have filled a power vacuum created by the decline of a bureaucratic model.

Second, the relationship between government and groups has changed to a more openly *political* system; that is, one where policy outcomes are the result of political competition between a range of inside and outside actors. In this competition, interest groups are a decided asset; so much so that they will be encouraged and enlisted by the bureaucracy to provide technical advice and assist in policy implementation. The bureaucracy is no longer regarded as having an information monopoly. Also, many types of policy can be implemented 'more easily, cheaply, and effectively if the relevant interest groups cooperate' (Wilson, 1992, p. 81).

Pross (1986, p. 243) also argues that the development of policy communities 'has transformed participating interest groups from useful adjuncts of agencies into vitally important allies' and the relationship between agency and interest group is more equal than it was. As a result, the policy system is more open and dynamic. It is hard to say which came first: whether the changes to a more open managerial system have led to an enhanced role for groups or whether, as Pross argues, events occurred the other way round. However, there is certainly greater commonality between groups and government, and between theories of groups and public management.

In another variant of the idea that groups and the bureaucracy have common interests, agencies within government can be seen as *representative* of outside interests, in that 'very few causes are completely without an administrative spokesman' (Goodsell, 1983, p. 138). In this view, agencies are competitors with each other inside the system, but act as representatives of outside interests. An aggrieved citizen can find the appropriate part of the bureaucracy, with its attendant interest groups, to be his or her representative. Goodsell (1983) asserts that bureaucratic representatives of this kind can be more accountable than is possible through the political system itself. This is a further extension of the policy community argument. It does raise some questions of political accountability in that the main arena for political conflict in the system as a whole becomes that between different parts of the bureaucracy. Certainly, agencies compete with each other on behalf of groups.

Beyond the policy community

The key policy community theorists put their ideas forward in the late 1970s and early 1980s. While still of value, there are other ideas that have come to fore since then, concerning the role of groups and how they might interact with governments. The policy community theorists might have paved the way by raising the possibility that, in considering where policy came from and how it was organized, the traditional accounts of policy-making had severe weaknesses.

Networks

It is already apparent from the discussion about interest groups and policy communities that particular interests are heavily involved in the development of policy, and even in its detailed implementation. This can be argued to have led to the idea of 'networks' and governance by network as a further stage beyond that of public management (see also Chapter 6). One definition of a network refers to 'initiatives deliberately undertaken by government to accomplish public goals, with measurable performance goals, assigned responsibilities to each partner, and structured information flow'; with the aim of producing 'the maximum possible public value, greater than the sum of what each lone player could accomplish without collaboration' (Goldsmith and Eggers, 2004, p. 8). While quite comprehensive, their definition could apply equally to collaboration, even co-production, indeed much of their discussion and many examples are about collaboration.

Rhodes goes somewhat further, stating that networks are a means of co-ordinating and allocating resources – a governing structure – in the same way as markets and bureaucracies operate (Rhodes, 1996; Bevir and Rhodes, 2003). In the interest group or policy community view of the world, government is a participant in the process – receiving information and working with interested parties; while in the network view as set out by Rhodes, it is the networks themselves that become the governing structure. The government is perhaps a passive participant, perhaps not very involved at all.

Salamon (2002) also comments that new forms of governance involve moving from agency networks and 'in shifting the focus in public problem solving from agencies and programs to generic tools, the *new governance* also shifts the attention from hierarchic agencies to *organizational network*' (p. 11) and adds (p. 12):

> The traditional concerns of public administration with the internal operations of public agencies – their personnel systems, budgetary procedures, organizational structures, and institutional dynamics – have become far less central to program success. At least as important have become the internal dynamics and

external relationships of the host of third parties – local governments, hospitals, universities, clinics, community development corporations, industrial corporations, landlords, commercial banks, and many more – that now also share with public authorities the responsibility for public programs operations.

Salamon argues that this is different from traditional public administration – which it is – but also different from the privatization and reinventing government movements.

Governments do rely increasingly on other actors to deliver services, to intervene on their behalf and to be, in many ways, a partner. This means a system of 'third-party government in which crucial elements of public authority are shared with a host of nongovernmental or othergovernmental actors, frequently in complex collaborative systems that sometimes defy comprehension, let alone effective management and control' (Salamon, 2002, p. 2). Third-party government – the new governance – emphasizes its 'collaborative nature, its reliance on a wide array of third parties in addition to government to address public problems and pursue public purposes' (p. 8). This network management is different from both traditional public administration and the new public management, and requires new skills in dealing with outside partners.

Mintzberg (2000) points out that, in the network model, 'government is viewed as one intertwined system, a complex network of temporary relationships fashioned to work out problems as they arise, linked by informal channels of communication' (p. 76). However, an apparent dependency on non-governmental partners does not necessarily mean any decline in the power of government. It is, rather, a realization that the formal, rational bureaucratic model is no longer appropriate and that it suits governments better to involve a wide range of actors in what they do. This involvement may be aimed at making government more efficient and effective rather than ceding any real power to the outside.

Collaboration and co-production

The traditional public administration approach to service delivery is for the government to deliver public services in ways largely determined by the bureaucracy itself, at times it finds convenient and with the underlying assumption of a one-way flow of authority from the bureaucracy to its clients. The recipients of public services did not have much of a role at all. Early managerial approaches aimed to involve clients and citizens, but really only in terms of consultation and participation. However, as the process of public sector reform has continued it has become apparent that more active forms of outside engagement can provide for better outcomes.

Collaboration is where various parties actively work together to solve a problem affecting all. Bardach (1998) defines it as 'any joint activity by two or more agencies that is intended to increase public value by their working together rather than separately' (p. 8). While this is a useful definition, there is no reason to limit collaboration only to agencies; indeed, collaborative public management 'may include participatory governance: the active involvement of citizens in government decision-making' (O'Leary *et al.*, 2009, p. 3). Often the issues may be narrow and the collaboration short-term; but sometimes the issue may be a perennial one requiring a more strategic approach. Even if 'collaborations are inherently more unstable, fragile, and idiosyncratic than hierarchical settings' (Norris-Tyrell and Clay, 2010, p. 10) there are benefits in working together from an early stage.

A neat distinction is made by Donahue and Zeckhauser (2006) in what they term 'collaborative governance'. They argue that a pure service contract is where the government retains control, and voluntary provision vests all discretion with the donor; in collaborative governance 'each party has a hand in defining not only the means by which a goal is achieved but the details of the goal itself' (p. 497). They argue that collaborative governance is increasingly consequential; indeed 'as demands for the creation of public value outpace governments' capacity to deliver it unaided – in health care, education, environmental preservation, employment and social welfare, and even security – the collaborative impulse intensifies' (p. 522).

Collaboration is, however, quite alien to bureaucratic practice. Collaboration 'values equality, adaptability, discretion, and results; the bureaucratic ethos venerates hierarchy, stability, obedience, and procedures' (Bardach, 1998, p. 232). Individuals may have the best intentions in terms of collaboration and to reach outcomes through that means. The best way to do this is with personal linkages, which again are quite different from standard bureaucratic practice, as Bardach argues (p. 268):

> The cutting edge of interagency collaboration is interpersonal collaboration. If interagency collaboration is supposed to create new value, that value will almost certainly be bigger and better if the people involved can work together easily and constructively. One barrier to doing so is the bureaucratic culture. It is at its core hostile to the required spirit of pragmatism ... Interpersonal collaboration is to a large extent a process of negotiation within a matrix of interpersonal trust.

People inside different agencies may wish to engage with others to find pragmatic results, but such collaboration cuts across the normal ways of working in a bureaucracy.

A further step is *co-production* – the realization that the delivery of certain governmental outcomes requires the citizenry to be quite active co-producers in contributing time, effort, information and compliance to the achievement of organizational purposes. As Alford (2009, p. 23) defines it:

> Co-production is any active behaviour by anyone outside the government agency which:
>
> - is conjoint with agency production, or is independent of it but prompted by some action of the agency;
> - is at least partly voluntary; and
> - either intentionally or unintentionally creates private and/or public value, in the form of either outputs or outcomes.

This definition applies to all kinds of co-producers, whether they are volunteers, clients, other government agencies, community organizations or private firms.

Some co-production is relatively low-level; for example, citizens may fill out at least part of their taxation forms themselves and this saves the government agency from having to do it. But in some cases, effective co-production is required for the agency to fulfil its very function. As Alford (2009, p. 3) argues about the police force:

> In the basic work of responding to crimes already committed, police officers rely on citizens to report offences, provide witness statements or even to intervene temporarily in socially threatening situations. More extensively, crime prevention relies on householders to secure their homes, install alarms and mark their goods, and beyond that to contribute to well-functioning communities in which antisocial behaviour is minimized. In these and a whole raft of other activities ... government organizations need ordinary people, who in many cases are their clients, to act in particular ways which contribute to the achievement of their purposes.

The same applies to a number of government agencies. Many people in the community assist the government in its mission one way or another; indeed, as with the police example, it would be hard for some agencies to function effectively without that involvement.

It follows that managers need to work actively with clients, client groups and the wider citizenry, and those managers 'who ignore their clients will miss potentially significant capabilities and resources' (Alford, 2009, p. 3). It does mean a different role for public servants in that their jobs are not simply about producing services; there is an additional role 'of influencing clients to co-produce' (p. 221). Public servants will need to find new skills, as Alford notes (p. 222):

> Not only are they suppliers of services, but also they are purveyors of motivators and facilitators to clients, to encourage them to contribute to production. This is likely to call for different kinds of skills on the part of the staff, such as those of client communication, negotiation, advice and consultancy.

Co-production, like collaboration, is another way of managing for results. It is not the only way; indeed, it would be quixotic to try to find any new 'one best way'. As Alford (2009) points out, the history of public management since the 1980s 'has been a story of governments and their officials trying to find a new orthodoxy – the one "right way" to manage in the public sector' and rather than trying 'to shoe-horn everything into a "one-size-fits-all" model, we need a variety of approaches to governing, one of which is client co-production' (p. 223).

Issues regarding over-reliance on the outside

Perhaps the extra focus of public managers on external constituencies should be regarded unfavourably because of its apparent subversion of the political process and the notion of an apolitical career service. Against this, public servants do exercise power and have political roles, even if these features were played down in the traditional model of administration. By recognizing these facts, the managerial model brings a healthy dose of realism to the relationship between the overall political system and the wider citizenry.

It has been argued that, unlike the traditional model of administration, public sector managers are now active participants in the external relations of their department or agency. There is a trend towards an active partnership between interest groups and the bureaucracy, a relationship in which each party needs the other. For the most part these have been beneficial changes, but not without some problems.

There are possible problems of accountability. When the politicians were nominally responsible for any problem arising from outside relationships, at least there was someone to blame. There may be gaps in the accountability system with the changes described here. If a problem arises from the bureaucracy's relationship with the outside world, both the public servant and the politician can claim it is not their fault. There are also substantial risks for public managers in their dealings with external constituencies. Public servants now have to realize that while there are benefits in being identified with their agencies, there are also costs, in becoming personally accountable. Related to this is the problem of politicization, in which career public servants become well-known partisans for policies in a party political sense.

Kettl (2009, p. 11)argues that networks can be seen as 'pluralism on steroids', noting that accountability is a particular issue:

> If no-one is clearly in charge – if government officials are not necessarily the prime movers of the network, and if, within government, public responsibility is fuzzy – how does accountability work? Who is responsible for defining, pursuing

achieving the public interest? Or have the worst fears of pluralism's critics come home with a vengeance? Has the government's role in defining public policy weakened?

This comment has a wider applicability than merely networks. All of these points apply to all the public sector's interactions with the outside world; there is a lot that can be achieved by better relationships and better collaboration of various kinds, but someone still needs to be finally accountable.

Another problem in dealing with outside influences in this political kind of way is that agencies, indeed governments, can become overly reactive. They may only respond to interest group demands instead of leading, or being proactive. They may allow, in effect, the interest groups to become the policy-makers. The old bureaucratic system at least aimed towards formal rationality, and would attempt this regardless of the views of the public. It is the same with the partnership between interests and the bureaucracy. In the United States system, the interaction between interest groups, the bureaucracy and the relevant Congressional Committee has been described as an 'iron triangle', one in which the three parties act in unison for each other's benefit. In this kind of process, the consumer and the taxpayer can be forgotten; some interest groups may never get anything, and agencies may be captured. However, the new views of interest groups are far more persuasive than the traditional view, in which the outside was to be ignored completely.

However, it is possible to overestimate the strength of interest groups and of involvement with the outside world. As Fountain (2001, p. 80) argues about networks: 'Inter-organizational networks have emerged in response to large-scale technological, economic, social, and political change. They have not replaced hierarchies, or bureaucracies ... Hierarchy, in both the state and the economy ... still holds final rule'. This statement also has greater applicability. While it is possible to gain better results than would occur if the outside is ignored, all parts of government, including the public service, have wider responsibilities than merely dealing with interest groups. Governments should engage with stakeholders; public servants should collaborate with interest groups, treat their clients as customers as far as possible, and participate in networks, at least to some extent. But they have a responsibility to the entire society that cannot be forgotten.

The reliance on groups

There are issues for the political and wider governmental system in regarding political competition as essentially about competition between groups. There are not only accountability issues but also other theoretical issues involved in the making of policy. More complete accounts of various theories of interest groups are readily available (Grant, 1989; Wilson, 1990; Dunleavy, 1991; Hrebenar, 1997; Thomas, 2001; Jordan and Maloney, 2007). For now, the discussion will be confined, briefly, to some theoretical perspectives.

For pluralists, competition between groups is beneficial to the policy-making process and even to outcomes. The main idea in pluralist theory is that governments themselves are not active participants in group processes and competition, but rather act as a kind of umpire, allowing rival groups to fight one another. Pluralist theory was derived in the United States, most particularly in the 1950s and 1960s (Truman, 1951; Bentley, 1967). If an issue arose in the public arena that had a particular interest group acting in its favour, then those opposing the matter would form their own interest group. No single group has power, and any government action results from interest group competition.

In some circumstances, pluralist tendencies can be seen to be at work in the interaction between government and groups, or between groups. However, it seems too much to claim that the existence of groups is itself an explanation and a justification of democracy, as has been asserted. Also, it seems unrealistic to argue that government is only a bystander; an umpire with no views of its own. Pluralism has difficulty in explaining that groups are not equal, or that some groups always have the ear of the government while others are ignored. There are similar problems if the relationship between government and groups fits a corporatist model of interest group behaviour. Big business, big government and big labour no longer represent that much of a society, and rarely do their interests seem in concert compared with society as a whole. Also, agreement between these three large groups is not necessarily in the interests of society as a whole. It could, for example, disregard the interests of consumers, small business or workers who are not in unions.

Allowing policy to be made by groups could arguably make government less effective. There are arguments that group competition is harmful to society as a whole and to the functioning of the political system. In different ways, though both are adherents of 'rational choice' economic theory (see Chapter 4), Olson (1965, 1982) and Stigler (1975) argue that interest groups may cause undesirable policy outcomes.

Olson contends (1965, 1982) that pluralism is illogical and the pluralist view is 'fundamentally flawed'. Potential groups would not necessarily turn into actual groups, as the organizer of a large group will not gain a large share of the benefit of a policy change when compared to the costs in both time and effort of organization. Rather than large groups being more important and more powerful, as pluralist theory argued, it is in fact small groups that dominate and are more successful in persuading the government to agree with their views. Small groups – special interest groups – represent only a narrow segment of society. They have little or no incentive to make sacrifices in the interests of the society and can best serve their members' interests by striving to seek a larger share of a society's production for themselves. And, indeed, small groups in society, especially those with collective economic interests, do seem to have power greater than their numbers would suggest.

Olson (1982) can be used to explain why it is that doctors' groups are far more powerful than the potential group of medical patients. Even if the sum total of concern about medical funding is greater among consumers, there is the problem of organizing when the benefit obtained by any one actual organizer will be small.

Large or 'encompassing groups', such as a high-level association ('peak') or council of unions, or an employers' association, may be more willing to make sacrifices for the benefit of the nation and their own long-term interest. But, Olson (1982, p. 41) argues: 'on balance, special interest organizations and collusions reduce efficiency and aggregate income in the societies in which they operate and make political life more divisive'. In other words, a society with many special interest groups will perform worse than one with none.

There is substantial explanatory power in Olson's theory, and it is only when it becomes rather more grandiose – interest group competition is regarded as *the* single reason for the rise and decline of nations – that there are some problems. However, the point that special interests may reduce aggregate economic efficiency provides a lesson in going too far in allowing groups to make policy.

Stigler's (1975) view of interest groups is that their intervention leads to poorer outcomes. His 'capture theory' argues that there is a co-optive relationship between an agency and the relevant interest groups. The regulatory agency of an industry will be *captured* by the industry it is supposed to be regulating, which then controls what it does. While it is unlike the other theories mentioned here, the theory of agency capture has had an impact on the process of deregulation. It has also been used to support the arguments of those who believe that bureaucracy is an inherently flawed instrument. However, Stigler goes too far. For him there are no examples of public benefit and no examples of public interest. All regulation, all interest group pressure being followed by a governmental response, he argues, leads to outcomes worse than if the government had not become involved. Even if Stigler's argument can be supported in some individual cases, the general case is overstated. He denies any chance for the political system to operate, as well as denying any possibility that political action in response to public demand can be beneficial.

The significance of Stigler's work, allied with that of Olson – both could be described as New Right economists – has been to give further theoretical backing to demands to reduce government involvement because of the persistence of links between government and interest groups. It became easier to cut assistance schemes that supported special interests, perhaps as a result of such theoretical arguments. It is also easier to deregulate, as capture theory predicts that any government regulation or regulatory agency will only make matters worse. Political leaders can declare that they will not be captive to special interests, and can use these arguments to reduce interest group power.

Conclusion

One part of the transformation in public sector management has been to focus much more on external constituencies. To look outside the organization and to manage the interaction with outside forces is at considerable variance with the traditional model of administration, which in its original form was truly rather insular. There are promises as well as some problems in this change of focus, but on balance, there are far more advantages than difficulties. Interest groups are no longer regarded by the bureaucracy as a nuisance and barely to be tolerated. This is a major change. Nowadays, interest groups are an active, resourceful and fundamentally useful part of the policy process. In the same way, the general change in orientation towards the outside world improves the bureaucratic process. After all, any public sector organization arose in the outside world as a response to the political process. A public organization exists in a social context beyond the organization itself, a context that contains threats to its budget and even its existence, as well as opportunities to advance its functions.

The management of external stakeholders and constituencies has become one of the major tasks of the public manager, one that has increased in importance in recent years and is likely to become even more important in the future. Public management is sometimes criticized as being narrow and focused only on economic results. It is argued here that public management is far from being narrow, but rather enhances political processes through more active engagement with parts of society that are affected. Public managers can co-opt or persuade interest groups to assist them; they can go into the public arena. In short, the game being played is one of politics, broadly conceived. It is bureaucratic politics, personal politics: any kind of politics. Public management is therefore more realistic than the traditional model, where public servants pretended they were not involved in politics and did not need to deal with the outside world.

Chapter 9

Accountability

Chapter Contents

- Introduction
- The idea of accountability
- Accountability in the private sector
- Accountability in the public sector
- Accountability in the traditional model
- A managerial model of accountability
- Accountability problems from public sector reform
- Conclusion

Introduction

The operations of the public sector do not exist in a vacuum, hermetically sealed from the rest of society. The political leadership, the public services and the public are closely tied to one another by institutional arrangements and political interaction. Whatever it is called – public administration or public management – the business of government is embedded in politics. There is a fundamental requirement in any long-lasting political system for there to be a line of accountability from the administration to the political leadership and to the citizenry. Indeed, it can be argued that 'accountability underpins civilization' (Donahue, 2002, p. 1). Senior managers need to be aware of politics, and knowledgeable about it: 'effectiveness as a public administrator is predicated on both an understanding of politics and of the political process and an ability to manage public programs in a political context' (Frederickson, 1989, p. 12). The political basis of the public service is sometimes forgotten. Books on public administration often treat the subject technically and separately from politics; indeed, the traditional model of administration attempted to depoliticize the public service. Politicians in power may assume that what they want will be carried out unquestioningly and administratively in a kind of master–servant relationship. Public servants from the traditional model claim that they merely administer and have no policy-making role, let alone any involvement in politics. Both politicians and bureaucrats would perpetuate the

185

myth, associated with the name of Woodrow Wilson, that policy and politics can be separated strictly from administration; and that administration can be purely instrumental. It is not. The way choices are made, the way policies are devised and administered, and the way that programmes are managed are all matters that are fundamentally political in nature. The political parts of government are established by varying legal and constitutional arrangements and in these some form of accountability will be required.

There is a certain tension in all the encounters between public servants and citizens, as both parties have powers in the exchange. The individual is subject to the law; the agency is aware that individuals have some powers of complaint and appeal if dissatisfied with their treatment. It is the system of accountability that ties the administrative part of government with the political part, and ultimately to the public itself. Any acts of the government are supposed to be, in the final analysis, acts of the citizens themselves through their representatives, and this 'requires a carefully designed structure of accountability that ensures for citizens the best efforts of those who act on their behalf' (Donahue, 1989, p. 222).

In the traditional model of administration, accountability at the bureaucratic and political level was supposed to be assured through the political process alone, usually only at elections. There are two reasons why this no longer applies. First, the narrow formulaic relationship of the politics/administration dichotomy set out by Woodrow Wilson is no longer realistic, if it ever was. The bureaucracy does much more than simply follow the instructions of the political leadership and it needs to be recognized as an active participant in the political process.

Second, while still remaining accountable to the public through the electoral process, the bureaucracy is increasingly accountable to the public itself for what it does. Such direct accountability is a major change and a key aspect of public sector reform. Demands for a client focus, more responsiveness from the bureaucracy and the personal responsibility of managers change the system of accountability of the public service, and indeed the relationship between government and citizen. It is realized increasingly that citizens are co-producers with governments, actively assisting in the creation of public value (Alford, 2009). Greater engagement of this kind does offer opportunities to deliver services better and to be more responsive to the needs of clients and the public as a whole. These changes do pose a challenge for the system of accountability. Even if the Wilsonian dichotomy between policy and administration proved to be mythical in practice, it was a justifying myth that suited the interests of politicians and public servants alike. Direct accountability, including accountability for results, therefore poses something of a challenge to accountability theory in general.

The idea of accountability

Accountability is one of those words that appears to convey a clear meaning, but on closer examination, the clarity becomes more elusive. Bovens (2007) describes accountability as 'an icon', a concept that 'has become less useful for analytical purposes, and today resembles a dustbin filled with good intentions, loosely defined concepts and vague images of good governance' (p. 449). But it is still useful, even necessary, to look at accountability, because even as its precise meaning may be hard to find, there is still an aspiration for real accountability in public management.

Accountability has a wider usage than in the public sector alone. Behn (2001) argues that 'when people seek to hold someone accountable, they are usually planning some kind of punishment' (p. 4). In common usage this is probably correct, although accountability should also include overall responsibility for both success and failure. 'Accountable' means, according to the *New Shorter Oxford Dictionary* (1993), 'liable to be called to account; responsible (*to* persons, *for* things)'. Bovens (2007) expands this further and defines accountability as 'a relationship between an actor and a forum, in which the actor has an obligation to explain and to justify his or her conduct, the forum can pose questions and pass judgement, and the actor may face consequences' (p. 450). Some parts of this very useful definition need further elaboration. The *actor* may be an individual or an organization; the *forum* can be an individual, an institution such as a parliament, or an agency, or, in the private sector, a board of directors; the *obligation* may be formal or informal; and the *questions* and *judgement* may lead to *consequences* that are either negative or positive. As Bovens (2007) notes, 'the possibility of sanctions – not the actual imposition of sanctions – makes the difference between non-committal provision of information and being held to account' (pp. 450–2). Accountability is, then, about explanation and justification to a forum with the possibility of sanction as a result.

Accountability in the private sector

Issues of accountability exist in the private sector as well as the public sector. Some kind of accountability is needed whenever there are hierarchical relationships, or a relationship between principals and agents, in order to ensure that those with authority act in ways that their ultimate owners wish. An agency relationship is 'a contract under which one or more persons (the principal(s)) engage another person (the agent) to perform some service on their behalf which involves delegating some decision making authority to the agent (Jensen and

Meckling, 1976, p. 308). The agent carries out tasks on behalf of the principals and reports to them on how they have been performed with the possibility of questions and sanctions. The agent – management – cannot be assumed to always act in the best interests of the principal – shareholders – and it is therefore necessary to establish incentive and monitoring regimes to reduce principal–agent problems, as the interest of each group may diverge. The extent of the reporting is a matter of some debate. Is the agent accountable, liable or merely answerable?

The private sector is presumed to have clear avenues of accountability available to it. The management of a company is expected to act for the benefit of its shareholders. By law and custom it is the responsibility of the board of directors to act in the interests of the company and, through it, the interests of the shareholders. As Donahue points out (1989, p. 43), this kind of accountability addresses problems of the relationships between principal and agent:

> One particularly significant device for overcoming agency problems is a *layered* structure of accountability – the profit-seeking, wage-paying private firm. Ownership is wholly or partially distinct from operations. Production workers are accountable to managers, and are paid a wage in exchange for time on the job. Managers, in turn, are accountable to owners, and are paid a salary for directing and supervising production. Finally, the owners are accountable to customers, and collect a profit – the excess of revenues over costs – in exchange for organizing and monitoring the whole process. From the customer's point of view a classic profit-seeking agency relationship prevails, but with layers of more complex contracts within it.

In all of these ways there is presumed to be a clear line of accountability from management to the board and, finally, to the shareholders.

There are several other accountability devices in the private sector that are not present in the public sector. First, private shareholders are able to trade in the equity capital of the enterprise, and fluctuations in the share price are a continuing measure of performance. Second, the company competes for capital on commercial terms. It faces the continual monitoring of its investment and borrowing programmes and is subject to the judgement of rating agencies, such as Moody's or Standard & Poor's, for this purpose. Third, there are threats of takeover or merger and the ever-present chance of insolvency. Fourth, the presence of competitors means customers will go elsewhere if they are dissatisfied. All these points mean that the private organization, particularly its management, has strong incentives to perform. Given the uncertainties of the business environment, it is normal for there to be little security of tenure for any employee. From the highest level down, no one is guaranteed their position in the company, with continued employment often being conditional on personal and company performance. Advocates of the private enterprise system of accountability would argue that there is a clear and well-understood set of incentives that should lead to enhanced personal and organizational performance.

Accountability relationships in the private sector have been increasingly seen as a *model* – the best available practice – for the public sector. There are two aspects to this. First, the privatization of parts of government was, at least in part, related to improving accountability. Contracting delivery functions to the private sector is argued to be more efficient because private managers are more accountable than public sector managers. There are supposed to be fewer agency problems: the owner of a business holding a contract has more incentive to perform than might be the case with the diffuse accountability of in-house provision. In this way, the private sector serves as the model of accountability for the private sector. Second, and in part as a result of the first point, some private sector accountability methods are used in the public sector. This does not mean that public agencies should sell shares or be subject to takeover. If this were true, they would no longer be in the public sector, but it does mean greater effort in developing performance indicators and formal contracting mechanisms as surrogate measures analogous to those used in the private sector. The introduction of private sector measures of accountability has meant less security of tenure for employees, on the grounds that, as in the private sector, there will be greater incentives for individuals to perform if they are not guaranteed a job for life. Again, the private sector serves as the model of accountability. It is easy to see why some might consider this desirable. Compared to the confusion of the public sector, and its apparent failures of accountability, private sector accountability relationships are relatively well known and straightforward.

Of course, the presumed superiority of private sector accountability is an ideal that may not work perfectly in practice. Management may ignore shareholders and treat the board as an irrelevance. The share price and credit rating are imperfect measures of performance. There may be goals other than profit being pursued. While the private sector has established procedures of accountability there is usually some gap between the theory of accountability and it being achieved optimally.

This gap has wider implications. Whenever there is some separation between principals and agents, there are potential problems of accountability. These may be greater in the public sector, because '(a) the principals do not typically seek to maximise profits, (b) there are no marketable ordinary shares in the firm, and hence no *market* for corporate control, and (c) there is no direct equivalent to the bankruptcy constraint on financial performance' (Vickers and Yarrow, 1988, p. 27). It is often argued that governmental institutions are neither responsible nor accountable when compared to the private sector, and this is one reason for reducing their size and influence.

Some parts of the public sector have greater accountability problems than others. For example, public enterprises – those parts of the public sector most comparable with the private sector – do seem to show accountability problems when compared to private companies doing similar things (see Chapter 7). Allowing the private sector to provide that good or service should then improve service delivery and efficiency by adopting the accountability mechanisms that exist in the private sector. This argument depends on the existence of better accountability in the private sector, and if the good or service in question is one that potentially could be supplied by the private sector.

There must be some differences between public and private forms of accountability. The private sector has no real equivalent to political accountability, for which precise measures are never likely to be found. Political accountability makes much of the public sector different in kind, rather than different in detail. As a result, public sector accountability is unlikely to emulate that of the private sector; and to demand this would be unrealistic. But as long as the private sector remains the model of accountability, the public sector will be both vulnerable to arguments that it is not accountable, and to reductions in its size and scope, made on grounds of accountability.

Accountability in the public sector

Any government requires a system of accountability to ensure that it acts in ways that are broadly approved by the community. Accountability is fundamental to any society with pretensions to being democratic. Perhaps this could be stated more strongly in reverse; being democratic *requires* a suitable system of accountability. Government organizations are created by the public, for the public, and need to be accountable to the public. The relationship between the citizenry and government can be regarded as another kind of principal–agent relationship because the citizens have given their consent to someone else to govern on their behalf. Having agreed to this, they then need to be satisfied that their interests are being served.

The relationship between government and citizen depends on the system of accountability, whereby the governmental organization carries out its function and the citizenry allows it to do so, but on condition that those powers are not exceeded, and that the government and its agencies are accountable. Government is distinguishable from other social institutions by its possession of coercive powers, backed ultimately by the police and the armed forces. Historically, citizens did not give up their own power lightly and insisted that the political or administrative actions of governments be supported by the citizens themselves. This is done in two ways. First, all governmental actions must be soundly based in law. These laws apply to everyone, not only to the citizens, but also to those in the apparatus of government itself. Second, some particular person inside the governing apparatus is accountable for each of the actions of government. A member of the society is presumed to be able to find someone in government to assume responsibility for every action, from the counter staff to the highest political level. Without both of these points working reasonably well, government and the bureaucracy could still operate, but the absence of accountability could mean that government and the bureaucracy are omnipotent, omnipresent and potentially corrupt. A system of accountability is an *exchange* arrangement where both governors and the governed exchange part of their power, and where each party needs the other.

Accountability is not the same as responsibility. Accountability means that there is someone in the organization who can accept the blame or praise for a decision or action. From the lowest levels of the public service to the highest, each member of staff is supposed to be accountable to a superior. Responsibility is usually regarded as operating in the other direction through the hierarchy; that is, everyone with subordinate staff is responsible for the actions of these subordinates. A Cabinet minister is 'responsible' for the actions of the staff in his or her department. Responsibility is a less precise concept than accountability, however, in that it is never completely clear exactly what a superior is responsible for, or how far their responsibility extends. If a subordinate staff member makes an administrative mistake, this does not necessarily mean that the supervisor is accountable for that mistake, even as he or she is 'responsible' for that staff member.

Kinds of accountability

There are many typologies of accountability relationships in the public sector. Behn (2001) states that there are three kinds of accountability: accountability for finances; accountability for fairness; and accountability for performance (p. 6). The first is the original kind of accountability, in the historical sense, as evident from its obvious links to the word 'accounting'. Financial accountability remains important in government and is quite straightforward, as Behn (2001, p. 8) argues:

> The managers and employees of any public organization have been entrusted with something quite valuable: the taxpayers' money. They have the responsibility – the obligation – to use these funds wisely. They ought to be held accountable for doing so. When they don't, they ought to be punished.

The second kind, accountability for fairness, is to Behn (2001, p. 9), again straightforward:

> The managers and employees of any public organization have been entrusted with something quite valuable – with ensuring our mutual commitment to fairness. Thus, they have the responsibility to treat all citizens absolutely fairly. They ought to be held accountable for doing so. When they don't, they ought to be punished.

Fairness also includes protection from abuses of power, so there are rules and procedures to prevent this. The third form of accountability is that of accountability for performance; the accomplishment of public purposes. As Behn argues about this kind (2001, p. 10):

> To hold a public agency accountable for performance, we have to establish expectations for the outcomes that the agency will achieve, the consequences that it will create, or the impact that it will have. We cannot do this with rules, procedures, and standards. To specify the level of performance we expect from a public agency, we need some kind of objective, goal, or target – a clear benchmark of performance. We need an explicit measure of how well the agency has done against the expectations we have set for it.

In practice, it is unlikely that all three forms of accountability will be able to be achieved at the same time. They may even be contradictory as compliance with the rules for financial and fairness accountability make it difficult for managers to achieve performance accountability (Behn, 2001, pp. 28–30).

Accountability for performance is quite controversial. One of the key reform changes has been to set performance standards for agencies, and even individuals, but trying to do this in government has been the subject of debate. But the principle is correct: accountability must include what a part of government produces and how well it does so. Accountability in the traditional model of administration was little interested in this aspect, being obsessed by procedure and process, and accountability in the financial and legal senses, rather than the achievement of results.

Romzek (1998, 2000) maintains that there are four different types of accountability relationships: hierarchical, legal, political and professional. These are useful distinctions, in particular in the context of public sector change.

1. *Hierarchical accountability.* Hierarchical relationships rely on supervisory and organizational directives, including rules and standard operating procedures, for the standards to which employees are answerable for their performance. It is based based on 'close supervision of individuals who have low work autonomy and face internal controls' (Romzek, 2000, p. 23). Obedience is the behavioural expectation. This type emphasizes directives that tell

employees what to do, through rules, standard operating procedures, supervision, and organizational directives. To Romzek, 'Traditional "merit"-based civil service systems that are organized around position classification schema exemplify a reliance on low discretion and supervisory control' (2000, p. 24).

2. *Legal accountability.* Legal accountability relationships emphasize compliance with some externally derived expectations or standards of performance and close scrutiny and oversight as the means by which employees are held to answer for their performance. The underlying relationship of legal accountability 'is that of a principal–agent; the accountability standard focuses on whether the agent has complied with the principal's (externally derived) expectations' (Romzek, 2000, p. 24).

3. *Political accountability.* Political accountability relationships are about satisfying key external stakeholders, such as elected officials, clientele and other agencies. These types emphasize accountability based on whether the administrators have been sufficiently responsive to the expectations of the agency's clients. The essential point is that the accountable official 'anticipates and responds to someone else's agenda or expectations – ones that are beyond the scope of supervisor–subordinate obligations or professional expertise' (Romzek, 2000, p. 27).

4. *Professional accountability.* Professional accountability relationships emphasize responsibility and deference to expertise. Performance standards are established by professional norms, accepted protocols and prevailing practices of one's peer or work group. The expectation is that 'discretion will be exercised responsibly and in a manner consistent with accepted norms of responsible practice' (Romzek, 2000, p. 26).

The four types of accountability may be present within the same organization. The same actors 'can be involved in different accountability relationships at different times, sometimes emphasizing obedience, and, at other times, deference to expertise, rule of law and/or responsiveness' (Romzek, 2000, p. 29). Moreover, differing accountability expectations can conflict with each other.

A key point that follows is that traditional accountability emphasized hierarchical and legal accountability where there is a low level of autonomy; the other two – political and professional accountability relationships – allow much higher levels of autonomy. Romzek (2000) argues that public sector reform attempts to move from a heavy reliance on rules and process towards discretion, flexibility and entrepreneurial behaviour; such changes 'reflect a shift in emphasis away from hierarchical and legal standards of accountability toward professional and political ones' (pp. 30–1). The other kinds may remain in place but are emphasized less. Romzek does warn that failure to align accountability relationships with government reforms will undermine the likelihood that the changes will be successfully implemented.

Accountability in the traditional model

It was argued earlier that accountability requires all governmental actions to be, first, firmly based in law and, second, that someone is finally accountable for all actions of government. In the final analysis, the voter in a democratic system is supposed to be able to assess the competence of the administration, political and bureaucratic, and to cast a vote accordingly. Also, as any action must be based in law, there is an avenue of accountability through the legal system. It is supposed that, through this system, individual bureaucrats will behave at all times according to established rules and can be prevented from exceeding their authority.

Within these precepts, political accountability means that politicians are finally able to be called to account by the ordinary citizenry, mainly through the act of voting. While the two basic points of accountability are generally followed by developed countries, there are significant differences in how they are approached by different political systems, particularly between parliamentary and presidential systems.

In a parliamentary, or Westminster, system, such as that in the United Kingdom, the public service is accountable through its hierarchy to a minister, who is in turn accountable to the Cabinet, then to Parliament and ultimately to the people. Every act of every public servant is therefore an act of the minister and the people who originally chose the minister through choosing the party that is elected to govern, with the government requiring a majority in the Parliament. The executive branch and the legislative branch are effectively fused. A minister is in charge of a department, and the hierarchical structure ensures normal bureaucratic accountability through the various levels. By this rather tenuous process, any act of the administration is considered to be an act of the collective will of the voters.

A presidential system, such as in the United States, offers a somewhat different framework of political accountability. First, the fact of a written constitution means that interpretation of the constitution, and laws made according to it, increases the importance of the judicial branch of government. Second, the effective fusion of the executive and the legislative branch, as in the Westminster system, is specifically ruled out in the United States, so that the Congress and the president are not formally linked. In the formal sense, the two branches of government are separate, though, in practice, there are usually quite strong informal links. Third, the federal system affects the system of political accountability. Under the constitution, powers are divided between the federal government and state governments, and voters are assumed to be able to exercise their powers of political accountability correctly; that is, be able to tell which level of government is responsible for particular functions.

The political accountability of the public service is, in theory, ensured in the United States, but in rather different ways from the Westminster system. A civil servant is part of the executive branch, so is accountable to the chief executive – the president or state governor – and, as this person is chosen directly by election, political accountability is ensured by a line extending from the public servant to the voter. Bureaucratic accountability should also be through the hierarchical structure to the people, technically via the president, but this is not the end of the story. The blurring of the branches means the bureaucracy is also dependent on the legislature and the courts. The agency is responsible to the chief executive, as that office is part of the executive branch. However, the governing legislation and funding of the agency is under the control of the legislature, so there is also accountability to the legislature and to elected members of it. The courts also have an important role in the accountability system. Administrative acts of any kind may be scrutinized to ensure that they conform to the constitution, particularly those parts related to human rights, and every citizen has the right to take court action against the government. Taking these points together, the United States bureaucracy is theoretically accountable – but separately – to the chief executive, the legislature and the courts. These separate accountabilities are likely to make the task of public management even more complex than in parliamentary systems.

Bureaucratic accountability in the traditional model

Traditional public administration had its own form of bureaucratic accountability. In this, the bureaucracy merely advised the political leadership on policy, and managed its resources as well as possible on behalf of the political leadership. Every public servant was technically accountable, through the hierarchical structure of the department, to the political leadership and eventually to the people. In addition, there was supposed to be a strict separation – the politics/administration dichotomy – between matters of policy, formally the province of politicians, and matters of administration, which were left to the public service (see also Chapter 3).

The model of separation between politics and administration is easy to understand and superficially attractive. Any act of the administration is attributable to the political leadership, and the public servant is merely an instrument carrying out the policy instructions that emanate from the political leadership. Behn (2001, p. 42) argues:

The public administration paradigm is internally consistent; the distinction between politics and administration permits the construction of a simple, appealing, hierarchical model of political accountability. Thus, despite its flaws, the old paradigm has one, big, advantage: political legitimacy. The accountability relationships are clear. The traditional public administration paradigm meshes well with our traditional paradigm of democratic accountability.

But there are some obvious problems. First, it is really only the politician who is accountable in this system as the administrator is neutral and anonymous, and not associated with particular policies. In a real sense the administration is not accountable at all as its leaders can say they carried out the policy diligently; if something went wrong it was the political leaders' fault. A bureaucrat can hide behind anonymity and thereby avoid accountability.

Second, there must be some point in the line of accountability where the political part of government meets the administrative part. The interface between the two is likely to be a source of problems, as each has a different culture, type of rationality and form of accountability. In a parliamentary system the key relationship is that between the minister and the departmental head. It is here that there are quite different conceptions of the nature of the game each is playing, a discontinuity in the process of administering policy. Any dealing within the bureaucracy occurs according to Weberian principles, in which every public servant at a particular part of the hierarchy has a specific position and role, and is accountable to a superior. Procedures, formal rules and systems are developed rationally and proceed up the hierarchy. At the top of this structure there is one person – the departmental head – who deals with the political leader of the department. At this point, the bureaucratic, rational part of government suddenly confronts the political part. Formal rationality faces political rationality. This link was always problematic, as the precise role of each was never clear. It could be argued that genuine accountability was not possible in the traditional model, as it often broke down at the interface of the political and the bureaucratic parts of government.

Third, despite obvious problems, there is some accountability in the traditional model, but it is accountability of a particularly narrow kind. While it is clear who is finally accountable in this system, it is accountability for errors rather than achievements. It aims to avoid mistakes, so encourages risk-averse behaviour. The convention of ministerial responsibility in Westminster systems – even if rarely followed in fact – was that a minister was ultimately responsible to Parliament for all the actions of his or her department, no matter how minor, and was compelled to resign over departmental errors whether or not they had prior knowledge of them. Though the precise status of ministerial responsibility is now unclear, with sanctions being uncertain or even arbitrary, the minister still does take some political responsibility for the actions of his or her department. But this provides no real *managerial* accountability for the achievement of results. Political leaders often had inadequate knowledge of lower-level functions and did not provide managerial oversight. Accountability was less than satisfactory when this lack of knowledge was reinforced by poor measures of performance. This was, at best, a negative system of accountability; avoiding errors is not the same as achieving something.

Finally, even if the traditional model of accountability was well understood and politically legitimate, there are very real questions about basing a theory concerning something as important as accountability, on a myth. As the public administration literature has attested for many years, there can be no realistic separation between politics and administration, between the political leadership and the administrators. It seems odd to find in this recognized myth the supposed foundation for accountability. Traditional public administration accountability requires a clear separation between those who give instructions and those who carry them out, and the latter have no responsibility for results. This is, and was, a nonsense. Basing accountability on the politics/administration dichotomy is a weak position from which to start. It is a most convenient fiction 'for once we confess to the unpleasant reality that, for civil servants to do their job, they *must* make policy decisions, we have to discard the public administration paradigm' (Behn, 2001, p. 64).

A managerial model of accountability

One of the main reasons for public sector reform was the perception, even by governments themselves, of the failure of the system of accountability under the traditional model of administration. Avoiding embarrassing mistakes is not the same as providing any positive incentive to improve efficiency. There are a number of changes involved in what could be called a managerial model of accountability.

The old form of accountability relied on the formal links provided through the hierarchical structure. Accountability in a managerial model is often more free-flowing, and more political. This is perhaps seen most easily in the United States system, where agencies have always had informal and indirect links beyond the formal ones within the executive branch and have operated in quite different ways from the model set out earlier. In the formal model, agencies are firmly under the control of the president. In the real world, their funding and even their future are dependent on Congress, and their range of action is circumscribed by the courts. Accountability in this model cannot be of the rigid kind set out by the formal organization chart. One of the major roles of any agency head is to work actively with all the institutions that affect its accountability, in order to maintain support for what it does. Though less easy to see, the same thing is becoming true in parliamentary systems. The relative openness of the bureaucracy, and the easier access to information, mean that there is a different kind of accountability at work. Accountability exists in the bureaucracy's relationship to clients, to its own managers, to its political leadership, and finally, though perhaps more contentiously, directly to the citizenry.

Reforms in the United Kingdom had the express aim of improving accountability. In the late 1960s, the Fulton Report argued that accountable management means 'holding individuals and units responsible for performance measured as objectively as possible'. Its achievement depended on 'identifying or establishing accountable units within government departments – units where output can be measured as objectively as possible and where individuals can be held personally responsible for their performance' (Fulton, 1968, p. 51). Fulton did not lead to immediate improvements in accountability but raised an important issue that was to be revisited with later reform.

An express aim for greater acountability was a major factor at work in the Thatcher Government's financial changes in the 1980s; specifically, there was 'the desire of some ministers to get a grip over their own departments: to ensure that the civil servants, for whose activities they were accountable to Parliament were actually accountable to them' (Carter *et al.*, 1992, p. 17). Gray *et al.* (1991) state that promoting accountable management was the 'guiding ideology' of the Financial Management Initiative in the United Kingdom, where 'authority and responsibility are delegated as far as possible to middle and junior managers who are made aware of and accountable for meeting their costs and other performance targets' (p. 47).

A managerial view of accountability adds direct accountability to the public. Political accountability still exists, but there is now greater accountability for results to politicians and the public, especially clients. There is less emphasis on the negative sense, which concentrated on the avoidance of mistakes. Management systems aim to fulfil government programme objectives, in which costs are visible and related to outputs. When public servants become involved in setting policy and monitoring progress towards objectives, they become managerially as well as politically accountable. While the political leadership certainly has a major role in determining goals and objectives – strategic leadership – the bureaucracy itself is required to meet targets. As Behn (2001, pp. 210–11) argues:

> We need to accept that accountability is not just about finances and fairness, but about finances, fairness, *and* performance. Traditional hierarchical accountability might make sense for finances and fairness. It might even make some sense when results are something that one person or one unit produces. It does

not make sense, however, in a non-hierarchical world of collaboratives. Thus we need a new mental model of accountability; we need to shift from the implicit conception of linear, hierarchical, uni-directional, holder–holdee accountability to an explicit recognition that we need mutual and collective accountability. And we need to do both of these things simultaneously – to shift our accountability emphasis from finances and fairness to finances, fairness, and performance while rethinking what accountability (for all three) might mean.

Under a managerial system the political leadership still wishes to achieve results, but does so with the assistance of advisers and the bureaucracy. There is also a blurred distinction between politicians and the public service itself, a practice that has been followed in the United States for many years. There it is common for politicians to be appointed to administrative positions, or for heads of agencies to become political figures with the express purpose of dealing with the political apparatus external to the agency. Provided there is a clear distinction between political and career appointments, such a system might actually improve accountability and is being more widely adopted elsewhere.

A client focus

Another change to the system of accountability in a managerial model is to improve the relationship with clients. In the old model, the only avenue of accountability was through the political leadership. There are now more direct links to the citizenry. These may be consultative, or through interest groups, or simply by the agency realizing it needs the support and approval of stakeholders. Public managers attempt to manage the relationship with clients as part of their normal duties, to see avenues of direct accountability in which the agency is itself responsible for dealing with its clients and improving service to them. The role of clients is seen increasingly as analogous to the role customers play in the private sector.

The client focus includes 'how far the needs of clients can be satisfied within the framework of policy; the comprehensibility and accessibility of administration; the openness of administration to client participation in decision-making; the availability of redress', and argues that overall economic efficiency depends on how responsively the public sector provides goods and services (OECD, 1991b, p. 7). This is a far more direct form of accountability than that existing under the traditional model of administration.

The traditional model was not particularly responsive to clients, and it had no real need to be. Concerns about managerial accountability alter this and, in turn, this leads to internal changes. Improving accountability led to a need for measurable results and responsiveness to clients; indeed, individual public managers began to focus on fostering client relations as a major part of their activities. A formal model of bureaucracy allows for no role for public servants in dealing with outside groups or improving responsiveness. Public management allows, and even *requires*, interaction with the outside, and aims for more direct accountability as a result.

Accountable management

The basic aims of a managerial approach are to achieve goals rather than merely comply with rules or procedures, to improve responsiveness to clients, and to inject a concern with costs and the most effective use of limited resources. Letting the managers manage means that accountability can be more direct. If the manager is given the resources to carry out a specific job and is personally responsible for achieving results, it should then be obvious later whether the task has been achieved or not. This becomes a system of accountable management.

Accountable management involves more than merely delegating a task to a manager. There does need to be: 'an agreed definition of tasks, measures of performance, appropriate organization and control of resources, systems for monitoring and reporting, and incentives and sanctions' (OECD, 1991b, p. 10). Once the broad parameters are established by the political leadership, it is the manager who is responsible for the organization achieving its objectives.

There are three parts to the adoption of accountable management. First, accountability will be improved by a clearer specification of what is actually done by all organizations within government. This means that achievement (or lack of achievement) of results should be quite transparent. Those in favour would argue that doing these things should help to improve management by providing incentives for organizations to achieve targets. In the traditional model there was never any real way of deciding whether results had been achieved, so public servants could and did hide unsatisfactory performance from both political and public gaze.

The second part is the personal side of accountability, as distinct from organizational. A manager is, by definition, someone who takes *personal* responsibility for the achievement of results. This may require some form of contractual arrangement so that targets are specified for the manager to work towards. As an OECD paper (1998a, p. 54) states:

> There have been some instances where it has been difficult to establish who is responsible for what and to whom, especially where separate agencies are set up at arm's-length from the Minister. In order to avoid confusion, which can damage good management as well as accountability, the underlying principle

should be that the most senior person is to be held accountable if he or she were involved or should have been involved. Specifically, this means senior management is not necessarily held accountable for an isolated instance of wrongdoing or poor service by a subordinate, but senior management would be held accountable if this were systemic, and especially if senior management did not take adequate preventative action. Once accountability is clarified along these lines, it should be possible to reconcile the need for proper accountability with devolution of responsibility.

In this way, senior managers would be accountable, but not unfairly or unreasonably. This is a more realistic form of accountability in that the most senior person in the organization actually carrying out a task is the accountable person. This is an explicit recognition that accountability to the public is often to be found at levels lower than that of the minister.

A third form of accountable management is that of retrospective accountability. The traditional model always had some retrospective mechanisms, particularly for financial probity. Behn (2001) claims that it should be possible to establish a similar retrospective accountability for performance (p. 105):

> It seems straightforward to adapt the existing, retrospective mechanisms for establishing democratic accountability for finances and equity to the new needs of creating a retrospective mechanism for establishing democratic accountability for performance. Trust but verify.

Behn's notion of trust deserves wider consideration. Trust is required of a manager, in that s/he is given a task to do and is then left to do it, in theory without detailed oversight. If later there is verification that the work has been done, that in no way takes away the sense of trust given to the manager in the first place. The alternative, seen in traditional bureaucracy, is to build up more and more detailed rules, manuals and procedures so that administrators merely follow these through in a machine-like fashion.

Fukuyama (1995) draws a distinction between those who operate according to rules, and professionals, where 'the concept of a professional serves as a prototype of a high-trust, relatively unregulated occupation' (p. 223):

> Past a certain point, the proliferation of rules to regulate wider and wider sets of social relationships becomes not the hallmark of rational efficiency but a sign of social dysfunction. There is usually an inverse relationship between rules and trust: the more people depend on rules to regulate their interactions, the less they trust each other, and *vice versa*.

For public management to be regarded as a profession there needs to be more trust and fewer detailed rules. Managers should be allowed to achieve their goals, but, for reasons of accountability, there still needs to be verification – 'trust but verify' – as noted earlier. The increased use of evaluation of programmes, of formal inquiries, assists this requirement for accountability. Public managers will be trusted to achieve results and to take formal responsibility for doing so, but the achievement of results will face verification, as it should.

Accountability may be enhanced by public sector reform. Both organizationally and personally, accountability may be improved because the principals – the politicians and the public – have far better information on the activities of their agents – the public service, while those agents are required to take responsibility for what they do and what they achieve. Managerial changes promise greater transparency, so that achievements of particular programmes can be seen better than was ever previously the case. Failure to achieve objectives should be more visible than under the old system. Yet there are problems of accountability, or potential problems arising from the reform process.

Accountability problems from public sector reform

A managerial model does lead to major changes in the system of accountability. It is arguable whether this will mean some diminution of accountability, but what seems certain is a change of emphasis away from traditional kinds of accountability. If public managers are responsible for the achievement of their own objectives, this may diminish political accountability. To the extent that the public servant is to be managerially accountable, does this not mean that the political leadership is less accountable? Pollitt and Bouckaert (2004) also contend that executive politicians have been rather cunning in making public managers responsible for achieving targets, but 'at the same time they have frequently retained powers of intervention so that, if things go badly wrong in the public eye, then the politician can appear to ride to the rescue with inquiries, inspection teams, restructurings, and all the other paraphernalia of crisis management' (p. 147). Perhaps politicians will no longer be considered responsible or accountable. Perhaps, too, the derogation of traditional accountability is so serious that the entire public sector reform programme is doomed to fail.

The first point to look at briefly is that of the relationship between new forms of accountability and democracy. As Minogue (1998, p. 17) argues:

> Modern public administration is not just about efficiency; it also involves ideas of democratic participation, accountability and empowerment. There is therefore a constant tension between two main themes: making government efficient and keeping government accountable. There is a corresponding tension between

the conception of people as consumers, in the context of relations between the state and the market; and the conception of people as citizens, in the context of relations between the state and society.

There may be a tension, as Minogue argues, but what he does not establish is that accountability in the political sense is any worse with public management than it was previously. Perhaps the citizenry can distinguish between the different roles of government; sometimes services are delivered, and sometimes regulation or governance. The former can be judged as consumers, while the latter cannot. In Westminster-style parliamentary systems the minister is presumed to be accountable for the acts of the administration and is politically accountable through the legislature. Managers do become more responsible for the operations of which they are in charge, rather than the minister who, while being politically accountable, can avoid blame (Hondeghem, 1998). In the United States, it has long been the practice that agency heads are themselves accountable, so any diminution of accountability might be less of a worry there.

A second issue is that accountability becomes that of the market rather than through democratic institutions. Peters (1996) argues that, 'rather than being defined as progressing upward through ministers and parliament and then to the people, accountability is defined increasingly in market terms' (p. 43). And, market accountability is more important than 'instruments such as parliamentary oversight and judicial reviews'. Peters adds that 'along with rules and hierarchy, these formalized mechanisms are often indicted as the means through which government organizations have avoided meaningful accountability' (p. 43). It is the case that agencies are now required to specify their progress towards agreed objectives and this is different from the traditional model. But this hardly seems revolutionary. One of the most important parts of traditional accountability is that of spending public money; any agency that cannot say why it is doing something and how well it is performing is not accountable. If defining accountability in market terms includes reporting performance, accountability would be improved rather than reduced. The different accountability mechanisms of the public sector have been used to evade accountability in the past, such as where the need to comply with outside mechanisms makes market-type accountability impossible. But again, any organization, public or private, has an obligation to justify its existence through meeting its objectives.

However, the creation of independent agencies operating at arm's length through a contractual or quasi-contractual basis may lead to a problem of political accountability in the same way as the delivery of services through explicit contracts by the private sector. Yet specifying what is to be done through a contract may be more transparent.

Simply exchanging public for private accountability will not necessarily solve problems, especially if the government and the contractor attempt to blame each other for the difficulties. Governments will still be held to account even when there are clear contractual arrangements or complete privatization. Governments will be accountable for conflict over the awarding of contracts if contractors fail to deliver.

A third, and related, problem might arise from the derivation of the managerial model of accountability from that of the private sector. There are real difficulties with accountability in the private sector, and obvious problems if this is to be emulated by the public sector. In the world of business, management often operates for its own benefit rather than that of its shareholders, and boards may be ineffective. However, the external presence of competitors to whom customers may turn if dissatisfied provides a powerful incentive to operate competently. Introducing contestability for government services may have a similar effect. None the less, there are problems of accountability in both sectors. What is needed is a case-by-case comparison between the two. In some circumstances, the public sector might be more accountable, and in others, the private sector.

A fourth problem might be that bureaucracies will gain effective power from the managerial changes. In dealing with bureaucracy, the citizen is only a small and minor participant in a complicated process competing against a huge apparatus with all the skills and all the force of the law behind it. Citizen victories are rare. Yet, despite occasional lapses, the bureaucracy does not dominate in the way it would if it were accountable to no one. It is more the case that the bureaucracy has actually lost power in recent years and the move towards transparency and greater accountability is potentially able to improve the lot of the individual's dealings with it. In theory, the citizenry of democratic countries have an enviable system of accountability or responsibility, one that people in other countries aspire to emulate. In practice, the theory may not work as well as is usually assumed. However, in this sense there seems to be no diminution of accountability in the public management model compared to the traditional model. If the citizen was relatively powerless under the old model, it remains to be seen whether s/he is worse off now.

Another possible problem is that, while the traditional accountability mechanisms have been displaced, there is no adequate replacement. Pollitt and Bouckaert (2000) argue that 'in the UK, but also in other Westminster-influenced systems, the additional pressures which NPM reforms have put on traditional concepts of public accountability have not been met with any clear and coherent new doctrine to cope with the new circumstances' (pp. 138–9). There is something in this claim. The new model might not have been articulated by politicians, but the idea of accountable management shows promise. Accountable management may not be as fair, in that managers might be sacked for things they did not do, or have to take the blame for a specific problem that is only a small part of a systemic problem outside their control. Perhaps fairness, however, is a concept that is itself unrealistic when the bureaucracy is seen as part of the political system.

The problems of accountability that have been discussed thus far are more potential than actual. Concerns may be expressed that the reforms will make accountability worse, but with little evidence that accountability in a more managerial public sector is any less than in the traditional model. At most, there may be a change of emphasis from compliance kinds of accountability to those based around achievement of results.

Conclusion

The system of accountability forms the key link between the administration of government and the political system. Traditional methods of accountability and responsibility were well celebrated but in reality left much to be desired. The separation between government and its administration – the politics/administration dichotomy – was always naïve and unrealistic, as was the system of accountability that followed from it; separating 'politics from administration inherently (if not consciously) obscures accountability' (Behn, 2001, p. 115).

Political accountability in the traditional model was a complicated and vague system that produced more questions than answers. It was a well-known system in which, in theory, ordinary citizens could bring the whole apparatus of government to account when they came to vote. While the precise details of political accountability may leave much to be desired, there is no evidence that this kind of accountability has diminished. When elections are held, a choice may be made, at least by some voters, based on what they thought of the government over its term in office. For the public service, however, and in comparison with the private sector sense, this kind of accountability alone is too sparse, too rare and too ineffective to ensure performance.

Bureaucracies have not regressed from being accountable under the old system to being unaccountable under the new one. There are many avenues of accountability, including some on the outside such as the media and the courts. Perhaps what is happening is the replacement of an inferior and unrealistic form of accountability by another kind.

There are possible problems of accountability following reform, though whether these are greater than in the traditional model remains to be seen. To begin with, traditional accountability could hardly be said to have worked particularly well, or even at all, so any change in accountability might be an improvement.

There is an obvious need to discard once and for all the notion that politicians make policy and the public service simply carries it out, and that, through this division of labour, accountability is ensured. If managers are to be recognized as being in charge, at least someone will be in that position. As Romzek comments (2000, p. 40):

> As a result of reforms, civil servants find themselves with fewer detailed directives; and they face much less certainty about the accountability consequences of their actions. Yet they must continue to accommodate expectations from several different legitimate sources and be answerable for their behaviour under any and all accountability relationships that are relevant. And they must be able to shift the accountability standard under which they answer for their behaviour, as needed.

There may be some cause for concern with accountability, but there is also a need to balance it with enhanced performance. Accountability needs to be *compared*. It is not the case that a perfectly accountable system is being replaced by one that is not. As Romzek (1998) argues, 'de-emphasizing inputs and processes and emphasizing outcomes and outputs does not necessarily mean more or less accountability from government administrators'. It means, rather, that 'different kinds of accountability relationships should be emphasized, ones that encourage entrepreneurial management, increased discretion and worker empowerment in daily operations, and greater responsiveness to key stakeholders and customers' (Romzek, 1998, pp. 215–16). The traditional model did offer political accountability, even if it was of an indirect, unsatisfactory kind, but with very poor managerial accountability in the sense of results. Public management allows for direct accountability to clients, greater responsiveness and transparency of results. Any diminution of political accountability might be more than compensated by an improvement in managerial accountability.

For bureaucratic accountability, a more realistic approach is to adopt 'accountable management', the idea that, in a way analogous to the private sector, public managers are themselves accountable for their own actions and those of their agencies. They are less able to deny their own responsibility by saying that all actions are politically accountable. A new form of accountability is developing in which relationships between the bureaucracy, clients, the legislature, the media and individuals are carried out directly, rather than always through politicians. Direct accountability of this kind offers advantages over what was previously in place. Together with an increased focus on output and its measurement, accountability in the new model might turn out to be far better than that of the traditional model of administration. As Holmes and Shand (1995) comment, 'If the people really responsible for making these decisions are held accountable, accountability is actually enhanced' (p. 564).

Accountable management should mean that those who do something are accountable for it, whether a manager or a politician. Indeed, the meaning of management, as discussed earlier, is that a manager organizes to achieve results and is personally responsible for doing so. Public managers are employed by the taxpaying public as agents to carry out particular functions and need, accordingly, to be accountable to their principals.

Chapter 10

Strategic Management

Chapter Contents

- Introduction
- Strategy
- Strategy in the private sector
- Strategy in the public sector
- Strategic planning models
- Strategic management
- Criticisms of strategy in the public sector
- Conclusion

Introduction

The traditional model of administration was notable for its inward focus and short-term perspective. Each of these shortcomings has been addressed to some extent as part of the change to public management, given that a concern for strategy is part of a manager's role (Allison, 1982). A strategic perspective considers the position of an organization within its external environment; it aims to specify clear goals and objectives; and it attempts to move away from routine management tasks to consider, in a more systematic way, longer-term considerations of where the organization will go and what it should do. Strategy is about setting a direction for the future.

The traditional model of public administration required little conception of strategy; serious forward planning was either not carried out or carried out in rather limited ways. Indeed, strategy of any kind would have been considered 'political', if thought of at all, and would therefore be a task reserved for political leaders, not administrators. Public servants 'administered' in the dictionary sense set out earlier, simply carrying out instructions issued by politicians. It was, and is, possible to administer without a sense of strategy, without any idea of optimizing resources to gain long-term objectives, and to follow instructions without any external focus. The traditional model missed out on the longer-term perspective and, by being preoccupied with process, often forgot there was a larger purpose, an overall goal, for any public organization.

It was realized by the early 1980s that those presumed to be responsible for strategy under the old administrative model – solely the politicians – were not always in a position to provide long-term strategic leadership for their agency. If public managers are to be held responsible for results as a part of their work, there needs to be some thought given as to how day-to-day results can aggregate into the overall purpose or mission of the organization. Therefore, a key part of public management is to determine overall strategy and set objectives, not just by governments, but also by the agency and its various parts. Political leaders more often demand that agencies and public servants consider the longer-term implications of programmes and policies. A concern with strategic management in the public sector does not mean usurping the role of politicians; it is most often done at their instigation and is really part of a general realization that the old separation of policy from administration is untenable. Objectives and priorities can be decided by the organization itself, perhaps in collaboration with the political leadership.

Without a sense of strategy, any organization lacks direction. Day-to-day activities do not add up to any coherent goal and short-term responses to issues followed by further short-term responses can lead to incoherence. Ideally, all activities undertaken help to further specified aims, and beyond them the overall purpose of the agency. Using ideas of strategy in the public sector is not necessarily straightforward and there are criticisms of the use of such notions. However, in the final analysis, the short-termism of the administrative era was more problematic. Having a systematic approach when deciding how to confront the future does offer the promise of improvement.

Strategy

'Strategy' is a term deriving from the military; referring to the objective of winning the war, as opposed to 'tactics' – the lower-level objective of winning a particular battle. Strategy has a longer view, sees the big picture, rather than just the short-term outlook. Strategy is a much better fit with management than it ever was with administration; indeed, having some explicit requirement for strategy and for external constituencies are the two biggest differences between administration and the 'general management function' (Allison, 1982).

There are several different kinds of strategy in terms of fields of study. There is continuing interest in military and international aspects of strategy, and in what is sometimes called 'grand strategy' (Kennedy, 1988), which looks at the longer-term competition between states. Strategy can be defined as game theory and in some usage that is its only definition (Dixit and Nalebuff, 1991). Important theoretical work started in the in the 1960s combining game theory with international politics over issues such as limited nuclear war (Schelling, 1960; Schelling, 2006). The usage here is more prosaic, with strategy being essentially about answering the question 'What do we do next?'

Strategy is 'not a detailed plan or program of instructions; it is a unifying theme that gives coherence and direction to the actions and decisions of an individual or an organization' (Grant, 2008, p. 4). There are different ways of conceptualizing strategy, though there are four common factors (Grant, 2008, pp. 7–9):

1. Goals that are simple, consistent, and long term.
2. Profound understanding of the competitive environment.
3. Objective appraisal of resources.
4. Effective implementation.

Strategic decisions share three common characteristics: 'they are important; they involve a significant commitment of resources; they are not easily reversible' (Grant, 2008, p. 14). Key aspects are purpose, resources and action. Another way of setting out the basic rules of strategy is that there are five key aspects: *purpose* – the *raison d'être* or overall aim of the organization's position at some point in the future; *capability* – internal organizational assets to be compared to those of a competitor; *will/leadership* – how far the organization and its leadership are able to push ahead; *terrain* – the field on which the contest will take place, or the competitive environment; and *tactics* – how to carry out the overall purpose, with day-to-day activities aggregating to the overall purpose.

Strategy in the private sector

Strategic concepts are widely used in private sector management. An analogy between warfare and business was made as long ago as the time of Socrates, who compared the duties of a general and a businessman 'and showed that both utilise plans to use resources to meet objectives' (Montanari *et al.*, 1989, p. 303). Contemporaneous with the time of Socrates, the Chinese work *The Art of War*, attributed to the perhaps mythical Sun-Tzu, set out strategic precepts that are still studied and used today (Sawyer, 2007).

Much more recent usage of strategy in business derives from Chandler (1962) and Porter (1980, 1990). Applications of strategy in the private sector are obvious enough, with considerable competitive advantage resulting from looking at the long term and the external environment, rather than always considering more immediate internal problems. Normal management processes may be adequate for ordinary operations but it is also necessary, from time to time, to reassess the fundamental reason why the organization exists, what it is trying to do and where it is going. Resources can then be focused on areas identified as having long-term strategic benefit and reduced in other areas of lesser long-term benefit. Without a sense of strategy, it would be all too easy to carry on as before, disregarding longer-term purposes.

Even given the intrinsic attraction of using strategic concepts in the private sector, it was really only in the immediate post-Second World War period that they began to be applied in a coherent way. Hax and Majluf (1984, 1996) identify five stages in the evolution of planning: budgeting and financial control; long-range planning; business strategic planning; corporate strategic planning; and strategic management. These defined stages are relevant to the present discussion, in particular the difference between strategic *planning* and strategic *management* and, later, for the complementarity of the five stages of planning in the private sector to the development of planning in the public sector.

Budgeting and financial control are rather limited forms of planning. Relying on immediate financial results can lead to a rather short-sighted approach to management, often no more sophisticated than spending a one-year budget allocation. Long-range planning, which began in the 1950s, is an improvement in that it includes multi-year projections of future sales. This made some sense in the immediate post-war period, with 'high market growth, fairly predictable trends, firms with essentially a single dominant business, and [a] relatively low degree of rivalry among competitors' (Hax and Majluf, 1984, p. 11), but is limited if these conditions are not met. Long-range planning does not work if there is a change in the external environment or strong competition, as the projections are not likely to be met. There are also problems in assuming that the future is a simple straight-line projection from past data points.

There are, then, three forms of strategic planning identified by Hax and Majluf, and these have some points in common. All identify an organizational mission, perform an environmental scan, specify a set of objectives, and produce a strategic plan to achieve these objectives.

The first type of strategic planning is business strategic planning. This originated in the 1960s, and is where the concepts of mission and environmental scan or analysis first appear. The *mission* of the business includes a clear definition of current and expected business scope, products, markets and expectation over a period of a few years. The mission involves a consideration of what business the organization is following. The *environmental scan* involves a detailed assessment of the organization's internal strengths, weaknesses, opportunities and threats. This would include items inside the organization: the skills of workers, managerial capabilities, type of plant, financial structures, the constraints of government and so on. However, the real advance is the undertaking of a dispassionate analysis of the external environment, covering market structures and trends, including those in other countries; the extent of technological change; threats from similar products or substitution; the capabilities of competitors; and anything else that affects the existence of the organization. *Objectives* are more specific aims resulting from the mission and environmental scan. Elements of strategy at a higher managerial level become objectives at a lower one. From the mission, environmental scan and specified objectives, a business strategy plan is derived for both the short and longer term, combined with resource allocation and performance measures.

The second form of strategic planning is corporate strategic planning. This emerged in the 1970s as a result of 'increased international competition, changing societal values, military and political uncertainties, discriminating buyers, and economic slowdown' (Toft, 1989, p. 6). Corporate strategic planning is more concerned with the higher levels of the organization than is business strategic planning, and in allocating responsibility among differing parts of the business. The strategic plan is specified in much more detail than in the first form of strategic planning.

Both business and corporate strategic planning have their limitations. Ansoff (1988) states that early experience with strategic planning 'encountered three serious problems: "paralysis by analysis", that is, when plans produced little result; "organizational resistance" to the introduction of strategic planning, and ejection of strategic planning if the support of top management was withdrawn or relaxed' (p. 166). The problems led to the third form of strategic planning: strategic management.

In the 1980s, strategic planning started to be replaced by 'strategic *management*', a more refined form that incorporates the strategic planning function, but extends it much further. The difference between them is that 'strategic planning is focused on making optimal strategy decisions, while strategic management is focused on producing strategic results: new markets, new products and/or new technologies' (Ansoff, 1988, p. 235). Strategic management is therefore more comprehensive; rather than merely drawing up a plan it aims at integrating planning with all the other parts of the organization. Strategic management is 'a way of conducting the firm that has as an ultimate objective the development of corporate values, managerial capabilities, organizational responsibilities, and administrative systems that link strategic and operational decision making, at all hierarchical levels, and across all businesses and functional lines of authority in a firm' (Hax and Majluf, 1996, p. 419). Strategic management aims to extend the strategic vision throughout all units of the organization, encompassing every administrative system. Instead of being mechanistic, it 'recognises the central role played by individuals and groups and the influence of corporate culture' (Toft, 1989, pp. 6–7). Also, prior to the mission statement, there should be a reasonably permanent vision of the firm articulated by the chief executive officer (CEO). This corporate philosophy 'has to provide a unifying theme and a vital challenge to all organizational units, communicate a sense of achievable ideals, serve as a source of inspiration for confronting daily activities, and become a contagious, motivating, and guiding force congruent with the corporate ethic and values' (Hax and Majluf, 1996, p. 255).

There are two main points in this. First, there needs to be greater integration between planning, management control and the organizational structure. Planning should not be regarded as a separate activity, relying on a separate planning department, but as a responsibility of management, and not to be isolated from the organization. Second, the organization needs to pay attention to its 'culture'. Plans still exist in strategic management, but more attention is paid to implementation because of the need to consider the human factors present in the organizational culture and affecting its management.

It is easy to see that strategic management fits the private sector and, if implemented well, would provide a company with an information base for making decisions that would not necessarily arise from normal operations. It can help an organization to step back from the normal management process or day-to-day activities and ask fundamental questions about the existence and future of the organization. There are other kinds of strategy used within the private sector, but strategic management is still the one most widely employed.

Strategy in the public sector

Despite supposedly deriving from the private sector – an arguable point, given its origins in the military – strategy has become used increasingly in the public sector. Public organizations do have long-term existences but often face problems in deciding their focus. They could conceivably benefit from a more strategic approach, though not without some modification of the private sector perspective. Some kind of planning in the public sector has been used for decades, and with the methods used following fairly closely the five stages of planning set out earlier for the private sector. Budgeting and financial control began very early in the public sector. This planning stage could be argued to be the quintessence of organizations in the traditional model of administration, where the main planning aim is simply to spend the budget allocation. Long-range planning was also used in the same way as in the private sector and with the same problems of forecasting. Strategic planning in the public sector is a phenomenon of the early 1980s – significantly later than its development in the private sector. It became commonplace for governments to require their agencies to prepare strategic plans. Strategic management was also adopted in the public sector, but, again, it followed the private sector with a gap of some years.

Strategic planning and strategic management as currently used do derive from the private sector. There may be more problems and constraints in public sector strategy compared to strategy in the private sector, and these 'range from constitutional arrangements to legislative and judicial mandates, to government-wide rules and regulations, to jurisdictional boundaries, to scarce resources, to political climate factors, to client and constituent interests' (McCaffery, 1989, p. 207). Direct importation may not work; strategic managers in the public sector 'should be wary of using private sector approaches that assume clear goals, profit or economic purposes, unlimited authority to act, secret development, limited responsibility for actions, and oversight through market mechanisms that signal financial results' and in public organizations 'many of these assumptions are not valid' (Nutt and Backoff, 1992, p. 23). Early formulations of strategy in the public sector tended to commit all these sins, but strategic management may prove to be the most promising approach, as it has in the private sector.

Strategic planning models

The earliest stages of a strategic approach in the public sector were based around strategic planning. A useful definition is that of Olsen and Eadie (1982, p. 4) in which 'strategic planning is a disciplined effort to produce fundamental decisions shaping the nature and direction of governmental activities, within constitutional bounds'. This definition stresses three points. First, strategic decisions are 'fundamental decisions', not low-level ones, as the latter can presumably be performed by normal bureaucratic means. Second, strategic decisions are specified as decisions which affect 'the nature and direction of activities' and the whole future of the organization. Third, there are limits to the scope of strategic planning of a political and constitutional kind, which is an immediate difference from a private sector context. Ideally, strategic planning does not subvert normal political or bureaucratic approaches but takes place within them.

In the early 1980s, Olsen and Eadie (1982) (see also Eadie, 1983), were among the pioneers who argued that strategic planning had a place in the public sector, which could learn much from the private sector about planning. They argue that the strategic planning process consists of the following basic components (p. 19):

- The overall mission and goals statements, which are formulated by an organization's executive management and provide the framework within which strategies are developed – the 'targets' toward which strategies are aimed.
- The environmental scan or analysis, consisting of the identification and assessment of current and anticipated external factors and conditions that must be taken into account when formulating the organization's strategies.
- The internal profile and resource audit, which catalogues and evaluates the strengths and weaknesses of the organization in terms of a variety of factors that must be taken into consideration in strategic planning.
- The formulation, evaluation, and selection of strategies.
- The implementation and control of the strategic plan.

There are obvious similarities in this model with strategic planning in the private sector. When compared to the private sector models set out earlier, it would seem to have most in common with the business strategic planning model.

A more comprehensive account of strategic planning is that provided by Bryson (1988, 2004). Bryson outlines ten steps in strategic planning (2004, pp. 32–51). The Bryson model is clearly a strategic planning model derived from the private sector, but with some variations to allow for the public sector context.

The first step for Bryson is initiating and agreeing on a strategic planning process. The second step is to consider the organization mandate, or what is specified in the establishing legislation of the public organization. This is one immediate difference from the private sector, where the mandate is in a sense without limit, in that it is quite common for a company with expertise in one area – say, steel – to diversify into the oil or food businesses. This is not the case in the public sector. Public organizations have *mandates,* specified in legislation, that limit the scope of their activity.

Box 10.1 The Bryson model of strategic planning

1. Initiate and agree on a strategic planning process.
2. Identify organizational mandates.
3. Clarify organizational mission and values.
4. Assess the external and internal environments to identify strengths, weaknesses, opportunities and threats.
5. Identify the strategic issues facing the organization.
6. Formulate strategies to manage the issues.
7. Review and adopt the strategies or strategic plan.
8. Establishing an effective organizational vision.
9. Develop an effective implementation process.
10. Reassess the strategies and the strategic planning process.

The third step is to make clear the organizational mission and values; why does the organization exist at all, and what is it trying to achieve? Public sector organizations may find it difficult to decide exactly what they do. For example, what is the precise aim of a social welfare department or a health department? However, a lack of clarity becomes a major weakness in an age in which clear goals and progress towards them are demanded by governments. Where strategic planning can assist is in making an organization or an agency specify what it is trying to achieve. As far as possible, though controversial in its implementation, its objectives and targets should be empirical.

Fourth, consideration of the external and internal environment involves essentially the same process as a SWOT analysis – strengths, weakness, opportunities and threats – as in the private sector. Public organizations exist in an environment that has both opportunities and threats. Public organizations in the administrative era were criticized for being overly insular, preoccupied with internal matters and not thinking about how or where their organization exists within government or society as a whole. A good strategic plan would discuss the opportunities or threats faced by the organization in the context of its external environment as well as its internal capability. Public organizations exist in an environment in which threats are ever-present. A good plan would point to these and do so in detail. It should go beyond the obvious to be a clear, comprehensive picture of where the organization fits into its broader environment.

A public organization is no different from one in the private sector when it comes to assessing its external environment, or in having a need to do so. There are differences of emphasis, as Nutt and Backoff (1992, p. 180) argue:

> The emphasis in the content of SWOTs varies markedly across sectors. First, firms have tight markets and weak political linkages. The reverse is true for public and third sector organizations; markets are loosely defined and authority systems impose constraints ... Second, firms are pulled toward opportunities and public and third sector organizations tend to be driven by threats.

This is a perceptive comment. Public organizations may be more reactive than proactive and respond more to threats, which means an expectation of a differing result from strategic processes.

The internal operations of the organization are also critical to its existence. If it has internal weaknesses it becomes harder to justify its continued operation in an atmosphere in which any excuse is used for making cuts. The internal environment assessment requires a thorough assessment of the capability of staff. This would include the quality and qualifications of staff, age, gender or other profiles in the hierarchy, departure rates, and less quantifiable measures including the state of morale. There should be an assessment of the extent of resources, particularly financial, but also the systems that are used, notably information systems, accounting systems and so on.

Fifth, Bryson looks to identify the strategic issues facing the organization. These should surface as a result of the environmental scanning activity. Strategic issues should be separated from day-to-day ones in some way, and need to be listed as they would form the basis of strategies to be formulated and implemented. A strategic issue could be a major staffing problem – say, for example, in a tax office where senior, experienced accounting staff are leaving for the private sector at far higher salaries. Another might be that a particular good or service being provided is now being contracted out to the private sector in some other jurisdiction, so that privatization might be considered in the future. A strategic issue is a major issue, one that affects the organization's future or ability to function.

Sixth, and following logically, strategies are formulated to manage the issues identified as being strategic. Formulating strategies – sometimes referred to as deriving an 'action plan' or 'action programme' (Hax and Majluf, 1996) – is where the strategic issues deriving from the previous steps are put into effect. In the above examples of strategic issues, a response to the staffing problem would be to offer more money or better conditions to encourage the accountants to stay. If an organization feels its existence is threatened by, for example, a requirement to contract-out, it would need to be pre-emptive, to make a case for its continuance, and as well to think of contingencies – other alternatives for the staff – if the worst happened.

Seventh, once strategies have been formulated, there may need to be an official decision to adopt them and proceed with implementation, most notably in large organizations. If a strategic plan is developed for an organization by a sub-group, its viability would need to be ratified. It could be argued that this is one reason why a strategic plan should not be constructed as a separate activity and with a separate strategic planning group.

Eighth, the organization needs to describe its vision of success – what it should look like once it has implemented its strategies successfully and achieved its full potential. A vision statement is often listed as one of the first requirements of formulating a strategic plan. Bryson (2004) comments that iterations of planning may be necessary before organizational members know what they want, and that 'the further along in the process a vision is found, the more fully articulated it is likely to be' (p. 49). The development of citizen's charters was intended to set out the parameters of a public organization's relationship with clients. Presumably, part of the idea is to provide a shared vision to those inside the organization to govern their behaviour.

Ninth, the plan needs to have embedded within it an effective implementation scheme. Strategies do not implement themselves, and carrying out the proposed activities is crucial to any strategic plan's success.

Tenth, and finally, the organization should 'review the strategies and the strategic planning process, as a prelude to a new round of strategic planning' (Bryson, 2004, p. 51). Strategies might not work; and it may be possible to improve the process itself in the next iteration. The desired outcomes include 'the maintenance of good strategies, modification of less successful strategies through appropriate reforms or plan revisions, and elimination of undesirable strategies' (p. 266). An effective strategic management system or performance management system can be constructed to assist in further iterations of the strategic plan and monitor progress towards targets.

In sum, strategic planning, as set out by Bryson, may offer much in a public sector context. A stages approach, proceeding logically through the various steps, would enable public sector agencies to produce plans in the way that is increasingly demanded by governments. But, as Bryson (2004) argues, 'the ultimate end of strategic planning should not be rigid adherence to a particular process or the production of plan'; instead, strategic planners 'should promote wise strategic thought, action, and learning on behalf of the organization and its key stakeholders' (p. 16). Planning does not take away from the political process; indeed, it should be regarded as an adjunct to the political process, albeit one with limits. These limits may be greater than in the private sector, a factor that changes the way plans are drawn up and what they contain, but does not diminish the value of the process.

Strategic planning does have limitations in the public sector, in precisely the same way as it did in the private sector. Frequently, the only product of the process in the early years of strategic planning in the public sector was to produce a formal document that was 'all too often the main, if not the sole product' (Eadie, 1989, p. 170). Bryson states that strategic planning is no panacea (2004, p. 15):

> Strategic planning is simply a set of concepts, procedures, and tools designed to help leaders, managers, and planners think, act, and learn strategically. Used in wise and skilful ways by a coalition of interested parties, it can help organizations focus on producing effective decisions and actions that create public value, further the organization's mission, meet organizational mandates, and satisfy key stakeholders ... Unfortunately, when used thoughtlessly, obsessively, or excessively formally, strategic planning can drive out precisely the kind of strategic thinking, acting and learning it was supposed to promote.

Strategic planning may not suit all organizations at all times. However, it is likely to be markedly better than planning by budget or simple forecasting. However, while strategic planning is widely used in government so too is strategic management, a more comprehensive approach again deriving from the private sector (see Elcock, 1996).

Strategic management

As noted earlier, the fifth stage in the evolution of planning in the private sector is that of strategic management. The public sector too has increasingly adopted strategic management as a result of limitations found with strategic planning.

Strategic management aims to integrate the planning function within the overall management task. Beyond this point, though, there are differing views as to exactly what is entailed in strategic management. As in the private sector, strategic planning involves analysing the environment for opportunities or threats, and formulating strategic plans to exploit any opportunities or cope with threats. Strategic management includes strategic planning, but it is 'a more inclusive concept, emphasizing dynamic interaction with the environment and an incremental methodology that allows for scanning the environment to choose the target that will yield the most benefit for the effort expended' (McCaffery, 1989, p. 194).

Bozeman and Straussman (1990) see four aspects to strategic management; they explain (pp. 29–30):

> As we use the term, strategic management is guided by four principles: (1) concern with the long term, (2) integration of goals and objectives into a coherent hierarchy, (3) recognition that strategic management and planning are not self-implementing, and most important, (4) an external perspective emphasizing not adapting to the environment but anticipating and shaping of environmental change. Strategic *public* management adds an additional ingredient: strategic thinking must be cognisant of the exercise of political authority.

The first two are essentially no different from strategic planning. However, the need for good implementation and greater interaction with the environment are persistent themes in the transition to strategic management. From these various perspectives, the changes from planning to management seem to be, first, greater care in developing the plan and what it represents; and, second, greater attention to implementation. Even here the differences from planning frameworks may not be huge, given that Bryson (2004) also includes these as part of strategic planning.

Strategic management includes strategic planning and a plan is formulated in a similar way as before. Nutt and Backoff (1992) set out six points for a strategic management plan (p. 152):

- depict the organization's historical context in terms of trends in its environment, its overall direction, and its normative ideals;
- assess the immediate situation in terms of current strengths and weaknesses and future opportunities and threats;
- develop an agenda of current strategic issues to be managed;
- design strategic options to manage priority issues;
- assess the strategic options in terms of stakeholders affected and resources required; and
- implement priority strategies by mobilizing resources and managing stakeholders.

Nutt and Backoff's first point is novel. The strategic management group is asked to 'reconstruct aspects of the history of the organization that have special significance'. In this, 'trends, events, and directions are examined, noting how they have changed in the past and may change in the future' (1992, p. 169). Organizations are regarded as having a history and a culture, both of which need to be considered in formulating strategy and are especially relevant in a public sector context.

The second, third and fourth points are similar to those found in a strategic planning model. The environmental scan is presumed to be more thorough, but this is a difference of emphasis, not kind. Strategic issues and options are similar to before, but the real difference is in the recognition of stakeholders and using them to implement strategy.

Implementation

Implementation refers both to the implementation of strategic management and the implementation of any strategic plan once it has been developed. Both of these will inevitably involve changes within the organization. Implementation may be more difficult in the public sector as 'publicness brings with it constraints, political influence, authority limits, scrutiny, and ubiquitous ownership' (Nutt and Backoff, 1992, p. 201).

The biggest implementation problem will be in convincing staff that a strategic focus is useful, and that the changes to follow will be beneficial in the long run. It should be possible for the plan itself to anticipate opposition, and to involve people from all levels of the organization. Organizations contain people who have their own culture, and convincing people or changing cultures are processes that need to be managed and not simply assumed. Strategic planning models tended to focus on the steps involved without any consideration of there being people involved. The process cannot be imposed; there must be ownership of the plan. Stakeholders too need to be managed. One key change from strategic planning to strategic management is the importance attached to stakeholders. This is different from 'the narrower concept of strategic planning; stakeholders are decision makers within the organization and its environment who have an interest in organizational performance and can help or hinder the choice and implementation of strategies' (McCaffery, 1989, p. 195).

There are some ways to improve the strategic management process. It is usually argued that having a separate planning branch to carry out the task is not the best way of formulating any strategy, as other parts of the organization then feel no ownership of it. This is one difference between some formulations of strategic planning and strategic management. Strategic planning does have connotations of planning as an exercise separate from the operation of the organization, to be carried out by specialists in planning. It is usually far better to have a strategic management team of five to ten managers, including the chief executive, but also including managers from levels below top management who are closer to operations (Bozeman and Straussman, 1990, p. 47; McCaffery, 1989, p. 196). Nutt and Backoff (1992) also refer to the strategic management group in an organization as being made up of 'people who represent interests and power centres internal and external to the organization' and which becomes the 'key source of ideas about change and how to make the change within the organization' (p. 152). The chief executive should be part of this group and have the overall responsibility for setting out, and attempting to achieve, the organization's strategy; indeed, this should be seen as his or her most important task.

The main aim of strategic management is to incorporate strategic thinking into management at all stages, instead of undertaking a one-off planning exercise to produce a document that might not be used. This integration is much harder to achieve, especially in government organizations; indeed, it is likely to mean that strategic planning is more used than strategic management (Toft, 1989, p. 6). One reason why it is hard to introduce strategic concepts into public organizations is that many of them have been static in operation and, more important, thought processes, for a long time. To make the change into a dynamic organization – one with expectations of change – requires a complete adjustment of the culture.

Public value and strategy

There is an open question for both strategic planning and strategic management as to the ultimate purpose of any public sector organization. Goal statements such as 'the public interest' may have their place but are ultimately vague. Also, while public agencies should obey the instructions of their political leaders, it is inarguable that most agencies have continuity far longer than can be accounted for by changes in the politicians nominally in charge. Public organizations should be seen as serving some kind of public purpose. What, then, is an agency trying to achieve, and how much scope does it have in determining what it is trying to achieve? To answer by saying that public servants simply obey the instructions of their political masters is to regress to nostrums of the traditional model of public administration.

A better answer is that agencies do things that the public wants, that the public values, and through mechanisms that have existed for a long time. Moore (1995) argues that agencies should seek the creation and maintenance of 'public value', a commodity analogous to the private value that is created in the private sector. As Moore contends (p. 20):

> In this view, public managers are seen as explorers who, with others, seek to discover, define, and produce public value. Instead of simply devising the means for achieving mandated purposes, they become important agents in helping to discover and define what would be valuable to do. Instead of being responsible only for guaranteeing continuity, they become important innovators in changing what public organizations do and how they do it. In short, in this view, public managers become strategists rather than technicians.

The idea has resonance. Bryson (2004), for example, argues that strategic planning can help public and non-profit organizations fulfil their missions, meet their mandates, and create real public value; it can also help communities serve important purposes, including the creation of public value (p. 332). Mulgan (2009) states that government strategy derives from paying systematic attention to: *purposes* – why they should act in the first place; *environments* – where they are seeking to achieve their goals, the contexts and capacities; *directions* – what they want to achieve; *actions* – how they are to achieve their goals; and *learning* – systems for understanding which actions did or didn't work, and with the overall goal to 'create public value' (pp. 4–5).

Public value may have a role in assisting public organizations to work out what they are trying to do. However, Rhodes and Wanna (2009) are critical of the public value approach (p. 162):

> We argue it mistakenly diagnoses the roles of management in the modern public sector. It invents roles for public servants for which they are not appointed, are ill-suited, inadequately prepared and, more importantly, not protected if things go wrong. It asks public managers to supplant politicians, to become engaged in the political process, and become the new platonic guardians and arbiters of the public interest.

The criticism is unfounded. It is better to see public value as an analogue of private value in private markets. Any agency should be aware of its place in the political system, and to make some effort to provide a service or good that the public values in some way.

Accountability issues have also been raised in terms of public value. Rhodes and Wanna (2009, p. 180) argue 'In public value approaches, public servants are encouraged to bypass the conventions of democratic politics and rely on their idea of what is in the public interest'. However, Moore (1995) anticipates this criticism and discounts it as supposing a 'rigorous distinction between policy and administration' that was theoretically and practically impossible and that if public managers could define public value more precisely, that this would 'help society make a virtue of necessity' (p. 21). And, in reality, public managers, like public administrators before them, have always been involved in making policy; it does not seem problematic to expressly require agencies to establish what public value they aim to produce in a strategic sense.

Criticisms of strategy in the public sector

Strategic planning and strategic management have not been without their critics. Some criticisms apply to strategic planning or management in general, as well as their application in a public sector context. A selection of criticisms is discussed below.

Overly simplistic

Perhaps the formal strategic planning process becomes overly simplistic in setting out all the complex things that governments do. Though the various steps follow logically, the analysis of a strategic situation is often not simply a matter of filling in the standard boxes. The headings can provide a framework for thinking about an organization's strategy, but does not, by itself, constitute a plan. The process of SWOT analysis is problematic in many circumstances. Despite any good plan requiring thorough organizational self-examination, it is usually difficult for an organization to really look at itself in a critical way, as this can be construed as a direct criticism of the current leadership. Being able to do so is necessary for a meaningful strategic plan. In the public sector, internal inadequacies as found by a SWOT analysis could well become issues seized upon by opposing politicians or the media. This tends to mean that examinations of internal capability are likely to be superficial.

Too rigid and slow-moving

The formal strategic planning process may be too rigid and slow-moving to respond adequately to a rapidly changing, turbulent environment (Olsen and Eadie, 1982, p. 66). In some cases, strategic management can be forced on to agencies in a rather rigid way. Also, a plan set in stone for many years will almost certainly fail as the environment changes around it. This problem should be able to be resolved by good implementation and updating of the plan at regular intervals, or by seeing strategic management as a continuous, rather than a cyclical, process. Also, the plan itself should not be the main product; it is the process of thinking about the organization in a strategic way that has real value.

The public sector context

There is often criticism of the application of strategic concepts to the very different public sector context from its original home in the private sector. Strategic management has been successful enough in the private sector to suggest that it is a model of some power and considerable validity, but there still may be problems in applying it to the public sector. There may be problems of goals, in that the public sector finds it hard to set goals or objectives for its activities. Any plan may become 'a symbolic or ornamental enterprise conscientiously undertaken, but with only slight impact on practical management' (Montanari *et al.*, 1989, p. 314). This is a real problem, particularly if the output of the process is only a document, rather than the process bringing a real change in management practices.

Issues of accountability

The perennial issue of accountability may conflict with strategic management. If the strategy is made by the organization this could be seen as usurping the input of the politician, thus causing problems of accountability. A good strategic plan would have to incorporate the very political basis of the public sector. Strategic planning and management do not replace political decision-making, but rather seek 'to improve on the rawest forms of political decision-making, however, by assuring that issues are raised and resolved in ways that benefit the organization and its key stakeholders' (Bryson, 1988, p. 70).

Setting objectives

It is difficult to set objectives in a public sector context. There are obvious difficulties in deciding what given public agencies do. To decide mission and goals is rarely easy and may not be meaningful. It could be argued that the objectives of public sector organizations are so imprecise as to make any strategy meaningless. There are two responses to this. First, the imprecision of objective setting may not be as different from the private sector as would normally be imagined. According to Ansoff (1988) objectives are 'one of the most controversial issues of business ethics', with some writers seeking to 'remove profit from its position as the central motive in business and replace it with doctrines such as equal responsibility to stockholders, long-term survival, or a negotiated consensus among various participants in the firm' (p. 28). This is some distance from the normal assumption that the private sector is motivated purely by profit. If the objectives of a firm are in reality 'a negotiated consensus of objectives of the influential participants' (p. 31), this is not really much different from a stakeholder perspective in the public sector.

Nutt and Backoff (1992) argue for the use of 'ideals' rather than objectives. As they state (p. 177):

> Our strategic management process uses ideals in place of goals. Goals are not used because they are typically ambiguous in public organizations and tend to remain so after clarification attempts ... However, leaving goals implicit makes it difficult to modify or even evaluate current practices. Without some concept of the organization's aims, all change becomes contentious and the organization's strategy tends to stay rooted in past practices and conventional wisdom. To provide targets that identify intentions, we use the notion of ideals. Ideals suggest aims that can be articulated in concrete terms to capture goal-like targets and offer ways to seek compromise among competing views that dictate what the organization is (or is not) about.

In this way, the strategic management process can go ahead without becoming bogged down in setting precise targets. There must still be ideals of some kind and these should be enough to make the strategy meaningful. There is real tension here between the fluidity of demands on public agencies and an imposed requirement for precision. Politicians or central agencies increasingly demand plans with clear goals and objectives as part of budgetary decision-making. In the longer term, it will become more difficult for agencies without clear goals to survive in the competition with other agencies for resources.

Short time horizons

It could be argued that the public sector has such short time horizons that any long-term perspective is bound to fail. Time perspective is a problem, but rather than this point dooming any strategic plan, it should be factored into the analysis for the plan. Any long-term view in a rapidly changing area does need to be updated constantly. Some private sector industries also change very quickly – computers, for example – but strategic management is still feasible and useful there.

There are other possible problems. Sufficient information may not be available to enable a plan to be developed. There may be a bias towards measurable activities in the strategic plan, to the possible detriment of those activities that are harder to count. Staff may be inadequately trained, and there is always the problem that even after it has been produced, the strategic plan sits gathering dust on a shelf and is not regarded as meaningful by the staff.

However, none of these criticisms is so damaging as to make a strategic perspective in the public sector useless. They may serve as a caution against expecting too much and point to the need for careful implementation with stakeholders. It should be a method of thinking above all else, as Bryson (2004, p. 15) argues:

> Strategic planning is no panacea ... Strategic planning is simply a set of concepts, procedures, and tools designed to help leaders, managers, and planners think, act, and learn strategically. Used in wise and skilful ways by a coalition of interested parties, it can help organizations focus on producing effective decisions and actions that create public value, further the organization's mission, meet organizational mandates, and satisfy key stakeholders ... Unfortunately, when used thoughtlessly, obsessively, or excessively formally, strategic planning can drive out precisely the kind of strategic thinking, acting, and learning it was supposed to promote.

Introducing a strategic perspective into the public sector is valuable if it is done sensibly, not too rigidly, involving stakeholders, and as an aid to management rather than being an end in itself. It is the case that the transition 'from bureaucratic organizations to strategy-led organizations that manage continuous improvement and responsiveness to the public will take some time to achieve' (Joyce, 2000, p. 229). After this is done, or even while it is managing the process, there should be positive effects on the organization with regard to focus and results, and ultimately its long-term future.

Mintzberg (1994) is critical of formalized strategic planning and argues that the use of simple, logical steps, combined with SWOT analysis, is not likely to lead to much in the way of strategic insight. Successful strategies are more likely to be *emergent*, deriving from existing circumstance rather than considered strategy, especially that deriving from a separate strategic planning group (pp. 24–7). However, at the end of a sustained critique of strategic planning, Mintzberg argues, 'Too much planning may lead to chaos, but so too would too little, and more directly' (p. 416). There is a more general lesson here. Formalized strategic planning or management may have problems, as noted. But those problems are likely to be fewer than those arising from having no focus, no strategy, no plan for the future, and no idea where an organization is going.

Conclusion

An enhanced concern with strategy is part of the change from the traditional model of administration to public management. No organization can automatically assume its future existence is guaranteed. Even if it might not face the immediate threat of going out of business if a product does not sell, as in the private sector, the difference between sectors in terms of a strategic imperative may no longer be that great. There is the constant threat of reorganization, amalgamation with some other agency, privatization, or the government deciding that the function is no longer needed. The absence of certainty is not altogether bad, as it concentrates attention on what the organization does in terms of goals and missions, and in aligning these with the government's overall strategic objectives. In theory, it should be possible to link the strategic planning process with other elements of public sector reform. From the strategic planning process, it should be possible to identify the areas of operation on which to concentrate. These can be identified as specific programmes, with separate funding and performance measures attached. At specific times, evaluation of success or failure can then be fed into the overall strategic planning process.

In the private sector, strategic management and planning are useful tools for management, though they have not proved to be a panacea. The same should be true in the public sector. Just thinking about the future is a useful exercise for public sector organizations, even though the traditional model of administration was not renowned for its long-term perspective. If the aims of strategic planning are to assist in the provision of information, it should prove useful. There have been some examples of poor strategic planning in the public sector, where this lesson was not absorbed. Strategic management should not be introduced in an overly rigid fashion. The process should include compromise, political constraints and political activities as an integral part rather than something that occurs outside the model.

Strategic planning or strategic management is not to be done on just one occasion. It is the planning process and strategic thinking that are important, not the plan itself. The use of strategic concepts should allow the organization, from top management down, to develop a shared vision for the future. It does not guarantee that mistakes will not be made. Strategic planning and strategic management simply give some direction and purpose to public organizations, something that is required in moving from public administration to public management.

Chapter 11

Leadership and Managing People

Chapter Contents

- Introduction
- Staffing in the traditional model
- Leadership
- Management of human resources
- Some problems with the HRM changes
- Conclusion

Introduction

Public sector reforms have affected many parts of government, including the way that offices are organized, how they are staffed, and how they are led. The operations of government may still take place in offices, which, apart from improvements in technology and fashions in furniture design, are basically similar to those of a hundred years ago. What are quite different, though, are the rules, procedures and terms and conditions relating to the people who work for the government. Despite some continuity with the traditional model of administration, there has been marked change in staffing and the systems of personnel and human resource management (HRM). In the era of the traditional model, as noted earlier, a government job promised tenure for life, normally following recruitment only at the base grade; promotion through the grades was through steady incremental advancement; the monitoring of individual performance was undemanding, and in many places it was difficult to dismiss poorly performing staff. Individual staff members made an implicit trade-off between, on the one hand, job security and generous retirement benefits, and, on the other, slow progress and relatively low pay. Over time, elaborate procedures and systems were built up, ostensibly to ensure fairness, as well as a belief that public sector jobs were, in some way, special.

As argued earlier, the most important factor in the transition from public administration to public management is that a public manager is personally responsible for the delivery of results. There are three key aspects that have emerged in terms of staffing as a result of this change.

The first is that the old terms 'personnel administration' and even 'personnel management' have been largely replaced by 'human resource management'. Personnel administration is more oriented towards process and procedure, whereas HRM takes a more strategic approach to finding and managing the right people for organizational purposes (see Legge, 2005). Even if there might have been a public sector version of HRM at the start of the reforms, a trend developed towards regarding HRM as a generic practice. Second, far more attention is paid to the monitoring of staff performance, through various systems of performance appraisal, to ensure that everyone in an office contributes to the achievement of results. Third, public sector organizations, as with the private sector even earlier, now actively seek out and develop leaders. This is very different from the traditional model of administration based on the theory of bureaucracy, where such personal attributes were not considered to be part of the model. An administrator is not a leader, other than incidentally. The very consideration of ideas of leadership in public management is a further sign of how far the management of government has moved from the traditional model.

Managerial reforms have altered staffing arrangements and conditions of service – in general, away from public servants having special terms and conditions and towards those that apply in the private sector. Changes affecting personnel have been controversial, particularly in the early stages of managerial reform. Those who were familiar with the old model found the changes to personnel systems – performance appraisal, short-term contracts, merit pay and so on – threatening to their long-established terms and conditions of work. Retirement benefits were reduced in many jurisdictions, with defined benefit schemes closed to new employees and retirement ages extended. However, and perhaps surprisingly, over the more than twenty years of public sector reform since the 1980s, what were once controversial personnel changes were gradually accepted, perhaps as a new generation of public servants came into government with different expectations. Newer public servants may have been less willing to accept the ideas of slow, incremental progress and low pay, but nor did they show as much loyalty; working in government became more of a job not much different from one in the private sector and much less a career or a vocation.

Human resource management, performance appraisal and leadership together mean that, even if the work of public servants takes place in offices, the way that those offices are staffed is quite different from what it once was. Performance appraisal and leadership, while linked, point to quite different things. On the one hand, public servants are more closely monitored and have lost some of their unusual terms and conditions of employment, while on the other hand, leadership is actively sought and a leader has real scope to make a difference and to deliver results. Many public managers finding themselves in that situation do rise to the challenge, even though they will have to take ultimate responsibility if results are not achieved. The staffing function of managers is quite different from personnel administration in the old model, albeit challenging in its own way.

Staffing in the traditional model

The Weberian model of bureaucracy regarded officials as forming a distinctive elite within society. Even though the idea that public servants were an elite declined somewhat over the twentieth century, there was certainly a distinctive way of dealing with the staff who worked inside an administrative system. Administrators followed instructions and followed the manuals. There could be no place for leadership in a strictly bureaucratic model when any semblance of personality in administration – and what Weber termed 'patrimonialism' – is to be removed from what is to be an impersonal system. There was instead a detailed set of standard personnel requirements that followed the bureaucratic theories of Max Weber almost to the letter. As discussed earlier (see Chapter 3), the individual public servant was to have a particular set of working conditions – for example, appointment for life, appointment by a superior authority and not elected, a positional appointment and promotion, old age security provided by a pension – and 'a career within the hierarchical order of the public service' (Gerth and Mills, 1970, pp. 199–203). The notion of a career service, common in many countries, followed these precepts almost exactly.

As an example, a typical description of a career service personnel model is that of the Commonwealth Government in Australia as described by the Coombs Commission in the mid-1970s as (RCAGA, 1976, p. 169) (see Box 11.1).

The normal practice until the 1970s in some countries, and even later in others, was for aspiring administrators to enter the public service direct from school after sitting an examination administered by a separate non-partisan government agency, be appointed to a position at the bottom of the hierarchy, gain regular promotions, often based on seniority, or seniority combined with 'efficiency', and, in principle, aspire to become a department head. Recruitment was carried out by merit, and appointment was to the service as a whole rather than to one department or agency. Lateral appointment to higher levels than the base grade was discouraged. Before 1976 in Australia there was a ceiling imposed such that no more than 10 per cent of new recruits could be university graduates. Careers were largely restricted to men as, until 1966 in that same country, women were forced to resign when

---

BOX 11.1   A typical career service personnel model

- *recruitment by merit* (however defined) to a
- *unified service* (intended to mitigate the evils which result from fragmentary service) subject to
- *independent, non-political control* of recruitment and of the conditions of employment; and where the rights of career public servants are protected by
- regulations which *discourage the recruitment of 'strangers'* to positions above the base grade, and by
- *legislated protection against arbitrary dismissal* (termination being only for cause and by due process). This unified service is characterized by
- *a hierarchical structure of positions* defined by
- a regular system of *position classification* of salaries (with incremental advancement within the salary ranges of particular positions), with the career public servant rising through this hierarchy of positions according to
- a system of *promotion by merit* subject to
- a system of *appeals against promotions* (designed to ensure that justice is seen to be done), the final reward for long and loyal service being
- a *distinctive retirement and pension* system

---

they married. Though no longer mandated, at the time of writing this is still common practice in Japan. The final point, and in accordance with strict Weberian principles, the reward for long and loyal service would be a distinctive retirement and pension system. In return for permanency of employment, usually for a lifetime, public servants accepted that they would be neutral, non-partisan and anonymous. For those on the inside, the traditional career service system was comfortable, not too hard and provided a steady career for those of a mind to follow the rules.

There are some advantages to this as a system of personnel administration. It provides a measure of stability for those within the system. It was designed to be non-partisan, while the principles of neutrality and anonymity fitted an administrative or technical view of public service. Appointment at the base grade and steady progression through the hierarchy, even promotion by seniority, should inculcate loyalty to the department and public service, and could reduce office politics. If promotion is by length of service, perhaps staff can work together instead of jockeying for recognition. In Japan, for example, what is termed the 'slow promotion' system routinely rewards all members of an incoming group of college graduates equally for at least ten years after entry.

However, as a system of human resource *management*, there are more problems than benefits in the traditional model. A system characterized by rigid hierarchy is unable to cope with rapid change and could (and did) become self-absorbed and claustrophobic. Personnel management should aim to select, appoint and develop the best available workers for the required tasks. Even though this matching cannot be done perfectly in any system, it would be hard to find an example where these three points were performed in a worse way than the traditional model of administration.

Taking recruits only at the base grade initially aimed at training them for a lifetime of service in an unusual occupation. What it meant in practice was that a cohort group would advance in parallel fashion until the ends of their careers, so that the persistent and unambitious public servants would become departmental heads, and the talented or impatient would leave. Unsatisfactory personnel selection devices such as seniority give the appearance of fairness, when all they really do is to reward the time-servers and punish the able. A system of promotion by seniority is an acknowledgement either that performance cannot be measured or that everyone has equal performance in administrative tasks. Both are damning of the personnel system that produced it – a system that almost guaranteed mediocrity.

The absence of performance measurement can also lead to other personnel problems. A clique of like-minded managers might develop, who then only hire or promote those of their own kind. These might be all males – which was frequently the case in the past – or chosen from a particular religious denomination or social set. Other social groups either found it hard to gain a foothold or to achieve advancement if they did. As with the practice of seniority, a workforce using such practices is unlikely to be a model of efficiency, but with the traditional model of administration such inefficiency could be hidden for many years, all because it was assumed that performance could not be measured.

A particular personnel problem in Britain was the emphasis placed on general ability rather than on specific skills that were deemed to be relevant to government. Even after the reform process was well under way, authority remained with generalist administrators (Zifcak, 1994, p. 166). If the United Kingdom was so anomalous in this regard, it is little wonder that the Thatcher Government began to question the management capabilities of its public service.

In the United States, the civil service system also had major problems in developing a management culture, as argued by Ingraham (1995, pp. 12–13):

> Virtually everything about the civil service system and its concomitant rules and regulations works against the development of a strong managerial culture and strong managers. The wrong incentives are in place and they are in the wrong places. The civil service system was not intended to be a flexible management system; true to its intent it is not.

Personnel systems in the traditional administrative era were obsessed with fairness rather than the ability to achieve a result. It was indeed designed not to be flexible, and that was what was achieved. As Ingraham also argues (1995, p. 11):

> The emphasis on rules and procedures has created an organizational environment in which applying rules and following procedures has been valued more highly than using discretion and flexibility effectively to mobilize resources to achieve organizational objectives. This distinction can be summarized by considering the differences between administration and management. The former describes the neutral civil servant applying the right rule at the right time, but not questioning the rule and certainly not exercising discretion in whether it should be applied. Management, on the other hand, connotes considerable authority, discretion in its use, and accountability for outcomes and product rather than to rules and regulations. Civil service systems generally create administrators, not managers.

It began to be perceived that the personnel system itself did not attract the right people to government service or promote the most able. While it may have bred capable administrators, what was needed was capable managers. The rigidity of the administrative structure makes it difficult to hire the right people as the selection procedures are cumbersome and usually beyond the control of the manager. It is similarly difficult to provide appropriate reward structures or to remove people who are not performing. In addition, the rules inhibit managers' ability to motivate subordinates (Bozeman and Straussman, 1990).

A career service model of personnel, widely used during the period of the traditional model of public administration, had its strengths but also its weaknesses. It was not surprising that doing something about the structures and procedures dealing with the people inside government was an early focus of managerial reform. In the outside world times had changed but inside the civil service there was little difference.

Leadership

One of the aspects of public management reform has been explicitly to seek out and encourage leadership, whereas this was discouraged in the traditional model of administration. Public management requires there to be an individual, a 'named person', who has specific responsibility for the achievement of results. In the strictly bureaucratic model, the only acceptable kind of leadership is that exercised by politicians; the public servants are merely followers, no matter what their level. Once the system changes, the personal qualities of public managers – their leadership skills – necessarily become important in the way that results are achieved. This is in complete contrast to Weberian bureaucracy, which aimed to be quite impersonal. There cannot be much of a role for leadership in a strictly bureaucratic system; indeed, there is not much of a role for any individual, other than to follow the rules impersonally and impartially. But once public managers are made responsible for results, the machine model of bureaucracy – including total impersonality – breaks down; if not immediately, then over time.

One obvious problem with the bureaucratic model is that organizations are made up of people, and people inevitably interact with each other. Impersonality is quite unrealistic. Of course, some traditional public administrators were leaders, and possibly highly effective ones, but leadership was not required by design and, if it did exist, was only an informal factor attached to a formalistic system that set out to remove any vestige of personal management. Traditional administration is really about the exercise of authority rather than leadership.

The emergence of concepts of leadership in the public sector should be seen as a reassertion of individual and personal attributes in management and, as a corollary, a reduction in the emphasis on management by formal rules. A manager must not only deliver, but also persuade subordinates to agree with the general parameters of the vision and to be inspired to achieve in turn, all for the overall benefit of the organization. The staff involved need to achieve and the manager needs to lead them. The delay in considering ideas of leadership was perhaps related to the previously held view that leadership does not have much of a role to play in a formal bureaucratic system (Javidan and Waldman, 2003). The emergence of leadership brings more realism into what actually happens in the workplace, once the decision is taken that managers are required to organize their people to deliver results.

There is no single agreed view about what leadership involves, particularly in a public sector context. Sometimes it refers 'to the possession of personal properties such as courage, stamina, or charisma' and at other times, it means 'a property of a position which dispenses power, authority, and responsibility' (OECD, 2001, p. 11). There are two somewhat contrasting ideas about leadership in this view. The first refers to some personal qualities a leader may possess that enable him or her to stand above others; and the second idea is that leadership is attached to a position. The two views lead to quite different conceptions of what might be involved in leadership in the public sector context. Here they will be used as the two overarching views of leadership in the public sector; the first we can call the 'personal' view of leadership, and the second, the 'positional' view.

Leadership as a personal attribute

Leadership can involve personal attributes; some individuals are regarded as 'leaders' and others are 'followers', with both qualities being almost innate. What Bennis terms 'basic ingredients of leadership' include a guiding vision; passion; integrity; trust; curiosity and daring (1989, pp. 40–1). All these characteristics have a connection to personality, individual thought or behaviour. They are 'personal' qualities, as opposed to attributes that come with position in a hierarchy. It follows that leadership in this sense, almost by definition, is not an attribute that is inherent to many people, just to those lucky few possessing innate qualities that make them leaders in contrast to the mass of followers.

The view of the leader as a person possessing extraordinary authority through personal charisma is associated most closely with the work of Max Weber. As noted earlier (see Chapter 3) Weber argued that charismatic authority was one of the three types of authority, along with traditional and rational/legal authority. Charismatic authority involves the personal qualities of an individual who is then able to lead others by the exercise of these attributes. As Weber described it (Gerth and Mills, 1970, p. 79):

> There is the authority of the extraordinary and personal 'gift of grace' (charisma), the absolutely personal devotion and personal confidence in revelation, heroism, or other qualities of individual leadership. This is 'charismatic' domination, as exercised by the prophet or – in the field of politics – by the elected war lord, the plebiscitarian ruler, the great demagogue, or the political party leader.

The charismatic leader leads and the followers merely follow anywhere the leader takes them, whatever the destination might be. As Weber notes, 'Charisma knows only inner determination and inner restraint. The holder of charisma seizes the task that is adequate for him and demands obedience and a following by virtue of his mission. His success determines whether he finds them' (Gerth and Mills, 1970, p. 246). If success is not found, the authority of the charismatic leader presumably falls away.

Weber recognized that charismatic authority can exist, and leadership can be based on charisma. But it is seen by him as being obsolete, as belonging to an earlier, pre-modern age. Even more than the traditional authority of a tribal chief, charismatic authority is essentially non-rational and cannot last. As Weber argues, 'It is the fate of charisma, whenever it comes into the permanent institutions of a community, to give way to powers of tradition or of rational socialization' (Gerth and Mills, 1970, p. 253). In other words, rational/legal authority – bureaucracy – inevitably takes over.

Weber regarded charismatic and traditional authority as being obsolete, patrimonial and inefficient compared to bureaucracy based on rational-legal authority. The bureaucratic system was set up precisely to avoid charismatic authority, and to replace any kind of personal authority with impersonal rules. To Weber, charismatic authority is temporary and less effective than the rationality to be found in bureaucracy (Gerth and Mills, 1970, p. 246):

> In contrast to any kind of bureaucratic organization of offices, the charismatic structure knows nothing of a form or of an ordered procedure of appointment or dismissal. It knows no regulated 'career', 'advancement', 'salary', or regulated and expert training of the holder of charisma or of his aids. It knows no agency of control or appeal, no local bailiwicks or exclusive functional jurisdictions; nor does it embrace permanent institutions like our bureaucratic 'departments,' which are independent of persons and of purely personal charisma.

In the wider political system, for much of the twentieth century and into the twenty-first, charismatic leadership has been associated with disorder rather than order. And this kind of charisma has usually been seen as something to be avoided by organizations, particularly those in the public sector.

The idea of charisma has made something of a comeback more recently, starting in the private sector. Charisma can be observed in management 'as an attribution made by followers who observe certain behaviors on the part of the leaders within organizational contexts' and this is 'not an attribution made about an individual because of his or her rank in the organization, but rather it is an attribution made because of the behavior he or she exhibits' (Conger and Kanungo, 1987, p. 639). Within government, leadership of this kind may be harder to measure, but clearly, it does exist.

In trying to achieve a result, a manager should be able to use whatever means are available, including leadership based on personal characteristics, personal interaction and personal political behaviour. With hindsight, it was unrealistic for the strict bureaucratic model to be so rigid about lack of personal involvement. Organizations are not inhabited by unthinking robotic beings, and how they relate to each other has an inevitable effect on the achievement of results.

Leadership as a positional attribute

The second view of leadership is that it is based on position within an organization. Achievement through leadership can be found inside organizations without the obvious exercise of personal qualities. A leader may be someone who is in a leadership 'position' rather than a person who is innately suited, through force of personality, to be in the position of leader. In other words, he or she is a leader, not by the innate possession of charisma, but simply because leadership of others is required by the nature of the job currently being undertaken. This kind of leadership is not to be disparaged; indeed, a leader in this sense may well be just as effective as the glowing, charismatic leader.

Heifetz and Laurie (1997) argue that the prevailing notion that 'leadership consists of having a vision and aligning people with that vision is bankrupt because it continues to treat adaptive situations as if they were technical: the authority figure is supposed to divine where the company is going, and people are supposed to follow', adding that leadership 'has to take place every day', that it 'cannot be the responsibility of a few, a rare event, or a once-in-a-lifetime opportunity' (p. 134).

A leader needs to work well with others, particularly in the modern-day public sector. A leader now may attain high levels of emotional intelligence and may also have skills and passions that can influence subordinates, but not necessarily be a leader possessing innately charismatic qualities. A leader may also have technical skills that are able to be learnt; notably in framing a vision or a strategy for the organization to follow, and persuading subordinates to accept the vision and contribute to its realization.

Moreover, changes in management practice have democratized the workplace and point to a flaw in the charismatic view of leadership. The view of the leader-as-dictator, the leader whom everyone else fears, is out of date. It is less acceptable now for authoritarianism to prevail, and such a leader would often be unacceptable to the rest of the staff. The idea of the leader who has all the wisdom for a group and to whom everyone defers does seem somewhat obsolete, as an OECD paper states (2001, p. 43):

> Under the old autocratic model, leaders could expect to solve the problem, announce the decision, and get compliance, based on their authority. But public sector leaders today must gain commitment, not just compliance, and therefore a collaborative style is needed. Leaders now succeed only if they can influence others, and quite often those whose support they need do not report to them.

Leadership should be able to occur without formal authority; indeed, that kind of leadership is much more in tune with an organizational culture that is participative.

There remains the question as to whether leadership in the public sector is largely personal or positional. An OECD report argues that the leadership profile includes: 'focusing on delivery of results, challenging assumptions, being open to learning from the outside, understanding the environment and its impact, thinking and acting strategically, building new patterns and ways of working and developing and communicating a personal vision of change' (OECD, 2005, p. 178). Some of these points are personal, and others may be more positional. The final point – communicating a personal vision of change – is clearly personal, whereas some of the other points could be regarded as being either positional or a combination of the two. A manager must achieve results, but could conceivably do so without any kind of charismatic authority, more as a result of being placed in charge, and that leadership is involved as part of being in charge.

Ingraham (2005) sets out ways that an excellent leader 'drives and supports performance in important ways', including the leader as communicator, the leader as the driver of performance, and as a shaper and reinforcer of performance. She adds that strong leadership in public organizations 'is going to be absolutely fundamental to keeping the future course as steady as possible' and leaders with 'vision, resolve, and frankly, pretty tough skins, will be key ingredients to performance success' (p. 395). These points could refer to either leadership as a personal attribute or leadership as a positional attribute, but the underlying view does seem to lean towards personal attributes such as vision and resolve. Someone in a leadership position may be able to gain the commitment of others based on their authority level, but they are also more likely to be effective if they bring some aspects of personality to that process.

Leadership and management

There may be some debate over the relative importance of leadership and management, as to whether leadership is a different and higher-level function than management. In the private sector literature, Kotter (1990) argues that leadership and management are two distinctive and complementary systems, each having its own functions and its own characteristic activities, but both are necessary for the management of complex organizations. Management is 'about coping with complexity' whereas leadership is 'about coping with change' (p. 104). Management involves planning and budgeting, setting a direction, organizing and staffing, aligning people and by controlling and problem solving, but leadership is about vision, motivation and inspiration – 'keeping people moving in the right direction, despite major obstacles to change, by appealing to basic but often untapped human needs, values, and emotions' (p. 104). For Kotter, management is about systems and processes, but leadership is about vision and coping with change.

In the public sector context, Fairholm (2004) agrees with Kotter in seeing management as being about organizational structures, making transactions and 'ensuring control and prediction', whereas leadership is about change and transformation, 'setting and aligning organizational vision with group action, and ensuring individuals a voice so that they can grow into productive, proactive, and self-led followers' (p. 588). However, the clear separation between management and leadership argued by Kotter and Fairholm may be less relevant in a public context. There are two aspects to this.

The first is that the tasks that Kotter (1990) ascribes to management fit, in the historiography of the public sector, the concept of public administration far more than public management. Kotter's planning and budgeting, setting a direction, organizing and staffing, and the like are similar to 'POSDCORB' – planning, organizing, staffing, directing, co-ordinating, reporting and budgeting (Gulick and Urwick, 1937) as key administrative functions in government. The private sector has no equivalent of a political leader in the person of the minister. In the public sector, there has always been a tension between the administrative and political parts of government. With public sector reform, administrative functions have become management functions, but while management functions may include the administrative and procedural ones listed by Kotter (1990), they also include strategy and other high-level functions reserved for leaders in the private sector.

The second point, and it has been mentioned before, is that leadership in the public sector takes place within parameters, within mandates, in a way that is not usual in the private sector. As Behn (1998b, p. 220) argues:

> I am advocating active, intelligent, enterprising leadership. I am advocating leadership that takes astute initiatives designed to help the agency not only achieve it purposes today but also to create new capacity to achieve its objectives tomorrow. I am advocating a style of leadership that builds both an agency's and its government's reputation for accomplishment and thus competence. Such leadership requires public managers to exercise initiative within the framework provided by their legal mandate.

The legal mandate is quite different from that of the private sector. Leadership occurs in government but it is a constrained kind of leadership as the mandate restricts freedom of action compared to the private sector. Leadership is then not so far away from management in the public sector context. Leadership is similarly flexible, perhaps even more so in the sense that a leader is expected to crash through obstacles, to be innovative, and to take the organization in a new direction.

It could be argued that leadership is a higher-order function than management, and that, in terms of the development of public management, a linear progression can be seen from administration to management and then to leadership. An alternative but equally valid view is that leadership is a part of the function and functionality of management, so that a manager also needs to be a leader. In the governmental context at least, a manager increasingly does need to be a leader. If a manager is to achieve results, s/he needs to exercise leadership. Moreover, the higher a manager rises in an organization, the more that leadership takes over from tasks better described as administration and day-to-day management. At the highest levels, political behaviour, in the broadest sense, and interpersonal relationships become more important in the achievement of results than do technical administrative or management skills.

If there is a big dividing line between the three concepts, it is between administration and management, or between traditional public administration and public management. Traditional public administration tried, at least in the ideal Weberian case, to take any personal dimension away from what a public servant does in practice. The reasoning was laudable, in that an impersonal administration based solely on rules and laws will make the same decision every time. But public administrators are people; they are men and women with personalities and with personal relationships of a kind with one another, and with the politicians and the public that they serve. A public manager has as one of his or her required attributes the ability to work with others in order to achieve results. Accepting the personal responsibility for doing so could be considered as leadership in action; through both personality and position. It may or may not be charismatic leadership, but leadership it is, and its absence makes it that much harder for the organization to achieve its goals.

Management of human resources

Managerial reforms have included significant changes in personnel systems in order to achieve better results. It has become easier to hire the right people, quickly and often with variations to the standard conditions of employment. Often contracts are used that can be of short duration. At the highest levels, it is more common for ministers to appoint their own senior staff, in what may be an extension to other countries of the American system of political appointees to the public service. The reward and incentive structure has changed, with performance pay being common. It is also easier to remove those who are not performing. The public services now cannot afford to have people who are not contributing, but the corollary is that good performers can be identified and rewarded. This means that unsatisfactory personnel devices such as seniority are disappearing, as is the dominance by particular social groups. Some countries have rigorous programmes of affirmative action and, while these have been driven by societal demands, they also have an efficiency aspect given that in the past talented people were excluded.

Ideas for changing personnel systems have been around for some time; indeed, the kinds of reforms eventually carried out had long been on the agenda. The Fulton Report in Britain in the 1960s (Fulton, 1968) recommended that the system be opened up, that outsiders be employed at all levels, and that the rigid hierarchical structure in which barriers were placed at several points be removed. Under the previous system, professional staff could not rise beyond a certain point, but this too was to change.

The Civil Service Reform Act of 1978 in the United States was similarly based on the view that management needed to be improved, and that managers would take greater responsibility for their organizations and their staff. The Act established merit pay and a new Senior Executive Service (SES). This was to be an elite of senior managers who would be appointed to the SES rather than to any specific position, with the aim of allowing a ready transfer between positions. It also introduced performance appraisal and performance pay, both of which have also been implemented in other countries. These represented an attempt to introduce the incentives common in the private sector into the public sector, to provide some tangible reward to the able. The Act also introduced new demotion and dismissal procedures, again with the idea of improving quality.

In general, there has been a move towards breaking down the rigid hierarchical structures and providing flexibility. Rather than secure lifetime employment, more employees at all levels face regular restructuring of their agencies, more movement, more redundancies and less certainty of tenure. Term appointments are likely at lower levels, permanent part-time work and flexible hours are more popular, and the special retirement benefits once enjoyed by public servants have steadily been reduced. More use is made of contracts for short-term employment rather than lifetime employment, and for contracting-out functions and positions once performed inside the system. Employees may no longer have public service conditions of employment. Public servants who assumed they had a steady job for life did find the adjustment difficult. Staff are increasingly recruited at all levels; indeed, base-grade appointment is becoming quite rare in some places. It is more common to recruit graduates rather than those having only a high school level of education. Even department heads may be recruited from outside the organization, including from outside the public sector.

Public sector employment has declined, at least in relative terms, though precise calculation is difficult because of definitions. From 1995 to 2005, the proportion of the labour force employed in the public sector (government and public corporations) declined in 9 of the 11 OECD countries for which data was available, with the Netherlands and Spain being the two exceptions (OECD, 2009, p. 66). Public sector employment in the UK fell from 6.5 million to 4 million between 1979 and 1999, though definitional changes make a strict comparison difficult to make (Greenwood *et al.*, 2002, p. 17).

Changes to human resource management practice were once controversial and resisted by both employees and unions. But at a time when flexibility, a mobile workforce and management by results are common in the private sector, it is difficult for public servants to insist on the personnel practices of a past age. Caiden (1982, p. 183) refers to 'the bulk of public employment where conditions are similar to those obtaining in the private sector' and this is in fact the case. Except, arguably, at the highest levels, most public servants carry out work that is quite similar to that done by office workers in business. Personnel practices peculiar to the public sector were introduced because government work was considered to be quite different; tenure was considered necessary to ensure frank and fearless advice. But the increase in size and function of government has meant that most public servants are engaged in service delivery analogous to that of the private sector, not policy advice, and the case for different standards of employment is less tenable.

It follows that personnel arrangements more like those in the private sector will become commonplace. According to Osborne and Gaebler (1992), public sector experiments have shown the success of 'broad classifications and pay bands; market salaries; performance-based pay; and promotion and lay-offs by performance rather than seniority', and that other important elements of a personnel system could include 'hiring systems that allow managers to hire the most qualified people ... aggressive recruitment of the best people; and streamlining of the appeals process for employees who are fired' (p. 129).

Public services now have better-educated people than they once did. Better methods of management and analysis as well as better recruitment and promotion procedures may make public sector managers more competent, especially when combined with improved use of new technology. The human resources available at the time of writing are certainly better than they were, when it was assumed that public administration required no special competence. Greater flexibility in promotion and improved performance measurement should allow the competent to rise faster. With the demise of the career service model, staff are less likely to spend their entire careers in one agency, or even in public service, but to move between public and private sectors.

For the ambitious and able, public service work is more interesting than it once was. Previously, capable people would often leave their jobs in frustration at the rigidity of the personnel system, and were often unwilling to wait their turn for promotion. Barzelay (1992) comments that public managers can have much more varied roles than previously (p. 132):

> The post-bureaucratic paradigm values argumentation and deliberation about how the roles of public managers should be framed. Informed public managers today understand and appreciate such varied role concepts as exercising leadership, creating an uplifting mission and organizational culture, strategic planning, managing without direct authority, pathfinding, problem-solving, identifying customers, groping along, reflecting-in-action, coaching, structuring incentives, championing products, instilling a commitment to quality, creating a climate for innovation, building teams, redesigning work, investing in people, negotiating mandates, and managing by walking around.

It could be argued that many of these tasks are merely derived from the private sector; that they are fads and are not relevant for government. What is more accurate is that the tasks specified by Barzelay are those of a manager rather than an administrator, with the role of the former being more varied and more interesting.

A public service does two main things. The first is to provide assistance and advice to the political leadership. The second is to deliver services, to implement the legislation that the present government or previous governments have passed. The two can be linked, in that insights found while delivering services can lead to information or anomalies that can be fed back to the political leadership for further attention and subsequent legislation. But conceptually the two are different. The traditional public administration provided for little distinction between them, so that the conditions of employment perhaps needed for the first – to provide frank and fearless advice, for example – required permanent employment and neutrality, aspects that were not really needed for the second service delivery role. They became conditions of employment, often negotiated by unions holding real power to make demands. And because some public servants needed to be permanent in order to remain neutral, it became commonplace in the old model that all public servants needed to be permanent, when this was never necessary.

What managerial reform has done, among other things, is to unpack the various kinds of public service work. The service delivery function is a production function, a management task, and little different from the private sector. There is a logistical task involved in sending out millions of social security payments but one no different in character from a major logistical task in, say, retail marketing. The recognition that service delivery was different from policy advice led to experiments in agencification (Pollitt *et al.*, 2004), in contracts, in using call centres or the like, and even providing government services through the private sector. It also led to the realization that not all public servants need to be permanent, nor is it required for all to have unusual and more generous conditions of service than other comparable jobs in the private sector. Moreover, those parts of the public sector close to the political action – policy positions, heads of agencies and so on – found it difficult to justify permanency when the political leadership did not want it.

Additionally, it was realized that the HRM function needed to be managed actively. Farnham (1999) states there are five key features of contemporary human resource management and employment relations emerging in the public services (p. 127):

> First, the personnel function is attempting to become more strategic than administrative in its tasks, but within resource constraints structured by the state. Second, management styles are tending to shift towards more rationalist, performance-driven ones, away from paternalist, pluralist ones. Third, employment practices are becoming more flexible and less standardized than in the past. Fourth, employment relations are becoming 'dualist', with most non-managerial

staff continuing to have their pay and conditions determined through collective bargaining, whilst public managers are increasingly working under personal contracts of employment. Fifth, the state is moving away from being a 'classical' model employer. In its place, it appears to be depending increasingly on HRM ideas and practices taken from leading-edge private organizations, whilst adapting them to the particular contingencies of the public services.

The organization's overall strategy, and even its very survival, are linked to the competence of key staff. What is often termed strategic human resource management in government seeks to integrate strategy with staffing and links in other areas such as industrial relations, recruitment, training, incentives and performance evaluation.

It would be feasible for an agency to contain only a small number of core officials and have its functions largely contracted out (Davis, 1997). This could be considered to be a return to the elite model proposed by Northcote–Trevelyan or Weber (see Chapter 3), but more likely is further rapid change and even more short-term positions in the public service taken up by managers who are equally comfortable in the public or the private sector. Perhaps there will be a floating population of policy advisers: sometimes in the bureaucracy; sometimes advising politicians; and sometimes working as consultants for one of the big accounting or consulting firms. Permanency and a career may be seen as archaic and not characteristic of many public service staff, who will transfer more readily into and out of the sector rather than being lifetime employees.

The task for public managers is more complex and challenging than it once was. A managerial public service may be more interesting for public servants than was the traditional model. As Caiden argues (1996, pp. 30–1):

> Few would want to return to the passive bureaucracy of the past, its conservatism, adherence to the strict letter of the law, reluctance to depart from precedent, undue weight given to respectability (read good connections), reliability (reputation for avoiding innovation), seniority (length of routine service), and group conformity. Such traits might have suited the tempo of past times but they need to be transformed to meet today's needs and to prepare for tomorrow's surprises.

In the best public services this transformation is indeed happening, and there is certainly no real possibility of returning to the rigidity of the past. But it is also the case that the transition period has been difficult for many public servants. The public sector is a difficult place to work at the best of times. Poor morale may be endemic, or at any rate hard to combat. The public service in future is likely to be much smaller, at least in relative terms, though it will probably have to offer higher salaries to compete for the scarce, competent staff it will need. Such a service might be much better, but trying to improve the perception of outsiders and to recover some respect from the community at large will be much more difficult.

Some problems with the HRM changes

Changes to the personnel system have affected everyone in government agencies. Some have argued that a public service career is not what it was. The notion of career service is disappearing, as is lifetime tenure or the inability to be dismissed. Promotion prospects are less certain, and there has been a bewildering series of reforms affecting morale. There are several points made by critics as to the changes in personnel systems.

Reducing conditions of service

Arguments have been put forward that there is a contradiction in the personnel sense between motivating public employees and reducing their conditions of service (Pollitt and Bouckaert, 2000, pp. 162–3). There is some point to this. At the same time as it is claimed that public sector reform will liberate managers and allow them to take responsibility, tenure is being removed, as are many of the special conditions of service once given to administrators. This means that working for the public sector is 'now less different from working for the private sector, and one should think about the implications of those changes' (Peters, 1996, p. 18). In earlier times, there was an implicit contract where public employees tended to be paid less than in the private sector but could trade this for greater permanency in their employment. Where employment conditions are made more like those in the private sector, the commitment of public employees to public service may well decline. The overall direction of change is 'that of reducing the distinctiveness of the rules governing many public service jobs' (Pollitt and Bouckaert, 2004, p. 80).

Performance management systems

One of the key reforms involving staff has been the introduction of more formalized systems of performance appraisal for individuals. It is incorrect to say that performance appraisal did not exist previously; it is more accurate to say that in earlier times performance appraisal was *ad hoc* rather than systematic. If a public manager is to be responsible for the achievement of results, it follows that what each staff member contributes towards the overall achievement needs to be assessed.

Performance appraisal systems of any kind may not be greatly appreciated by the staff whose performance is to be assessed. Even if the private sector has established ways of measuring individual performance and the public sector has set out to emulate these, it is more difficult to measure the performance of personnel in the public sector. The public sector has also, historically, been somewhat obsessed with the idea of 'fairness' and in setting out procedures and processes that are impartial and transparent. On the other hand, it could be argued that 'fairness' in reward structures is a peculiarly public service view of the world, that the private sector hardly has 'fair' reward structures and that some unfairness may be the price to be paid for greater flexibility.

The review of personal performance can become an instrument of control. Horton (1999) observes that 'civil servants are now more obviously managed, with the personal review acting as an instrument of control, although it is more often presented as an instrument of consultation and individual empowerment' (p. 153). Pollitt and Bouckaert (2000) argue that managers have more freedom but are simultaneously under greater scrutiny (p. 138):

> Beneath the surface, the process of letting – or making – public managers manage has not been so simple. There have been countervailing currents and considerable centralization, partly through the establishment of evermore sophisticated performance indicator and target regimes, underpinned by rapidly advancing information technologies ... Executive politicians have transferred their focus for control from inputs to outputs, via processes. This may account for the somewhat ambiguous responses from public service managers themselves – they have experienced greater freedom to deploy their inputs (e.g., switching money from staff to equipment, or *vice versa)* but at the same time they have felt themselves under closer scrutiny than ever before as far as their results are concerned.

Public managers have greater scope to do things and to achieve results; but with this has come increased attention as to whether results have actually been achieved. By itself this may not be a big problem, but it is very difficult for public managers if they are expected to achieve results while following the same detailed procedures as in the bureaucratic model. Management freedom to act does need to be meaningful, but no one can escape verification after the fact that results have been achieved.

Some kind of performance appraisal is used in all sectors and is accepted by employees as part of what they have to do. It is no longer tenable for public servants to argue that their sector is so special that it should not have formal appraisal.

Performance pay

Another problem has been the idea of providing incentives by means of extra pay. Even if performance pay is a good idea in the abstract, it has been hard to implement in a fair and reasonable way. It could be used to reward favourites and may cause resentment in those who consider themselves worthy of extra reward but get none. Performance pay has generally not worked well, especially when it has been set up within a rigid system of hierarchical levels. Staff may become resentful over not getting performance pay of even very small amounts – as little as 5 per cent of salary, say – as they see the achievement of an award for performance as a signal of their worth. The denying of it or the perception of unfairness in allocation can lead to disengagement.

Problems of morale

The series of unrelenting attacks on government and bureaucracy, followed by a series of bewildering changes including those of performance measurement and personnel changes, has caused problems of morale, notably in the early reform era. Public administration in its Golden Age was a valuable and valued profession, and one with substantial prestige. By the early 1980s, this was no longer the case in many countries, and individual bureaucrats had to cope with antipathy from the citizenry. Some of the morale problems of public servants may be part of a larger problem. Attacks on the bureaucracy, even on government as a whole, might be part of some general disaffection with the idea of politics and government. The lack of regard for the bureaucracy probably did lead to a lack of sympathy from the public about public sector change and made managerial reform easier than it could have been, but probably exacerbated the problem of public service morale.

Demoralized workers are obviously less effective, so improving overall performance means attention must be paid to problems of morale. Pollitt (2001) argues that lower-level staff 'show less enthusiasm for enacted reforms than do the "mandarins" at the top' (pp. 476–7). This should not be a surprise. The old administration was quite comfortable and easy, and a great place to work for those valuing stability. The managerial workplace is more difficult; it is more rewarding for those who are capable, but less comfortable for those looking for an easy life. In this respect it is much more like the private sector. As an OECD paper states (1998a, p. 48):

> Some public servants also profess to be concerned about the disruption that change inevitably brings, and the number and speed of changes. The fact is, however, that the amount of structural adjustment in the public sector is typically no greater than is being experienced elsewhere in the economy, and the pace of change has speeded up everywhere.

There might have been a gradual improvement of morale inside the system as the expectations of workers changed to resemble those of private sector employees. If public servants do not expect to be employed for life, they should have fewer morale problems than those earlier employees who thought they would enjoy lifetime tenure. As the reforms proceeded, expectations of staff did seem to change. This has positive effects in that flexibility in staffing has been the result. Flexibility, however, works both ways. Without an expectation, or even desire, for long-term employment, good staff would stay for a short time and then leave for another job in the private sector or in a different part of government. Perhaps the result of all the changes will be improved quality in the public sector, and this development will satisfy both citizens and public employees. It will be necessary, however, to treat staff as the valuable resources they are. Old-style authoritarianism is most often counterproductive in dealing with good staff, as they will simply leave.

In the abstract, how human resource management is carried out, and who can be hired to do the work at the next level down, should be to the responsibility of the manager to decide. In practice, personnel systems remain highly bureaucratic and with detailed rules that, while they allow more scope for managers than in the administrative model, are a long way from giving the manager a free hand. At the same time, though, public sector organizations have focused much more attention on leadership, on who should become a leader, their scope of action once they have achieved a leadership position, even the idea of embedding leadership throughout an organization and at all levels.

Conclusion

Personnel management has moved some distance away from the methods of the traditional model, where, in the name of equity, personnel procedures almost guaranteed mediocrity. In general, the competence of public servants is high, probably higher than it was previously. Staff are hired with better qualifications and there are now very few hired at the base grade. The jobs themselves are often more interesting and rewarding than they once were. There seem to be sufficient people willing to accept flexibility and who do not value career-length tenure as much as they did previously. There is more monitoring in the sense of performance appraisal systems, but good staff accept the need to show achievement.

Even if there were problems in setting up new systems, the direction of human resource management in government is quite clear. Since the 1980s there has been an inexorable movement towards the terms and conditions of employment in the private sector rather than seeing public employment as being axiomatically different. If certain changes encounter difficulties, they will be superseded by further changes in the same direction, rather than going back. Second, comparisons should not look at how well the reforms work in the abstract, but rather how well they compare with what went before. In this regard, all the changes mentioned here are far better than those that existed under the traditional model of administration. In that model, there were systems of personnel management but these were of rather dubious quality.

The most fundamental capability of any organization is that held by its people. It could be argued that a public manager must do more than carry out the requirements laid down in the legal mandate, as no matter how carefully legislation is drafted there is always room for individual judgement and leadership of others. The administrative model was clearly inadequate in this regard, as any possibility of individual discretion or scope was removed as completely as possible. Taking personality out of the management of government was always completely unrealistic as it is, and always was, people with personalities who did the work and interacted with one another.

It is increasingly clear that highly successful managers in the public sector operate in ways that are sometimes outside the formal management structures and procedures. Only by including some aspects of charismatic authority, including ideas of leadership, can this be understood. A leader may well have charismatic qualities that allow him or her to progress to high positions, but equally someone who is placed in a high position may have to develop leadership skills by virtue of being in a job where leadership is required.

The administration of government was always in the hands of people, but the systems that were commonplace in the traditional model were set up almost to perpetuate a system where those who were mediocre rose to the top and talented employees would leave. This is no longer the case. With the breaking down of the hierarchy often seen as being advantageous for an organization, leadership can be demonstrated merely by being able to get people working together without a hierarchy, and without authority needing to be exercised.

It is a fundamental role of any leader, and any manager, to find, train, nurture and promote the next generation of managers and leaders. While no personnel management system can do all these things perfectly, it is not hard to make the case that the traditional model of administration did none of them well. Public management does at least allow the possibility of improvement in this most important function.

Chapter 12

Financial and Performance Management

Chapter Contents

- Introduction
- The government budget
- Traditional financial management
- Financial management reform
- Performance management
- Some criticisms of financial and performance management
- Problems with the accounting changes
- Conclusion

Introduction

Financial management is central to the very operation of government. Any governmental activity needs money in order to operate; indeed, the ability to raise taxation and spend it is a factor that sets the institution of government apart from other parts of society. There are very few parts of governmental activity not reliant in some degree on money extracted from taxpayers and used for public purposes. Raising and spending money are not narrow, technical operations. The ability to use resources determines the very nature and extent of government activity, as well as the winners and losers in the political competition for financial favours. A party or group elected to govern has access to the government's taxation revenues to spend, while a loser in the election does not. With increased pressure to provide services and to contain or reduce its costs, the budgetary process is even more of a battleground, one in which different parts of the bureaucracy compete no less than in the community at large. A reality of government is that there is always an internal political game for resources, played by agencies as advocates and moderators of political demands, which can be just as intense as party politics.

Budgeting has become linked more closely with agency and programme performance. Even if some kind of expectation of performance was present in the traditional administrative model, it did tend to be

250

rather unsystematic. With managerial reform, performance management was used increasingly and with explicit links being made to the financial management system in what became known as performance budgeting. Agencies would enter into a bargain where money was allocated through the budget to carry out particular activities, but with conditions set in terms of expectations of delivery. If those expectations were met, then the manager had delivered on what was promised. The undeniable need to account for performance arguably went too far. Performance indicators were developed at all levels, measuring – variously – targets, outputs, outcomes, staffing, indeed almost anything that could be measured. In theory, the system worked well, but the reality was often some distance from the theory. Measuring performance was good practice, but a bewildering array of indicators may well have obscured whether anything real had been achieved. Performance measures in some places did lead to management by arbitrary target, where a target would be set but without any obvious way of reaching it. Measuring performance is a fundamental part of allowing managers to manage, but this kind of reform did not proceed smoothly and did alienate some public servants as well as some elements of the public. However, despite difficulties in implementation, there had still been a substantial advance from the rather primitive financial and performance management found in the traditional model of administration.

Reforms to financial management have been one of the key aspects of overall public sector reform. Financial management is now closely related to performance management; indeed, the budget process is sometimes referred to as performance budgeting (OECD, 2007). The early reforms often appeared under a broader strategy, such as the Financial Management Initiative (FMI) in the United Kingdom in 1982, or the Financial Management Improvement Programme (FMIP) in Australia (see Zifcak, 1994).

Financial management reforms have generally worked well, even if they have not necessarily worked perfectly. For all the issues that have arisen with accrual accounting, performance indicators, programme budgeting and so on, what they have done is to provide far more information for decision-makers about the short- and long-term consequences of budgetary decisions.

The government budget

The government budget is the centrepiece of government financial management and the locus of activity for the bureaucracy as a whole. In this one document the estimates, revenues and expenditures for the budget sector of the government – excluding government trading enterprises and some capital transactions – are set out in the form of accounts. Budgets have several functions, ranging from the simple recording of government financial transactions to a major role in determining the health of the entire economy.

In the simplistic, 'most literal sense, a budget is a document, containing words and figures, which proposes expenditures for certain items and purposes' (Wildavsky, 1979, p. 1). However, any budget is much more than this, as Wildavsky continues (p. 2):

> In the most general definition budgeting is concerned with the translation of financial resources into human purposes. A budget, therefore, may be characterized as a series of goals with price tags attached. Since funds are limited and have to be divided in one way or another, the budget becomes a mechanism for making choices among alternative expenditures.

By allocating money for some purposes rather than others, the government may alter the very shape of the society. As demands for government spending are always far greater than its capacity to pay for them, there must be some way of deciding between those who will be favoured in terms of financial resources and those who will not. The process is innately political. There may be technical ways of deciding where to locate, say, a new hospital, but there is no technical way of choosing between a hospital and a school, or between a school and a road. Governments must in some way reconcile funding between quite diverse and competing political demands. At the highest level of government, the only way of deciding who is to be favoured by spending, or penalized by particular forms of taxation, is through the imperfect, sometimes irrational, method of political bargaining. Therefore, the budget must ultimately be a political document and procedures must allow for this reality.

For convenience, it is customary to divide budget functions into two parts: economic and financial (Musgrave and Musgrave, 1989), which will be discussed below.

Economic functions of the budget

Economic functions are concerned with how the government, through the budget, influences the entire economy. A government tries to achieve a great deal with its overall financial management, so what inevitably results is a compromise between conflicting aims. Through its budget, a government tries to do many things: to set the level of public activity in the economy; to put in place a reasonable distribution of income and wealth; and to provide some control of the overall level of economic activity. These are usually described as policies for *allocation*, *distribution* and *stabilization*. A further indication of the innate compromise in a budget is that these economic functions can at times conflict with each other.

Allocation policy

This aspect concerns the relative size of the public and private sectors and who does what. In other words, the budget sets out both the overall level of government activity and specifies which activities are to be carried out publicly rather than privately. Both government expenditure and taxation policies influence the allocation and distribution of resources in the private sector. For example, a decision to raise public expenditure on road construction will have widespread effects on the private sector by directing benefits to contractors, concrete manufacturers and their employees. Also, a tax applied to a particular good in the private economy is likely to affect its consumption and thus also its levels of employment and profitability.

Arguments about the size of government are really about the system of allocation. The view that government spending and taxation consume too high a proportion of economic activity suggests there might be a distribution between sectors that is better than the present one. When a government controls a large proportion of economic activity, shifts in its spending have a substantial effect on the private economy. However, there is really no *a priori* or explicitly rational level of government spending and taxation that all citizens accept as being fair and reasonable. All a government can do is to compare intuitively the electoral costs of imposing particular levels of taxation with the electoral benefits of expenditure, as well as the flow-on effects from any budgetary change.

Distribution policy

Governments attempt to redress to some degree the inequalities in wealth and income between citizens. This is typically done by assisting those with lower incomes with payments, in part derived from taxing higher-income earners. The major part of distribution policy is the provision of social welfare, including transfer payments to certain classes of citizens, but all other budgetary decisions have some distributional consequences. A tax benefit given to a particular group, such as farmers, is distributional in exactly the same way as are direct payments for social security. As with allocational decisions, the level of transfer payments and the effects on particular groups cannot be determined technically. As Musgrave and Musgrave (1989) state: 'the answer to the question of fair distribution involves considerations of social philosophy and value judgment' (p. 10). In other words, there is no technical solution; rather, one of political preference. Some on the Right even argue that a fairer distribution necessarily leads to a poorer economy by reducing profitability and investment. In practice, as there is no agreement on what a desirable distribution between sectors or income groups should be, arguments about 'fairness' in distribution are inherently controversial and perennial matters of political debate.

Stabilization policy

This is where the government aims to improve the overall economy through budgetary policy. It is probably the most difficult of the economic functions of the budget. All government spending and taxation decisions have marked effects on the private sector, so, by varying these policies and their aggregate levels, an attempt can be made to influence the entire economy. After 1945, with the widespread use of Keynesian economics, Western governments explicitly accepted responsibility for promoting full employment, price stability, economic growth and a stable balance of payments. They try to do this, to some extent at least, by using the government budget to achieve these outcomes.

Government fiscal policy is important for providing stability for the economy. While spending and taxation have economic effects of their own, the net balance between them – the deficit or surplus – is of major importance. Keynesian economic theory argues that, if the budget is in deficit – expenditure is greater than revenue – the whole economy can be stimulated by a multiplier of the budget deficit. If the economy is overheated, then the government can, in theory, budget for a surplus to slow the economy. The budget balance can also affect the net debt position of the government, and can cause reactions in the private sector, especially in financial markets.

From the 1970s there was something of a change in the intellectual respectability of the Keynesian model. Relying on the government budget to manage the economy originally represented an economic revolution in that budgets did not have to be balanced every year. By varying its budget balance a government could, in theory, ameliorate the damaging affects of the boom and bust business cycle. The Keynesian model promised much and was successful for some time, but the coincidence of high inflation and high unemployment in the mid-1970s produced a reassessment. The orthodoxy became that of 'neoclassicism', with the emphasis being placed on reducing government, balancing the budget and letting market forces find a desirable economic equilibrium. When the global financial crisis (GFC) hit in 2008, governments in many countries were forced to return to Keynesian prescriptions to prevent a downward spiral in their economics, and they ran up large budget deficits. For the most part, this did prevent the crisis becoming even worse, but it imposed a debt problem that will take many years to recover to more normal levels.

Financial functions of the budget

Accounting for revenue and expenditure is the second of the key functions of the budget. Balance sheets need to be drawn up for the whole of government activity, in exactly the same way as in the private sector. The financial functions of the budget are: first, an evaluation of total government and public authority expenditures within the budget sector; and, second, to act as the legislature's instrument of accountability and control over the government in its handling of financial matters. The first of these is a pure accounting function to set out estimates of receipts and expenditures, while the second is an important part of the system of accountability.

From its earliest days, the most important role of the legislature has involved government finance. Through a process beginning with Magna Carta in 1215, the English Crown agreed to consult the nobles when taxation was contemplated. A long struggle between the English Crown and Parliament gradually led to the latter's approval being necessary when taxation was raised, and the spending of it was in turn required to be reported back to Parliament. Even now, Budget Day is traditionally the most important day of the British parliamentary calendar. Other countries, particularly those with a British heritage, have a similar financial reliance on the legislature. A United States president must obtain Congressional approval for spending and has a limited veto over Congressional spending.

The financial part of the budget is where the accounts of the government are reconciled, and where revenue and expenditure items are set out for public scrutiny. The main steps in budgeting are: *formulation* – where the budget is drawn up; *authorization* – the formal approval by the legislature; *execution* – where it is carried out; and *appraisal* – an assessment of how it performed. The budget involves legislation; any government spending or taxation measures must be firmly based in law.

There are significant differences between countries: in the United Kingdom and other parliamentary countries, the government is firmly in control of its financial resources; it can dominate all four budgeting steps, with almost total control of the first three. This is not the case in the United States. The greater degree of separation of the powers – legislature, executive and judiciary – means that, while the president can propose a budget, the Congress is not obliged to accept any part of it. Congress can also pass its own budget measures, something unknown in Westminster systems, where, by convention, only the government can initiate spending measures. The long period of very large United States government budget deficits after the 1980s was in large part caused by the government not being able to control its budget, and a breakdown in the system of compromises between Congress and the

White House. The entire Federal government sometimes closed down for several weeks, such as in 1995, when no agreement was reached on the budget and, as civil servants cannot be paid without authorization from Congress, they could not work. Even if such an event is rare in the United States, it points to a key difference with parliamentary systems, where a government that could not pass its budget would have to resign.

Traditional financial management

The traditional model of administration had its own form of financial management, one ideally suited to an administrative view of government. There are several main features of the traditional budget, also called the *line-item* or *input* budget. First, money is allocated to particular items or types of expenditure that are the major inputs to the task of administration. These typically include money for staff, equipment, postage and all incidental items used to run the department. Second, the budget contains a comparison between income and expenditure for the previous financial year. A typical line-item budget is only for one year in advance, but with some cursory comparison with the year before. Third, there is a marked tendency for the budget for the forthcoming financial year to be based solely on the record of the previous one. This is *incremental* budgeting; that is, the budget represents a series of incremental increases on the previous year, usually to allow for inflation.

The line-item budget does have some points in its favour. It is a good *control* mechanism, though it is difficult to transfer spending between items, and managers have little flexibility. As Wilenski (1982, pp. 168–9) points out, the traditional budget is:

> First, an ideal mechanism to limit expenditure to the amounts and to the items voted in the appropriations. Secondly, it provides a certain degree of flexibility if across-the-board cuts have to be made mid-year for macro-economic purposes. Third, the traditional budget makes budgeting easier and more manageable: arguing from a historical base is easier than having to justify each item from scratch; choice is routinised, conflict about objectives and methods of achieving them, which might otherwise reach unmanageable proportions, is strictly limited so that the budget is in fact prepared in time. Finally, supporters of the traditional budget claim that it is adaptable to all economic circumstances and conditions.

The system is conducive to a meticulous form of financial supervision, in that it can easily be seen whether money was spent on the items for which it was voted. It also fits in well with an annual budget cycle, where agencies are asked to compare their actual expenditure with the amount allocated, and then to make estimates as to what those items and additional ones will cost in the forthcoming year. Across-the-board cuts can be made quite readily, such as, for example, by issuing an edict to cut all travel costs by, say, 10 per cent. There is even some advantage to incremental budgeting, in that the funding for the following year starts with a base in the current year, reducing most argument to major budgetary changes only.

However, the advantages of line-item budgeting are insufficient to outweigh its faults. The smallest amount of government expenditure may be accounted for in the traditional budget, but by itself this kind of retrospective control does nothing to improve *managerial* efficiency. Managers may be too concerned with demonstrating that they have spent the money 'correctly', or have spent exactly the monies allocated, irrespective of whether their expenditure was either efficient or achieved its purposes, whatever they might have been.

There are several problems with line-item budgeting. First, it is not clear from budget figures what departments or agencies actually do, or whether they do it well; that is, the system stresses *inputs* rather than *outputs*. There is no necessary relationship between input costs and the achievement of any goals, as inputs and performance are not related in any documentation. Second, line-item budgeting is quite short-term, usually for only one year in duration. This means that items of long-term budgeting tend to continue unchanged and are not considered in any detail. Instead of spending being decided on a basis of assessed need, it tends to be carried out incrementally, with inadequate critical appraisal. With such a short-term view of the budget there is often no idea of the future cost of new programmes into a second, third or even a tenth year. Third, the specific items of expenditure within a budget are quite rigid in that managers have little flexibility in moving resources from one kind of spending to another. If amounts are allocated to particular inputs they are invariably spent, otherwise the budget for the following year might be reduced. Departments may employ extra staff, or spend money on items that are unnecessary, just to use up the allocation. Even if expenditure on a particular item is no longer needed as the budget year progresses, there is still a tendency to spend the money, for fear of a reduced allocation in the following year. Finally, the paucity of information in the traditional budget means that politicians have only a limited ability to make major changes, and only limited data linking costs to achievements. Neither political leaders nor the public have any satisfactory way of judging whether taxpayers' money is serving desired ends, or is doing so efficiently or effectively. As a result of these various flaws, there have been substantial changes to the system of financial control as part of wider public sector reform.

Financial management reform

As noted earlier, the traditional budget makes no express link between the allocation of money and performance. As this is its main failing, it seems an obvious reform to link the budget in some way with outputs and performance. The deficiencies of the line-item budget led to demands for better forms of budgeting, mainly by governments arguing that the traditional method of budgeting did not provide enough information for decision-making purposes.

The early years of financial reform were not encouraging. As far back as the Hoover Commission in the United States (1949), performance budgeting was advocated for the military. It failed there, as did other attempts in the 1950s. The comprehensive 'planning, programming, budgeting' (PPB) system was introduced into the US Defense Department in 1961 and extended to other federal agencies by President Johnson in 1965. The initiative did not survive the Nixon Administration and, by 1971, 'PPB as a major budget system and even as an acronym was allowed to die a quiet death', with the main reasons for its failure being (Lee and Johnson, 1989, p. 84):

> The lack of the leadership's understanding of and commitment to using programme budgeting tended to deter success, as did an agency's general 'underdevelopment' in the use of analytic techniques. Agencies administering 'soft' social programmes had difficulty devising useful programme measures. Bureaucratic infighting also reduced the chances of successful implementation.

The demise of PPB is sometimes used as an argument against any comprehensive financial management system, though it was probably a heroic effort and unrealistic to introduce such a reform without the requisite information systems.

Another attempt at more rational budgeting was that of 'zero-based budgeting' (ZBB), introduced by the United States Department of Agriculture in 1962. The basic idea is that no assumption should be made that future spending is related to past spending, so that the department or agency must justify its *entire* budget each year. On becoming president in 1977, Jimmy Carter mandated ZBB for all federal agencies, but in fact ZBB was never applied as expected as a comprehensive management approach. It did not revolutionize budgeting approaches and was abandoned by the Reagan Administration in 1981. The main reasons for its failure were the waste of administrative time in producing massive amounts of documentation to justify the total budget, and the practical political problems of cutting programmes.

More recent public management changes have included a series of adjustments to government finance, which are, collectively, far more than was attempted in earlier financial reforms. Box 12.1 sets out a comprehensive set of these financial changes. Some of them are not just

---

> ## Box 12.1   Public financial management reform
>
> 1. Improvement in financial reporting systems, including accrual-based financial statements following recognized accounting standards.
> 2. Measurement of performance through performance indicators, benchmarking and other means.
> 3. A market-based management system with the pricing and provision of public services based on normal commercial criteria.
> 4. Devolution of budgets to operating areas.
> 5. More systematic and detailed auditing of past performance.

financial reforms, and overlap with other reforms. The main reforms will be considered separately.

Financial reporting by performance

As the name suggests, performance budgeting is about bringing performance information into the budget process; it is 'a form of budgeting that relates funds allocated to measurable results' (OECD, 2005). In the early 1990s, governments tried to regain some control over their budgeting process in a way that was different from the PPB-type reforms of an earlier generation, which were mainly about policy planning and analysis of programmes. The more recent reforms are management oriented and focus on what organizations do and produce, and on the means for holding them accountable for performance.

Programme budgeting aims to direct funding more towards the achievement of actual policy objectives or outputs. Government activities are divided into the hierarchical structure of programmes, sub-programmes, activities and components (if necessary). Appropriations can then be made to particular programmes according to the priorities of the government of the day. Instead of funding *inputs* to the administrative process, as in the traditional budget (salaries, overtime, postage and so on), identifiable *programmes* are funded. Management reporting systems can then be based on the programme structure to encourage better feedback on programme performance, and allow, in principle, for the evaluation of the effectiveness of managers and staff. This, or the extension of programme budgeting to funding outcomes, depends on the establishment of suitable performance indicators. The proper development of objectives, programme structures and performance indicators is a difficult and time-consuming task for all levels in an organization, but it is a logical extension of the change from government administration to government management.

There are several advantages in the programme budgeting approach over the traditional, line-item approach. First, it allows for a better allocation of resources. The political leadership can to some extent reassert its control over budgeting; budget choices should be able to be made more explicitly by politicians in terms of national objectives. Under the old system, there was insufficient knowledge of what had actually been achieved, as the allocation of financial resources was not related to the work done or to any particular goal. Second, forward planning is enhanced. Programme costs may be extrapolated for some years ahead, which can enable a clearer appreciation of the ongoing cost of pursuing government objectives. Under a one-year system, it may be tempting to undertake new expenditure for political reasons, without worrying too much about longer-term costs. Third, better management practices can be expected, arising from the comparisons of objectives with achievements, not only financial, but also other measures of performance that go with them. Finally, budgets are public documents in which the government accounts for the money advanced to it by taxpayers. Presenting information in a programme form and relating objectives to performance and resources used can improve the link between government and the public. This should also assist in improving the accountability of the government in general, and the public services in particular.

Another important budgeting change involves the preparation of detailed budget estimates for multiple years rather than the more usual single year. This is another generally successful reform. In Australia, for example, forward estimates have been prepared since 1972; since 1983, their format has been greatly improved, and published in time to assist the following year's budgetary process. Forward estimates provide the government and the public with information on the level and composition of spending over the following three years, and with quite comprehensive forecasts of spending and revenue beyond that. Rather than comprising 'wish lists' from departments, they now represent a realistic assessment of government spending, both overall and on particular programmes, that will occur in the absence of policy changes. This enables the long-term costs of programmes to be estimated more efficiently. The longer-term perspective has been extended even further, through intergenerational reports that project programme costs for up to 40 years, assuming that there will be no policy changes.

Accounting reforms

Traditional budgeting is based on cash; that is, revenue received and outlays paid out in the one year. What is termed 'accrual accounting' is more sophisticated as it includes the value of assets in a more comprehensive way. Its major objective is to compare the total of economic costs incurred during a reporting period against the total economic benefit accrued in that period. In other words, the value of assets is included as well as their depreciation, so that a more complete picture of the government's financial position is known in a way similar to the situation in the private sector. There follows a more meaningful comparison of financial inputs to policy outcomes, Accountability is to be improved through the incorporation of performance measures, and there is the opportunity to predict and monitor longer-term impacts of government decisions.

Accrual accounting was implemented as early as 1992 in New Zealand, but it was only during the late 1990s that other jurisdictions tried it. In Australia, the federal government started using it in 1999–2000 as did the state governments at around the same time (Carlin and Guthrie, 2001). The United Kingdom adopted the system in 2000. An OECD paper declares that there are necessary conditions for it to work (1997, p. 25):

> Two conditions must prevail for accrual accounting to be more than a bookkeeping exercise: managers must have genuine choice in deciding whether to bear the costs; and the costs they are charged must have an impact on the financial resources available to them ... The second condition is that costs affect the resources available to the agency. If an agency were charged for depreciation, this cost should reduce the resources otherwise available for operations.

Accrual accounting requires that the full costs be charged to operating units, including accommodation and assets used, in other words, the full economic cost of operating that unit. In principle, accrual accounting would by itself drive substantial reform; as Kettl (2005) notes, 'accrual accounting, especially in the Westminster countries, has been an important tool in making government more transparent' (p. 46). However, accrual accounting is difficult to bring about and, if implemented badly, could impose a similar rigidity to that of the traditional model. It does, however, offer an improved accounting system to go along with other parts of public management, though there are real difficulties in implementation (Guthrie *et al.*, 2005).

Another aspect of accounting is the more intense use of auditing than was previously the case. Public sector auditing once concentrated on financial probity by managers, rather than whether a programme or agency was serving any useful function. Performance auditing can address this by making an assessment of programme outcome as well as financial probity.

Devolution of budgets

There is also a shift away from detailed regulations and compliance management towards giving individual managers greater control over their own budgets as part of their overall responsibility to achieve results. Instead of the allocation of photocopiers across branches, for example, being decided centrally, it becomes the responsibility of a line manager to decide if that section wishes to buy a photocopier or a computer, or use the money for a completely unrelated purpose. In principle, a one-line budget could be given to a particular manager to then manage the resources as s/he chose. As Thompson (1997, p. 6) observes:

> In the private sector, operating budgets are primarily a means of motivating managers to serve the policies and purposes of the organization to which they belong. Budgets convert an organization's commitments into terms that correspond to the sphere of responsibility of administrative units and their managers and provide a basis for monitoring operations, evaluating performance, and rewarding managers.

A similar principle can be applied to government. A manager needs to produce results, and the budget is the main resource allowing this to be done. This has generally worked quite well. In principle, the devolution of real budget authority to managers is inarguable; in practice, however, it has not been so easy for central agencies to let the manager manage and devolve budget authority as completely as might be desired. Common reforms include provision for any savings realized to remain with the spending agencies and not automatically be re-appropriated by the central budget office.

In general, the financial reforms aim to make the public sector more like the private sector in terms of how it deals with money. As Kamarck (2000, pp. 246–7) asserts:

> Performance-based budgeting, the use of new accounting systems, and the general interest in accountability exhibited by some of these reform movements are part and parcel of an effort to bring the public sector's financial management more in line with commonly accepted practices in the private sector. Like civil service reform, many of the experiments in financial management reform seek to close the gap between the public and the private sector.

It could be argued that private sector financial management has its own problems and should not be used as a model. However, it is still more rigorous than the public sector was under the traditional model of public administration. Financial management is concerned most of all with providing information to enable decisions to be made. The newer forms of financial management do this rather better. Governments may still make decisions for political reasons, but will be informed of the actual cost and over a longer period of time than the single year of the traditional model.

Performance management

When public managers are themselves personally accountable for the achievement of results, it follows that there needs to be some kind of assessment to decide whether results have been achieved. By any standard, performance management in the traditional model of administration was inadequate, and this applies to both the performance of individuals and the organization itself. Measures that did exist were *ad hoc* and far from systematic. There are difficulties in measuring performance in the public sector compared to the private sector, but it seemed that little effort was being made. Perhaps it was assumed that results would follow from bureaucratic organization, so that any explicit measures were unnecessary. There was often no idea what was produced, how well it was produced, who was to take the praise or blame, or even who was a good worker. In any case, an administrator does not need to worry about performance as all s/he is doing is carrying out instructions, and performance measurement is the problem of those giving the instructions. Evaluation of programmes or people was infrequent and inadequate, with no idea of progress towards objectives, if indeed there were any clear objectives. Monitoring performance was particularly weak in the traditional model, and other internal management components, notably the budget, were aimed at monitoring inputs and not outputs or the performance of objectives.

Reforms to performance management are a particularly important part of managerial reform. Indeed, Kettl (2005) argues that public sector reforms 'converge remarkably on a single driving theme: measuring performance, especially program outcomes' (p. vii). Agencies are now expected to develop 'performance indicators'; that is, some way of measuring the progress the organization has made towards achieving declared objectives. Statistical measures can be developed in any organization, though there are more difficulties in practice in the public sector than are usually experienced in the private sector. Performance of staff is also measured more systematically than before. The performance appraisal system aims to measure the performance of individual staff, even to the extent of defining the key contributions expected over the year, which are then compared with actual achievement at the end of the year. This can extend to rewarding or sanctioning staff according to progress towards agreed objectives. Informal methods of appraisal are considered to be ineffective and lead to inferior organizational outcomes. There is a general aim to monitor and improve the progress of staff and agencies towards achieving objectives.

As noted earlier in the chapter, one of the starting points in performance management was the Financial Management Initiative (FMI) in the United Kingdom that aimed at promoting in each department (UK Treasury and Civil Service Committee, 1982):

An organization and a system in which managers at all levels have:

- a clear view of their objectives; and means to assess, and wherever possible, measure, outputs or performance in relation to those objectives;
- well-defined responsibility for making the best use of their resources, including a critical scrutiny of output and value for money; and
- the information (particularly about costs), the training and the access to expert advice which they need to exercise their responsibilities effectively.

In the FMI, financial management, performance and personnel management were linked by the FMI into a new system that involved the specification of objectives for all government policies and for individual units within the bureaucracy; precise allocation of costs to activities and programmes; and 'the development of performance indicators and output measures which can be used to assess success in achieving objectives' (Carter *et al.*, 1992, p. 5).

Performance indicators became a new movement within the public services. Indicators were established for all kinds of activities. Indeed, in some offices, a bewildering number of them were used – often far too many. However, if central government 'is to maintain control over the implementation of policies while at the same time decentralising day to day responsibility, the performance indicators become an essential tool: it is necessary to centralise knowledge about key aspects of performance in order to be able to decentralise activity' (Carter *et al.*, 1992, p. 179).

Further reforms in the UK led to the adoption of Public Service Agreements (PSAs) in 1998. These were based on four principles of public service performance:

- Clear, outcome-focused national goals, set by the government.
- Devolution of responsibility to public service providers themselves, with maximum local flexibility and discretion to innovate, and incentives to ensure that the needs of local communities are met.
- Independent and effective arrangements for audit and inspection to improve accountability.
- Transparency about what is being achieved, with better information about performance, both locally and nationally. (OECD, 2007)

Performance indicators are open to criticism for trying to specify the unspecifiable, given the inherent difficulties of measuring performance in the public sector. Managers will argue that the benefits brought by their particular organization cannot be quantified, or that empirical measurement distorts what it does by focusing only on those things that can be quantified and are able to be processed by the information system (Bellamy and Taylor, 1998). This may be a danger, but can be overcome by setting measures directly related to the organization's overall success. Also, once objectives are set they should not be irrevocable, but be useful, parsimonious and easily understood.

Having such measures is necessary to be able to judge the manager's achievement of results, as is characteristic of public management, even though there are limitations as to how far this can be extended. There are difficulties in measuring performance, and these are greater in the public sector, but this does not mean that no attempt should be made. The original idea of the managerial reformers was to provide some surrogate measure for the use of profit and other measures in the private sector. Without some attempt at measuring performance, the other aspects of the managerial programme will not work. It is important, however, that performance measures be developed for the specific needs of the public sector (see Talbot, 1999). There is much more in the literature about criteria for good performance indicators. They should be: sensitive to change; precisely defined; understandable by users; documented in the sense of being recorded; relevant; timely; feasible; and comply with co-ordinated data processes and definition (Van Dooren *et al.*, 2010, pp. 60–1).

However, even if it is unlikely that any single performance measure will be as useful as the final determination of profit is in the private sector, there are several reasons why performance measures will continue to be used in government. First, while some public servants may see the use of indicators as a threat, they can provide an opportunity by pointing to good practices and good performance, both of which may be rewarded. Second, as any public activity is under threat of being cut or removed completely in the economic climate at the time of writing, a function or position in which measures of performance are inadequate is much more vulnerable. Every agency needs to be able to demonstrate some 'public value' (Moore, 1995). Third, there is little point in setting clear objectives, or funding programmes accordingly, unless there is some means by which progress towards objectives can be monitored. There has been so much capital invested in these other changes that performance measures will be insisted upon.

There are many reasons to measure performance. Behn (2003) finds eight primary purposes: to evaluate, to control, to budget, to motivate, to promote, to celebrate, to learn and to improve, and adds, 'the public manager's real purpose – indeed the only real purpose – is to improve performance' with the other points 'simply means for achieving this ultimate purpose' (p. 588). Performance management is now more often considered to be a part of financial management rather than a completely separate exercise. Agencies are given specified tasks to carry out, along with the budget and performance measures to ascertain whether the task has achieved its aims.

Some criticisms of financial and performance management

The financial and performance changes were controversial, though with lengthy experience now, they can no longer be claimed to be novel. In some countries, the financial and performance reforms have become so embedded in government activity that a critique of them can seem anachronistic. Despite the widespread adoption of programme budgeting, for example, there are still criticisms that the old-style budget was better. And as far as performance management is concerned, it would only be a very long-serving public servant who would have any memory of a time before performance appraisal and indicators.

Budget reform

The most prominent critic of programme budgeting was Wildavsky (1979), notably in reference to the PPB reforms of the 1960s in the United States, discussed above. For Wildavsky, programme budgeting has failed 'everywhere and at all times' (p. 198). His general argument is that programme budgeting is an attempt to impose rationality on what is basically an irrational (or highly political) process. Yet his criticisms may not be as universal as he has suggested. They greatly overstate what programme budgeting can actually do, because, as pointed out earlier, the final budget decisions are necessarily political, in that choices must be made between totally dissimilar activities. Programme budgeting, at least as it is now being implemented, simply provides far more *information* for the politicians who finally make the decisions. At the point of decision, their choices may still be irrational, though more information obviously helps decision-making. Also, Wildavsky's criticism of PPB is likely to be far more applicable to the United States – where budgetary responsibility is diffuse or evaded totally – than to parliamentary systems, where the executive has a more complete control over its budget. Results in parliamentary countries point to more success than might be suggested by American experiences in the 1960s and 1970s. Programme budgeting does require considerably more information about the activities of the agencies than is required for traditional line-item budgeting, so it is not easy to implement. But even if there are difficulties in its implementation, programme budgeting offers far better information on which to base budgetary decisions.

Traditional budgeting was characterized by incrementalism, with some theorists (such as Wildavsky, 1979) arguing that this was beneficial. Complete rationality in budgeting would require the listing of all the ways in which money could be spent, enumerating the advantages and disadvantages of each, and then selecting the highest-ranking preferences and funding them accordingly. No government could conceivably do this, for two reasons. First, budgeting in a democracy is, and must be, a political rather than a technical process, which means that a completely technical system such as PPB would probably fail. Second, budgeting is necessarily composed of commitments, such as social security entitlements, which cannot be changed rapidly. The amount of ongoing commitment in any budget is variously estimated at around 90 per cent or 95 per cent of total spending. Accordingly, any policy change is likely to involve small shifts, characteristic of incrementalism.

In practice, the performance-based budget may be more limited than it appears. In principle, the budget becomes more rational but in practice there may be a façade of reform, behind which the old form of incrementalism survives. While being far from ideal, a budget process that is not completely mechanistic is more realistic in an innately political environment. Incremental budgeting could be considered, above all, as a response to inadequate information, so that, if better information is provided, choices can be made in other than incremental fashion. Other influences will make their way into the process, but ultimately a budget is an inherently political process, as it should be.

The traditional budget gave only a minor role to political leaders in any case. It denied them adequate information to make decisions and provided no systematic record of the achievement of results. Budget reforms, as with other reforms to the management of the public sector, have improved the position of the political leadership. Budgetary decisions may still be made in a political manner, and for political reasons, but can be more precisely targeted. The traditional budget was also ideal for public servants to conceal possible reserves of money, hoarding these as resources to fall back on in hard times. This could occur in the absence of good information about where money was being directed. With better information, the expenditure control system has been tightened from above.

Problems with the accounting changes

Perhaps the biggest change in accounting rules within government has been the adoption of accrual accounting. This is difficult to implement in government, even though it makes accounting more complete. How is it sensible, for example, to value a 100-year-old government asset that was long ago paid for – say, a bridge or a dam – at its current replacement value? Pollitt and Bouckaert (2000) argue that 'the application of accruals systems is not equally straightforward for all different types of service and circumstance, and reform can create perverse incentives as well as advantages' (p. 69). This is undoubtedly the case. Accrual accounting reforms are 'more than neutral, technical, disinterested activities' (Carlin and Guthrie, 2001, p. 89). They can drive organizations in a managerial direction, into market-based activities, and can alter the distribution of power within and between organizations. However, the same could be said of any form of change. It is entirely possible that financial management changes will affect the power relations between line managers on the one hand, and central agencies and political leaders on the other. But it would equally be possible to argue that this will improve rather than lessen accountability compared to the old system.

The biggest difficulty is that of implementation. Adopting accrual accounting can provide more transparency, better relate outcomes to inputs and so on, but the task of putting a system together is difficult. It has become commonplace for agencies to maintain two sets of accounts, one on an accrual basis and the other on a cash basis, and to manage using both. Particularly because of problems of implementation, it is argued that such systems 'can provide welcome assistance in the effort to improve public management practices' but 'will not constitute the panacea suggested by some central agency rhetoric' (Carlin and Guthrie, 2001, p. 98). As more jurisdictions use accrual accounting it will become easier to determine the worth of this particular reform, but it is one that takes a lot of work to put into effect.

Problems in measuring performance

There are some obvious problems in the implementation of performance measurement in the public sector. It is difficult to design adequate measures of performance and there have also been problems in the types of performance indicators that have been used. Measures need to be meaningful but parsimonious, and to have a direct impact on the operations of that part of the public sector. Poorly chosen performance measures may result in management being focused on achieving satisfactory results only through the measures used rather than the best possible performance by the organization as a whole. In addition, despite the attractions of a rigorous system of performance appraisal of staff in identifying both good and bad performers, it is difficult to design a system that provides reliable comparisons and is accepted as a fair one by all those involved.

Another significant point is that the widespread use of performance measures has not improved relations with the citizenry. Referring to the United Kingdom, Flynn (2007) argues that 'the biggest disappointment for government must have been the disconnection between improvements in performance and the level of public satisfaction' (p. 149). For example, despite figures showing that levels of crime are reduced and public safety greater than ever, members of the public often believe they are less safe than previously. Statistics by themselves are not enough.

Perhaps too much can be claimed for the use of performance indicators. Rather than being performance *measures* – perfect surrogates for profit in the private sector – they are in fact *indicators* of performance, which are simply pointers to good or bad performance, and do not try to measure it precisely. Not measuring performance is now inconceivable, but there are many better ways in which performance indicators can and should be used. As well as indicators of overall progress towards objectives or the achievement of financial targets, there should be indicators of customer or client satisfaction, or the speed and level of service delivery. Indicators should aim at measuring programme effectiveness, client perception and other factors, and should be outwardly focused rather than only being meaningful to those inside the public service. It is easy to criticize performance management and to find real problems with the way it is operationalized (see Van Dooren *et al.*, 2010), or to discuss at length but inconclusively (Bouckaert and Halligan, 2008). However, it would now be inconceivable to try to manage in the absence of some kind of performance regime.

The global financial crisis

The global financial crisis that started in 2008 has led to significant issues for many governments in managing their finances. Government debt re-emerged as a critical problem, especially for those countries that already had high levels of debt before the GFC struck. In the G20 as a whole, budget deficits swung from 1.1 per cent of the group's collective gross domestic product (GDP) in 2007 to 8.1 per cent in 2009. The budget deficit in both the United States and the United Kingdom was above 11 per cent of GDP in 2010. Gross debt in the United States was 83 per cent of GDP in 2009 and was predicted to rise to over 100 per cent by 2012 (information online from the White House). This is historically a very high level only exceeded previously in wartime. Some countries – Greece, the Republic of Ireland, Iceland, Italy, Portugal and even Spain – faced the possibility of a sovereign debt crisis and a long period of adjusting the government budget.

High debt levels inevitably place pressure on the government budget, meaning that there is even more pressure to make the public sector more efficient. Government debt needs to be maintained through the government budget, and eventually to be repaid through the same source. If a country has debt levels of 10 per cent of GDP, it would need to find between 0.3 per cent and 0.5 per cent to service that debt – reflecting the long-term bond rate – to stay at the same debt level, and slightly higher if it intends to repay. Most countries would not find this a difficult burden. However, if a country has debt levels of 100 per cent of GDP, it follows that the government would need to take from the government budget an amount equal to the long-term bond rate in order to stay at the same level compared to GDP. Even standing still poses a big problem for government budgets. With the advanced economies in the G20 averaging more than 100 per cent of gross government debt in 2010 (IMF, *Fiscal Monitor*, May 2010) the pressure to reduce government spending would only increase.

In the United Kingdom, for example, where government spending is around 50 per cent of GDP, merely standing still requires something of the order of 10 per cent of the budget to service interest payments alone, leading to a squeezing of expenditure in other areas. The problems engendered are exacerbated when particular items of expenditure are ruled out from suffering cuts. Prior to the 2010 election, the incoming government had promised to not impose cuts on the National Health Service (NHS). What this does is to make for much bigger cuts in other areas. As *The Economist* (14 August, 2010) noted:

> with interest payments rising because of huge borrowing, and the NHS ring-fenced from real cuts, the departments responsible for other public services face cuts of 25% by 2014–15. If defence and schools are to be spared such harsh treatment – by limiting cuts to 10%, say – the others face a real squeeze of 33%.

Government action to deal with budget deficits will mean that, over time, taxes may have to rise in the developed countries, but as they are already at high levels, further increases could reduce economic activity. Austerity measures will have to be put in place. To add to this, ageing populations are more costly in terms of health care and inevitably pay less tax. All of these points taken together mean that the management of government will itself have to be much more efficient. As Van Dooren *et al.* (2010, p. 5) argue:

> The financial crisis may further institutionalize performance management. The nature of the crisis has already changed from a financial to an economic crisis. It is unclear how it will transform in the future, but it seems plausible that a fiscal crisis will follow upon current deficit spending. With public finance under pressure, the need to assure and demonstrate value for money of public programmes will be reinforced.

It seems inarguable that financial stringency will persist for some considerable time. In turn, if money is scarce there is even greater pressure than has been the case in recent decades to manage government more efficiently; 'an agenda of "more for less" seems here to stay' (OECD, 2009, pp. 30–1). The prospect of budget deficits extending for many years is likely to mean even further pressure to cut the costs of operating government. While this will mean ongoing cuts to programmes, it will also mean pressure to reduce the public service itself or, at the very least, for real managerial efficiency to be demonstrable.

Conclusion

Financial management in government is not only about delivering cuts or about relating performance in service delivery to financial goals. It is about using money for public purposes: raising it, spending it, and reconciling the accounts. Financial management is, and always was, fundamentally a political process; any claim that financial management reform takes away from political decision-making is specious. Rather than usurping the political process, financial and performance management reform aims to enhance it by providing more and better information to political leaders. Political leaders may still indulge in pork-barrelling or in making wild promises they have no intention of keeping, as is their right. However, more sophisticated financial and performance management can make it clearer than it was before reform as to what the costs will be. Governments with better information can make better spending and taxing decisions and, in principle, allow for choices to be made between activities.

Financial management has been transformed, at least in some countries, from a traditional system that provided little information and did so in an opaque way, to one where more precise data can be provided to aid decision-makers. The problem with the traditional budget systems was that there was insufficient information as to either the purposes of the spending or how well or badly such purposes had been met. The information as to what was achieved by the application of resources was so poor that it led to many of the other sub-optimal features of the traditional model of administration. It was thought to be too difficult to measure performance in government, if indeed this had even been considered. The real purpose of any agency became to spend its budget allocation with little thought as to why or for whom, what was produced and whether or not it was efficient or effective in achieving goals. Even if an agency had a function and attempted to carry it out, any evaluation of what resulted tended to be quite unsystematic. Wildavsky (1979) opposed rationality in budgeting, but times have changed; information systems have greatly improved; and no longer is it sustainable to avoid financial reform merely because it is hard to do.

Performance budgets set out the costs of identifiable programmes, which, along with associated measures, allow for decisions to be made as to whether they are achieving their purposes. Accrual accounting allows for the long-term consequences of spending to be calculated more precisely by its effects on the overall balance sheet as it includes changes in asset values. Of course, financial management reforms are not perfect; of course, there are problems in precisely setting the performance measures; and of course, accounting systems can be used to reinforce power structures. They can also be used to hide facts or to deceive, as has occurred even in the private sector. But more information allows for better decisions to be made, though it does not guarantee them. In a democratic system such decisions are made, for good or ill, by elected governments. Traditional financial systems allowed civil servants to hide the true state of the accounts from their supposed masters. Having transparent accounts may well increase the power of political leaders as well as central agencies, but is ultimately more accountable to the people. This is clearly better than when there was so little information that the best form of accounting was by cash and the best form of budget was by input only with an amount set aside for salaries, a smaller amount allocated to other inputs such as postage and telephone calls, and with no requirement to measure performance. Old-style, traditional budgeting did not provide sufficient information for real choices to be made. And even with new financial systems in place, there is nothing to stop a government from making a bad budgetary decision. It will, however, be made aware of the long-term consequences in a way that was not possible before.

Chapter 13

E-government

Chapter Contents

- Introduction
- Technology and the traditional model of administration
- The beginnings of e-government
- E-government stages
- The impact of technological change on bureaucracy
- E-government and public sector reform
- Problems of e-government
- Conclusion

Introduction

The information technology (IT) (later also known as information and communication technology – ICT) revolution that began in the last two decades of the twentieth century saw a real transformation in the economies of many countries. New industries were created producing both software and hardware, older ones disappeared through disintermediation and, while overall productivity increased, there were unsettling effects for many workers. There were equally far-reaching effects on the operations of government. Developments in the private sector led to the invention of the terms 'e-business' and 'e-commerce'; and parallel developments in the operations of government led to the term 'e-government' being coined, to refer to the specifics of the IT revolution in government, as well as to something of a specialist area within public management.

E-government may refer to 'the use of information technology, in particular the Internet, to deliver public services in a much more convenient, customer-oriented, cost-effective, and altogether different and better way (Holmes, 2001, p. 2). A broader definition of e-government is that 'it encompasses all use of digital information technology (primarily computers and networks) in the public sector' (Heeks, 2006). The technologies can include video conferencing, touch-tone data entry, CD-ROMs, the internet and private intranets, as well as other technologies such as interactive television and internet access via mobile phone and personal digital assistants, and social networking sites such as Twitter and Facebook.

The changes induced in the operations of government by technology are far-reaching. Public organizations have generally been early adopters of technology, from the typewriter to the photocopier and early mainframe computers. In 2000, a special survey by *The Economist* noted 'Within the next five years it [e-government] will transform not only the way in which most public services are delivered, but also the fundamental relationship between government and citizen. After e-commerce and e-business, the next Internet revolution will be e-government' (24 June 2000). Eight years later, another survey by the same news magazine was more sanguine about what had been achieved, arguing:

> Technology can give politicians and officials a better idea of what the public wants and how to provide it, just as it has done in the private sector. But just as the private sector's adoption of new technology involved a number of pitfalls, some e-government ventures have been ill-starred. Citizens are right to be suspicious about technology that can make government all-encompassing, and they should demand a lot more of government as a monopoly provider of public services. (*The Economist*, 14 February 2008)

The development of e-government came at the same time as public sector reform in many countries. As Bellamy and Taylor (1998) state, 'The patterns of organizational change which are so commonly associated with the information age are remarkably consistent with the patterns associated with current forms of managerialism in public administration' (p. 37). And it is doubtless the case that e-government did promise much in the era of managerial reform. However, in two ways, the promise has not been realized quite as well as might have been thought possible at the start of the twenty-first century.

The first issue has been serious design and implementation problems in many jurisdictions, which have meant that the actual delivery of e-government has been less than stellar. As *The Economist* survey results showed, 'Although putting information on the web ... has worked, our special report shows that "e-government" - using the interactivity and speed of the internet to provide public services - has so far mostly meant high costs and poor returns' (14 February, 2008). Many government IT projects have failed (Heeks, 2006), even as they may have made suppliers and consultants wealthy.

The second issue relates to what has happened in the business community in terms of IT. For a time, the private sector saw e-business and e-commerce as something new and separate from business itself. By 2000, the speculative bubble that resulted led to what became known as the 'dot com crash' as the prices of stock market listings in IT companies fell dramatically, creating a recession in the United States. What had happened was that there never really was anything separate and different from business called 'e-business', or anything separate from commerce called 'e-commerce'. And business fundamentals reasserted themselves. The integration of IT within business meant that all businesses were now 'e-businesses' and all commerce was now 'e-commerce', and to such an extent that the special names were no longer needed. It follows that e-government may no longer need to be seen as a separate field from government. As IT processes are embedded within government, and government processes are inevitably related to the usage of IT, perhaps public management and e-government are becoming indistinguishable. The key question about e-government is not whether it is useful or has been far-reaching, but whether it is truly novel, whether it is a technological enabler such as an office calculator, or if it is indeed quite different from normal government.

The great promise and potential of e-government is that services can be delivered by governments more efficiently and effectively. The expectation of e-government has been that internet-enabled systems will cut costs significantly and provide a better service; the reality is often, however, that government IT projects are costly failures, with poor specification and implementation (Heeks and Bhatnagar, 1999; Heeks, 2006). And the greatest cause of failure is poor management rather than the use of technology. E-government can reinforce existing management structures, but could also provoke a complete rethink of how services should be delivered. This latter possibility has some distance to go.

Technology and the traditional model of administration

During the time of the traditional model, public organizations were often technological leaders, using the latest in equipment as soon as it became available. The telegram and the telephone became very important for communication both within and outside government services, and government departments were early adopters and assiduous users of both. The nineteenth-century theory of bureaucracy actually depended on, and was quite consistent with, such contemporary inventions. As Fountain (1999, p. 142) states:

> Organizational forms developed by state and industry ... were rendered possible by technological achievements that underlay the Industrial Revolution. The steam engine, telegraph, telephone, and early adding machines all made possible bureaucracy as well as the inter-organizational forms underlying business and government using vertical integration and spatially dispersed headquarters and field organizations. Technological developments did not determine these forms in an inevitable fashion, but they made them possible and, in some cases, completely logical.

The traditional model of public administration was entirely consistent with the technology then available.

A central part of Weberian bureaucracy is the concept of 'the office' – a place where officials go to work, where the public goes for its interactions with the agency, and where records are kept. The office is also the central place for organizational technology and for processing information. As Weber describes it (Gerth and Mills, 1970, p. 197):

> The management of the modern office is based upon written documents ('the files'), which are preserved in their original or draught form. There is, therefore, a staff of subaltern officials and scribes of all sorts. The body of officials actively engaged in a 'public' office, along with the respective apparatus of material implements and the files, make up a 'bureau'.

The 'scribes' and the 'apparatus of material implements and the files' refer to the available technology. The office is the repository of the files: these store information; they are required to record precedents so that the agency makes an identical decision when circumstances match an earlier occasion, and are used to process claims for regular benefits such as pensions. The basic technology of communication at that time was that of a single document, initially written by hand, created by the technology of the quill pen, and later by the typewriter and the typing pool. There was essentially a single copy of a document and a single file, with the papers in a file passed up and down the hierarchy to gain approval or to provide information. Subsequently, the files were kept in a central repository and drawn upon as needed. The passage of single pieces of paper induced transaction costs by having to proceed from desk to desk. Copies could be made laboriously, if at all – initially by hand – and the later invention of carbon paper only allowed a small number of copies to be made before the quality deteriorated so far as to be unreadable.

For many years the overall system worked well, in the sense of organizational structures being designed around the available technology. With the benefit of hindsight it can be argued that the bureaucratic model was an ideal fit with the technology of a single document. And there were relatively few major changes in office technology until at least the 1960s. The plain paper photocopier was a major advance over the carbon copy but this was a mere refinement, rather than such a major development requiring totally different organizational systems.

The public sector was an early user of the telegram and telephone. Even if the nineteenth-century equipment now seems rather primitive, it was a very big jump from what had been in use previously. But the telegram and telephone are also essentially single-copy or user implements, just like a letter. They were truly revolutionary when they were invented, but the way they were used by the government did not change much for close to a century. They simply became further parts of the apparatus, reinforcing the power of the bureaucratic office. Even the arrival of the fax machine did not mean much of a change. It was only when the widespread use of interlinked computers within government became common that a further revolution took place. Earlier changes could be incorporated into the agency with little effect on power structures or the way the office was organized.

From the 1960s, governments became assiduous users of computers, but in a limited, linear, batch-processing way. Computing was regarded as a separate activity within an agency, staffed by experts, but operated in a way that was analogous to a typing pool. The early use of computers had little impact on organizations, as they were introduced in ways that reinforced existing boundaries, as Bellamy and Taylor (1998, p. 11) explain:

> Here, in these early days of government computing, was affirmation by machine of the centralized forms of bureaucratic organization which prevailed at the time. The mainframe computer was being used to process data which had central, corporate functionality. It offered no challenge to the hierarchical and centralized structures by which it was surrounded. Indeed, its effect was to sustain and even to reinforce those features of large-scale bureaucracy. Its reason for being was simple automation; the accomplishment of large-scale data processing tasks at lower costs than hitherto.

The information and communications revolution changed all that. Only with personal computers on every desk, as has become common within government, combined with intranets and access to the internet, has there been any serious impact on organizational structures. The public sector's approach began to change: technology was 'now being viewed as a key component in improving the way the public sector conducted its business and provided service to citizens' (Seneviratne, 1999, p. 45).

By the 1990s, the potential was there for an IT revolution to change the office and its management within government. There was no longer as much of a need for the kind of office that Weber had described. The files could be distributed and kept virtually; staff did not have to be at their desks the whole time; and expert systems could do much of the processing. Given the spread of IT, 'the necessity for people to be in a common setting in order to share the characteristics of an organization has diminished ... therefore, forming alternatives to traditional organizations has become practical' (Peters, 1996, p. 9).

In a networked age, formal structures designed for nineteenth-century technology are unlikely to remain relevant. One of the more substantial, even if unrealized, promises of the IT revolution is the possibility of organizing government agencies in a different way. Some of this has occurred with a flattening of hierarchical structures, a hollowing out of middle management, but government departments most often keep their existing organizations in terms of scope. Information technology, particularly but not exclusively the use of computers, can change management; even the hierarchy itself. Managers do not need to wait until an item makes its way through the hierarchy; copies appear on their own computer screens. Information and data of all kinds can be gathered and transmitted cheaply, and transformed into performance information, which, in turn, allows management to be decentralized, even as it is able to be monitored by senior management. Records are kept electronically so that they are accessible from many different locations at the same time. Investments in IT have resulted in less worker time spent in processing routine work. Some public servants use their computers from home instead of going to an office. Local offices become less necessary, as a seamless service can be provided remotely through call centres or over the internet; and where services do need to be provided locally, a number of agencies can share facilities and even staff.

However, the existence of a technology does not, by itself, determine the desired outcomes. There is no automaticity to organizational change. The existence of technology does not, by itself, determine the predicted outcomes; it is rather that the technology makes changes possible. Indeed, the major challenge for governments is not in developing better technology but in 'reorganizing and restructuring the institutional arrangements in which those transactions are embedded' (Fountain, 2001, p. 6). All too often, e-government changes take place within existing organizational boundaries instead of taking a wider look at how technology can assist in delivery as a governmental totality.

The beginnings of e-government

As noted earlier, in the late 1990s, e-commerce and e-business were terms adopted as descriptions of the fundamental changes taking place as businesses adapted to working with the internet. In the early stages, a business would simply place information about their firm and its products on a website; and later there would be interaction, such as the ability to place orders over the internet and ways of using the information as a resource. So-called 'dot com' companies were set up to exploit opportunities that arose from what was seen as a different way of doing business. One result was a stock market bubble as stock prices soared for companies that had no real prospect of making money, thus leading to the 'dot com crash' of 2000. However, what may have been forgotten in the boom and bust of the internet economy was that, for many firms, their way of doing business had been transformed. Even if business-to-consumer (B2C) sales were slow to take off initially, firms such as Amazon showed that retailing could be carried out profitably through the internet. Other retailers then had to alter their practices. Business-to-business (B2B) links have grown very rapidly, and while start-ups may have found the environment more difficult than it first appeared, established companies have had to make fundamental changes to their operations. Interestingly, the very success of IT-enabled business challenged the idea that there is something special and different about e-business or e-commerce. Perhaps all business has become e-business; it would now be an unusual company that was immune to the IT revolution.

A similar situation is occurring in government, but with a time lag compared to e-business. The products of government – overwhelmingly services – are often quite suited to electronic delivery when compared to the problems of organizing the delivery of goods. It might have been expected that governments would be leaders in electronic delivery, but the private sector was the pioneer. Once it had started, though, the greater service provided by private e-business as the result of techno-logical change led to demands for governments to do the same (OECD, 1998b). If banking at all hours via automated teller machines (ATMs) or the internet could become the norm, why should the consumers of government services have to queue only in working hours for quite similar services?

Bellamy and Taylor (1998) argue that there are three stages in the development of information and communication technologies in gov-ernment (see also Heeks, 1999). The first stage is *automation* where the aim is to use machines to reduce the costs of existing, mainly paper-based work, and with information only as a by-product (Bellamy and Taylor, 1998, pp. 38–40). This characterizes the early phases of managerialism.

A second stage is that of *informatization* described as a shift from automation to 'an emphasis on the information that can be liberated' (Bellamy and Taylor, 1998, p. 46). In this stage, the new information resources allow the integration of data from a number of sources, permit the significant enhancement of organizational intelligence, allow greater flexibility in arranging who may access and exploit information resources, and how information-dependent processes are undertaken and permit 'new kinds of interactive communications within and between organizations (including between organizations and their sup-pliers or customers)' (Bellamy and Taylor, 1998, p. 47).

The third and final stage is that of *transformation* described as 'using business process re-engineering to totally reorganize across boundaries, to share data' (Bellamy and Taylor, 1998, pp. 51–3). This last stage could be regarded as the goal of e-government. Delivery services can be organized by 'life event', or for particular groups, such as elderly people or students, instead of organization by department or agency. The dream is 'the simple but hugely potent claim that liberating the power of new technology will drive down the costs of public services and, at the same time, help to rebuild relationships between governments and their citizens' (Bellamy and Taylor, 1998, p. 64).

By the late 1990s, rapid changes in technology did start to affect the organization of government. In the United States, the reinventing government movement of the earlier 1990s did foresee that organizational changes would need to be made, following its explicit aim of creating a government that would work better and cost less. Technology was a way to do this. Osborne and Gaebler (1992) argued that bureaucracies designed earlier in the century 'simply do not function well in the rapidly changing, information-rich, knowledge-intensive society and economy of the 1990s' (p. 12). Bringing this about was no trivial task, though the possibility of a technological revolution in government did arrive somewhat later with the internet.

In the UK in 1996, the government launched *Government Direct*, a Green Paper about the electronic delivery of services. This prospectus was 'said by ministers to herald a new phase of public service reform' (Bellamy and Taylor, 1998, p. 10). A few years later, at the end of the 1990s, distributed computer networks with a personal computer on the desk of every public servant, intranets and greater use of the internet, meant that what was foreseen in the early 1990s had now become possible.

E-government stages

There are different ways of classifying e-government interactions. In the development of e-business, the earliest phases were those where information only was provided and later there were two-way transactions. There are also different kinds of interaction possible between government and other parties, notably with citizens, businesses and other government agencies. There is a reasonably agreed set of developments dependent on the level of interaction enabled:

- *Information.* The first stage involves departments and agencies posting information about themselves for the benefit of external users. Websites provide information in a passive way, outlining the purposes of the public organization and how to contact it. This information does not include real provision of services. Websites are provided by departments rather than functions and have limited capacity for updates. This is the most common form of website.
- *Interaction.* These sites then become tools for two-way communication, allowing citizens to provide new information about themselves (for example, change of address), gathered using instruments such as

e-mail. It is no longer necessary to telephone or write a letter to contact the government. Content files present information about more issues, functions and services, which can be downloaded; forms may be downloaded and completed offline and posted in the normal way. However, feedback is limited. There are large numbers of such sites in existence, many of which depend on the relatively low-level technology of e-mail.

- *Transaction*. A formal quantifiable exchange of value takes place, such as paying a licence or a fine, or filing a tax return. This level allows for tasks, previously carried out by public servants, to become web-based self-services, though they may require off-line channels for completion.
- *Transformation*. Government services may be provided through the integration of government services and provide a path to them based on citizens' needs, replacing the traditional structure of department or agency. Through a portal, the information systems of all departments and agencies can be linked to deliver integrated services in a way that avoids users having to understand the agency structures of government.

The government of Singapore, admittedly with the geographical advantage of small size, has proceeded furthest towards the highest level, that of transformation. Electronic road pricing started in 1998; a charge was made to enter some parts of the city, and prices alter according to time of day and the level of congestion. The Singapore government set up the e-Citizen portal in 1999 as an initiative of the Ministry of Finance. By 2010, the portal had become in many ways the main communication channel for government services in a country that has much experience in IT. Citizens and permanent residents obtain a single password for various transactions with government. The services available through the portal vary from taxation matters, to registering a business, paying licence fees and traffic fines, to accessing cultural events. Singapore also has its own secure on-line payment system. Services available are divided into seven 'towns' of like services instead of the government departments to which they might belong. In addition, the government provides drop-in centres so that those without computers can still gain access. Singapore has also installed a fibre optic network across the whole city-state to enable very fast broadband access.

In the United States, the site *usa.gov* provides a single, if somewhat conventional, gateway for users to all government websites, and for all levels of government. Even if it is more about letting citizens know what services are available rather than involving transactions – though there are some entitlements that can be applied for – *usa.gov* does provide access to a wide range of information, and uses Facebook and Twitter as additional access channels.

Many governments are still at relatively low levels of interaction, rather than enabling transactions or providing portals. However, first- or second-stage sites are important as they provide information to citizens to a greater extent than was common in old-style bureaucracy. Much more change is engendered by third- and fourth-stage interactions.

Government-to-citizen links (G2C)

There are a number of ways in which e-government facilitates the link between government and citizen. Service delivery systems may be linked with life events and citizen needs. For example, many of the compliance tasks involved in foreign travel can be linked with each other on the same website. Passports, visas, health warnings and vaccinations may be accessed together when someone, or their agent, books travel. It is much easier, as noted earlier, to renew vehicle or drivers' licences or pay fines through links of this kind. E-government allows public agencies to provide many services whenever its clients require them and without having to attend an office in person. Renewing of licences, changes of address or even completing forms for provision of welfare can be done on-line. It is also much cheaper to provide services this way.

Providing services more conveniently reinforces the view of the citizen as customer. For many services this is an appropriate perspective. Correlating information about location, status, dependants and other demands on government enhances the ability to identify an individual's current situation and anticipate future needs, though there are obvious dangers if insufficient attention is paid to privacy and security. Customer resource management techniques allow a closer relationship with citizens – for good or ill – by making better use of information already collected through techniques such as data warehousing and data mining.

Another, relatively unsung, part of G2C is the greater availability of information on government services that can be accessed by citizens. Even if much of this is essentially one-way, there is much more information available that is more easily accessible than previously under the traditional model of administration. In the traditional model, information was held centrally and released only grudgingly, usually by printed reports that were difficult to obtain and did not encompass much of the inner workings of government. It is now much more common for information of all kinds to be released as it is completed, in downloadable form for anyone to access.

Government-to-business links (G2B)

E-business in the sense of electronic exchanges involving commercial and fee-for-service transactions is a rapidly growing sector of the economy in a number of countries. In manufacturing, large companies such as Ford and General Motors (GM) use the internet to source parts and require their suppliers to adapt their internal workings to comply. Public organizations too are placing significant resources into delivery and procurement systems for their interactions with business. If using the internet is becoming more common in the private sector for B2B interchange, it is hardly surprising that governments would wish to do the same. Increasingly, governments are requiring suppliers to operate as e-businesses.

Government contracts are, in most countries, a substantial part of private sector business. However, there are transaction costs incurred by businesses in knowing that a contract has been called and in complying with the tender requirements. The complexity of government tendering can lead to higher tender prices as there may be relatively few companies willing to go through the procedures involved. Competition may be lessened as a result. Such transaction costs can be reduced by e-government. The Australian government and some US states have encouraged e-business practices within public agencies by charging a fee to companies that submit paper proposals. It is even possible to have on-line reverse auctions where suppliers can compete with each other for the lowest price, with the possibility of making more than one bid in the time allowed. Procurement of standard items such as stationery is much easier and cheaper through placing orders to contractors on their websites, and companies wishing to gain government contracts have every incentive to comply with a requirement that orders be processed on-line. There can be significant cost savings to be made by governments in the area of procurement. Moving from paper-based to web-based processing of documents and payments 'typically generates administrative cost savings of roughly 50 per cent – more for highly complex transactions' (Fountain, 2001, p. 5).

Government-to-government links (G2G)

Government agencies increasingly use electronic links between one another to improve service delivery. This is not altogether new, but capability has been enhanced in part by using the internet, or a standard programming language such as XML to overcome problems of incompatible computer systems. Other parts of the same government, other levels of government, and even the governments of other nations may benefit from the electronic exchange of information. In the case mentioned earlier of foreign travel, it would also be possible for the booking of travel or requesting a passport or visa to trigger a set of other government-to-government information flows, ranging from immigration or customs checks to dealing with security concerns.

There are already sophisticated exchanges of data between governments and these can be enhanced by e-government.

An example is Centrelink in Australia, an agency created in 1997 for the purpose of delivering services. These are provided for a number of dissimilar departments – Social Security, Employment, and Education – with the agency acting as a contractor for service delivery. Citizen needs cross the boundaries of departments. Services for the elderly, for example, are provided by several agencies. By linking these through e-government, a better overall service could be delivered; after all, it is the service that is important rather than its agency home, with the citizen unlikely to understand the nuances of organizational structures. In this way information flows can cross departmental boundaries. E-government can allow government agencies to work together more effectively, though there do need to be adequate safeguards for privacy and security.

Government-to-citizen – and citizen-to-government – links have become much more important. Government services do need to be available to every eligible person rather than only those with access, so there is a need to provide channels in addition to the internet, including ordinary mail and telephone. This is unlike the situation in the private sector, where someone without the required access can simply be ignored. On the other hand, the much smaller number of businesses who deal with governments can be forced into compliance if they wish to gain government business.

Occasionally there is reference to a fourth category, government-to-employee (G2E) and there are certainly ways in which government agencies have organized their internal operations using computer systems for greater efficiency (see Yong, 2005). Internal forms are processed on-line instead of being paper-based and so on; however, this could be considered more a part of normal internal operation than a new aspect of e-government.

The impact of technological change on bureaucracy

From the discussion so far, it is clear that, with these changes, there must be impacts on a system of bureaucracy designed for an earlier technological era. There were several imperatives driving the public sector reforms, as discussed in earlier chapters. Technology was certainly one of these, not least because the private sector's use of ICT led to demands for better service from government. As Kamarck (2000, p. 235) points out:

> The information revolution in the private sector raised expectations on the part of the public and made rule-bound, paper-based governmental bureaucracies

seem old-fashioned and unresponsive. At mid-century the organization of the Pentagon and the organization of General Motors were not terribly different. But as organizational theory in the private sector evolved and produced a new information age theory of organizations, public sector insistence on traditional bureaucracy seemed all the more obsolete.

One effect of e-government is that organization can be based on information flow rather than hierarchy. Governmental clients or 'customers' may not be aware of the precise boundaries between what one agency or another does, particularly with regard to service delivery. And the citizenry cannot be relied on to have a detailed knowledge of the activities of different levels of government. E-government allows services to clients to be grouped together. Initially, a website could be constructed to provide information and contact across a number of agencies; and later the agencies themselves could be altered to conform to the flow of information.

It is often argued that organizations need fewer middle managers as a result of such technological change, and there is evidence to back up this claim. Middle managers are the contact points between higher and lower levels, with their main roles being, first, to process information from below and pass it on to higher levels; second, to transmit information and instructions downwards from higher levels; and third, to supervise staff. Higher-level staff now gain their information directly, often in automated form, and lower-level staff do not need the close supervision they once did – whether someone is working efficiently can often be monitored electronically and his or her outcomes become obvious. Bureaucracy in the power relation sense remains in place; hierarchy does not disappear, but does not need so many levels. Managers can be delegated tasks; their performance still needs to be monitored by higher levels but without a need for detailed supervision.

There may be less of a need for lower-level public servants altogether. For example, a number of countries allow for on-line lodgement of tax returns. In Australia, some 90 per cent of income tax returns were lodged electronically during 2009–10 by tax agents using the Australian Taxation Office's electronic lodgement system, or by individuals using the electronic tax system. There are organizational effects: on-line lodgement reduces the time taken to process returns, and greatly reduces the staff needed to process paper forms, including the data entry of details. Much of the data needed is keyed into the relevant parts of the database by the client, which means that it can be processed directly by the assessor, rather than anyone else being needed at lower levels to prepare the data. There is less of a need to hire base-grade or casual staff, as was once the norm, to process forms after the due date for submission of tax returns. Tax office staff are able to spend more time on assessing the return itself, rather than dealing with the documentation.

A further effect on hierarchy is that the use of powerful database software enables higher-level tasks to be done by lower-level staff. As Fountain (1999, p. 139) observes:

> Knowledge workers and knowledge work have replaced simple, repetitive, clerical tasks required in paper-based bureaucracy. Case workers, whose desktop computing capacity provides access to several databases and powerful analytic tools, perform work previously disaggregated into several positions. In some cases, automated tools allow relatively simple employees to make sophisticated evaluations. Task integration due to information technology has resulted in a collapse in the number of job categories and simplification of the position classification system in the federal bureaucracy.

A tax assessor, in the same example, would be assisted by his or her own powerful computer system, with expert systems software included, by search engines, and by relational databases, and would be able to be more productive than was once the case. If many of the functions can be carried out by lower-level staff, with assistance from software, resources can be diverted to higher tasks and to difficult cases rather than being used for routine processing. This points to an effective devolution of authority, even as there is enhanced capability to monitor results at higher levels.

There are, then, several points relating to personnel and career structures: there is less of a need for base-grade staff, the greater capability of lower-level staff, fewer middle managers and, perhaps, greater scope for higher-level staff. As a result of these changes, there are flow-on effects for the career structures of public servants. Other effects include 'modifications to supervisory roles, transformation of hierarchical relations, and, at a deep cultural level, modernization of the nature of authority structures and systems' (Fountain, 1999, p. 139). Knowledge workers are more likely to take advantage of flexible arrangements, as consultants or contractors, and to earn high salaries without necessarily being career public servants. At the same time, however, lower-level staff are now not needed in large numbers.

The 'office' in the Weberian sense has also changed. With remote-access technology there is no necessity for staff to proceed to a central point to use the office's equipment. Staff may work from home just as effectively, and staff of welfare agencies who carry out, for example, home visits, need not be out of contact. Part-time work is facilitated by ICT. Already, virtual teams working from disparate locations and home-based working are well established in some governments. There can be a 'logical office' or a 'virtual corporation' rather than an actual one, so that location in different cities or even countries becomes irrelevant to the work carried out (Bellamy and Taylor, 1998, p. 36). This is not universally welcome, however, as out-workers may have difficulty in operating logical offices because of dislocation, and miss out on socializing with co-workers or being involved in vital office politics. However, such changes are already being implemented in government organizations.

The bureaucratic organization may change dramatically as the result of e-government. What remains will still be a bureaucracy but one that is quite different. As Fountain (1999, p. 146) argues:

> It is certain that a solid core of hierarchy and functional specialization will remain in information-based organizations. But the control apparatus that required multiple layers in the chain of command has been greatly simplified, with gains in accountability, through information technology. With information systems that render employee behaviour largely transparent, hierarchical authority is relieved of the task of physically observing employees. In a transparent system shirking is obvious, as is greater output. Hierarchical authority takes on the more important task of direction setting in turbulent environments, keeping officials current with environmental changes and ensuring the alignment of task, technology, human resources and goals.

The governmental working environment will be very different if all these changes to the system of bureaucracy occur. As Fountain (2001) comments, 'to the extent that knowledge is power, this fundamental structural shift has important implications for authority and power in government' (p. 60). There will be opportunities for some but threats for others. There is likely to be more intellectually challenging work to do, but, on the other hand, an ever-present electronic monitoring of performance could cause some unease among staff.

E-government and public sector reform

It could be argued that e-government is the latest instalment in public sector reform – even, perhaps, moving beyond public management to a completely new kind of management. What is beyond doubt is that there are effects caused by e-government on the operations and theories of public sector management.

E-government offers a way of operationalizing the theoretical changes of managerialism, while the way e-government is to work – the focus on service delivery, involvement of the private sector through contracts – is a long way removed from the precepts of traditional public administration. Some may see public sector reform and e-government as separate movements, but in reality they are mutually reinforcing. It would be conceivable for a more hierarchical, bureaucratic organization to implement the new technologies, but without the subsequent organizational changes they would be unlikely to work very well. A traditional model of e-government would be similar to the 'automation' phase described earlier; computer systems would be used merely to improve processing time without changing the organization.

E-government can assist public sector reform by providing better information to managers. It could even be argued that substantive reform would not be possible unless the required information was available and it is, moreover, essential for that information to be of good quality, to be provided in a timely way, and to be sufficiently robust to enable highly sophisticated analyses to be performed subsequently. Governments have a wealth of data, much of which could be used to greater effect through data-mining and other techniques to make the raw data meaningful in a policy sense; indeed, 'public services must not only be computerized, they must be informatized' (Bellamy and Taylor, 1998, p. 48).

Digital era governance

There is a fundamental question as to whether e-government is yet another new model of public management, or whether it is simply part of a wider picture of public sector reform. Some argue that e-government may be a new stage. Lenk and Traunmüller (2001), for example, assert that 'electronic government is clearly transcending new public management in that it implies new bold and comprehensive approaches to administration modernization beyond managerialism and a few theories borrowed from economics' (p. 71). Dunleavy *et al.* (2005) contend that what they term 'digital era governance' has superseded new public management (NPM), which is suggested by them to comprise three integrating themes: disaggregation, competition and incentivization. These integrating themes are declared to be failures and therefore NPM is declared to be 'dead' (Dunleavy *et al.*, 2005, p. 468).

Dunleavy *et al.* then argue that digital era governance is the replacement for NPM. This is characterized by 'reintegration', 'holism' and 'digitalization': reintegration means rolling back the disaggregation of NPM to include such points as joined-up governance and 're-governmentalization'; holism is to include client-based or needs-based reorganization, one-stop provisions, 'ask-once' processes, interactive and 'ask-once' information-seeking, data warehousing, pre-emptive needs analysis, end-to-end service re-engineering and agile government processes; and digitalization elements include electronic service delivery and e-government, new forms of automated processes, radical disintermediation, active channel streaming, customer segmentation, mandated channel reductions in order to move towards co-production of services, quasi-voluntary compliance, do-it-yourself forms and tax-paying, and open-book government (Dunleavy *et al.*, 2005).

Of most relevance for our present purposes is the argument of Dunleavy *et al.* that e-government will lead to more centralization – reintegration – of government. Their idea is that there will be large, indeed very large, government computer installations that will then require formal bureaucracy to reassert itself. They argue that differences from earlier IT reforms in the current period involve the internet, e-mail and 'the generalization of IT systems from only affecting back-office processes to conditioning in important ways the whole terms of relations between government agencies and civil society' (2005, p. 478). For them, 'the advent of the digital era is now the most general, pervasive, and structurally distinctive influence on how governance arrangements are changing in advanced industrial states' (p. 478).

It is not entirely clear, however, from the Dunleavy model how or why bureaucracy will be reasserted. It is only an assumption that centralization of functions will lead to greater efficiency, and that large computer facilities will enhance bureaucracy. What has happened in reality is more of a story of large-scale failure as big governmental computer projects ultimately cost far more than had originally been estimated, and often do not deliver on their promise. Equally plausible is that there will be further decentralization, and that open source software using the 'cloud' will obviate the need for centralization of the kind put forward by Dunleavy *et al.* (2005).

The idea that e-government is a new form of management taking over from other, earlier models of public administration and public management may come to fruition, but it is not really persuasive. E-government does focus on service delivery to customers, as does managerialism. Even if it is possible that e-government may become more important than public management, it is more likely to be seen as an enabler of managerial reform rather than a totally separate model of reform. In the same way that e-commerce and e-business are disappearing from the lexicon, so too will e-government as a description, because it will be inconceivable to manage government any other way.

Problems of e-government

E-government does have the potential to be a new phase in the government reform process that began in the 1980s. Much has been promised since then, particularly by computer companies and consultants touting for business, but the reality is more prosaic. There are potential problems with e-government, as with any part of the reform process.

The digital divide

While the numbers of people connected to the internet shows remarkable growth, there are still many in society who are not connected and never will be. There are whole societies where even access to a telephone would be an IT revolution. There is a potential problem that such citizens could be bypassed or left behind by their more adept neighbours. This is not as much of a problem for e-business as it is for e-government. A private provider of a good or service can decide to exclude those who do not wish (or are unable) to be on-line, but governments cannot do so. They must make their services available to everyone and on similar terms regardless of the level of technological understanding their clients may possess. Even if most tax returns are submitted electronically there still need to be ways of submitting them by ordinary mail. Some governments provide free internet terminals in libraries or other public places, but it is still the case that there will be some governmental clients without any access. In addition, some people see no benefit in becoming computer literate. It will remain necessary to continue other channels for government communication – no matter how much they cost – such as telephone call centres, ordinary mail, and assistance for those unable or unwilling to interact with their government on-line.

Another aspect of the digital divide is that people in developing countries have less access than those in developed ones, exacerbating differentials between rich and poor nations. The lowest usage of the internet and e-government is in developing countries. While there has been remarkable growth in mobile telephone network coverage – to 77 per cent of the world's population – Africa has perhaps only one internet user per 100 people (World Bank, 2005). Though governments in such circumstances are trying to bridge the gap it is obviously more difficult than in developed countries.

Privacy and security

The advances in ICT does offer much to governments as well as providing enhanced service delivery for their clients. However, the problem is that 'these capabilities have the potential for surveillance and control' (Bellamy and Taylor, 1998, p. 86). Safeguarding privacy and security are important aspects of e-government.

E-government does bring with it an enhanced surveillance capability over citizens in a society. While it is technically possible for files to be shared between agencies for efficiency reasons, this also imposes problems of privacy. Internet or e-mail usage is recorded and able to be traced far more easily than ordinary mail or telephone calls; the former leave electronic traces and can be stored for long periods of time in an easily accessible form. All e-mails can be searched for key words of interest to police or intelligence agencies, whereas intercepting telephone calls or mail in the traditional way is much more labour intensive and usually confined to a those suspected of major crimes. It is technically possible for many more people to be under surveillance electronically with the same level of police resources. The FBI in the United States, for example, has programs to tap the World Wide Web and can collect data and read the e-mails of criminal suspects

(Holmes, 2001). The police in the United Kingdom have powers under the Regulation of Investigatory Powers Act passed in 2000 to require internet service providers to install interception devices on e-mail and internet activity and relay it back to a government monitoring centre.

Computer security is also problematic. When documents were in paper form their security could be ensured merely by safeguarding the files in a registry or in storage, but when files are held on computers their security can be compromised. Hackers have been able to find their way into government computers. The security systems for the electronic use of credit cards are insufficient and there would need to be some form of digital signature or other safeguards implemented before the payment of fines or accounts over the internet can become more widely accepted.

The increased use of Global Positioning Satellite (GPS) data means that it is becoming far easier to track where individuals are located at any time. GPS could be used for real-time road-use tolling, as it is now technically possible to charge individual road users for their actual use of such facilities. Peak hour users can be charged at higher rates. But the location of individual vehicles at any given time would raise issues of privacy. Face recognition can be combined with closed-circuit television (CCTV) monitoring to track individuals; indeed, 'efficient government can be repressive government' (*The Economist*, 16 February, 2008).

A further issue with privacy and security is that of ownership and usage of information, especially with the widespread contracting-out of IT. According to Bellamy and Taylor (1998, p. 155), more than 30 per cent of Britain's central government IT was contracted out, and such contracts put a few companies 'in a strategically powerful position in relation to information age government' – and further:

> They also expose important issues about the control and exploitation of personal data on UK citizens which are now flowing into computer installations run by commercial companies. These flows of information raise sensitive questions about data stewardship. Especially data ownership and data privacy, but they also raise questions about the nature and efficacy of control over the commercial value of customer datasets, questions which have not been publicly aired or resolved.

Through data mining, and in combination with modern marketing techniques, government information can be used to target particular kinds of products. It would be possible, if a register of births was in private hands, for direct mail to be used to sell baby products. Without safeguards it would be possible for an agency involved in the delivery of health care services to sell on its data to insurance companies, who could then use patient records to determine risk. It could be argued that governments could themselves use such information for commercial purposes, but there is likely to be greater concern over privacy if the information is controlled by a contractor. There will be a continued need for legislative and ethical standards, but they must be very tightly specified to stop the private sector using government information in this way. Privacy and security are major problems for e-government.

Governments have another issue to deal with, and that is the major difficulties raised in trying to keep its own sensitive information private. A DVD (optical storage disc) or memory stick can contain gigabytes of information; and they can easily be concealed should a whistle-blower or other person wish to provide information to the media or someone else outside. When government files are on-line, large amounts of information can be issued without even being printed out. For example, in late 2010, some 250,000 American diplomatic documents were sent to the whistle-blower organization WikiLeaks, and parts of these were subsequently published by the media. The ability to exchange information on this scale dwarfed what spies were able to do during the Cold War. In a Weberian bureaucracy, maintaining secrecy was always assumed to be one of the great strengths of the model; but technological change may mean a completely different approach to secrecy in government and to maintaining the integrity of government information.

Implications of e-government for politics

E-government may lead to changes in the political system as well as to the internal operations of government. Terms such as 'electronic democracy', 'digital democracy' or 'democracy.com' (Kamarck and Nye, 1999) are becoming more common. There are those who advocate referenda carried out by e-mail or website vote. Political parties are already assiduous users of websites and social networks; and e-mails to politicians have largely replaced earlier mail and telephone responses on issues.

However, there is no sign that e-government is leading to a more informed public in a political sense. On-line petitions can be put together very quickly and the use of social networks can mobilize people to protest. But they can also lead to lowest-common-denominator politics. Even if the articulate and informed always receive disproportionate attention in any political system, relying on electronic responses to political issues would disenfranchise large numbers of voters. The result could be a kind of populism and, as has been shown in a number of countries, the use of the internet makes it easier for extremists to organize and gain attention. The system of representative democracy has evolved over centuries and, for all its faults, continues with the support of most of its people. There are real problems with the idea of electronic democracy.

Difficulties with implementation

It is, of course, possible that the e-government changes will not happen, and there are major hurdles to overcome. There may be active resistance from staff. Also, government IT strategies have tended to be very expensive, exacerbated by a tendency to make poor systems choices, and to lock-in to short-lived technologies. Much money has been wasted, and failure is common (Heeks, 2006). Indeed, as *The Economist* has argued, e-government 'has yet to transform public administration' and 'its most conspicuous feature has been a colossal waste of taxpayers' money on big computer systems, poorly thought out and overpriced' (*The Economist*, 16 February 2008). There have been endemic problems in trying to agree on standards, whether they should be open or proprietary, and the continued difficulties of communication across different kinds of computer. The standards issue may be able to be addressed by the internet itself, as it operates across different kinds of computer hardware and software.

A more systemic problem is the distance between hype and reality. Bellamy and Taylor (1998) argue that 'despite the powerful hyperbole which surrounds the notion of an information age, heroic scenarios for reinventing government through the application of ICTs are fundamentally misleading' (p. 93). Computers by themselves are not an answer to management problems. As *The Economist* (16 February 2008) noted: 'Badly managed organizations with computers will stay badly managed. That has been the lesson from private business, and it equally applies to the public sector, where e-government has barely begun to scratch the surface of what is possible. That is reason for disappointment, but also for hope.'

It was always an assumption that because IT systems could conceivably foster managerial change, that they would indeed do so. Realizing the dream is much more difficult. It is axiomatic that any movement, any reform, will be modified by its implementation and it is undoubted that the institutional inertia within government bureaucracy makes it even harder to adapt to change. But it would be a sclerotic society or organization that allows for no attempt at change at all on the grounds that it is all a bit too hard to implement.

Conclusion

In some respects, e-government can be considered a second managerial reform, another stage in the public sector reform movement that began in the 1980s. It does present a further challenge to the traditional model of public administration and, if implemented well, will transform the way public services are organized and delivered. The greatest potential of e-government is in operationalizing the theoretical changes, in changing from public administration to public management, as described in earlier chapters. Contracting-out requires sophisticated monitoring systems; new budgeting and accounting systems require good information technologies, as does performance management. E-government can assist in realizing the theoretical changes of public sector reform.

E-government does provide the opportunity to bring about the changes that were foreshadowed in the early days of public sector reform. The use of ICT in government is proceeding apace and may lead to even more changes to the operations of government than have been seen thus far in the reform process. That having been said, it cannot be argued as yet that e-government is the management reform that will supplant or surpass other public sector reforms. It reinforces public management but is not a replacement; e-government is basically like any technology – a tool to assist managers to do their work better. It is an enabler of management, and an enabler of managerial change, but not a revolution in its own right.

Chapter 14

Public Management in Developing Countries

Chapter Contents

- Introduction
- The traditional model in developing countries
- Problems with the administrative model
- Public sector reform
- Problems with the managerial model
- Conclusion

Introduction

Even if substantial public sector reform is appropriate for developed countries, there is still the question as to whether the kinds of managerial changes adopted in that setting are applicable in developing countries. It cannot be assumed that a style of management begun in the developed countries of the West would necessarily work in such a different setting. It is possible that public management and managerialism are culturally bound in a way that restricts their utility in less-developed countries.

Developing countries followed the traditional model of public administration during and immediately following independence. Strict hierarchies were the norm, and all the familiar bureaucratic conditions of service prevailed. Staff were recruited by examination to lifetime careers, many different layers made for an overly heavy bureaucracy typically slow to move and, in accordance with Weberian principles, the bureaucracy was a prestigious and relatively well-paid elite even in the poorest of countries. Almost all developing countries were once colonies of one European power or another, with centralized bureaucratic administration characterizing colonial governance.

In addition, along with a bureaucratic approach to administration at independence, most developing countries adopted the principle of a strong state sector in the economy, in many cases allied with the then-prevailing ideas of socialism and Marxism. It was thought that the fastest way of achieving economic growth was through government ownership of enterprises, intervention in the private economy, and dominance by a bureaucratic technocracy. In general, this strategy failed. As the World Bank (1997, p. 2) argued:

> In a few countries things have indeed worked out more or less as the tech-nocrats expected. But in many countries outcomes were very different. Governments embarked on fanciful schemes. Private investors, lacking confidence in public policies or in the steadfastness of leaders, held back. Powerful rulers acted arbitrarily. Corruption became endemic. Development faltered, and poverty endured.

Government loomed large in economic activity, but did not have the competence or standing to be successful and its larger role enhanced the power of the bureaucracy even more than in Western countries. Government became by far the most important societal actor, controlling the details of the economy in addition to its normal functions. This needed to change.

Following the end of the Cold War and a global turning away from statist and socialist ideas, most of the developing world, with some notable exceptions such as North Korea, adopted principles of free markets and participation in the world trade system. In addition, there are many more countries adopting democratic elections in comparison with the one-party states that were previously common. As part of these changes and under the direct encouragement of international financial institutions such as the World Bank and the International Monetary Fund (IMF), many developing countries followed, to a greater or lesser extent, principles of market liberalization, including cutting the size of the public sector and restructuring state-owned enterprise. There are arguments for and against managerialism in developing countries. On the one hand it can be argued that public sector reform is appropriate for developing countries as 'the basic principles are relevant for every country' (Holmes and Shand, 1995, p. 577). On the other hand, however, it can be argued that 'sophisticated reforms such as market testing and internal markets are unlikely to work outside developed economies' (Minogue, 1998, p. 34). Whether managerial principles will work in developing countries is far from clear. However, the traditional model of public administration, based on the model of bureaucracy combined with state ownership of key industries, was not a great success in developing countries either.

The traditional model in developing countries

It almost goes without saying that the public sectors of developing countries can be characterized as following the traditional, bureaucratic model of public administration. Weberian bureaucracy and Taylor's scientific management were successful exports to developed and less-developed countries alike, and formed the basis of the model adopted in the period following independence. There must be some speculation as to why this occurred to the extent it did. Perhaps the prescriptions of the traditional model struck a chord with earlier forms of administration, or perhaps the inherent elitism was familiar. Some of Weber's ideas came from the Orient; it could be argued that China, for example, had its own long history of bureaucracy going back as far as Confucius, and with some continuity today (Aufrecht and Li, 1995, pp. 175–82). It is more likely, though, that at the time of its adoption in the post-independence period, the traditional model of administration was in fashion everywhere, including in the headquarters of former colonial powers, where the new national leaders were usually trained. Perhaps public servants in developing countries thought that, by emulating the administration apparently successful in the West, they could imitate developed countries' economic and social success.

The role of government

Developing countries emerged from independence in the 1950s and 1960s, with governments playing the largest role in the economy and society. It was a time in which state-dominated economic development was seen as the most appropriate way of developing, as it was in the post-war period in France and the United Kingdom, the countries with the largest number of colonies. Keynesian thinking was dominant in the West at the time, and a large and active state seemed to offer the best means of governing. As the World Bank (1997, p. 23) stated:

> The new interventionist credo had its counterpart in the development strategy of the day, adopted by many developing countries at independence, which emphasized the prevalence of market failures and accorded the state a central role in correcting them. Centralized planning, corrective interventions in resource allocation, and a heavy state hand in infant-industry development were part and parcel of this strategy. Economic nationalism was added to the mix, to be promoted through state enterprises and encouragement of the indigenous private sector. By the 1960s, states had become involved in virtually every aspect of the economy, administering prices and increasingly regulating labour, foreign exchange, and financial markets.

In addition, the apparent success of the Soviet Union and China in the 1950s and 1960s, with their own models of economic development, seemed to provide an alternative system for many developing countries. In rhetoric at least, Soviet and Chinese socialism appeared to promise a path for developing countries and, with the Third World an ideological battleground during the Cold War, advice and assistance could be obtained by choosing to follow one side or the other. Many countries chose the socialist side and gained some benefits, such as the TanZam Railway (now the Tazara Railway), constructed by the Chinese in Tanzania in the early 1970s. Tanzania tried to follow other parts of the Chinese model, though the latter began, from 1978, to make its own transition to participation in the market system. Superpower conflict through Third World surrogates also meant the transfer of military equipment, often at the cost of programmes to alleviate poverty; this led to the military itself becoming an important part of the bureaucracy and even the economy in many developing countries.

Bureaucracies were particularly important in developing countries, but at a cost to the nation. Public employment accounted for more than 50 per cent of non-agricultural jobs in Africa, 36 per cent in Asia and 27 per cent in Latin America, and in 1986 the wage bill for Guinea's civil servants accounted for 50 per cent of total current expenditure (Smith, 1996, p. 221). The bureaucracy often operated at a remove from its own society, and constituted an elite with more in common with its counterparts in the West and with foreign corporations than with its own people. Though not part of the traditional model, corruption became endemic as public servants pursued their own interests. Public service pay was often low and it became common – as, for example, in Indonesia – for public servants to have additional jobs in the private sector as well as being in government employ. The sanctions against corruption were weak, so it is hardly surprising that individual public servants sought to enrich themselves.

The bureaucratic model

The bureaucratic model in developing countries can be argued to have largely failed, and with the roots of its failure found most often prior to independence. Colonial governments used bureaucratic means to administer their colonies, often by using indigenous civil servants, at least at the lower levels. Even if higher levels remained firmly in the hands of expatriates or the home government, a system of administration was put in place and this system continued with little change into the post-independence period. As Turner and Hulme (1997, p. 222) comment:

> In countries such as Bangladesh, the current administrative laws are usually those introduced by the British 50 to 100 years ago. South Asian civil servants commonly claim that 'their system' follows 'the British system': such claims are made with pride and are to demonstrate the pedigree and quality of their civil services. They fail, though, to note that they are based on a British colonial model (rather than the British domestic model) and that, 50 years on, modifications might well be desirable.

After independence, many lower-level colonial civil servants became senior officers in the public services, often as a result of the principle of seniority being rigidly acquired from the colonial government, but they were ill-equipped for their new role. The bureaucracy was large and important but did not have the institutional support to work effectively.

Regardless of ideology, the form of government adopted resembled that of colonial regimes, which made it doubly difficult for developing societies to overcome their colonial legacy. This problem was exacerbated because the bureaucracy was often the sole source of expertise and knowledge, particularly of a professional and technical kind, and could dominate even when there was a strong government and competing political parties. The practice of public administration became familiar to public servants and citizens alike. Weberian bureaucracy found fertile domains in the developing countries, but this was not without its problems, particularly when combined with underdeveloped political institutions. As Grindle (2000) argues 'whether because of the artificial and partial grafting on of western institutions by colonial powers or the ravages of chronic public sector poverty, rule by corrupt leaders, or institutional incapacity and decay, government institutions in most developing countries have never worked particularly well' (p. 189).

As Smith (1996) points out, 'a universal feature of colonial government was that it developed bureaucracies while neglecting legislatures, parties, local councils and other bodies able to maintain control and accountability' (p. 181). An administrative system can and did work for most of the twentieth century in the developed world, though with the limitations discussed in earlier chapters. But when bureaucracy is the only developed institutional actor, as in much of the developing world, a serious imbalance can and does arise. Administration requires instructions to be given clearly to enable an administrator to carry them out. However, if instructions are not clear, because of the inadequacies of the political system, or if political leaders are erratic, as is often the case, bureaucracy gains power. When bureaucracy, particularly administrative bureaucracy, is the most powerful institutional actor it rules without political constraint. But it is rudderless in the strategic sense without input from the political leadership. The separation of politics from administration may have been successful in developed countries for a long period, but in developing countries these principles have been inadequate because of the underdevelopment of the political system. Only if the political and administrative systems are in some kind of balance can Wilson's prescription have some utility.

As a result, the administrations of developing countries became true bureaucracies, meaning government by bureau; government by officials. There may even have been a 'bureaucratic mode of production' in which, as Smith (1996, pp. 235–6) notes:

The bureaucracy controls and manages the means of production through the state. It provides the necessary organization. It proliferates opportunities for bureaucratic careers by the creation of public bodies needing public managers – marketing boards, development corporations and other parastatal organizations and their subsidiaries. It articulates an ideology of state ownership and planning. It organizes the means of its own reproduction by passing on to the offspring of bureaucrats disproportionately advantageous opportunities to obtain the qualifications needed for entry into bureaucratic occupations and therefore the new class.

The bureaucracy maintained sole ownership of technical knowledge in the various sectors from agriculture to mining and industry. The bureaucracy was the sole employer of professional experts, most of them trained in the country of the former colonial master. There were no other institutions that could compete. As the sole source of knowledge it is easy for the bureaucracy to assume that it knows best, and that its experts need to be able to impose their solutions on to the various problems of development.

Some of these problems also occur in Western countries, particularly where bureaucracies involve technical experts. Yet these have other sources of information, a tradition of the bureaucracy being quite firmly subservient to the political leadership, as well as formal and informal rules to ensure ethical behaviour. In developing countries, the bureaucracy is superior to the rest of society. The principles of examination led to a closed bureaucracy open only to elites, formally educated (often in the West), but operating at a remove from their society of origin.

Public enterprise

In the post-independence period, governments were the prime agents of economic development, providing infrastructure, and producing goods and services, often provided through the mechanism of the public enterprise. Developing countries used public enterprises to a greater extent than was the case in most Western countries. For example, in 1977, Tanzania's 400 state-owned enterprises accounted for 38 per cent of gross fixed capital formation, similar to that of Ethiopia (Jorgensen, 1990, p. 62).

Initially there were some good reasons for this greater use of public enterprise. There was a chronic shortage of capital and capital markets such that private ownership would necessarily mean foreign ownership. Also, in many cases, no one from the private sector was interested in providing utility services for nation building, so for the nation to have necessary infrastructure it would need to be provided through the public sector. It was hard to develop exports without adequate port facilities or rail links, while the cities required reliable electricity supplies and telecommunication links. In addition, at the time of decolonization, in the 1950s and 1960s, public enterprise was considered to be an appropriate form of organization, unsurprisingly in view of the major role given to public enterprise in the former colonial powers such as the United Kingdom and France. At a time when public utilities in European countries were in public hands, allied with the expectation that public enterprise could be used to advance the cause of socialism, it was natural that Tanzania or Bangladesh would develop a large public enterprise sector. Indonesia even gave public enterprise a protected role in its constitution. India saw industrialization as the key to reducing poverty, and state ownership of industry as the means to control industrial development.

Much of the reliance on public enterprise was misplaced and the results were not what had been anticipated. Instead of serving as an agent of national development, many public enterprises served only the interests of their managers and workers. In 1991, public enterprises accounted for 23 per cent of formal employment in Africa and only 3 per cent in Asia, and in general, the poorer the country, the larger the relative size of the sector (Turner and Hulme, 1997, p. 176). Even if it could be argued that infrastructure needed to be provided through public hands, there seemed to be little justification for government ownership of jute factories in Bangladesh, mines in Africa or national airlines almost everywhere.

In some countries, public enterprises controlled almost all economic activity. From the late 1960s, the public enterprise sector in Zambia represented about 80 per cent of all economic activity, with the private sector accounting for the remaining 20 per cent (Kaunga, 1993). The sector was structured with one enterprise, Zimco, a holding company, controlling the other businesses, and with the government in turn, particularly the Zambian president, controlling Zimco. This meant that the government, and particularly the president, could control the greater proportion of economic as well as political activity. If economic success had followed, the public enterprise sector would have been lauded. However, Zambia declined; from 1960 to 1990 there was an average annual growth rate of −1.9 per cent compared to an average real increase of 2.9 per cent for other low-income countries (Simpson, 1994, p. 212).

Despite some successes, public enterprises in developing countries have been characterized by low profitability, poor returns on investment, and lack of strategy. There were a number of problems: managers were poorly trained and lacked direction; there was an inefficient organizational structure with 'overstaffing common; inadequate financial control systems; weak oversight by the government; political interference; and the "opportunistic misuse" of state-owned enterprises by private individuals, bureaucrats or joint-venture partners' (Jorgensen,

1990, p. 62). Loss-making enterprises were a significant burden on government budgets, with central government subsidies to state-owned enterprises not being spent on more urgent needs.

By the early 1980s, the popularity of the instrument of the public enterprise was in decline, allied to some general questioning of the economic role of government. Privatization was adopted by many developing countries in the 1980s following the apparent success of the programme in the UK. While privatization is under way in many developing countries it is difficult for the private sector to overcome its problems of insufficient capital or expertise.

Development administration

Particularly in the period following the Second World War, a single model of administration for developing countries was followed, termed 'development administration', a speciality within the broader field of public administration. The idea was to apply to developing countries the administrative theories and procedures derived from the former colonial countries to 'modernize' their economies, accelerating development to become equivalent, eventually, to the West. This approach included the various features of the best administrative practice available in the developed countries, which was the traditional model of public administration. A technocratic bureaucracy following rational/legal principles as set out by Weber would be all that was needed to overcome tribal authority and superstition, combined with the application of technical expertise to agriculture and industry. It was all rather patronizing, reflecting 'the naive optimism and ethnocentricity of modernization theory, that there were straightforward technical solutions for underdevelopment and the West possessed them' (Turner and Hulme, 1997, p. 12).

While the motivations of the practitioners of development administration were high, there were problems, as Dwivedi and Henderson (1990, pp. 13–14) note:

> Development administration was supposed to be based on professionally oriented, technically competent, politically and ideologically neutral bureaucratic machinery ... The ostensible output was modernization – induced and predictable social change following Western perceptions – preceded by institution-building and modernization of the indigenous bureaucratic machinery to undertake developmental tasks ... But what was missing from the expected picture-perfect imitation in the Third World was the necessary set of conditions for bringing about a number of social, economic, cultural and political changes. These included an expanding economic base, a tax base, professionally trained manpower, political legitimacy, cultural secularization, universalism, a relatively open society, and a strong political superstructure capable of governing.

The principles of development administration were those of the pre-vailing model of administration in the West – that of formal bureau-cracy. Despite the different models of economic development followed in Tanzania, India, Pakistan or the Pacific region, the familiar precepts of a Weberian system were to be found almost universally.

Development administration largely faded as a speciality within public administration in the mid-1970s as its theories and assumptions came under attack (Turner and Hulme, 1997, pp. 12–17), and a similar kind of demise had befallen its allied discipline, development economics (Krugman, 1995). There were intellectual problems in trying to carve out a separate speciality and at times the arguments between different theorists seemed to ignore the fact that there were real problems in the administration of developing countries.

Problems with the administrative model

The traditional model of administration did not serve developing coun-tries particularly well. Features which worked in the West, notably political neutrality and incorruptibility, were not followed as rigor-ously in the Third World, and the bureaucracy, while maintaining the appearance and institutions of the traditional form, tended to serve particular elite, ethnic or religious interests. Above all, it served itself. While there is some argument about the model of public choice as applied to the bureaucracy in the West, in the developing world it could scarcely be denied that bureaucrats looked after their own inter-ests first. Also, it was rare that the performance of public servants was evaluated in a systematic way and there were manifest problems of accountability, with no one taking responsibility for negative out-comes.

How much of the problem can be attributed to the bureaucratic model itself? It could be argued that what was happening was not the problem of the model, but was rather that its precepts were being per-verted, as exemplified by the problem of corruption. While this is pos-sible, it is more the case that the flaws in the model were exacerbated in developing countries. It was always naïve to think that bureaucrats would be impersonal, neutral arbiters and not involved in either poli-tics or looking after themselves. The problems could be argued about in developed countries, but in developing countries their effects could be seen in corruption and other forms of self-enrichment. While not unknown in developed countries, problems of corruption were worse in developing ones. As Huque (1996, p. 23) argues:

> Public administration itself is susceptible to corruption since officials exercise a substantial amount of power. There are possibilities for acquiring improper

benefits by interpreting or bending rules in favour of certain groups or individuals. All governments seek to have in place a number of safeguards for deterring and dealing with corruption within administrative agencies. At the same time, public administration has to develop ways and means to prevent and detect corruption in other sections of society. Much of the benefit of rapid economic growth or a stable political order may be lost in the growing tide of corruption.

How could it be expected that public servants would stay out of politics as the model naïvely assumes they should, when the bureaucracy was the most powerful political force and many of the political leaders were inept? How can Weber's model of rational-legal authority apply when the rule of law is itself weak?

Compounding these problems was the fact that developing countries failed to thrive under the traditional model of administration, and the failures were more often than not failures of governance. In part because of the apparent failures of the traditional model of administration, developing countries began to experiment with other forms. If the key characteristic of the traditional model is bureaucracy and the key characteristic of new public management is the use of markets, it was clear that developing countries had begun to discard the traditional model at the same time as they began to adopt market approaches more generally.

Public sector reform

Developing countries started to change their attitudes to public sector management in large part following the public sector reforms that began in the developed world in the 1980s. The World Bank's *World Development Report* raised the issue of government capacity in 1983, arguing that 'development failures and disappointments were now seen not simply as the result of inappropriate policy choices but also because state institutions were performing poorly' (quoted in Turner and Hulme, 1997, p. 105). This was to be a persistent theme in subsequent reports on development.

The role of government

In response to questioning regarding the role and size of government in the 1970s and 1980s (see Chapter 2), the idea became popular that the best government was minimal government in the developing world as well as in developed countries. Many countries saw the need to further define the role of government in order to move away from central planning and allow for economic liberalization, the privatization of public enterprises and to change the management of government. Some of this was in response to continuing failure to develop or pass on economic benefits to the society as a whole instead of only to a narrow elite, and some was in response to demands made by international agencies requiring market reforms and public sector cuts.

Developing countries found themselves undergoing various kinds of structural adjustment to satisfy international agencies, notably the World Bank and the IMF. The various structural adjustment programmes, at least in their initial stages, were not particularly successful. There seemed to be an assumption that, merely because neo-classical economic theory prescribed a minimal role for the state, all that was needed for economic development to occur was to cut the public sector. It seemed that another orthodoxy – the simple reduction of state activity – was to replace the previous orthodoxy of development administration. It also seemed that the result would be no better.

The shift to state minimization did not work as intended. Even the World Bank (1997), one of the institutions whose prescriptions had led to this impasse, for which it must share some blame, could comment later (p. 24):

> As often happens with such radical shifts in perspective, countries sometimes tended to overshoot the mark. Efforts to rebalance government spending and borrowing were uncoordinated, and the good was as often cut as the bad. To meet their interest obligations, countries mired in debt squeezed critically important programmes in education, health, and infrastructure as often as – or more than – they cut low-priority programmes, bloated civil-service rolls, and money-losing enterprises.

It was simple, but also simplistic, to say that government just needed to be cut. What was more important was that government should be efficient, facilitative and appropriate to its circumstances rather than merely small. This change in attitude led the funding agencies to change their perspective on the role of government. In the 1990s, development specialists 'were concerned about building institutions for democratic accountability as well as for economic regulation and management' (Grindle, 2000, p. 189). And, following a period in which policy seemed to be based on the assumption that all developing countries needed was to reduce the role of government to the bare minimum, the World Bank began to emphasize public sector reform.

In 1997, the World Bank argued that 'an effective state is vital for the provision of the goods and services – and the rules and institutions – that allow markets to flourish and people to lead healthier, happier lives'. The need for government to provide a suitable institutional framework seemed to be forgotten during the 1980s and early 1990s, when developing countries were urged simply to reduce the size and scope of government. The change of stance in the World Bank and other international organizations was a recognition that markets require good governance and government in order to work effectively.

Indeed, the key economic role for the government may well be to create an institutional framework that lowers the costs of transacting; 'a well-functioning economy requires a well-functioning government' (Yeager, 1999, p. 41).

Several institutions are required for markets to function well and these are provided by governments as part of the infrastructure of society. Perhaps the biggest lesson of the transition to a market system in Russia and the former Eastern bloc countries was the need to establish key institutions to govern markets. In most cases, the early years of these countries transitioning to a market economy were years of failure, not usually because of markets themselves failing, but more often the result of a failure of institutional arrangements that are taken for granted in Western countries. There were political failures, failures of regulation, including insufficient planning for what would replace public enterprises, and failures within public services. Two key features – enforcement of contracts and property rights – are argued to be the most important institutions that enable markets to prosper. The existence of a legal system for contracts is the single most important feature, as without that markets are not likely to get beyond low-level transactions. Property rights are desirable and will be demanded once markets become established.

Yet other institutions can enhance the operations of markets. Grindle (2000) adds 'independent central banks and tax agencies, stock markets, and regulatory bodies for privatised industries and financial institutions' to contracts and property rights (pp. 180–1). Additional institutions such as independent central banks, stock market and other economic regulation are obviously useful, but are not as fundamental as is a legal system to enforce contracts and property rights for buyers and sellers. A country that established a legal system which could operate independently to enforce contracts and to ensure property rights would be one well on the way to being a market society. Other institutions, such as democratic elections, antitrust regulation and so on are helpful, but are not necessarily needed prior to the existence of a market society.

If in the traditional model government was large and all-powerful, governments in developing countries would now have to accept a more facilitative role. In its *World Development Report* of 1997, the World Bank asserted:

> An effective state is vital for the provision of the goods and services – and the rules and institutions – that allow markets to flourish and people to lead healthier, happier lives. Without it, sustainable development, both economic and social, is impossible. Many said much the same thing fifty years ago, but then they tended to mean that development had to be state-provided. The message of experience since then is rather different: that the state is central to economic and social development, not as a direct provider of growth but as a partner, catalyst, and facilitator.

Markets were to be encouraged, not discouraged, and the role of government was as a facilitator in economic development rather than a competitor.

The role of government was to change from that in the post-independence period, but was also quite different from the 'small government' approach tried in the 1970s and 1980s. Stiglitz (2001) argues that there is a new agenda for development (p. 346):

> It sees governments and markets as complements rather than substitutes. It takes as dogma neither that markets by themselves will ensure desirable outcomes nor that the absence of a market, or some related market failure, requires government to assume responsibility for the activity. It often does not even ask whether a particular activity should be in the public or the private sector. Rather, in some circumstances the new agenda sees government as helping to create markets ... In other areas ... it sees the government and the private sector working together as partners, each with its own responsibilities. And in still others ... it sees government as providing the essential regulation without which markets cannot function.

This relatively pragmatic approach is a long way from the earlier view that government simply needed to be minimized. Attention would also need to be paid to the management competence of government.

Changes in management

In the earlier structural adjustment period, there was a real problem of administrative competence in implementing international assistance programmes, and this inadequacy was itself a reason for the failure of many of them. There were some signs that the international institutions recognized the problem and this led them to set up programmes to improve governmental performance, with the World Bank, the United Nations and the OECD offering various programmes aimed at improving the management of the public sector. How the institutions of government were organized and, importantly, how the managerial competence of public managers should be developed, were to be explored instead of the usual programmes of privatization and spending cuts. No longer, it seemed, was government merely to be minimized as part of a programme of structural adjustment; it was also to be improved. The theoretical framework used seemed to draw from new public management.

In its landmark 1997 development report the World Bank (1997, pp. 79–80) wrote:

> Many lower income countries have been unable to provide even the most rudimentary underpinnings of a rule-based civil service. Their formal systems often resemble those of industrial countries on paper. But in practice informality remains the norm. Merit-based personnel rules are circumvented, and staff are

recruited or promoted on the basis of patronage and clientelism; budgets are unrealistic and often set aside in any case by ad hoc decisions during implementation. At bottom, all these problems can be traced back to weaknesses in the underlying institutions; poor enforceability of the rule of law both within and beyond the public sector; a lack of built-in mechanisms for listening to, and forming partnerships with, firms and civil society; and a complete absence of competitive pressure in policymaking, the delivery of services and personnel practices.

The World Bank (1997) report called for three essential building blocks. First, 'strong central capacity for formulating and coordinating policy', including visions, goals and strategic priorities regarding the place of politicians and the public service alike; second, an 'efficient and effective delivery system', setting the balance between flexibility and accountability, including contracts for contestable services, better performance and client feedback; and third, 'motivated and capable staff, with incentive structures to motivate them to perform well, including merit-based recruitment and promotion, adequate pay, and a strong esprit de corps' (p. 81). All these elements are to be found in the public management model, but not in the traditional model of administration.

Dealing with corruption

The propensity to be corrupt needs to be assumed to be the same everywhere, rather than as a problem confined to developing countries. However, such societies have had greater problems than others with corruption, but the main reason is inferior management practices, rather than behavioural or other norms. Management systems need to be designed by assuming that public officials will be corrupt unless the system design itself either prevents it or raises the relative cost to such a high level that such behaviour is less likely to occur. It follows, then, that better management can lead to reduced corruption.

Manion argues that corrupt payoffs can be reduced by two main strategies: enforcement and institutional design, with a third strategy being education, to increase the 'psychic costs' of corruption. As Manion (2004, pp. 16–17) argues:

> *Enforcement* strategies reduce corrupt payoffs by increasing the likelihood that corrupt officials and their accomplices in society are discovered and, when discovered, punished with severity commensurate to the corrupt act. Enforcement strategies increase resources devoted to monitoring and detection, increase punishments for corruption, or both ... Anticorruption reform through *institutional design* restructures transactions to lessen incentives ... and opportunities to transact corruptly.

In particular, for those parts of government that offer licences and permissions, government may leave the field altogether as well as legalizing activities that generate corruption, such as off-track betting on horse-racing. Manion (2004) also argues that bureaucracies may be reorganized so that 'several officials supply the same government service' (p. 17). Also, such practices as sealed competitive bids for procurement and the like need to be embedded in all parts of government.

The standard ways mentioned for dealing with corruption are to: first, find malefactors and prosecute them, and, second, try to advance the notion of a transparent political structure that encourages accountability. While these may be useful and worthy, they do not go far enough, unless the institutional design aspect is extended to be about management, system design and process mapping, rather than just about greater democracy and transparency, as is more usual.

Most often, it appears that corruption is quite opportunistic, resulting from someone seeing a gap in a system; in other words, an administrative failing. If payment systems, tendering rules, appointments of staff, and budget and accounting systems – all the ways that government bureaucracies operate – were designed as if the staff involved in their operation would be corrupt if the opportunity presented itself, better results could be achieved. In Hong Kong, for example, staff from the Independent Commission Against Corruption (ICAC) participate in the design of government programmes as 'full participants in the initial design of procedures, policies, and legislation' with staff bringing to that process 'their specialized knowledge and a single concern: the implications for corruption' (Manion, 2004, p. 52). In addition, ICAC was given the power to investigate and make recommendations with regard to management systems and practices, not necessarily related to any ongoing investigation of illegal activity. Even as there was more enforcement and education of the community about corruption, having anti-corruption officials present when programmes were in the design phase to put forward their views from a corruption prevention perspective can greatly reduce the later incidence of corruption.

Contracting-out can also be used to reduce corruption. Providing a contracting process is run well and precisely what is to be delivered can be spelt out clearly, a contract could reduce corruption. For example, in 1996, the government of Mozambique contracted with the British firm Crown Agents to run the customs and excise in that country. This contract was aimed specifically at reducing corruption as well as at training and other longer-term benefits after the contract had ended. The point generally is that public management systems and their design do need to be able to be examined in order to reduce the chance of corruption occurring. Corruption of the opportunistic kind can be dealt with by better management above all else; that is, better public management.

Problems with the managerial model

There are a number of possible problems in adopting managerial reforms in the public sectors of developing countries, which are dealt with individually below.

Institutional arrangements

It is one thing to adopt a market and managerial approach, but quite another to have markets that work. Developing countries often have little experience of the operation of markets, and there is a range of factors required before markets can be effective. Markets are ineffective without the rule of law, for example, to ensure compliance with contracts. Yet it could be argued that many people in the developing world are natural traders, with a history of commerce dating back over many centuries and that these instincts were stifled during the period of command economies. But, until capital markets develop or domestic entrepreneurs appear, a market economy may mean greater domination by foreigners and foreign corporations.

There are obvious problems in moving to contractual arrangements for the delivery of services if the rule of law and the enforcement of contracts are not well established. Contracting works best where its outcomes are easy to specify. Where goals are vague and not able to be clearly set down in writing, or where corruption is endemic, using contracts is not likely to succeed. Without establishing the appropriate preconditions, the World Bank (1997) points out that the new public management 'must be introduced cautiously' (p. 97):

> If informal norms have long deviated significantly from formal ones (with regard to personnel practices, for example), simply introducing new formal rules will not change much. Where countries have been unable to establish credible controls over inputs, giving managers greater flexibility will only encourage arbitrary actions and corruption. And where specialized skills are in short supply, performance contracts and other output-based contracts for complex services may absorb a large share of scarce bureaucratic capacity to specify and enforce them. Nevertheless, countries can begin by providing greater clarity of purpose and task and by introducing performance measurement on a selective, sequential basis. When output measurement is strengthened and credible controls over inputs are instituted, managers can be granted more operational flexibility in exchange for greater accountability for results.

Contracting has major problems in the West, so without the other changes noted it would seem difficult for developing countries to move away from formal bureaucracies. A phased approach would seem likely to be more successful than to assume that sudden shifts can be made.

Privatization of public enterprise

There may be particular problems concerning the privatization of public enterprises, even if such enterprises have generally failed in the developing world. As Price (1994, p. 253) comments:

> Policy changes reflect a complete change in development philosophy, from a state-centred to a market-centred approach, and have consequently redefined the relation and boundary between the public and private sectors. As in the UK, where privatisation began, this is largely a reaction to perceived government failure in organising the public sector to the benefit of the economy at large (rather than any particular interest group). There is a danger that the public sector baby will everywhere be thrown out with the bath water, and that in discovering government failure states and agencies forget that market failure is also rampant.

As has been shown on occasion in the West, some public enterprises are well managed and serve governmental and societal purposes as well as commercial ones. An unvarying requirement for privatization, as usually set out by the World Bank, does not allow case-by-case circumstances for privatization to be specified. If a case-by-case approach is suitable for Western countries why should it not be allowed for developing countries? There are circumstances in which privatization will inevitably mean foreign ownership or ownership by one particular ethnic group, thus risking societal cohesion. Even if privatization is generally beneficial, there may be circumstances in which it is not. If markets are undeveloped, privatization will mean foreign ownership, and public utilities will need to be carefully regulated.

In addition, privatization is difficult to manage, and developing countries might not have the administrative capacity to do this successfully. While there are many examples of successful privatization, there are also many others that were not a success. Even the pro-privatization World Bank could point to poor examples. Guinea privatized 158 public enterprises between 1985 and 1992, but this change proceeded without a clear programme or legal framework; procedures for competitive bidding and accounting were not made clear; assets were often sold for much less than their value; and successful bidders were offered terms that sometimes included monopoly licences and the like (World Bank, 1995, p. 244). It is all very well to argue for the privatization of public enterprise, but in developing countries implementing such a policy successfully is no trivial task.

Corruption

Changing from bureaucracy to markets might seem to risk making corruption endemic, though corruption might be reduced 'by cutting back on discretionary authority'; and reform 'of the civil service, restraining political patronage, and improving civil service pay have also been shown to reduce corruption by giving public officials more incentive to play by the rules' (World Bank, 1997, p. 9). The reality is, however, that the bureaucracy remains more important than in Western countries, and that in order for the market-oriented changes to work, a powerful institution will have to give up a substantial amount of its power and, in the absence of other power centres in the polity or markets, will have to do so voluntarily.

There may be opportunities for unscrupulous people in the managerial system, notably in the case of contracting, but there were opportunities too in the traditional model of administration, as developing countries have shown, in such areas as the allocation of licences and permits, as well as in governmental purchasing. Whether greater ethical problems do occur as the result of managerialism will not be known for some time. However, if the benefit of the old system was its high standards of behaviour, its weakness was that results were only incidental. Greater transparency and freer availability of information should be sufficient incentive devices for the maintenance of high ethical behaviour by managers. But it does no good to insist that countries with problems of corruption should follow old-style bureaucratic processes and procedures when these have failed in the past. Similarly, it does no good, if improving management is one of the best ways of reducing corruption, to then reduce the allowable scope of good management.

The public sector reforms since the 1980s have attracted some criticism on the grounds they may lead to an increase in corruption. According to Hood (1991), the new public management 'assumes a culture of public service honesty as given' and 'its recipes to some degree removed devices instituted to ensure honesty and neutrality in the public service in the past (fixed salaries, rules of procedure, permanence of tenure, restraints on the power of line management, clear lines of division between public and private sectors)' and the extent to which the change 'is likely to induce corrosion in terms of such traditional values remains to be tested' (p. 16). On the other hand, deLeon and Green (2004) argue that there are several constructs that would be useful in combating the excesses of political corruption, including 'community-owned government, competitive government, mission-driven government, and results-oriented government that is enterprising, anticipatory, and decentralized' as well as 'modern accounting and management information systems' (p. 240). Anti-corruption policies could 'include a restructuring of the state to reduce its role through privatization and deregulation' (Rose-Ackerman, 1999, p. 220). Done well, this would transfer the risk to the private sector, but done badly – that is, without adequate regulation – what was once public sector corruption could just as easily become private sector corruption.

A single model

There is a sense that there is yet another single model of development that all must follow. This being a mistake in the old model of development administration is hard to deny, but it does seem that to make developing countries once again follow another single Western model is likely to be problematic. As Turner and Hulme (1997, p. 240) state:

> Whatever the reasons – naivety, historical and environmental blindness, or ideology – a powerful international lobby is promoting a 'one size fits all' approach to public sector reform in spite of the evidence accumulated from organizational and management theory and from empirical study that the outcomes of planned changes in organizations are conditioned by many contingent factors, especially those in the organization's environment. In some contexts, the NPM may yield its promised benefits, but in others the possibility of it contributing to reduced performance, and even political instability must be recognized.

Too much can be claimed for any model. In the same way as the bureaucratic model failed in its attempts to impose a single view of modernization on disparate developing countries, the managerial model may fail in a similar way. There are differing national perspectives and these need to be respected. However, the managerial model should allow for differing approaches in a way that the bureaucratic model does not, as the basic prescription is to manage for results but with the precise method able to be varied.

Expectation

Public sector reform does offer much to developing countries, at least in comparison to the bureaucratic model, which failed in that context. However, by itself it is unlikely to be able to overcome the manifest problems of developing countries. Any kind of management can be expected to do too much, and this expectation can itself lead to failure. Certainly, if developing countries are forced to adopt a single unvarying model of public management, the result is unlikely to be successful. There are problems of institutions, the rule of law, inadequate capital and retail markets, insufficient educated staff and so on. Moreover, developing countries have different histories and capabilities, and are not homogeneous.

If as part of the change to a market economy, institutional arrangements to enforce contracts, provide for competition and so on can be adopted prior to new kinds of public management, there is little reason to argue that the only kind of management suitable for developing countries is the old bureaucratic kind. It is patronizing in its own way to argue that traditional bureaucracy is the only way that developing countries are capable of managing, particularly when the administrative model failed so signally in the past.

Conclusion

Many developing countries seem intent on following some kind of managerialism as an organizing principle for their public sectors. This is happening as a result of encouragement from the World Bank and other international agencies in an effort to overcome both the endemic problems of development and the failure of earlier models of development economics and development administration.

Developing countries need a stronger private sector and stronger markets before going too far into public sector reform. These neither develop overnight nor do so without certain fundamentals that are related only obliquely to the administrative system, such as adherence to the rule of law, laws to maintain competition and prevent the emergence of monopolies, and competent staff. All three of these are frequently lacking in the developing world, and to assume that simply turning activities over to the private sector will work without any other change is wishful thinking. Markets require a competent and appropriate public sector if they are to work at all. In general, though, the traditional bureaucratic model did not serve developing countries very well, and a change to public management accompanied by increased use of the private sector should help the transition of developing countries into more developed ones.

Chapter 15

Conclusion: Paradigms in Public Management

Chapter Contents

- Introduction
- Paradigms in public management
- The traditional administrative model as a paradigm
- New Public Management as a paradigm
- Public management as a paradigm
- Issues in public sector reform
- Conclusion

Introduction

The argument here is that the traditional model of administration is obsolete and has been replaced by public management, and that this change represents a change of paradigm in the internal management of the public sector. In the beginning the reforms may well have been theoretically and ideologically driven, based on public choice and other economic theories, and including attacks on the traditional practices and conditions of public servants. And once the reform process had begun it continued into areas that might have once seemed sacrosanct. However, as the reforms continued into the later 1990s and beyond, they were less ideological and more about greater efficiency – an old public administration value – and more too about engaging with the citizenry. Many countries adopted their own reform programmes based more upon finding better ways of managing and getting results than following some ideological predilection as to the appropriate role of government in society. If the idea put forward by doctrinaire economists in the early 1980s was that government could be reduced to a bare minimum (Friedman and Friedman, 1980), it became harder to find many adherents to that view thirty years later, other than among a few extremists. Instead, there has been a relatively pragmatic division between things that governments and public services do well, and things that the private sector does well.

315

There are two key aspects to this concluding chapter. The first is to examine further the vexed question of paradigms. It is argued here that, either using the ordinary meaning of the word or the usage associated with the work of Kuhn (1970), the term paradigm is appropriate for both the traditional model of administration and that of public management. It follows that the change from the one to the other can be characterized as a paradigm shift. However, it is argued in addition that the specific kind of public management reform commonly known as New Public Management (NPM) (Hood, 1991) is not a paradigm in its own right. There was never a clear enough specification of NPM; there was little identifiable advocacy or even academic synthesis. And if there ever was an NPM era, it has now passed, while public management continues.

The second key aspect is to assess public management reform as a whole. Even as individual chapters have addressed some of the criticisms made against reform, there is still the totality to be looked at one more time. Has reform been successful, or do the critics have a point? Public sector reforms attracted academic critics from the start, with trenchant disapproval from one writer or another regarding every conceivable aspect of reform. Arguments about NPM have raged for years within academia, though these arguments and even the term itself had little impact on practice or practitioners. It could be argued that the main utility of the appellation of NPM was as a handy label for critics to bundle together disparate changes and attack them as a whole; a whole that has either passed or never really existed. Public sector reforms have been regarded by critics, variously, as an assault on democracy, an ideological movement, merely a fad, and have only achieved a derogation of morale within the public services where change has been tried. The general argument here is that some criticisms have been valid, some have been overly strident, and others have missed the mark completely.

And yet, taking a longer view, the public sector in the second decade of the twenty-first century is vastly different from that of the penultimate decade of the twentieth century. Regardless of their critics, governments went ahead with change. Reforms can fail and often do (Pollitt and Bouckaert, 2004, pp. 6–8), with the period after a reform being crucial to any long-term success (Patashnik, 2008). While specific NPM-style reforms can be criticized and even some aspects discarded, it is without doubt that more general forms of public management reform have not only continued but have become part of the mainstream.

Paradigms in public management

One of the more interesting parts of the debate over managerial reform has been whether the changes – and even the most fervent of critics agree that there has been change – are sufficient to constitute a paradigm shift. Some have argued that there is paradigmatic change (for example, Barzelay, 1992; Osborne and Gaebler, 1992; Holmes and Shand, 1995; Behn, 1998a, 2001; OECD, 1998a; Borins, 1999; Mathiasen, 1999). Others argue that there has been no change of paradigm or universal movement of change (for example, Pollitt, 1990, 1993; Hood, 1995, 1996; Lynn, 1997, 1998, 2001a, 2001b; Pollitt and Bouckaert, 2000, 2004; Gruening, 2001). It may be more useful to look again at what a paradigm is, and whether the idea of competing paradigms in the broader field of public administration has some validity.

Some writers are uncomfortable with the word 'paradigm'. As Behn (2001) argues, 'The world is divided into two camps: people who use the word *paradigm* daily and those who detest it' and notes further 'the word does appear to be appropriate to this context under the third definition from *Merriam Webster's Collegiate Dictionary* (tenth edition): "a philosophical and theoretical framework of a scientific school or discipline within which theories, laws, and generalizations and the experiments performed in support of them are formulated"' (pp. 230–1). Writing in the mid-1970s, Frederickson (1980) was able to find five paradigms for public administration (pp. 35–43), clearly indicating that he had no qualms regarding the use of the term.

Lynn (1997), however, remarks that 'The variation in the models of reform being tried around the world strongly suggest that *there is no new paradigm*, if by paradigm we use Thomas Kuhn's original definition: achievements that for a time provide model problems and solutions to a community of practitioners' (p. 114). Lynn quotes Kuhn (1970, p. 43) to the effect that paradigms are 'a set of recurrent and quasi-standard illustrations of various theories in their conceptual, observational, and instrumental applications'. According to Behn (2001), 'Lynn then argues that there is no "community", no "accepted theoretical canon", and no "accepted methods of application" and concludes that "one cannot find evidence to support a claim of widespread transformation, much less a claim that a new paradigm has emerged"' (p. 234). In Lynn's view it appears that a paradigm is to be regarded as a large hurdle to jump, requiring agreement among all its practitioners – a more or less permanent way of looking at the world (see also Gruening, 2001).

Much of the modern usage of the word 'paradigm' derives, as Lynn notes, from Kuhn (1970). However, Kuhn does not define paradigm clearly and uses the word in several different ways. A paradigm does not mean one set of views that everyone must agree on, rather views that exist for a time and are revealed in the discipline's practices. Within economics, for example, there would be few quibbles referring to the 'classical paradigm', the 'Keynesian paradigm', the 'neo-classical paradigm' or the 'Marxist paradigm'. These are all sets of ideas that identify a school of thought within the broader discipline of economics and can even exist at the same time as each other. Instead of a paradigm being a generally agreed framework among all the practitioners of a science, it is actually a contested idea. It does not require agreement among all practitioners; and there are often competing paradigms in the same field.

The traditional administrative model as a paradigm

There are different views as to whether what is referred to here as the traditional model of public administration can be considered a paradigm. To Behn (2001), the traditional model of administration does qualify as a paradigm, and, as he continues, 'certainly, those who support traditional public administration would argue that they have a "discipline," complete with "theories, laws, and generalizations," that focus their research' (p. 231). In this sense the traditional model of administration is clearly a paradigm; it constituted a series of ideas that had currency for a time. Behn argues elsewhere that the intellectual heritage of the 'current public administration paradigm comes from the thinking, writing, and proselytizing of Woodrow Wilson, Frederick Winslow Taylor, and Max Weber' (Behn, 1998a, p. 134). That these men are the key theorists of the traditional model of administration was discussed earlier (see Chapter 3).

Another theorist to see the traditional model as a paradigm was Ostrom. In his book, *The Intellectual Crisis in American Public Administration* (1974, 1989), Ostrom (1989) argued that the traditional model had problems, was in crisis, and called for a new approach. He said that 'the sense of crisis that has pervaded the field of public administration over the last generation has been evoked by the insufficiency of the paradigm inherent in the traditional theory of public administration' (p. 15). To Ostrom, Weber's theory of bureaucracy 'was fully congruent with the traditional theory of public administration in both form and method' (p. 8) and he pointed out the problems of bureaucracy and lack of intellectual coherence in public administration. The idea of crisis was explicitly drawn by Ostrom from Kuhn (1970), who had stated that paradigm testing occurs 'only after the sense of crisis has evoked an alternate candidate for paradigm' and that testing occurs 'as part of the competition between two rival paradigms for the allegiance of the scientific community' (p. 145). Ostrom (1989) held that the traditional model was a paradigm and nominated an alternative derived from economics (pp. 11–19).

However, Pollitt and Bouckaert (2004) consider that 'the idea of a single, and now totally obsolete, *ancien regime* is as implausible as the suggestion that there is now a global recipe which will reliably deliver 'reinvented' governments' (p. 63). Lynn (2001b) also disagrees that there ever was such a traditional model, stating (pp. 146–7):

> That there was an old orthodoxy has ... become the new orthodoxy. The essence of traditional public administration is repeatedly asserted to be the design and defence of a largely self-serving, Weberian bureaucracy that was to be strictly insulated from politics and that justified its actions based on a technocratic, one best way 'science of administration'. Facts were to be separated from values, politics from administration, and policy from implementation. Traditional administration is held to be sluggish, rigid, rule bound, centralised, insular, self-protective, and profoundly antidemocratic.

Based on an examination of the literature, Lynn argues that there were many theories in this period, not just one; and many ways of approaching public administration rather than only one model. However, any examination of public administration practice in the classical period, perhaps particularly in settings other than the United States, would show that it was indeed hierarchical and bureaucratic, that it was based on scientific management and that it did aspire to the principles of separation of politics from administration as set out by Wilson.

In another paper, Lynn (1997) argues against the idea of a post-bureaucratic paradigm, stating that this would mean 'a fundamental transformation in the historic role of the nation state'. He says, 'if the post-bureaucratic paradigm is rational/legal in the Weberian sense, then a post-bureaucratic paradigm must be founded on a different basis of legitimacy: perhaps different forms of rationality, different jurisprudential principles, a different allocation of property rights' (pp. 109–10). Perhaps a Weberian bureaucracy is regarded as being necessary for the modern nation state. However, Lynn overstates the case in three ways. First, market rationality is a valid alternative in many settings and a familiar one in that it is the central organizing feature of the private sector. Second, public sector reform does not mean totally overthrowing the system of government, the rational/legal authority of jurisprudence and property rights. Third, a reformed government would still be bureaucratic even if there was only a very small public service to carry out its functions through contract. In other words, public management does not require a different basis of legitimacy.

To move completely away from a rational/legal paradigm would indeed require a different form of legitimacy but that has never been in prospect. Managerial reform has been most of all about internal change. Governments are still elected by the normal means and not from a totally different form of politics. Some parts of government can and should be provided bureaucratically, but this does not mean that *all* government functions and services must be provided in that way, nor does it mean that *all* public servants need be employed for life under the career service model. One of the key aspects of public sector reform has been to push the envelope regarding those functions that should be provided by a bureaucracy and those that should not, those to be contracted out and those that would be provided ineffectively if they were. A totally different system of government does not follow from a change to some services being provided by other than bureaucratic ways.

Lynn (2001a) contends that the profession of public administration 'mounts an unduly weak challenge to various revisionists and to the superficial thinking and easy answers of the policy schools and the ubiquitous management consultants' (p. 155). He continues 'basic political and legal issues of responsible management in a postmodern era are inadequately defined and addressed. Such a result ill becomes a profession that once owned impressively deep insight into public administration in a representative democracy' (p. 155). Such is the fate of old paradigms. The decline of one school of thought occurs as a result of the rise of an alternative. Or as Kuhn (1970) points out, 'the decision to reject one paradigm is always simultaneously the decision to accept another, and the judgment leading to that decision involves the comparison of both paradigms with nature *and* with one another' (p. 77). The problem with the traditional model of administration was that its underlying theories lost support and lost relevance, so much so that the defence of the old model indeed has been weak. It is not the case that in a single moment everyone decided that public administration had been superseded; it is more the case that paradigms gradually change. A paradigm based on formal bureaucracy, separation of politics from administration and 'one best way' thinking, combined with unusual employment practices, now seems dated and old-fashioned. But a paradigm it was; and one with its own long and distinguished history.

New Public Management as a paradigm

It would be tempting to regard what was termed 'New Public Management' (Hood, 1991) as an opposing paradigm to the traditional model of administration (see Gow and Dufour, 2000). That is not the argument here, however. It is asserted, rather, that NPM is not a sufficiently concrete term, with its own advocates and defenders, to constitute a paradigm. There are three reasons for this: first, there is an almost total absence of identifiable advocates; second, NPM is too vague in content to be useful, with almost every discussant having his or her own version – often wildly different from the opinions of others

– of what it is; and third, and a corollary to the first one, NPM has become a term used almost exclusively by critics of public sector reform.

The advocacy of NPM

It is normally the case that a new approach or a new theory has some identifiable person or people putting it forward. For example, the New Public Administration in the 1960s and 1970s could claim as advocates those who were at the Minnowbrook Conference in 1968 and subscribed to its manifesto (Marini, 1971). Even if a movement arises seemingly spontaneously, there are usually advocates or synthesizers even if there is no single originator or theorist. However, NPM has neither been theorized nor defended so that it can be considered to have been a coherent theory from the start. There has been some commentary from within the bureaucracy (Holmes and Shand, 1995; Horn, 1995; Scott, 2001), even if the term is not used by them, but there is, overall, an absence of advocacy.

Hood's original description of NPM (1991) was that of a perceptive observer who had noticed what appeared to be a set of reasonably consistent reforms coming from the British government. The real novelty was in the linking together of different changes and attaching a name to them. Hood should not be regarded as the key advocate or theorist of NPM, indeed, as he maintained some years later (Hood and Peters, 2004, p. 268):

> No general theoretical treatise emerged from the academic world as the 'bible' of a new approach to public sector managerialism (many of the early ideas came from practitioners such as the New Zealand Treasury) ... but the coherence of the emerging ideas and practices also attracted some debate and attention, as well as attempts to explain the emergence of an apparently new agenda ... Like most divinities, NPM turned out to be somewhat mystical in essence, as no two authors of that era listed exactly the same features in enumerating its traits.

There are several important points here. For a start, Hood and Peters argue that there has been no general theoretical treatise encapsulating the movement; second, the early ideas came from practitioners; third, practitioners from the New Zealand Treasury, in particular, are supposed to have had a major role; fourth, NPM became 'somewhat mystical'; and fifth, no two authors list exactly the same features for NPM. It is interesting that a major survey of the field a number of years later could find no general theoretical treatise.

The reference to New Zealand and its Treasury does deserve further examination. There was once a time when Wellington was a destination of choice for public servants from other countries wanting to observe the radical reforms that had taken place there (see Boston *et al.*, 1996), even if the lessons were often not particularly relevant (Schick, 1998). But the New Zealand experiment of the 1980s was not a general theoretical exercise; it was, rather, a practical response to an immediate crisis. As Graham Scott, head of the Treasury in New Zealand at the time, notes, the reforms there in the 1980s were driven by ministers and their senior officials, with the impetus being the difficult economic circumstances the country found itself in at that time. Rather than New Zealand being the laboratory for a bold experiment in new ways of managing, it was the government – politicians and officials together – responding to pressing problems. As Scott (2001, p. 35) argues:

> New Zealand's politicians drove the reforms for practical reasons. The newly elected Labour government of 1984 had powerful forces for change in the combination of a discal squeeze and capable ministers enthusiastic to improve the performance of the economy and government. Economic growth was low, debt and inflation were rising, there was a large fiscal deficit and the economy was caught in a web of distorting industry subsidies and regulation. The government was a large player in the economy, supplying many goods and services that were considered by some politicians to be better provided by the private sector such as telecommunications, railways, airline services, construction, farming and forestry. Concerns about the quality of policy advice, inefficient government enterprises, the level of government spending and a lack of accountability in the large bureaucracy fuelled a desire for change.

Ideas to assist in solving what were manifest problems were sought from other disciplines, including economics and private management, apparently after deciding that old-style administration was unhelpful in addressing the problems New Zealand faced. As Scott (2001, p. 25) explains:

> Officials, particularly in the Treasury, drew on ideas from institutional theory, financial and accounting theory and practice and the eclectic, pragmatic literatures on public and private management. There is a common theoretical thread running through these applied disciplines, which is the economics of institutions.

It is stretching a point to regard New Zealand practitioners as the originators of NPM. No one in the New Zealand Treasury set out to develop (nor were they the founders of) a new theory of public management that would take the world by storm. All they were trying to do was to solve public problems and, as they found the existing model of administration to be inadequate, they looked for answers from other disciplines.

Neither can Osborne and Gaebler (1992) be regarded as the originators of NPM. They do not use the term at all. Their ten principles of entrepreneurial government have been seen as sharing a concern with NPM in 'competition, markets, customers and outcomes' (Rhodes,

1996, p. 46), but that is all. There may be some similarities, but it is simplistic to conflate the two or to say that Osborne and Gaebler are the key theorists of NPM. Their book is really about innovation in public sector management, illustrated by cases involving cutting red tape, drawn mainly from American local government. It was a popular and influential book for a time among politicians and senior bureaucrats in some jurisdictions. However, this is much more likely to be a symptom of perceived problems in the old style of administration than a clear and coherent programme for the future.

Who, then, did advocate NPM? Gruening (2001) discusses the theoretical foundations of NPM, but does not put forward a candidate for the innovation; indeed, his main point is that the theories involved were not new. This is a recurring theme. Stark (2002) argues that they are new, even if some of the aspects are not. Hood (1991) contends that the new managerialism is 'hype' rather than 'substance', and that nothing has really changed. In his view, new public management has 'damaged the public services while being ineffective in its ability to deliver on its central claim to lower costs'; and it was 'a vehicle for particularistic advantage' to serve the interests of an elite group of top managers, and could not claim to be as universal as its advocates suggested (1991, pp. 8–10). Hood later repeated the criticism, arguing that it was 'more that the packaging was new, not the ideas inside' and that NPM could be considered a 'cargo cult' (1994, p. 135).

Management consultants are sometimes enlisted as the agents of change, though without convincing evidence (see Lapsley, 2009). In all of this, what is absent is a coherent theorist putting the ideas forward. It seems to be assumed in the literature that everyone knows what NPM means without a theorist or agreed theory. Perhaps providing the packaging made it real. But if there was no advocate and no general theoretical treatise, perhaps it never really happened.

Specifying NPM

There have been many and varied specifications of NPM. A selection of views of NPM – there are simply too many to refer to them all – shows that agreement is not likely to be found as to what NPM ever included.

Behn (2001) defines the new public management paradigm as 'the entire collection of tactics and strategies that seek to enhance the performance of the public sector – to improve the ability of government agencies *and* their nonprofit and for-profit collaborators to produce results' and sees it as 'a worldwide phenomenon but with different strategies employed in different governments in different situations' (p. 26). This is very broad view that could apply just as well to any public sector reform rather than NPM specifically.

Rhodes (1991), drawing on Hood (1991), saw managerialism in Britain as a 'determined effort to implement the "3Es" of economy, efficiency and effectiveness at all levels of British government' and commented (Rhodes, 1991, p. 1):

> The 'new public management' has the following central doctrines: a focus on management, not policy, and on performance appraisal and efficiency; the disaggregation of public bureaucracies into agencies which deal with each other on a user-pay basis; the use of quasi-markets and contracting out to foster competition; cost-cutting; and a style of management which emphasises, amongst other things, output targets, limited-term contracts, monetary incentives and freedom to manage.

This view largely focuses inside the organization and implies that substantial changes are required, especially for personnel working in the system.

Hartley and Skelcher (2008) argue that NPM is an 'ideologically rooted cluster of activities, techniques and aims' derived from the United Kingdom and adopted in other countries. They maintain that (pp. 13–14):

> Any number of academics have now analysed the goals, activities and processes of 'new public management' and have broadly characterized this as the application of particular private sector management techniques to the public sector, often underpinned by a neo-liberal and public choice theoretical framework. In NPM, there is a strong emphasis on markets and market-like mechanisms (such as contracting out services, market testing of service delivery and private finance initiatives); a greater emphasis on performance management, more devolved financial management, and an emphasis on making the public services more efficient through a host of generic management techniques and activities.

Hall and Holt (2008) argue that NPM has been 'variously described as a doctrine, philosophy, movement and paradigm'; its theories are 'underpinned by two theories: public choice theory and neo-Taylorism' as well as 'public entrepreneurship (derived from Osborne and Gaebler)' (p. 22).

These definitions have little in common with each other, and the lack of commonality is noted by some other theorists. Fountain (2001) refers to NPM as 'a loose collection of policy and management initiatives designed to increase efficiency, accountability, and performance in bureaucratic states largely through greater use of markets and market-based management systems' (p. 19). Christensen *et al.* (2007) similarly argue that NPM 'is actually a rather loose concept encompassing several different administrative doctrines' as well as being 'rather contradictory'. Van Thiel *et al.* (2007) argue that NPM is a highly ambiguous concept. For them (p. 197):

> NPM is like a chameleon: it constantly changes its appearance to blend in with the local context ... Such adaptability is possible, because NPM is not a coherent set of ideas and tools. The ideas might be the same, but the underlying story differs all the time.

Another view is that there 'was not so much a single coherent agenda as a term coined to capture a set of changes which, when taken together added up to a fundamental shift in public service delivery' (Eliassen and Sitter, 2008, p. 94). These authors argue that the reforms drew from a critique based on economic theory, with the actual reforms including: 'first, *reorganization* of the public sector with a view to improving information and control (including performance indicators, disaggregation and separating purchasing from providing); secondly, increasing *competition*; thirdly, *incentives-based management* in the public sector (including private sector pay and flexibility)' and 'more discretionary power to managers, and clearer demarcation between political and operational accountability' (Eliassen and Sitter, 2008, p. 101). While this is a good effort at being comprehensive, their list is far from coherent, as they themselves say, and is far from indicating a truly novel programme of reform.

Meier and O'Toole (2009) combine a proposal for something they term 'evidence-based public management' with trenchant criticism of each of what they term the ten 'proverbs' of NPM. These proverbs consist of yet another idiosyncratic set of what NPM is about, even though the authors admit in a footnote that NPM is 'less a coherent approach than a loosely linked cluster of ideas and reforms' (p. 19).

There are too many more views to mention, many very different from each other, and many quite idiosyncratic. All these writers admit, at least implicitly, that they cannot define the term NPM. A loose collection of initiatives, or a loose and contradictory concept, should not a movement make; nor a paradigm. That there has been public sector change and reform is undoubted, but to give this a single name and acronym, applicable to all countries and circumstances where reform has taken place, is a serious distortion of reality.

Criticisms of NPM

There are some quite extreme criticisms of NPM. What these show, among other points, is the difficulty of pinning down exactly what NPM is, or was. Argyriades (2003, p. 523) declares that NPM is against social justice and human rights, and draws a very long bow in linking NPM to the terrorist attack on the World Trade Centre in 2001, as well as the collapse of Enron. He argues of NPM that 'drawing support from the Theory of Public Choice, it discarded all such concepts as *public or general interest* which, since the Age of Enlightenment, provided the underpinnings of State and public service'.

Lapsley (2009) asks if NPM is 'the cruellest invention of the human spirit' and this after another odd characterization of NPM as being about the role of management consultants, the development of e-government, the emergence of the 'audit society' and the increasing importance of risk management.

Even if these claims are somewhat overstated, they do point to a real problem in getting a handle on NPM at all. Some writers define NPM in an unusual way in order to then be able to declare it dead. For example, Dunleavy *et al.* (2005) claim that the three chief integrating themes in NPM are disaggregation, competition and incentivization. While this characterization of NPM is idiosyncratic, they then declare all of these not to have worked – according to very strange criteria and with a simple tick box as the only evidence.

In 1998, Lynn (1998) argued that NPM will fade away, stating, among other points that 'fundamental differences among reforms will begin to eclipse superficial similarities', that 'the term "new" would become inconvenient' and that there would be demand for 'a fresh theme' and adds that 'most of us could write the New Public Management's post mortem now' (p. 232). Much of what Lynn predicted has indeed occurred. There have been differences in reforms across countries (Pollitt and Bouckaert, 2004), even if they have tended to have been in the same direction. And, after two decades, the movement is 'no longer "new"' (Schedler *et al.*, 2004, p. 4). Other themes that have arisen, including leadership, collaboration, co-production, governance, and other attempts to establish some new acronym, including those for 'new public service' (Denhardt and Denhardt, 2011), 'new public governance' (Osborne, 2006, 2010), and 'digital era enhanced governance' (Dunleavy *et al.*, 2005).

In sum, the discipline has moved away from NPM, but it might be more useful to regard NPM as an invention by its critics; one that might have had some currency for a time but without an advocate or an agreed content. NPM is no longer a useful term; and nor is it a paradigm.

Public management as a paradigm

Any new paradigm must be based on very different premises from its predecessor. If public management is to be regarded as a new paradigm, there is a need to look further into what is involved in it, in order to assess its candidature as a paradigm. It would be necessary, in particular, to look at key differences from the traditional model of public administration, differences so significant that a case can be made for a paradigmatic shift.

An OECD report (1998a) describes the managerial reforms as a new paradigm and sets out the key points involved (p. 13):

> In most Member countries public management reform has involved a major cultural shift in response to a new paradigm of public management, which attempts to combine modern management practices with the logic of economics, while still retaining the core public service values. This new management paradigm emphasizes results in terms of 'value for money', to be achieved through management by objectives, the use of markets and market-type mechanisms, competition and choice, and devolution to staff through a better matching of authority, responsibility and accountability.

These points do represent marked departures from the public administration paradigm. Kettl (2002) argues (of NPM), 'while scholars debated whether it, in fact, represented a new paradigm or part of a continual battle to reconcile old ideas, there was little doubt that it represented an approach substantially different from public administration' (p. 93). The same applies to broader public management.

Public management is very different from public administration. Decentralized management is very different from a rigid bureaucratic hierarchy. A greater client focus contrasts with the traditional model, where client interests were only incidental, and allowing choice and competition is anathema to the traditional model. The use of market instruments for delivery is different from bureaucratic delivery, while a focus on results and their measurement is very different from hoping that results will follow from structure and process. In addition, the requirement for a manager to achieve results is very different from an administrator merely following instructions. Public management does allow for a greater role for markets and economics, both eschewed by public administration, but the concept of value for scarce public money is an old administrative value as much as a managerial one. And, in retrospect, it does seem odd that the discipline of economics was avoided by public administration as a matter of principle.

Even if public management is quite different from public administration, it is equally important not to regard public management as being the same as its NPM variant (see Hartley and Skelcher, 2008). As noted earlier, NPM cannot be considered a paradigm as it is so loosely and variously specified that it is free of agreed content. It also suggests a programme of action that is unvarying, that is simply rolled out by a league of management consultants. Public management can change over time and place, and in response to circumstances. It is the management that takes place in the public sector, taking into account that management is different from administration.

The most profound change from public administration in a paradigmatic sense, and a point made repeatedly in previous chapters, is that public managers are required to achieve results and to take personal responsibility for doing so. By itself, this shift leads to much of the subsequent managerial change. Once a manager is required to achieve results and with some personal accountability for doing so, it then becomes necessary to be able to measure whether results have been achieved. If public managers are now more accountable, it needs to be clear quite what they are accountable for, and what is still in the ambit of the political leadership.

Any set of reforms needs to be looked in a wider historical sense. The reforms since the mid-1980s can be argued to follow previous change rather than to break away from it completely. Rugge (2003) finds NPM to be quite consistent with overall administrative reform over a much longer period of time. As he points out (p. 120):

> Under the watchword of 'new public management' an effort has been made to renew the organization and the operation of public administration, basically on the model of the private corporation. Historical perspective may provide some grounds for de-emphasizing the novelty of both the regulative and the managerial state. As far as regulation is concerned ... it has never ceased to play a decisive role in the relations between the state and relevant societal actors. And it was often abandoned because it had proven ineffective or costly or both. As to managerialism, it has been a permanent goal of many administrative reformers in the last hundred years, starting with the attempt to introduce the teachings of Taylorism into the public office.

Rugge is correct. The overall goal of recent reform may well have been to deliver services better and more efficiently, but this goal is far from new.

Public management, as distinct from public administration, may be a lasting kind of reform. Managerial reforms were initially imposed by politicians and governments highly unimpressed with the quality and management of their public services. Some inside the system might have been carried along by the tide, but it was governments responding to community perceptions of public servants that drove the biggest changes. This is very different from earlier internal management reforms. The history of public administration is replete with failed experiments and failed techniques, most with their own acronyms such as: planning, programming, budgeting (PPB); zero-based budgeting (ZBB); and management by objectives (MBO). Instead of public management merely being a fad to which, like all fads, public servants pay lip service, it is argued there have been fundamental changes that have recast the role of public managers.

If public management is simply the management that is carried out in the public sector and its principles and theories are pragmatic above all else (see Alford and Hughes, 2008), it could be declared to not be a paradigm. However, if public management is compared over a number of facets with public administration, the difference is much more pronounced. The most fundamental point is that a public manager is required to perform a given function, to deliver results, and is personally accountable. This is very different from public administration, where public servants were mere administrators carrying out assigned tasks on behalf of the political leadership, and could evade direct accountability. If public administration was a paradigm, then a case can be made for public management also to be one.

Issues in public sector reform

Earlier chapters considered some of the critiques made of public sector reform, and some of the contrary arguments put forward as they refer to particular facets of change. At this point, though, there are some general issues about the whole movement for managerial change.

The ideological basis of managerialism

It has been argued that public sector reform is ideological (Dunleavy, 1994; Kearney and Hays, 1998; Minogue, 1998). Pollitt (1993, p. 49) argues that managerialism is 'the acceptable face of new-Right thinking concerning the state' and that ideological considerations may be part of the argument for reducing government through marketization. However, the ideological nature of public sector reform, certainly evident in the Thatcher and Reagan years, diminished later in the 1990s.

Public sector reform did not stop after Thatcher; in fact it had barely started. What happened was that the intensely ideological attack on the role of government in society was replaced by intensified efforts to improve its management. In New Zealand and Australia, the most radical of the public service changes were introduced by Left governments, and the movement was more about management and responding to economic crisis than new Right ideology. As the reform movement has spread, any party-political aspect seems harder to show, indeed reform 'seems now to have no evident coupling to a specific point on the traditional 'right-left' political spectrum' (Jones *et al.*, 2001, p. 3). Kettl (2005) also comments, 'Perhaps surprisingly, the movement did not have clear ideological roots in terms of governing party. Sometimes the argument came from the left, as in New Zealand; sometimes it came from the right, as in the United Kingdom' (p. 17).

Other parts of the managerial programme are not notably ideological. Performance management might be considered new-Right 'neo-Taylorist' ideology, but it could also reflect an older tradition of ensuring value for scarce public money. Flexibility in personnel practices might be argued to be ideological, but could also be a realization that traditional administrative employment practices are now irrelevant for other reasons. It could be argued that opposition to public sector reform is itself driven by ideology.

The impact on democracy

One serious criticism of public sector reforms is that they are against the precepts of democracy. Terry (1999) suggests that there is a moving away from the values of equity and democracy upon which public administration was founded (p. 276):

> While economy and efficiency are important values, one must not lose sight of the fact that responsiveness, equity, representation and the rule of law are highly prized in the US constitutional democracy ... Proponents must be reminded to carefully consider their attempts to minimize the differences between the public and private sectors. The blind application of business management principles and practices can undermine the integrity of public bureaucracies and so threaten our democratic way of life.

Terry (2005) argues that NPM philosophy and practices 'have contributed to an increasingly hollow state with *thinning* administrative institution' and these 'fragile institutions lack the integrity and, in turn, the capacity to effectively serve the public good', raising 'troubling questions about the long-term stability of the U.S. constitutional democracy' (p. 428). The case is not incontrovertible, as it would need to be proved that 'responsiveness, equity, representation and the rule of law' are any less valued than they were under traditional bureaucracy. It is also unsafe to argue that public administration had any such democratic or equity value at all. In some countries and at some times it might have had, but public administration has shown that it has been an instrument of great power possible to be used for any governmental purpose. In any case, it could be argued that all that is being put forward by managerial reform is to be more focused on how money is being spent and making sure that desired results are achieved. March and Olsen (1995) argue that there are two perspectives about democratic governance, the exchange perspective and the institutional perspective, with the former currently being dominant (pp. 5–6). Perhaps concentration on an exchange approach takes away from the institutional perspective, thereby reducing democracy.

It could be argued, on the other hand, that several of the major changes would, if carried out fully, improve the functioning of the democracy. Having a loyalty to the nation above and beyond that of the government of the day was a view held by some senior public administrators during the time of the traditional model of administration. If politicians have reasserted their role as a result of public sector reform, this could be argued to be an enhancement of democracy rather than a reduction. As an OECD paper (1998a) maintains, 'The public management reforms are not responsible for any problem of democratic deficit, rather they are part of the solution' (p. 56). There is to be more transparency, and enhancement of the role of elected politicians, while the focus on service quality and consultation increase opportunities for public involvement. It is also possible that public sector reforms were driven, in some countries, by a desire for greater democracy. Kamarck (2000) argues that 'the second driver of governmental reform is democratization', citing South Africa in the transition from apartheid, and Poland in its decentralization (pp. 233–4). She has a point. The traditional bureaucratic system had major problems with accountability – it is by no means clear that the new model is any less accountable, or any less democratic, than its predecessor.

One concern for democracy may be with the reduction in governmental scope. Politics needs to remain the art of the possible, and public administration the art of carrying out the possible. Any reduction in the allowable agenda for political action is a reduction in democracy. Perhaps democracy can be reduced by a reduction in political accountability; as public managers are themselves accountable for results, politicians could avoid accountability. But all that is being put forward is a new way of organizing within government, in that, whatever the extent of reform, what remains is the legal structure of a bureaucratic state. Public management is merely a tool for governments to use to improve the management of their public sector. There is no claim for any difference in the way that governments are chosen; in other words, no alteration in democratic regime.

An international movement

Whether the public sector reforms constitute a worldwide phenomenon is a point of some controversy. A survey of the world's 123 largest countries 'shows that significant government reform is going on around the world and that, to a remarkable degree, similar kinds of reform efforts exist in very different countries' (Kamarck, 2000, pp. 249–50). Kettl (2000, p. 1) also comments:

> Since the 1980s a global reform movement in public management has been vigorously under way. The movement has been global in two senses. First, it has spread around the world to nations including Mongolia, Sweden, New Zealand and the United States. Second, it has been of sweeping scope. Governments have used management reform to reshape the role of the state and its relationship with citizens.

Pollitt and Bouckaert (2000) argue that, instead of there being a global movement, different countries implement the changes in different ways. In their view, some countries are more open to the 'performance-driven, market-favouring ideas than others' particularly the Anglo-Saxon countries, whereas the more statist continental European countries have been more cautious (pp. 60–1; see also Kickert, 1997, 2000). Continental nations have not been immune to change, but have been slower rather than not acting at all. The point that there is a different pace to change is inarguable in 'a reform movement as varied as the nations of the world' (Kettl, 2005, p. 8). National political institutions may be more or less helpful to reform. British, Australian and Canadian prime ministers work within political institutions that are much more amenable to making government reform measures stick than is the case for American presidents. New Zealand went further than other countries partly because it has fewer institutional constraints. Management reforms must fit within a nation's model of governance and 'they must be supported by the political system for the administrative reforms to succeed' (Kettl, 2000, p. 32).

Changes were often introduced in difficult economic times, against opposition, but were carried through. Particular points may have been different, and the timing certainly was different, but the direction of change and its underlying theory do point to some similarities. The reforms in different countries may have varied in their details but they have been in the same direction, and this has been driven by the exchange of ideas and theories. As Kettl (2005, p. 76) states:

> There are intriguing signs that governments around the world are moving to new systems of accountability built on the measurement of outcomes; to new approaches to service delivery based on partnerships with for-profit and non-profit organizations; to aggressive innovations in information technology; and to new strategies of engaging citizens in governance.

It is unnecessary to establish that change is irresistible, uniform and global. More pertinent is the view of public sector reform as involving similar policy instruments, as Boston *et al.* (1996, p. 2) maintain:

> Although the rhetoric might have varied around the world, most of the recent efforts at governmental reinvention, restructuring, and renewal have shared similar goals – to improve the effectiveness and efficiency of the public sector, enhance the responsiveness of public agencies to their clients and customers, reduce public expenditure, and improve managerial accountability. The choice of policy instruments has also been remarkably similar: commercialization, corporatization, and privatization; the devolution of management responsibilities; a shift from input controls to output and outcome measures; tighter performance specification; and more extensive contracting out.

Kettl (2000) also argues that 'the movement has been striking because of the number of nations that have taken up the reform agenda in such a short time and because of how similar their basic strategies have been' (p. 1).

In looking at instruments and strategies, there is a degree of commonality between the reforms of various countries. What has changed most is the underlying theory rather than the specifics. It would be absurd to demand, for example, that all countries simultaneously adopt an identical model of performance appraisal and at the same time for a claim of similarity to be justified. Pollitt (2001), for example, argues that 'performance indicator systems have sprouted up in most countries and, for the optimistic, these may appear to hold out the prospect of pinning down performance improvements so that, eventually, international comparisons will be routine' (p. 488). Pollitt asserts that there are major problems and differences between countries in the use of performance indicators. But what is more important, surely, is that a large number of countries around the world have decided that systematic performance appraisal is necessary to address their performance and incentive structures, and that this is novel in itself. They may – most probably will – then adopt their own schemes in their own time, but the underlying theoretical change of now regarding performance appraisal as being important, rather than the reform specifics, is where countries have converged.

Pollitt (2000) argues that reform ideas 'have also varied considerably from country to country, and certainly the priority given to different components (e.g. privatization, contracting out) has fluctuated enormously' (p. 184). Obviously, a nation with little public enterprise, such as the United States, is not going to have much to privatize, but the underlying theory that privatization is a good thing, or rather that government ownership of enterprises is not, is very widely spread in developed and developing countries alike. The convergence is one of ideas, not of details. Governments find lessons from other jurisdictions and then apply them, with modifications, in their own contexts.

There does seem to be a directionality to public sector reform. If there were not, it might be expected that the kinds of management in different countries would be more random than it is. Some countries would be moving towards even more bureaucracy, or the nationalization of industry but not its privatization. That the evidence for this has not been observed suggests that there is a direction to reform. Even as the movement may generally be away from traditional administration, the extent of reform and its pace are decided by individual countries.

Public management as a practical discipline

A further issue is whether public management is to be regarded as a practical discipline, one in which academic research and debate have the ultimate aim of improving the performance of the public sector. Along with many other disciplines, public administration in its academic sense may be somewhat removed from its practice, but the debate over management reform widened the gap. Practitioners complain that much of what is written in journals or books is irrelevant to their work. Academic criticism of their management practice can be, and is, dismissed by real public managers as another irrelevance. This poses a problem for the public management academic community; its discipline is intended to be practical and yet its criticisms of current actual practice divide it from its area of interest.

Actual public management practice and academic discussion of it seem to be on divergent paths and to the detriment of both. As Kettl (2002, p. 18) comments:

> Public cynicism, rising expectations, more complicated programs, and political crossfire combined to create imposing challenges for government managers. Many of the old theories seemed to fit poorly, and hard-pressed managers scrambled for fresh insights. When they looked to public administration theory, they found few answers that fit their new challenges well. Many managers, in fact, felt strangely alone, jury-rigging tactics to fit their own situations. They had little sense of which managers shared their problems and which solutions fit which problems best. While many public administration scholars rejected the lively arguments in Osborne and Gaebler's *Reinventing Government*, many practitioners eagerly embraced their message of hope. The result was a growing gap between those who *taught* public administration and those who *lived* it.

Public administration academics faced a real danger of being seen as increasingly irrelevant in terms of their contribution to practice. Kettl (2002) continues: 'Public officials were charting their own course into the twenty-first century, largely without intellectual or moral support from academia' (p. 21).

It is apparent that public sector reform came from governments themselves, including their own public managers, seeking more responsiveness and better results. In New Zealand, it was the politicians who 'drove the reforms' for practical reasons and that 'concerns about the quality of policy advice, inefficient government enterprises, the level of government spending and a lack of accountability in the large bureaucracy, fuelled a desire for change' (Scott, 2001, p. 35). Rubin and Kelly (2005) argue that part of the reason for some of the reforms is 'because they seem to give elected officials more policy control, more policy tools' (p. 586). Pollitt and Bouckaert (2004, p. 19) make a similar point. The real leaders of reform have been from within the system and with little input from academics, or, at least, academics from the spheres of public administration or public management. In addition, defenders of managerial change have tended to be practising public managers, albeit in many cases with considerable academic qualifications and skills (see Keating, 1988; Paterson, 1988; Holmes and Shand, 1995; Horn, 1995; Scott, 2001).

If academic public administration, or even public management, once had a privileged position with regard to government, they did seem to lose some of this in the debates over public sector reform. Practical public managers now quite clearly draw from many disciplines – law, economics, political science, private and public management, to name but a few – and are likely to make up their own minds about the utility of what they find. Public administration no longer has a special role. It has doubtless been a source of frustration for some that public administration or public management theory have not been as highly valued as, for example, private management, institutional economics (Scott, 2001), transaction cost economics (Horn, 1995) or other disciplines. But practitioners have tasks to carry out, problems to solve and can and will draw on 'whatever works' in order to do those things (Alford and Hughes, 2008).

Even as there has been increasing criticism of public management practice by academics, the operations of governments have continued in the direction of reform. The caravan has moved on. New staff are employed under new terms and conditions. The generation that even knew the rigid bureaucratic model is rapidly disappearing, and younger public servants just get on with their work, wondering what all the fuss was about. As Schedler *et al.* (2004, pp. 3–4) comment:

> Many criticisms of 'neo-managerialism' seem to us valid, but they risk falling on deaf ears in the practitioner arena as new management methods are implemented in both developed and developing nations. What were a decade ago thought to be new management techniques and methods have become commonplace.

There are obvious risks in alienating practitioners from what should be their academic community of interest. One of the biggest problems for academic public management in the future is if it becomes widely regarded by public servants as irrelevant to what they do.

Conclusion

At this point, the aims of the book should be reiterated. The basic idea has been to compare the traditional model of public administration with public management following what is now a lengthy period of reform. It has been argued that the traditional model had so many weaknesses that it no longer deserves to be the model describing and prescribing the relationship between governments, the public services and the public.

The administrative paradigm, as a system of production, has outlived its usefulness and is unlikely to be revived. For a variety of reasons, the traditional model of public administration has been replaced by a new model of public management. This involves much more than mere public service reform. It means changes to the ways that public services operate, changes to the scope of governmental activity, changes to time-honoured processes of accountability, and changes to the academic study of the public sector. The main change is one of theory; sufficient, it is argued, to constitute a new paradigm. The process of managerial reform continues; the wider effects of it on not only the public sector but also the entire political system may still have some distance to travel.

Should public sector reform be abandoned and there be a return to the traditional model? Or is there perhaps another model, yet to be invented, that will overcome the problems of both? The traditional model is looked on with a good deal more nostalgia than it really deserved: it was inefficient, ineffective and needed to be replaced. The criticisms of traditional public administration are not new; they have always been there. Pollitt and Bouckaert (2000) assert that there were problems with the earlier traditional model:

> Our conclusion is *not* that the negative features of the 'traditional model' are fantasies, with no basis in reality. Every reader can probably vouchsafe some personal experience testifying to the capacity of public (and private) bureaucracies to work in infuriatingly slow and inefficient ways. However, it is a long – and unjustified – leap from there to the idea that the governments of the industrialised world previously operated their public sectors as Weberian-style traditional bureaucracies, and are now able to move, without significant loss, to a new, modern type of organisation which avoids all the problems of the past.

It has never been argued that there can be a shift to a new model without significant loss. It is rather that, in most of the areas that interest government – cost, efficiency, service delivery, and responsiveness – public management can deliver more than the old model. In some areas, the old model may be argued to have been better – democratic accountability, stability and fairness – though it remains to be seen whether the new model is in practice any worse than the old one on these points.

The traditional model of administration is argued here to be obsolete and to have been replaced by public management. However, public management, or any theory insisting that the public sector requires its own specialized form of management, is itself under threat from the idea that management is *generic* and technocratic. This argument is that management is the same anywhere, and that the public and private sectors are sufficiently similar for expertise to be readily transferable. Indeed, a particular kind of manager, such as a human resource manager, may regard him/herself as a professional in that area, and whether s/he is employed in the public or the private sector is relatively unimportant. This genericism points to a real threat for public management. Unless it can be established that the public sector is distinctive enough to require its own form of management, public management of any kind may become as marginalized as traditional public administration.

Almost thirty years after the beginnings of the current era of public sector reform, some fundamentals remain. In contrast to suggestions in the earlier, more ideological phase of reform, government cannot and should not disappear, as it serves functions that benefit the public and does so through mechanisms that no other institution can emulate. It also follows that the management of government is different from that in the private sector, though the line cannot be drawn as distinctly as some public servants might wish. For some senior levels, the intrusion of politics makes the management task more difficult, but for others at the service-delivery end, the task is not greatly different from a similar function in the private sector. And service delivery functions can be improved by using standard private sector management methods.

In sum, the reforms have worked, but not perfectly, but then that is not unusual; the whole purpose of undertaking reform is to seek out improvement rather than perfection. As Pollitt and Bouckaert (2004) point out, public management reform 'consists of deliberate changes to the structures and processes of public organizations with the objective of getting them (in some sense) to run better' (p. 8). It is in fact difficult to say in any precise way whether public sector reform has been successful and the administration now runs better. The counterfactual of a control public service that has not reformed does not exist. However, if an observer could make a simultaneous comparison of the public sector of, say, the early 1980s with one of today that had been through significant change, it is most likely that real improvements in many areas would be perceived in the latter. There would also be continuity with past practice, rather than a complete and disruptive change. But it would be most likely that the observer would be able to see the need for further reforms. Public managers are under ever-increasing pressure to do even more with fewer resources and the only way to do this in a sustained way is to undertake further management reform. Perhaps reform should be seen as a continuous process. Public management is not a programme, not a single way of looking at the world. It is, rather, what happens when a public manager is required to achieve results and to take personal responsibility for their achievement. By itself, this is very different from the traditional model of public administration.

References

Aharoni, Yair (1986) *The Evolution and Management of State-Owned Enterprises* (Cambridge, MA: Ballinger).

Alford, John (2009) *Engaging Public Sector Clients: From Service-Delivery to Co-Production* (Basingstoke: Palgrave Macmillan).

Alford, John and Hughes, Owen E. (2008) 'Public Value Pragmatism as the Next Phase of Public Management', *American Review of Public Administration,* 38, June, pp. 130–48.

Allison, Graham (1982) 'Public and Private Management: Are They Fundamentally Alike in All Unimportant Respects?', in Frederick S. Lane (ed.) *Current Issues in Public* Administration (New York: St Martin's Press).

Anderson, James E. (1984) *Public Policy Making,* 3rd edn (New York: Holt, Rinehart & Winston).

Anderson, James E. (1989) 'Government and the Economy: What is Fundamental?', in Warren J. Samuels (ed.) *Fundamentals of the Economic Role of Government* (New York: Greenwood Press).

Ansoff, H. Igor (1988) *The New Corporate Strategy* (New York: John Wiley).

Argyriades, Demetrios (2003) Values for Public Service: Lessons Learned from Recent Trends and the Millennium Summit', *International Review of Administrative Sciences*, 69, 4, pp. 521–33.

Aufrecht, Steven E. and Li Siu Bun (1995) 'Reform with Chinese Characteristics: The Context of Chinese Civil Service Reform', *Public Administration Review,* 55, 2, pp. 175–82.

Ayres, Ian and Braithwaite, John (1992) *Responsive Regulation: Transcending the Deregulation Debate* (New York/Oxford: Oxford University Press).

Bandy, Gary (2011) *Financial Management and Accounting in the Public Sector* (London: Routledge).

Bardach, Eugene (1998) *Getting Agencies to Work Together: The Theory and Practice of Managerial Craftsmanship* (Washington, DC: Brookings Institution Press).

Bardach, Eugene (2009) *A Practical Guide for Policy Analysis: The Eightfold Path to More Effective Problem Solving*, 3rd edn (Washington, DC: CQ Press).

Barzelay, Michael (1992) *Breaking Through Bureaucracy: A New Vision for Managing in Government* (Berkeley and Los Angeles: University of California Press).

Baumol, W. J., Panzar, J. and Willig, R. (1982) *Contestable Markets and the Theory of Industry Structure* (New York: Harcourt Brace Jovanovich).

Behn, Robert D. (1998a) 'The New Public Management Paradigm and the Search for Democratic Accountability', *International Public Management Journal,* 1, 2, pp. 131–64.

Behn, Robert D. (1998b), What Right Do Public Managers Have to Lead?', *Public Administration Review,* 58, 3, May/June, pp. 209–24.

Behn, Robert D. (2001) *Rethinking Democratic Accountability* (Washington, DC: Brookings Institution Press).

Behn, Robert D. (2003) Why Measure Performance? Different Purposes Require Different Measures', *Public Administration Review,* 63, 5, September/October, pp. 586–606.

Bellamy, Christine and Taylor, John A. (1998) *Governing in the Information Age* (Buckingham: Open University Press).

Bennis, W. (1989) *On Becoming a Leader* (London: Hutchinson).

Bentley, A. (1967) *The Process of Government* (First published 1908) (Chicago: University of Chicago Press).

Bevir, Mark and Rhodes, R. A. W. (2003) *Interpreting British Governance* (London: Routledge).

Black, Nick (2001) 'Evidence-based Policy: Proceed with Care', *British Medical Journal,* 323, 7307, pp. 275–9.

Blau, Peter M. and Meyer, Marshall W. (1987) *Bureaucracy in Modern Society,* 3rd edn (New York: Random House).

Borins, Sandford (1999) 'Trends in Training Public Managers: A Report on a Commonwealth Seminar', *International Public Management Journal,* 2, 2, pp. 299–314.

Boston, Jonathan (ed.) (1995) *The State under Contract* (Wellington, New Zealand: Bridget Williams Books).

Boston, J., Martin, J., Pallot, J. and Walsh, P. (1996) *Public Management: The New Zealand Model* (Auckland: Oxford University Press).

Bouckaert, Geert and Halligan, John (2008) *Managing Performance* (London: Routledge).

Bovens, Mark (2007) 'Analysing and Assessing Accountability: A Conceptual Framework', *European Law Journal,* 13, 4, July, pp. 447–68.

Boyne, George (2002) 'Public and Private Management: What's the Difference?', *Journal of Management Studies,* 39, 1, pp. 97–122.

Bozeman, Barry (1979) *Public Management and Policy* (New York: St Martin's Press).

Bozeman, Barry and Straussman, Jeffrey D. (1990) *Public Management Strategies* (San Francisco: Jossey-Bass).

Braithwaite, John (2006) 'Responsive Regulation and World Economies', *World Development,* 34, 5, pp. 884–98.

Bryson, John M. (1988) *Strategic Planning for Public and Non-Profit Organizations* (San Francisco: Jossey-Bass).

Bryson, John M. (2004) *Strategic Planning for Public and Non-Profit Organizations*, 3rd edn (San Francisco: Jossey-Bass).

Caiden, Gerald E. (1981) 'Administrative Reform', in G. R. Curnow and R. L. Wettenhall (eds) *Understanding Public Administration* (Sydney: Allen & Unwin).

Caiden, Gerald E. (1982) *Public Administration,* 2nd edn (Pacific Palisades, CA: Palisades Publishers).

Caiden, Gerald E. (1991) *Administrative Reform Comes of Age* (Berlin and New York: Walter de Gruyter).

Caiden, Gerald E. (1996) 'The Concept of Neutrality', in Haile K. Asmerom and Elisa P. Reis (eds) *Democratization and Bureaucratic Neutrality* (Basingstoke: Macmillan).

Carlin, Tyrone M. and Guthrie, James (2001) 'Lessons from Australian and New Zealand Experiences with Accrual Output-Based Budgeting', in Lawrence R. Jones, James Guthrie and Peter Steane (eds) *Learning from International Public Management Reform*, Vol. IIa (Oxford: Elsevier Science).

Carter, Neil, Klein, Rudolf and Day, Patricia (1992) *How Organisations Measure Success* (London and New York: Routledge).

Chandler, Alfred D. (1962) *Strategy and Structure* (Cambridge, MA: MIT Press).

Christensen, T., Lie, A. and Lægreid, P. (2007) 'Still Fragmented Government or Reassertion of the Centre?', in Tom Christensen and Per Lægreid (eds) *Transcending New Public Management: The Transformation of Public Sector Reforms* (Aldershot: Ashgate).

Conger, J. A. and Kanungo, R. N. (1987) 'Toward a Behavioral Theory of Charismatic Leadership in Organizational Settings', *Academy of Management Review*, 12, 4, pp. 637–47.

Copley, F. B. (1923) *Frederick W. Taylor: Father of Scientific Management*, Vol. 1 (New York: American Society of Mechanical Engineers).

Crozier, Michel (1964) *The Bureaucratic Phenomenon* (Chicago: University of Chicago).

Davis, Glyn (1997) 'Implications, Consequences and Futures', in Glyn Davis, Barbara Sullivan and Anna Yeatman (eds) *The New Contractualism* (Melbourne: Macmillan).

deLeon, Peter (1988) *Advice and Consent: The Development of Policy Sciences* (New York: Sage).

deLeon, Peter (1997) *Democracy and the Policy Sciences* (Albany, NY: State University of New York Press).

deLeon, Peter (2006) 'The Historical Roots of the Field', in Michael Moran, Martin Rein and Robert E. Goodin (eds) *The Oxford Handbook of Public Policy* (Oxford: Oxford University Press).

deLeon, Peter and Green, Mark T. (2004) 'Political Corruption: Establishing the Parameters', in *Strategies for Public Management Reform: Research in Public Policy Analysis and Management*, 13, pp. 229–58.

Denhardt, Janet V. and Denhardt, Robert B. (2011) *The New Public Service: Serving Not Steering*, 3rd edn (Armonk, NY: M. E. Sharpe).

Denhardt, Robert B. (1981) 'Toward a Critical Theory of Public Organisation', *Public Administration Review*, 41, 6, pp. 628–35.

Dixit, Avinash K. and Nalebuff, Barry J. (1991) *Thinking Strategically: The Competitive Edge in Business, Politics, and Everyday Life* (New York: W. W. Norton).

Doern, G. Bruce (1995) *Fairer Play: Canadian Competition Policy Institutions in a Global Market* (Toronto: C. D. Howe Institute).

Donahue, John D. (1989) *The Privatisation Decision: Public Ends, Private Means* (New York: Basic Books).

Donahue, John D. (2002) 'Market-based Governance and the Architecture of Accountability', in John D. Donahue and Joseph S. Nye, Jr. (eds) *Market-Based Governance: Supply Side, Demand Side, Upside and Downside* (Washington, DC: Brookings Institution Press).

Donahue, John D. and Zeckhauser, Richard J. (2006) 'Public–Private Collaboration', in Michael Moran, Martin Rein and Robert E. Goodin (eds) *The Oxford Handbook of Public Policy* (Oxford: Oxford University Press).

Downs, Anthony (1957) *An Economic Theory of Democracy* (New York: Harper & Row).

Duffield, Colin F. (2010) 'Different Delivery Models', in Graeme A. Hodge, Carsten Greve and Anthony E. Boardman (eds) *International Handbook on Public–Private Partnerships* (Cheltenham: Edward Elgar).

Dunleavy, Patrick (1991) *Democracy, Bureaucracy and Public Choice: Economic Explanations in Political Science* (London: Harvester Wheatsheaf).

Dunleavy, Patrick (1994) 'The Globalization of Public Services Production: Can Government Be "Best in World"?', *Public Policy and Administration*, 9, 2, pp. 36–64.

Dunleavy, Patrick, Margetts, Helen, Bastow, Simon and Tinkler, Jane (2005) 'New Public Management is Dead – Long Live Digital-Era Governance', *Journal of Public Administration Research and Theory*, 16, 3, pp. 467–94.

Dunsire, Andrew (1973) *Administration: The Word and the Science* (London: Martin Robertson).

Dwivedi, O. P. and Henderson, Keith M. (1990) 'State of the Art: Comparative Public Administration and Development Administration', in O. P. Dwivedi and Keith M. Henderson (eds)

Public Administration in World Perspective (Ames, IA: Iowa State University Press).

Eadie, Douglas C. (1983) 'Putting a Powerful Tool to Practical Use: The Application of Strategic Planning in the Public Sector', *Public Administration Review*, 43, pp. 447–52.

Eadie, Douglas C. (1989) 'Identifying and Managing Strategic Issues: From Design to Action', in Jack Rabin, Gerald J. Miller and W. Bartley Hildreth (eds) *Handbook of Strategic Management* (New York/Basel: Marcel Dekker).

Elcock, Howard (1996) 'Strategic Management', in David Farnham and Sylvia Horton (eds) *Managing the New Public Services*, 2nd edn (London: Macmillan).

Eliassen, Kjell A. and Sitter, Nick (2008) *Understanding Public Management* (London: Sage).

Elmore, Richard F. (1986) 'Graduate Education in Public Management: Working the Seams of Government', *Journal of Policy Analysis and Management*, 6, pp. 169–83.

Erridge, Andrew (2009) 'Contracting for Public Services', in Tony Bovaird and Elke Löffler (eds) *Public Management and Governance*, 2nd edn (London/New York: Routledge).

Fairholm, M. (2004) 'Different Perspectives on the Practice of Leadership', *Public Administration Review*, 64, 5, pp. 577–90.

Farazmand, Ali (1996) 'Introduction: The Comparative State of Public Enterprise Management', in Ali Farazmand (ed.) *Public Enterprise Management: International Case Studies* (Westport, CT: Greenwood Press).

Farnham, David (1999) 'Human Resources Management and Employment Relations', in Sylvia Horton and David Farnham (eds) *Public Management in Britain* (London: Macmillan).

Farnham, David and Horton, Sylvia (eds) (1996) *Managing the New Public Services*, 2nd edn (London: Macmillan).

Finer, S. E. (1997) *The History of Government from the Earliest Times* (Oxford: Oxford University Press).

Flynn, Norman (1997) *Public Sector Management*, 3rd edn (New York: Harvester Wheatsheaf).

Flynn, Norman (2007) *Public Sector Management*, 5th edn (London: Sage).

Foster, C. D. (2001) 'Civil Service Fusion: The Period of "Companionable Embrace" in Contemporary Perspective', *Parliamentary Affairs*, 54, pp. 425–41.

Fountain, Jane E. (1999) 'The Virtual State: Toward a Theory of Federal Bureaucracy in the 21st Century', in Elaine Ciulla Kamarck and Joseph S. Nye (eds) *Democracy.com? Governance in a Networked World* (Hollis, NH: Hollis Publishing).

Fountain, Jane (2001) *Building the Virtual State: Information*

Technology and Institutional Change (Washington, DC: Brookings Institution Press).

Frederickson, H. George (1980) 'The Lineage of New Public Administration', in Carl J. Bellone (ed.) *Organization Theory and the New Public Administration* (Boston, MA: Allyn & Bacon).

Frederickson, H. George (1989) 'How Politics Affects Public Programs', in Robert E. Cleary, Nicholas Henry and Associates (eds) *Managing Public Programs: Balancing Politics, Administration and Public Needs* (San Francisco: Jossey-Bass).

Frederickson, H. George (2005) 'Whatever Happened to Public Administration? Governance, Governance Everywhere', in Ewan Ferlie, Laurence E. Lynn, Jr. and Christopher Pollitt (eds) *The Oxford Handbook of Public Management* (Oxford: Oxford University Press).

Friedman, Milton and Friedman, Rose (1980) *Free to Choose* (Harmondsworth: Penguin).

Fry, Brian R. (1989) *Mastering Public Administration: From Max Weber to Dwight Waldo* (Chatham, NJ: Chatham House).

Fukuyama, Francis (1995) *Trust: The Social Virtues and the Creation of Prosperity* (London: Hamish Hamilton).

Fulton, Lord (1968) *The Report of the Committee on the Civil Service* (The Fulton Report) (London: HMSO).

Gerth, H. H. and Mills, C. Wright (eds) (1970) *From Max Weber: Essays in Sociology* (London: Routledge & Kegan Paul).

Giddens, Anthony (2002) *Runaway World: How Globalisation is Reshaping Our Lives*, 2nd edn (London: Profile Books).

Gillespie, Richard (1991) *Manufacturing Knowledge: A History of the Hawthorne Experiments* (New York: Cambridge University Press).

Gladden, E. N. (1972) *A History of Public Administration* (London: Frank Cass).

Goldsmith, Stephen and Eggers, William D. (2004) *Governing by Network: The New Shape of the Public Sector* (Washington, DC: Brookings Institution Press).

Goodsell, Charles (1983) *The Case for Bureaucracy: A Public Administration Polemic* (Chatham, NJ: Chatham House).

Goodsell, Charles (1990) 'Emerging Issues in Public Administration', in Naomi B. Lynn and Aaron Wildavsky (eds) *Public Administration: The State of the Discipline* (Chatham, NJ: Chatham House).

Gore, Al (1993) *The Gore Report on Reinventing Government: Creating a Government that Works Better and Costs Less,* Report of the National Performance Review (New York: Times Books).

Gow, James and Dufour, Caroline (2000) 'Is the New Public Management a Paradigm? Does It Matter?', *International Review of Administrative Sciences*, 66, pp. 573–97.

Graham, Cole Blease and Hays, Steven W. (1991) 'Management Functions and Public Administration – POSDCORB Revisited', in Steven J. Ott, Albert C. Hyde and Jay M. Shafritz (eds) *Public Management: The Essential Readings* (Chicago: Lyceum Books/Nelson Hall).

Grant Robert M. (2008) *Contemporary Strategy Analysis*, 6th edn (Oxford: Blackwell).

Grant, Wyn (1989) *Pressure Groups, Politics and Democracy in Britain* (London: Philip Allan).

Gray, Andrew and Jenkins, Bill with Andrew Flynn and Brian Rutherford (1991) 'The Management of Change in Whitehall: The Experience of the FMI', *Public Administration*, 69, 1, pp. 3–19.

Greenaway, John (2004), 'Celebrating Northcote/Trevelyan: Dispelling the Myths', *Public Policy and Administration*, 19, 1, pp. 1–14.

Greenwood, John, Pyper, Richard and Wilson, David (2002) *New Public Administration in Britain* (London: Routledge).

Greve, Carsten (2007) *Contracting for Public Services* (London: Routledge).

Greve, Carsten and Hodge, Graeme (2007) 'Public–Private Partnerships: A Comparative Perspective on Victoria and Denmark', in Tom Christensen and Per Lægreid (eds) *Transforming New Public Management* (Aldershot: Ashgate).

Grindle, Merilee S. (2000) 'Ready or Not: The Developing World and Globalization', in Joseph S. Nye and John D. Donahue (eds) *Governance in a Globalizing World* (Washington, DC: Brookings Institution Press).

Gruening, Gernod (2001) 'Origin and Theoretical Basis of New Public Management', *International Public Management Journal*, 4, 1, pp. 1–25.

Gulick, Luther and Urwick, Lyndall (eds) (1937) *Papers on the Science of Administration* (New York: Institute of Public Administration).

Guthrie, James, Olson, Christopher, Jones, L. R. and Olson O. (eds) (2005) *International Public Financial Management Reform: Progress, Contradictions, and Challenges* (Greenwich, CT: Information Age).

Hall, Mark and Holt, Robin (2008) 'New Public Management and Cultural Change: The Case of UK Public Sector Project Sponsors as Leaders', in Paul Windrum and Per Koch (eds) *Innovation in Public Sector Services* (Cheltenham: Edward Elgar).

Halligan, John (2007) 'Reform Design and Performance in Australia and New Zealand', in Tom Christensen and Per Lægreid (eds) *Transcending New Public Management: The Transformation of Public Sector Reforms* (Aldershot: Ashgate).

Hartley, Jean and Skelcher, Chris (2008) 'The Agenda for Public Service Improvement', in Jean Hartley, Cam Donaldson, Chris

Skelcher and Mike Wallace (eds) *Managing to Improve Public Services* (Cambridge: Cambridge University Press).

Hax, Arnoldo C. and Majluf, Nicholas S. (1984) *Strategic Management: An Integrative Perspective* (Englewood Cliffs, NJ: Prentice-Hall).

Hax, Arnoldo C. and Majluf, Nicholas S. (1996) *The Strategy Concept and Process; A Pragmatic Approach* (Upper Saddle River, NJ: Prentice-Hall).

Hayek, E. A. (1944) *The Road to Serfdom* (Chicago: University of Chicago).

Heeks, Richard (ed.) (1999) *Reinventing Government in the Information Age: International Practice in IT-enabled Public Sector Reform* (London: Routledge).

Heeks, Richard (2006) *Implementing and Managing e-Government: An International Text* (London: Sage).

Heeks, Richard and Bhatnagar, Subhash (1999) 'Understanding Success and Failure in Information Age Reform', in Richard Heeks (ed.) *Reinventing Government in the Information Age: International Practice in IT-enabled Public Sector Reform* (London: Routledge).

Heifetz, R. A. and Laurie, D. L. (1997) 'The Work of Leadership', *Harvard Business Review*, 75, 1, pp. 124–34.

Held, D., McGrew, A. G., Goldblatt, D. and Perraton, J. (1999) *Global Transformations: Politics, Economics and Culture* (Cambridge: Polity Press).

Hicks, U. K. (1958) *Public Finance* (London: James Nesbit).

Hodge, Graeme (2000) *Privatization: An International Review of Performance* (Boulder, CO: Westview Press).

Hodge, Graeme, Greve, Carsten and Boardman, Anthony (eds) (2010) *International Handbook on Public–Private Partnerships* (Cheltenham: Edward Elgar).

Hogwood, Brian W. and Gunn, Lewis A. (1984) *Policy Analysis for the Real World* (Oxford: Oxford University Press).

Holmes, Douglas (2001) *E-Gov: E-Business Strategies for Government* (London: Nicholas Brealey).

Holmes, M. and Shand, D. (1995) 'Management Reform: Some Practitioner Perspectives on the Past Ten Years', *Governance,* 8, 5, pp. 551–78.

Hondeghem, Annie (1998) 'Introduction', in A. Hondeghem (ed.) *Ethics and Accountability in a Context of Governance and New Public Management* (Amsterdam: IOS Press).

Hood, Christopher (1991) 'A Public Management for All Seasons?', *Public Administration,* 69, 1, pp. 3–19.

Hood, Christopher (1994) *Explaining Economic Policy Reversals* (Buckingham: Open University Press).

Hood, Christopher (1995) 'Contemporary Public Management: A New

Global Paradigm?', *Public Policy and Administration*, 10, 2, pp. 104–17.

Hood, Christopher (1996) 'Exploring Variations in Public Management Reform of the 1980s', in Hans A. G. M. Bekke, James L. Perry and Theo A. J. Toonen (eds) *Civil Service Systems in Comparative Perspective* (Bloomington and Indianapolis, IN: Indiana University Press).

Hood, Christopher (2005) 'The Word, the Movement, the Science', in Ewan Ferlie, Laurence E. Lynn and Christopher Pollitt (eds) *The Oxford Handbook of Public Management* (Oxford: Oxford University Press).

Hood, Christopher and Peters, Guy (2004) 'The Middle Aging of New Public Management: Into the Age of Paradox?', *Journal of Public Administration Research and Theory*, 14, 3, pp. 267–82.

Horn, Murray J. (1995) *The Political Economy of Public Administration: Institutional Choice in the Public Sector* (Cambridge: Cambridge University Press).

Horton, Sylvia (1999) 'The Civil Service', in Sylvia Horton and David Farnham (eds) *Public Management in Britain* (London: Macmillan).

Hrebenar, Ronald J. (1997) *Interest Group Politics in America*, 3rd edn (Armonk, NY: M. E. Sharpe).

Hughes, Owen E. (1998) *Australian Politics*, 3rd edn (Melbourne: Macmillan).

Hughes, Owen E. and Deirdre O'Neill (2001) 'Managerialism in Victoria', in L. R. Jones, James Guthrie and Peter Steane (eds) *International Public Management Reform: Lessons from Experience* (Oxford: Elsevier–JAI Press).

Hughes, Owen E. and Deirdre O'Neill (2008) *Government, Business and Globalization* (Basingstoke: Palgrave Macmillan).

Huque, Ahmed Shafiqul (1996) 'Administering the Dragons: Challenges and Issues', in Ahmed Shafiqul Huque, Jermain T. M. Lam and Jane C. Y. Lee (eds) *Public Administration in the NICs: Challenges and Accomplishments* (London: Macmillan).

Ingraham, Patricia W. (1995) *The Foundation of Merit: Public Service in American Democracy* (Baltimore, MD: Johns Hopkins University Press).

Ingraham, Patricia W. (2005) 'Performance: Promises to Keep and Miles to Go', *Public Administration Review*, 65, 4, pp. 390–5.

Isaac-Henry, Kester, Painter, Chris and Barnes, Chris (1997) 'Introduction', in Kester Isaac-Henry, Chris Painter and Chris Barnes (eds) *Management in the Public Sector: Challenge and Change*, 2nd edn (London: International Thomson Press).

Jacoby, Henry (1973) *The Bureaucratization of the World* (Berkeley, CA: University of California Press).

Javidan, M. and Waldman, D. A. (2003) 'Exploring Charismatic

Leadership in the Public Sector: Measurement and Consequences', *Public Administration Review*, 63, 2, pp. 229–42.

Jensen, Michael C. (2000) *A Theory of the Firm: Governance, Residual Claims, and Organizational Forms* (Cambridge, MA: Harvard University Press).

Jensen, Michael C. and Meckling, William H. (1976) 'Theory of the Firm: Managerial Behavior, Agency Costs and Ownership Structure', *Journal of Financial Economics*, 3, pp. 305–60.

John, Peter (1998) *Analysing Public Policy* (London and New York: Pinter).

Jones, L. R, Guthrie, James and Steane, Peter (2001) 'Learning from International Public Management Reform Experience', in Lawrence R. Jones, James Guthrie and Peter Steane (eds) *Learning from International Public Management Reform Experience*, Research in Public Policy Analysis and Management, Vol. 11A (Oxford: Elsevier Science).

Jordan, A. G. and Maloney, William A. (2007) *Democracy and Interest Groups: Enhancing Participation?* (Basingstoke/New York: Palgrave Macmillan).

Jorgensen, Jan J. (1990) 'Organisational Life-Cycle and Effectiveness Criteria in State-owned Enterprises: The Case of East Africa', in Alfred M. Jaeger and Rabindra N. Kanungo (eds) *Management in Developing Countries* (London and New York: Routledge).

Joyce, Paul (2000) *Strategy in the Public Sector* (Chichester: John Wiley).

Kaboolian, Linda (1998) 'The New Public Management: Challenging the Boundaries of the Management vs. Administration Debate', *Public Administration Review*, 58, pp. 189–93.

Kakar, Sudhir (1970) *Frederick Taylor: A Study in Personality and Innovation* (Cambridge, MA: MIT Press).

Kamarck, Elaine Ciulla (2000) 'Globalization and Public Administration Reform', in Joseph S. Nye and John D. Donahue (eds) *Governance in a Globalizing World* (Washington, DC: Brookings Institution Press).

Kamarck, Elaine Ciulla (2002) 'The End of Government As We Know It', in John D. Donahue and Joseph S. Nye, Jr. (eds) *Market-Based Governance: Supply Side, Demand Side, Upside and Downside* (Washington, DC: Brookings Institution Press).

Kamarck, Elaine Ciulla and Nye, Joseph S. (eds) (1999) *Democracy.com? Governance in a Networked World* (Hollis, NH: Hollis Publishing).

Kamenka, Eugene (1989) *Bureaucracy* (Oxford: Basil Blackwell).

Kanigel, Robert (1997) *The One Best Way: Frederick Winslow Taylor and the Enigma of Efficiency* (New York: Viking).

Kaunga, E. C. (1993) 'Privatization in Zambia', in V. V. Ramanadham (ed.) *Privatization: A Global Perspective* (London and New York: Routledge).

Kay, John and Vickers, John (1990) 'Regulatory Reform: An Appraisal', in Giandomenico Majone (ed.) *Deregulation or Re-regulation: Regulatory Reform in Europe and the United States* (London: Pinter/New York: St Martin's Press).

Kearney, Richard C. and Hays, Steven W. (1998) 'Reinventing Government, the New Public Management and Civil Service Systems in Comparative Perspective', *Review of Public Personnel Administration,* 18, 4, pp. 38–54.

Keasey, Kevin, Short, Helen and Wright, Mike (2005) 'The Development of Corporate Governance Codes in the UK', in Kevin Keasey, Steve Thompson and Mike Wright, (eds) *Corporate Governance: Accountability, Enterprise and International Comparisons* (Hoboken, NJ: Wiley).

Keating, Michael (1988) '"Quo Vadis"? Challenges of Public Administration', *Australian Journal of Public Administration,* 48.

Keeling, Desmond (1972) *Management in Government* (London: George Allen & Unwin).

Kennedy, Paul (1988) *The Rise and Fall of the Great Powers: Economic Change and Military Conflict from 1500 to 2000* (London: Unwin Hyman).

Kennett, Patricia (2008) 'Introduction', in Patricia Kennett (ed.) *Governance, Globalization and Public Policy* (Cheltenham: Edward Elgar).

Keohane, Robert O. and Nye, Joseph S. (2000) 'Introduction', in Joseph S. Nye and John D. Donahue (eds), *Governance in a Globalizing World* (Washington, DC: Brookings Institution Press).

Kettl, Donald F. (2000) *The Global Public Management Revolution: Keys to High-Performance Government* (Washington, DC: Brookings Institution Press).

Kettl, Donald F. (2002) *The Transformation of Governance: Public Administration for Twenty-First Century America* (Baltimore, MD/London: Johns Hopkins University Press).

Kettl, Donald F. (2005) *The Global Public Management Revolution,* 2nd edn (Washington, DC: Brookings Institution Press).

Kettl, Donald F. (2009) 'The Key to Networked Government', in Stephen Goldsmith and Donald F. Kettl (eds) *Unlocking the Power of Networks* (Washington, DC: Brookings Institution Press).

Kickert, W. (1997) 'Public Governance in the Netherlands: An Alternative to Anglo-American "Managerialism"', *Public Administration,* 75, pp. 731–52.

Kickert, W. J. M. (2000) 'Public Governance in Europe: A Historical-

Institutional Tour d'horizon', in O. van Heffen, W. Kickert and J. Thomassen, J. (eds) *Governance in Modern Society* (Dordrecht: Kluwer).

Kjaer, Anne Mette (2004) *Governance* (Cambridge: Polity).

Klijn, Erik-Hans and Koppenjan, Joop F. M. (2000) 'Public Management and Policy Networks: Foundations of a Network Approach to Governance', *Public Management*, 2, 2, pp. 135–58.

Klijn, Erik-Hans, Edelenbos, Jurian, Kort, Michiel and van Twist, Mark (2008) 'Facing Management Choices: An Analysis of Managerial Choices in 18 Complex Environmental Public–Private Partnership Projects', *International Review of Administrative Sciences*, 74, p. 251.

Kooiman, J. (1999) 'Social-political Governance' *Public Management*, 1, 1, March, pp. 68–92.

Kooiman, Jan (2003) *Governing as Governance* (London: Sage).

Kotter, J. P. (1990) 'What Leaders Really Do', *Harvard Business Review*, 68, 3, May–June, pp. 103–11.

Krugman, Paul (1995) *Development, Geography, and Economic Theory* (Cambridge, MA: MIT Press).

Kuhn, Thomas S. (1970) *The Structure of Scientific Revolutions* (Chicago: University of Chicago Press).

Lan, Zhiyong and Rosenbloom, David H. (1992) 'Editorial', *Public Administration Review*, 52, 6.

Lane, Jan-Erik (1995) *The Public Sector: Concepts, Models and Approaches*, 2nd edn (London: Sage).

Lapsley, Irvine (2009) 'New Public Management: The Cruellest Invention of the Human Spirit?', *Abacus*, 45, 1, pp. 1–21.

Lasswell, H. D. (1971) *A Pre-View of Policy Sciences* (New York: Elsevier).

Lee, Robert D. and Johnson, Ronald W. (1989) *Public Budgeting Systems*, 4th edn (Rockville, MD: Aspen Publications).

Legge, Karen (2005) *Human Resource Management: Rhetorics and Realities* (Basingstoke: Palgrave Macmillan).

Lenk, Klaus and Traunmüller, Roland (2001) 'Broadening the Concept of Electronic Government', in J. E. J. Prins (ed.) *Designing E-government: On the Crossroads of Technological Innovation and Institutional Change* (The Hague: Kluwer Law International).

Lindblom, C. (1968) *The Policy-Making Process* (Englewood Cliffs, NJ: Prentice-Hall).

Lynn, Laurence E. (1987) *Managing Public Policy* (Boston, MA: Little, Brown).

Lynn, Laurence E. (1996) *Public Management as Art, Science and Profession* (Chatham, NJ: Chatham House Publishers).

Lynn, Laurence E. (1997) 'The New Public Management as an

International Phenomenon: Questions from an American Skeptic', in Lawrence R. Jones, Kuno Schedler and Stephen W. Wade (eds) *International Perspectives on the New Public Management*, Advances in International Comparative Management, Supplement 3 (Greenwich, CT: JAI Press).

Lynn, Laurence E. (1998) 'The New Public Management: How to Transform a Theme into a Legacy', *Public Administration Review*, 58, pp. 231–7.

Lynn, Laurence (2001a) 'Globalization and Administrative Reform: What Is Happening in Theory?', *Public Management Review*, 3, 2, pp. 191–208.

Lynn, Laurence (2001b) 'The Myth of the Bureaucratic Paradigm: What Traditional Public Administration Really Stood For', *Public Administration Review*, 61, 2, pp. 144–60.

Manion, Melanie (2004) *Corruption by Design* (Cambridge, MA: Harvard University Press).

March, James G. and Olsen, Johan P. (1995) *Democratic Governance* (New York: The Free Press).

Marini, Frank (ed.) (1971) *Toward a New Public Administration: The Minnowbrook Perspective* (Scranton, PA: Chandler Publishing).

Mathiasen, David G. (1999) 'The New Public Management and its Critics', *International Public Management Journal*, 2, 1, pp. 90–111.

Mayo, Elton (1933) *The Human Problems of an Industrial Civilization* (New York: Viking Press).

McCaffery, Jerry L. (1989) 'Making the Most of Strategic Planning and Management', in Robert E. Cleary, Nicholas Henry and Associates (eds) *Managing Public Programs: Balancing Politics, Administration and Public Needs* (San Francisco: Jossey-Bass).

McCraw, Thomas K. (1986) 'The Historical Background', in W. Knowlton and Richard Zeckhauser (eds) *American Society: Public and Private Responsibilities* (Cambridge, MA: Ballinger).

Meier, Kenneth J. and Hill, Gregory C. (2005) 'Bureaucracy in the Twenty-first Century', in Ewan Ferlie, Laurence E. Lynn, Jr. and Christopher Pollitt (eds) *The Oxford Handbook of Public Management* (Oxford: Oxford University Press).

Meier, Kenneth J. and O'Toole, Laurence J. (2009) 'The Proverbs of New Public Management: Evidence from an Evidence-Based Agenda', *American Review of Public Administration*, 39, 1, pp. 4–22.

Merton, Robert K. (1968) *Social Theory and Social Structure*, 3rd edn (New York: Free Press).

Michalski, Wolfgang, Miller, Riel and Stevens, Barrie (2001) 'Governance in the 21st Century: Power in the Global Knowledge Economy and Society', in *Governance in the 21st Century* (Paris: OECD).

Minogue, Martin (1998) 'Changing the State: Concepts and Practice in the Reform of the Public Sector', in Martin Minogue, Charles Polidano and David Hulme (eds) *Beyond the New Public Management: Changing Ideas and Practices in Governance* (Cheltenham: Edward Elgar).

Minogue, Martin, Polidano, Charles and Hulme, David (1998) 'Introduction: The Analysis of Public Management and Governance', in Martin Minogue, Charles Polidano and David Hulme (eds) *Beyond the New Public Management: Changing Ideas and Practices in Governance* (Cheltenham: Edward Elgar).

Mintzberg, Henry (1994) *The Rise and Fall of Strategic Planning* (Englewood Cliffs, NJ: Prentice Hall).

Mintzberg, Henry (2000) 'Managing Normatively', in Henry Mintzberg and Jacques Bourgault (eds) *Managing Publicly* (Toronto: Institute of Public Administration Canada).

Monroe, Kristen Renwick (ed.) (1991) *The Economic Approach to Politics: A Critical Assessment of the Theory of Rational Action* (New York: HarperCollins).

Montanari, John R., Daneke, Gregory A. and Bracker, Jeffrey S. (1989) 'Strategic Management for the Public Sector: Lessons from the Evolution of Private-Sector Planning', in Jack Rabin, Gerald J. Miller and W. Bartley Hildreth (eds) *Handbook of Strategic Management* (New York/Basel: Marcel Dekker).

Moore, Mark (1995) *Creating Public Value: Strategic Management in Government* (Cambridge, MA: Harvard University Press).

Moran, Michael, Rein, Martin and Goodin, Robert E. (eds) (2006) *The Oxford Handbook of Public Policy* (Oxford: Oxford University Press).

Mosher, Frederick C. (1982) *Democracy and the Public Service*, 2nd edn (New York: Oxford University Press).

Mueller, D. C. (1989) *Public Choice II: A Revised Edition* (Cambridge: Cambridge University Press).

Mulgan, Geoff (2009) *The Art of Public Strategy* (Oxford: Oxford University Press).

Mullins, Laurie J. (1996) *Management and Organisational Behaviour*, 4th edn (London: Pitman).

Musgrave, Richard A. and Musgrave, Peggy B. (1989) *Public Finance in Theory and Practice*, 5th edn (New York: McGraw-Hill).

Nagel, Stuart S. (1990) 'Conflicting Evaluations of Policy Studies', in Naomi B. Lynn and Aaron Wildavsky (eds) *Public Administration: The State of the Discipline* (Chatham, NJ: Chatham House Publishers).

Newbold, Stephanie P. and Terry, Larry D. (2008) 'From the New Public Management to the New Democratic Governance', in Ricardo S. Morse and Terry F. Buss (eds) *Innovations in Public Leadership Development* (Armonk, NY: M. E. Sharpe).

Niskanen, William A. (1971) *Bureaucracy and Representative Government* (Chicago: Aldine-Atherton).

Niskanen, William A. (1973) *Bureaucracy: Servant or Master?* (London: Institute of Economic Affairs).

Niskanen, William A. (1994) *Bureaucracy and Public Economics* (Aldershot: Edward Elgar).

Norris-Tyrell, Dorothy and Clay, Joy A. (2010) *Strategic Collaboration in Public and Nonprofit Administration* (Boca Raton, FL: CRC Press).

Nutley, Sandra M., Davies, Huw and Walter, Isabel (2002) *Evidence Based Policy and Practice: Cross Sector Lessons From the UK*, Working Paper 9, ESRC UK Centre for Evidence Based Policy and Practice, Research Unit for Research Utilisation, St Andrews University, UK.

Nutley, Sandra M., Walter, Isabel and Davies H. T. O. (2007) *Using Evidence: How Research Can Inform Public Services* (Bristol: Policy Press).

Nutt, Paul C. and Backoff, Robert W. (1992) *Strategic Management of Public and Third Sector Organisations: A Handbook for Leaders* (San Francisco: Jossey-Bass).

OECD (1991a) *Public Management Developments: 1991* (Paris: OECD).

OECD (1991b) *Serving the Economy Better,* Occasional Papers on Public Management (Paris: OECD).

OECD (1997) *Modern Budgeting* (Paris: OECD).

OECD (1998a) *Public Management Reform and Economic and Social Development,* PUMA (Paris: OECD).

OECD (1998b) *Information Technology as an Instrument of Public Management Reform: A Study of Five OECD Countries,* PUMA (Paris: OECD).

OECD (2001) *Public Sector Leadership for the 21st Century* (Paris: OECD).

OECD (2005) *Modernising Governance* (Paris: OECD).

OECD (2007) *Performance Budgeting in OECD Countries* (Paris: OECD).

OECD (2009) *Government at a Glance* (Paris: OECD).

O'Leary, Rosemary, Gazley, Beth, McGuire, Michael and Bingham, Lisa Blomgren (2009) 'Public Managers in Collaboration', in Rosemary O'Leary and Lisa Blomgren Bingham (eds) *The Collaborative Public Manager: New Ideas for the Twenty-first Century* (Washington, DC: Georgetown University Press).

Olsen, Johan P. (2005) 'Maybe It Is Time to Rediscover Bureaucracy', *Journal of Public Administration Theory,* 16, pp. 1–24.

Olsen, John B. and Eadie, Douglas C. (1982) *The Game Plan: Governance with Foresight* (Washington, DC: Council of State Planning Agencies).

Olson, Mancur (1965) *The Logic of Collective Action* (Cambridge, MA: Harvard University Press).

Olson, Mancur (1982) *The Rise and Decline of Nations* (New Haven, CT: Yale University Press).

Osborne, David and Gaebler, Ted (1992) *Reinventing Government: How the Entrepreneurial Spirit is Transforming the Public Sector* (Reading, MA: Addison-Wesley).

Osborne, Stephen (2006) 'Editorial: The New Public Governance?', *Public Management Review*, 8, 3, pp. 377–87.

Osborne, Stephen (ed.) (2010) *The New Public Governance? Critical Perspectives and Future Directions* (London: Routledge).

Ostrom, Vincent (1974) *The Intellectual Crisis in American Public Administration*, Revd edn (Tuscaloosa, AL: University of Alabama Press).

Ostrom, Vincent (1989) *The Intellectual Crisis in American Public Administration*, 2nd edn (Tuscaloosa, AL: University of Alabama Press).

Parsons, Wayne (1995) *Public Policy: An Introduction to the Theory and Practice of Policy Analysis* (Cheltenham: Edward Elgar).

Patashnik, Eric M. (2008) *Reforms at Risk: What Happens after Major Policy Changes Are Enacted* (Princeton, NJ: Princeton University Press).

Paterson, John (1988) 'A Managerialist Strikes Back', *Australian Journal of Public Administration*, 47, 4, December, pp. 287–95.

Patton, Carl V. and Sawicki, David S. (1986) *Basic Methods of Policy and Planning* (Englewood Cliffs, NJ: Prentice-Hall).

Peters, B. Guy (1996) *The Future of Governing: Four Emerging Models* (Lawrence, KS: University of Kansas Press).

Peters, B. Guy and Pierre, Jon (1998) 'Governance Without Government? Rethinking Public Administration', *Journal of Public Administration Research and Theory*, 8, 2, pp. 223–43.

Peters, Thomas J. and Waterman, Robert H. (1982) *In Search of Excellence* (New York: Warner Books).

Pierre, Jon and Peters, Guy (2000) *Governance, Politics and the State* (Basingstoke: Palgrave Macmillan).

Pollitt, Christopher (1990) *Managerialism and the Public Services: The Anglo-American Experience* (Oxford: Basil Blackwell).

Pollitt, Christopher (1993) *Managerialism and the Public Services: Cuts or Cultural Change in the 1990s*, 2nd edn (Oxford: Basil Blackwell).

Pollitt, Christopher (2000) 'Is the Emperor in His Underwear? An Analysis of the Impacts of Public Management Reform', *Public Management*, 2, 2, pp. 181–99.

Pollitt, Christopher (2001) 'Clarifying Convergence: Striking Similarities and Durable Differences in Public Management Reform', *Public Management Review*, 3, 4, pp. 471–92.

Pollitt, Christopher (2003) *The Essential Public Manager* (Maidenhead: Open University Press).

Pollitt, Christopher and Bouckaert, Geert (2000) *Public Management Reform: A Comparative Analysis* (Oxford: Oxford University Press).

Pollitt, Christopher and Bouckaert, Geert (2004) *Public Management Reform: A Comparative Analysis*, 2nd edn (Oxford: Oxford University Press).

Pollitt, Christopher, Talbot, Colin, Caulfield, Janice and Smullen, Amanda (2004) *Agencies: How Governments Do Things through Semi-Autonomous Organizations* (Basingstoke, Palgrave Macmillan).

Popper, Karl (1965) *The Logic of Scientific Discovery* (New York: Harper & Row).

Porter, M. E. (1980) *Competitive Strategy* (New York: Free Press).

Porter, Michael (1990) *The Competitive Advantage of Nations* (London: Macmillan).

Price, Catherine (1994) 'Privatisation in Less Developed Countries', in Peter M. Jackson and Catherine Price (eds) *Privatisation and Regulation: A Review of the Issues* (London/New York: Longman).

Pross, Paul A. (1986) *Group Politics and Public Policy* (Toronto: Oxford University Press).

Pross, Paul A. (1992) *Group Politics and Public Policy*, 2nd edn (Toronto: Oxford University Press).

Pusey, Michael (1991) *Economic Rationalism in Canberra: A Nation-Building State Changes Its Mind* (Melbourne: Cambridge University Press).

Putt, Allen C. and Springer, J. Fred (1989) *Policy Research: Concepts, Methods and Appreciations* (Englewood Cliffs, NJ: Prentice-Hall).

Quade, Edward S. (1982) *Analysis for Public Decisions*, 2nd edn (New York: Elsevier).

Rainey, Hal G. (1990) 'Public Management: Recent Developments and Current Prospects', in Naomi B. Lynn and Aaron Wildavsky (eds) *Public Administration: The State of the Discipline* (Chatham, NJ: Chatham House).

Ranson, Stewart and Stewart, John (1994) *Management for the Public Domain* (London: Macmillan).

RCAGA (Royal Commission on Australian Government Administration) (1976) *Report* (Canberra: Australian Government Publishing Service).

Rees, Ray (1984) *Public Enterprise Economics*, 2nd edn (London: Weidenfeld & Nicolson).

Rehfuss, John (1989) 'Maintaining Quality and Accountability in a Period of Privatisation', in Robert E. Cleary, Nicholas Henry and Associates (eds) *Managing Public Programs: Balancing Politics, Administration and Public Needs* (San Francisco: Jossey-Bass).

Reid, J. (1983) *Review of Commonwealth Administration* (The Reid Report) (Canberra: Australian Government Publishing Service).

Rhodes, R. A. W. (1991) 'Introduction', *Public Administration,* 69, 1, pp. 1–2.

Rhodes, R. A. W. (1996) 'The New Governance: Governing without Government', *Political Studies,* 44, pp. 652–67.

Rhodes, R. A. W. (2000) 'Governance and Public Administration', in Jon Pierre (ed.) *Debating Governance: Authority, Steering and Democracy* (Oxford: Oxford University Press).

Rhodes, R. A. W. and Wanna, John (2009) 'Bringing the Politics Back In: Public Value in Westminster Parliamentary Government', *Public Administration,* 87, 2, pp. 161–83.

Richardson, J. J. and Jordan, A. G. (1979) *Governing Under Pressure: The Policy Process in a Post-Parliamentary Democracy* (Oxford: Martin Robertson).

Ritter, Gerhard (1983) *Social Welfare in Germany and Britain: Origins and Development* (Leamington Spa: Berg).

Romzek, Barbara S. (1998) 'Where the Buck Stops: Accountability in Reformed Public Organizations', in Patricia W. Ingraham, James R. Thompson and Ronald P. Sanders (eds) *Transforming Government: Lessons from the Reinvention Laboratories* (San Francisco: Jossey-Bass).

Romzek, Barbara S. (2000) 'Dynamics of Public Sector Accountability in an Age of Reform', *International Review of Administrative Sciences,* 66, 1, pp. 21–44.

Rose, Richard and Peters, B. Guy (1978) *Can Government Go Bankrupt?* (New York: Basic Books).

Rose-Ackerman, Susan (1999) *Corruption and Government: Causes, Consequences and Reform* (Cambridge: Cambridge University Press).

Rosenau, James N. (1992) 'Governance, Order and Change in World Politics', in James N. Rosenau and Ernst-Otto Czempiel (eds) *Governance Without Government: Order and Change in World Politics* (Cambridge: Cambridge University Press).

Rosenau, James N. (1997) *Along the Domestic–Foreign Frontier: Exploring Governance in a Turbulent World* (Cambridge: Cambridge University Press).

Rosenbloom, David (1986) *Public Administration: Understanding Management, Politics and Law in the Public Sector* (New York: Random House).

Rubin, Irene S. and Kelly, Joanne (2005) 'Budget and Accounting Reforms', in Ewan Ferlie, Laurence E. Lynn and Christopher Pollitt (eds) *The Oxford Handbook of Public Management* (Oxford: Oxford University Press).

Rugge, Fabio (2003) 'Administrative Traditions in Western Europe', in

B. Guy Peters and Jon Pierre (eds) *The Handbook of Public Administration* (Los Angeles and London: Sage).

Salamon, Lester M. (2002) 'The New Governance and the Tools of Public Action: An Introduction', in Lester M. Salamon (ed.) *The Tools of Government: A Guide to the New Governance* (Oxford/New York: Oxford University Press).

Savas, E. S. (1982) *Privatizing the Public Sector* (Chatham, NJ: Chatham House).

Savas, E. S. (1987) *Privatization: The Key to Better Government* (Chatham, NJ: Chatham House).

Sawyer, Ralph D. (2007) *The Seven Military Classics of Ancient China* (New York: Basic Books).

Schachter, Hindy Lauer (1989) *Frederick Taylor and the Public Administration Community: A Re-evaluation* (Albany, NY: State University of New York Press).

Schedler, Kuno, Jones, Lawrence R. and Mussari, Ricardo (2004) 'Assessment of Public Management Reform and Strategy', in Kuno Schedler, Lawrence R. Jones and Riccardo Mussari (eds) *Strategies for Public Management Reform*, Research in Public Policy Analysis and Management, Vol. 13 (Bingley: Emerald), pp. 1–15.

Schelling, Thomas C. (1960) *The Strategy of Conflict* (Cambridge, MA: Harvard University Press).

Schelling, Thomas C. (2006) *Strategies of Commitment* (Cambridge, MA: Harvard University Press).

Schick, Allen (1998) 'Why Most Developing Countries Should Not Try New Zealand's Reforms', *World Bank Research Observer*, 13, 1, pp. 123–31.

Scott, Graham (2001) *Public Management in New Zealand: Lessons and Challenges* (Wellington: New Zealand Business Roundtable).

Self, Peter (1993) *Government by the Market: The Politics of Public Choice* (London: Macmillan).

Seneviratne, Sonal J. (1999) 'Information Technology and Organizational Change in the Public Sector', in G. David Garson (ed.) *Information Technology and Computer Applications in Public Administration: Issues and Trends* (Hershey, PA: Idea Group Publishing).

Simon, Herbert (1957) *Administrative Behaviour*, 2nd edn (London: Macmillan).

Simon, Herbert (1983) *Reason in Human Affairs* (Oxford: Blackwell).

Simpson, E. E. (1994) *The Developing World*, 2nd edn (London: Longman).

Skelcher, Chris (2005) 'Public Private Partnerships and Hybridity', in Ewan Ferlie, Laurence E. Lynn and Christopher Pollitt (eds) *The Oxford Handbook of Public Management* (Oxford: Oxford University Press).

Smith, Adam (1976) *An Inquiry into the Nature and Causes of the Wealth of Nations* (Book 2), ed. Edward Cannan (Chicago: University of Chicago Press).

Smith, B. C. (1996) *Understanding Third World Politics: Theories of Political Change and Development* (Bloomington/Indianapolis, IN: Indiana University Press).

Smith, Steven Rathgeb (2005) 'NGOs and Contracting', in Ewan Ferlie, Laurence E. Lynn and Christopher Pollitt (eds) *The Oxford Handbook of Public Management* (Oxford: Oxford University Press).

Spann, R. N. (1981) 'Fashions and Fantasies in Public Administration', *Australian Journal of Public Administration*, 40, pp. 12–25.

Sparrow, Malcolm (2000) *The Regulatory Craft: Controlling Risks, Solving Problems and Managing Compliance* (Washington, DC: Brookings Institution Press).

Stark, Andrew (2002) 'What *Is* the New Public Management?', *Journal of Public Administration Research and Theory*, 12, 1, pp. 137–51.

Stigler, George (1975) *The Citizen and the State* (Chicago: University of Chicago Press).

Stiglitz, Joseph E. (1989) *The Economic Role of the State* (Cambridge, MA: Blackwell).

Stiglitz, Joseph E. (2001) 'An Agenda for Development for the Twenty-First Century', in Anthony Giddens (ed.) *The Global Third Way Debate* (Cambridge: Polity Press).

Stillman, Richard J. (1987) *The American Bureaucracy* (Chicago: Nelson-Hall).

Stillman, Richard J. (1991) *Preface to Public Administration: A Search for Themes and Direction* (New York: St Martin's Press).

Stokey, Edith and Zeckhauser, Richard (1978) *A Primer for Policy Analysis* (New York: W. W. Norton).

Szymanski, Stefan (1996) 'The Impact of Compulsory Competitive Tendering on Refuse Collection Services', *Fiscal Studies*, 17, 3, pp. 1–19.

Talbot, Colin (1999) 'Public Performance – Towards a New Model?', *Public Policy and Administration*, 14, 3, pp. 15–34.

Tarschys, Daniel (2001) 'Wealth, Values, Institution: Trends in Government and Governance', in *Governance in the 21st Century* (Paris: OECD).

Taylor, Frederick Winslow (1911) *Principles and Methods of Scientific Management* (New York: Harper).

Terry, Larry D. (1999) 'From Greek Mythology to the Real World of the New Public Management (Terry Responds)', *Public Administration Review*, 59, 3, pp. 272–7.

Terry, Larry D. (2005) 'The Thinning of Administrative Institutions in the Hollow State', *Administration and Society*, 37, 4, September, pp. 426–44.

Thaler, Richard H. and Sunstein, Cass (2009) *Nudge: Improving Decisions about Health, Wealth and Happiness* (New York: Penguin).

Thomas C. S. (ed.) (2001) *Political Parties and Interest Groups: Shaping Democratic Governance* (Boulder, CO: Lynne Rienner).

Thompson, Fred (1997) 'Defining the New Public Management', in Lawrence R. Jones, Kuno Schedler and Stephen W. Wade (eds) *International Perspectives on the New Public Management*, Advances in International Comparative Management, Supplement 3 (Greenwich, CT: JAI Press).

Toft, Graham S. (1989) 'Synoptic (One Best Way) Approaches of Strategic Management', in Jack Rabin, Gerald J. Miller and W. Bartley Hildreth (eds) *Handbook of Strategic Management* (New York/Basel: Marcel Dekker).

Truman, David (1951) *The Governmental Process* (New York: Knopf).

Turner, Mark and Hulme, David (1997) *Government Administration and Development: Making the State Work* (London: Macmillan).

Uhrig, J. (2003) *Review of the Corporate Governance of Statutory Authorities and Office Holders* (The Uhrig Review) (Canberra: Commonwealth of Australia).

UK Treasury and Civil Service Committee (1982) *Efficiency and Effectiveness in the Civil Service* (London: HMSO).

US House of Representatives (2008) *United States Government Policy and Supporting Positions*, Committee on Governmental Reform, US House of Representatives, 110th Congress, 2nd Session.

Van Dooren, Wouter, Bouckaert, Geert and Halligan, John (2010) *Performance Management in the Public Sector* (Abingdon, Oxon/New York: Routledge).

Van Thiel, S., Pollitt, C. and Homburg, V. (2007) 'Conclusions', in C. Pollitt, S. Van Thiel and V. Homburg (eds) *New Public Management in Europe* (Basingstoke: Palgrave Macmillan).

Vecchio, Robert P. (2006) *Organizational Behavior*, 6th edn (Mason, OH: Thomson/Southwestern).

Vickers, J. and Yarrow, G. (1988) *Privatization: An Economic Analysis* (Cambridge, MA: MIT Press).

Volberda, Henk W. (1999) *Building the Flexible Firm: How to Remain Competitive* (Oxford: Oxford University Press).

Walsh, Kieron (1995) *Public Services and Market Mechanisms* (London: Macmillan).

Weimer, David L. and Vining, Aidan R. (2011) *Policy Analysis*, 5th edn (Boston, MA: Longman).

White, Leonard D. (1953) *The Jacksonians: A Study in Administrative History* (New York: Free Press).

Wildavsky, Aaron (1979) *The Politics of the Budgetary Process*, 3rd edn (Boston, MA: Little, Brown).

Wilenski, Peter (1982) 'Budget Innovation and Reform', in D. J. Hardman (ed.) *Government Accounting and Budgeting* (Sydney: Prentice-Hall).

Williamson, Oliver E. (1986) *Economic Organization: Firms, Markets and Policy Control* (London: Wheatsheaf).

Williamson, Oliver E. (1996) *The Mechanisms of Governance* (Oxford: Oxford University Press).

Wilson, Graham K. (1990) *Interest Groups* (Oxford: Blackwell).

Wilson, Graham K. (1992) 'American Interest Groups in Comparative Perspective', in Mark P. Petracca (ed.) *The Politics of Interests: Interest Groups Transformed* (Boulder, CO: Westview Press).

Wilson, James Q. (1989) *Bureaucracy: What Government Agencies Do and Why They Do It* (New York: Basic Books).

Wilson, Woodrow (1941) 'The Study of Administration', *American Political Science Quarterly*, 56.

World Bank (1995) *Bureaucrats in Business: The Economics and Politics of Government Ownership* (New York: Oxford University Press).

World Bank (1997) *World Development Report 1997* (Washington, DC: The World Bank).

World Bank (2005) *Financing Information and Communication Infrastructure Needs in the Developing World: Public and Private Roles*, Working paper No. 65 (Washington, DC: World Bank).

Yeager, Timothy J. (1999) *Institutions, Transition Economies, and Economic Development* (Boulder, CO: Westview Press).

Yong, James S. L. (2005) *E-Government in Asia* (Singapore: Marshall Cavendish).

Zifcak, Spencer (1994) *New Managerialism: Administrative Reform in Whitehall and Canberra* (Buckingham: Open University Press).

Index

accountability 8,12, 26, 53–4, 60–1,
    90, 93, 98, 101, 131–2, 156–7,
    168, 175, 180–1, 185–207
  and democracy 101, 194–5,
    202–3
  and responsibility 53–4, 191
  bureaucratic 195–7, 205
  direct to public 186, 198–9,
    200–2, 205–7
  for fairness 191–2
  for finance 191
  for performance 191–2, 201
  hierarchical 192–3
  in managerial model 90, 93, 98,
    101, 197–202, 205–7
  in private sector 8, 12, 26, 131–2,
    187–90, 204
  in public sector 8, 12, 168,
    190–207
  in traditional model 60–1, 185–6,
    193–7
  legal 192–3
  managerial 197–202
  political 192–3, 194–5, 205
  possibility of sanctions 187
  private sector as a model
    189–90
  problems 98, 202–5
  public enterprise 63–4
  types of accountability 191–4
accountable management 186, 198–9,
    200–2, 205–7
accrual accounting 101, 260–1,
    267–8, 271–2
administration 1–4, 43–73
  definition 3–4, 59
  see also public administration
adverse selection 31
agents and principals see
    principal–agent theory
Aharoni, Y. 164

Alford, J. 93, 167, 179–80, 186
Alford, J. and Hughes, O. 16, 328,
    335
Allison, G. 9, 76–8, 168–71, 208–9
allocation 252–3
Anderson, J. 22–4, 109
Anglo-American democracies 79, 141
anonymity of public servants 53–4,
    64, 84, 84, 97, 172
Ansoff, H. I. 212, 224–5
antitrust regulation see competition
    policy
arbitrary administration 50
Argyriades, D. 325–6
attack on the public sector 9–11,
    20–1
Aufrecht, S. and Li, S. 297
Australia 6, 36, 38–9, 79, 82, 155,
    158, 230–1, 260–1, 283, 285,
    329
  Centrelink 284
  Coombs Commission 230–1
  Reid Report 79
authority 48, 123, 128–9, 142
  types of 48
authorizing environment 138
Ayres, I. and Braithwaite, J. 150

Bandy, G. 151
Bangladesh 301
Bardach, E. 26–7, 110–11, 178
Barzelay, M. 81, 242, 317
Baumol, W., Panzar, J. and Willig, R.
    161
behavioural theories 70, 94
Behn, R. 59, 61–2, 66, 82, 90–1, 187,
    191–2, 195–7, 198–9, 201, 205,
    239, 265, 317–18, 232
Bellamy, C. and Taylor, J. 264, 274,
    277, 279–80, 286, 288, 290–1,
    293

benefit–cost analysis, *see* cost–benefit
    analysis
'benign big gun' 150
Bennis, W. 234
Bentley, A. 182
Bevir, M. and Rhodes, R. 129–33,
    136–8, 176
Bismarck, O. von 341
Black, N. 116
Blau, P. and Meyer, M. 68
Borins, S. 317
Boston, J. *et al.* 11–12, 81, 84,
    321–2, 332
Bouckaert, G. and Halligan, J. 87,
    269
Bovens, M. 187
Boyne, G. 9
Bozeman, B. 55, 57, 64
Bozeman, B. and Straussman, J. 8, 64,
    67, 76, 219, 221, 233
Braithwaite, J. 150
Bryson, J. 91, 215–8, 222, 224, 226
budget cuts 38, 41, 269–70
budget functions 252–6
budgeting and financial control
    planning 211, 213
budgets 11, 25, 27, 38–40, 69–71,
    250–72
    accountability to legislature 255
    and debt 11, 269–70
    and financial management reforms
        258–62
    a political document 251–2, 271–2
    criticisms of financial reforms
        266–72
    devolution 261–2
    economic functions 252–4
    entitlements 267;
        financial functions 255–6
    forward estimates 260
    incrementalism 256, 266–7
    in traditional model 256–7
    line-item 256–7
    maximization 69–71
    PPB system 258
    problems with traditional model
        257
    programme 258–60
    United States 255, 258

Westminster countries 255–6
zero-based 258
bureaucracy 5, 43–73, 83–4, 135–7,
    166–74, 229–41, 275–8, 284–7,
    292, 296–300
    and absence of leadership 53, 66,
        229–30, 233–41
    and democracy 62–3
    and impersonality 49–50, 51, 68,
        230, 233–4
    and informal networks 64–5
    and interest groups 166–7, 173–4,
        178
    and legal framework 69
    and markets 70, 83–4, 137
    and office politics 70, 93, 169,
        171, 173–4, 184
    and scientific management 55–6
    and secrecy 62–3, 292
    and technological change 135–6,
        275–8, 284–7
    and 'the files' 49
    as an elite 64
    as societal villain 71
    as system of power 63–4, 66–9,
        101
    in developing countries 296–300
    internal focus 169–70
    position of the official 50–2
    principles 48–50
    problems of 59–73
    public choice and 69–72
    staying power 67
    technical superiority 52, 63–6
    Weber's theory 43–73;
        see also Weberian bureaucracy
bureaucratic mode of production
bureaucrats *see* bureaucracy
Bush government 36

Cadbury Report 132
Caiden, G. 6, 54, 65, 241, 244
Canada 29, 38–9, 158, 174
careers service 230–1
Carlin, T. and Guthrie, J. 261, 268
Carter, N., Klein, R. and Day, P. 83,
    198, 264
Chandler, A. 210
change imperatives 9–15

charismatic authority   48, 234–7, 249
   obsolescence of   235–6
China   25, 44, 297
Christensen, T., Lie, A. and Laegreid, P.
   324
client focus   90, 93, 139, 172,
   199–202, 282
Clinton government   36, 82
coercive power of government   7–8,
   22, 127–8
collaboration   76, 93, 177–81
   and bureaucracy   178
competition between providers   86,
   92–3
competition policy   23, 146, 149
Compulsory Competitive Tendering
   (CCT)   93, 153–4
contemporary political economists   *see*
   public choice
Conger, J. and Kanungo, R.   236
contestable market theory   92
contracting-out   13–14, 40, 74, 88–9,
   98, 138, 144–5, 151–7, 283,
   309–11
contractualism   92–3
coordination   8, 168–9, 171
Copley, F.   55
coproduction   167, 177–81, 186
   definition   179
corporate failures   20, 26
corporate governance   20, 26, 131–2
corruption   44, 47, 72, 99–100, 298,
   303–4, 308–9, 311–2
cost–benefit analysis   109, 121
criticisms of public management   2–3,
   75, 94–102
Crozier, M.   65
culture   213, 220–1

Davis, G.   92
debt   11, 269–70
decision-making   109
deLeon, P.   112–13, 120
Denhardt, R.   119
Denhardt, J. and Denhardt, R.   326
developing countries   295–314
   and administration   302–3
   and public management   304–14
   and socialism   295, 297–8

problems of public management
   303–4
public enterprise   301–2
traditional model   295–303,
   307–8, 310–4
dichotomy between politics and
   administration   *see* politics/
   administration dichotomy
digital era governance (DEG)   15,
   288–91
disaggregation   86–7, 98–9
distribution   253–4
Dixit A. and Nalebuff, B.   209
Doern, B.   149
Donahue, J.   125, 137, 154, 185–6
Donahue, J. and Zeckhauser, R.   112,
   178
Downs, A.   32
Duffield, C.   155–6
Dunleavy, P.   12, 15–16, 71, 99, 182,
   329
Dunleavy, P. *et al.*   135, 288–9,
   326
Dunsire, A.   54
Dwivedi, O. and Henderson, K.
   302–3

Eadie, D.   214
early administration   44–6, 50
e-business and e-commerce   273,
   278–80, 283
economic rationalism   11, 35
   see also neo-classical economics
economics   11–15, 69–72, 80, 82–4,
   94–5, 103–5, 111–13
   and public management   11–15,
   82–4, 94–5
   and public policy   103–5, 111–13
   behavioural theories   94
   deductive approach   83
   new institutional   14
   principals and agents   13
   public choice   12, 69–72
   transaction costs   13–14
education   29
e-government   14–15, 273–94
   and public management   287–9,
   294
   and politics   292–3

e-government (*cont.*)
  as another new model   274–5,
    288–9
  as enabler of reform   289, 294
  beginnings   276–80
  defined   273
  digital divide   287–90
  government-to-business (G2B)
    282–3
  government-to-citizen (G2C)   282
  government-to-government (G2G)
    283–4
  privacy and security   290–2
  problems   274–5, 289–93
  stages   279–84
efficiency   51–2, 59–60, 62, 64–6, 68,
    70, 72, 80, 83, 101, 162–3
Egypt   44
eightfold path   110–11
Elcock, H.   219
electronic government   *see* e-government
Eliassen K. and Sitter, R.   325
Elmore, R.   117
employment conditions   6, 229–30,
    241–5
entrepreneurial government   81,
    137–8
environmental scan   211–12, 216–17,
    220
Erridge, A.   154
ethical issues   75, 99–100
Ethiopia   300
evidence-based policy   104, 116–7
external constituency management
    93, 166–84
  in managerial model   166–72,
    176–80, 184
  in traditional model   93, 166–7,
    169–70
  need for external focus   93, 167–9
  press and public   168, 170–1
  problems of managerial model
    180–4
externalities   30, 149–50

fad or fashion   4
Fairholm, M.   238
Farazmand, A.   157
Farnham D.   243–4

Farnham, D. and Horton, S.   10
financial management   92, 250–72
  and accounting reforms   260–1,
    267–8, 271–2
  and performance   251, 265
  devolution of budgets   261–2
  problems of reform   266–72
Financial Management Initiative   198,
    251, 263–4
'files, the'   49
Finer, S.   127
Flynn, N.   8, 10, 79, 93, 268–9
Foster, C.   53
Fountain, J.   14, 181, 275, 278, 283,
    286–7, 324
France   29, 36, 64, 140, 158, 297,
    301
Frederickson, H. G.   16, 123, 125,
    142–3, 185, 317
Friedman, M. and R.   11, 31, 33, 35,
    148, 315
Fry, B.   55, 57
Fukuyama F.   201
Fulton Report   79, 198, 240
functions of general management
    76–8, 168

General Motors   11, 20, 27, 285
generic management   95–6, 101–2
Germany   10, 34, 38–9, 159
Gerth, H. and Mills, C. W.   5, 44,
    48–53, 55, 62, 230, 235–6, 276
Giddens, A.   14
Gillespie, R.   56
Gladden, E.   44, 47
global financial crisis (GFC)   11,
    26–7, 36, 40–1, 132, 145, 147–8,
    157, 160, 254, 269–70
globalization   14
goal displacement   65
Golden Age of public administration
    58–9, 65, 247
Goldsmith S. and Eggers, W.   65,
    176
Goodsell, C.   71, 121, 175
Gore Report   82
governance   2, 3, 16, 20, 26, 76,
    123–43, 176–7
  and government   123–4, 127–9

governance (*cont.*)
  and steering   125–6, 130, 138, 141–3
  as corporate governance   20, 26, 131–2
  as good governance   129–30
  as networks   129, 136–41, 176–7
  as new political economy   131
  as New Public Management   129–30, 132–6, 141–2
  as socio-cybernetic system   129–31
  definition   123–32
  digital era   135
  in international relations   123, 128–30
  not new   123–5
  standard meaning of   124–5, 132, 141–3
  tight and loose   141–2
  usefulness   141–3
government   7–11, 19–42, 81–4, 123–8, 142–5, 204
  and authority   127–8, 142
  and business   144–5, 164–5
  and economics   11, 81–4
  and governance   123–4, 127–9
  as economic problem   11
  basic functions   22–4
  budget *see* budgets
  coercive power   7–8, 22, 127–8
  instruments of   24–8
  loss of power   128–9, 142, 204
  makes a comeback   20, 36–7
  phases in history   32–8
  production   24–5, 27–8, 157–64
  provision   24–5, 27
  role of government   19–42
  size and scope   38–41
  universal membership   22
Gow, J. and Dufour, C.   320
Graham, C. and Hays, S.   59
Grant, R.   210
Grant, W.   182
Gray, A. and Jenkins, B.   198
Greenaway, J.   47
Greenwood, J., Pyper, R. and Wilson, D.   241
Greve, C. and Hodge, G.   155
Grindle, M.   147, 299, 305–6
Gruening, G.   317, 323

Gulick, L. and Urwick, L.   58–9, 61, 238–9
Guthrie, J., Olson, O. and Humphrey, C.   261

Hall, M. and Holt, R.   324
Halligan, J. and Bouckaert, G.   87
Hartley, J. and Skelcher, C.   324, 327
Hawthorne experiments   56–7
Hayek, F.   11
Hax, A. and Majluf, N.   211–13, 217
health care   29, 116
Heeks, R.   135, 273–5, 279, 293
Heeks, R. and Bhatnagar, S.   275
Heifetz, R. and Laurie, D.   236–7
Held, D. *et al.*   14
Hicks, U.   21
hierarchy   59–60, 63–4, 67–8, 278
Hodge, G.   162
Hodge, G., Greve, C. and Boardman, A.   154–6
Holmes, D.   273, 291
Holmes, M. and Shand, D.   10, 35, 91, 96, 99, 206, 296, 317, 321, 334
Hondeghem A.   203
Hogwood, B. and Gunn, L.   105, 109, 114–5
Hong Kong   309
Hood, C.   3, 7, 75, 80–1, 85–9, 99–100, 151, 312, 316–17, 320–3
Hood, C. and Peters, B.   88, 321
Horn, M.   321, 334–5
Horton, S.   81, 246
Hrebenar, R.   182
Hughes, O.   79
Hughes, O. and O'Neill, D.   14, 144, 151
human relations   56–9
human resource management   *see* personnel
Huque, A.   303–4

ideological basis of managerialism   20, 40, 315, 329
imperatives of change   9–15
imperfect information   30–1
impersonal administration   44, 50–2, 91, 234, 240

implementation 100–1
Indonesia 298, 301
informal networks 64–5
information and communication
    technology 15, 84, 100, 135,
    273–94
    see also e-government
infrastructure 22–3, 301–2
Ingraham, P. 232–3, 237–8
input focus of traditional model
    65–6, 256
institutions 146–7, 305–6, 310, 332
instruments of government 24–8,
    157–64
    production 24–5, 157–64
    provision 24–5, 252–3
    regulation 24–6, 144–51
    subsidy 24–5
interest groups 166–84
    and capture 183–4
    as bureaucratic allies 170–1, 173,
    175
    definition 172
    encompassing interests 183
    policy communities 173–4
    problems of reliance 180–4
    special interests 182–3
International Monetary Fund 10, 82,
    129, 296, 305–7
Isaac-Henry, K. Painter, C. and Barnes,
    C. 20
Italy 10

Jackson, A. 45
Jacoby, H. 63
Japan 38–9, 64, 159, 231
Javidan, M. and Waldman, D. 234
Jensen, M. 13, 131
Jensen, M. and Meckling, W. 13,
    187–8
John, P. 111, 113, 115
Jones, L., Guthrie, J. and Steane, P.
    329
Jordan, A. and Maloney, W. 182
Jorgensen, J. 300–1
Joyce, P. 226

Kaboolian, L. 84
Kakar, S. 54

Kamarck, E. 14, 137–9, 157, 262,
    284–5, 331
Kamarck, E. and Nye, J. 292
Kamenka, E. 44, 64
Kanigel, R. 55
Kaunga, E. 301
Kay, J. and Vickers, J. 30
Kearney R. and Hays, S. 329
Keasey, K., Short, H. and Wright, M.
    131
Keating, M. 334
Keeling, D. 79
Kennedy, P. 209
Keohane R. and Nye, J. 123, 126,
    128
Kettl, D. 6–7, 11–12, 15, 46, 54,
    89–90, 103, 129–30, 135, 138–9,
    142, 172, 180–1, 261, 263, 327,
    329, 331–2
Keynesian economics 11, 20, 34, 254,
    297, 318
Kickert, W. 331
Kjaer, A. 125
Klijn, E.-H. and Koppenjan, J. 136
Klijn, E.-H. *et al.* 155
Kooiman, J. 126
Krugman, P. 37, 303
Kuhn, T. 316–8, 320

laissez-faire society 22, 32–4
Lan, Z. and Rosenbloom, D. 80
Lane, J.-E. 71
Lapsley, I. 323, 326
Lasswell, H. D. 109
leadership 2–3, 53, 66, 68, 76,
    128–9, 228–30, 233–40, 248–9
    and bureaucracy 53, 66, 229–30,
    233–4
    and public management 128–9,
    233–40, 248–9
    and traditional model 66, 90–1,
    228–30, 248
    as personal attribute 234–6
    as positional attribute 236–8
Lee, R. and Johnson, R. 258
Left, the 32, 80
Legge, K. 229
Lenk, K. and Traunmüller, R.
    288–9

'let the managers manage'   85, 90,
      200–1
lifetime employment   63–4, 84
Lindblom, C.   118
long-range planning   211, 213
Lynn, L.   15, 48, 69, 105–6, 113, 115,
      117–18, 317, 319–20, 326

Magna Carta   255
management   3–4, 14–15, 24, 61,
      73–8, 84–5, 90–1, 101–2,
      199–200, 228–9, 233, 237–8,
      245–6, 262, 337
   achievement of results   4, 61, 73–6,
      84, 90–1, 199–200, 228–9, 233,
      237–8, 245–6, 262, 337
   and technology   14–15, 135–6,
      275–8, 284–7
   by objectives (MBO)   85
   definition   3–4, 76–8
   external constituency   166–84
   generic   95–6, 101–2
   human resources   *see* personnel
   meaning of   3–4, 76–8
   personal responsibility for results
      4, 61, 73–6, 84, 90–1, 199–200,
      228–9, 233, 237–8, 245–6, 262,
      337
managerial accountability   197–202
managerialism   2–3, 16, 40, 75,
      78–85, 92–102, 307–15, 329–33
   and economics   3, 94–5
   and new contractualism   92–3
   as international movement   331–3
   beginnings   78–83
   criticisms   2–3, 75, 94–102
   ethical problems   75, 99–100
   ideological basis   20, 40, 315, 329
   in developing countries   307–14
   problems   2–3, 75, 94–102
   theoretical basis   7, 83–5
   see also public management, New
      Public Management
managing external constituencies
      77–8, 166–84
   and managerial model   78, 166–7,
      170–2, 176–80, 184
   and traditional model   77–8, 93,
      166–70

coordination   8, 168–9, 171
   need for external focus   93, 167–9
   the press and public   78, 168,
      170–1
managing internal components   77–8
March, J. and Olsen, J.   330
Manion, M.   308–9
Marini, F.   321
market-based public administration
      80
market failure   24, 28–31, 149–50,
      157–9
   externalities   30, 149–50
   imperfect information   30–1
   merit goods   29
   natural monopoly   30, 145, 157–9
   public goods   28–9
market principle   20, 35, 70–1, 137–8
market testing   74, 88
Marxism   33, 295, 318
Mathiasen, D.   317
Mayo, E.   56–7
McCaffery, G.   214, 219, 221
McCraw, T.   22
Meier, K. and Hill, G.   67, 70
Meier, K. and O'Toole, L.   325
mercantilism   32–3
merit goods   29
Merton, R.   65
Michalski, W., Miller, R. and Stevens,
      B.   128
ministerial responsibility   54
Minnowbrook Conference   321
Minogue, M.   202–3, 296, 329
Minogue, M. Polidano, C. and Hulme,
      D.   130
Mintzberg, H.   140, 177, 226
missions and goals of an organization
      211, 216
Monroe, K.   71
Montanari, J., Daneke, G. and Bracker,
      J.   210, 224
Moore, M.   138, 221–3, 265
moral hazard   31
morale problems   100–1
Moran, M., Rein, M. and Goodin, R.
      104
Mosher, F.   45–6, 47
Mozambique   309

Mueller, D. 12
Mulgan, G. 222
Mullins, L. 3
Musgrave, R. and Musgrave, P. 21–2, 28, 252–3

Nagel, S. 109, 119–20
natural monopolies 30, 145, 157–9
neo-classical economics 11, 35–6, 254
neo-Taylorian management 57, 96–7, 324, 329
nepotism 44–5
net benefit maximization 115
Netherlands 99, 140–1
networks 129, 136–41, 174, 176–7, 180–1
neutrality of public servants 53–4, 64, 84, 97–8, 169, 172
new contractualism 92–3
new paradigm *see* paradigm
New Public Management 3, 7, 16, 20, 40, 75, 80–9, 94–102, 129–36, 315–29
   as an alternative paradigm 75, 316, 320–6
   as a tendency 88–9
   as a term 7, 16, 75, 86–8, 134–6
   as governance 129–30, 132–6
   as unvarying model 94
   critics and criticisms 94–102, 321, 325–6
   disaggregation 86
   ethical problems 75, 99–100
   ideological basis 20, 40, 315, 329
   lack of advocacy 321–3
   no agreement on content 75, 86, 89, 134–6
   no theoretical treatise 88, 320–3
   not novel 88, 326
   problems of model 99–100, 134–6, 320–6
   theoretical basis 83–5
   see also managerialism, public management
New Public Governance 135–6, 326
New Public Service 326
New Right ideology 20, 32, 37, 41, 72, 80, 183–4, 329

New Zealand 6, 36, 38–9, 79, 81–2, 87–8, 99, 261, 321–2, 329, 332, 334
   economic crisis 81, 321–2
Newbold, S. and Terry, L. 125
Niskanen, W. 69–71
Norris-Tyrell, D. and Clay, J. 178
North Korea 296
Northcote–Trevelyan Report 46–7, 54, 244
Nutley, S., Davies, H. and Walter, I. 104
Nutley, S., Walter, I. and Davies, H. 104, 116
Nutt, P. and Backoff, R. 214, 216, 219, 221, 225

objective setting 74, 212, 224–5
OECD 38, 41, 82–3, 116–17, 127, 199–200, 234, 237, 247, 251, 259, 264, 270, 317, 326–7, 330–1
   nations 19, 241
'office, the' 49, 228, 276–8, 286–7
office politics 70, 93, 287
O'Leary, R. *et al.* 178
Olsen, J. 69, 71
Olsen, J. and Eadie, D. 214–5
Olson, M. 182–3
'one best way' thinking 5–6, 54–6, 61, 93, 97, 105, 138, 167, 180
organizational behaviour 56–9, 64–9
Osborne, D. and Gaebler, T. 81–2, 133–4, 242, 280, 317, 322–4, 334
Osborne, S. 16, 135, 326
Ostrom, V. 70, 83–4, 137, 318
outcomes 88–9

paradigms 315–37
   defined 316–18
Parsons, W. 104
Patashnik, E. 316
Paterson, J. 334
patrimonialism 2, 50, 230, 235
patronage appointments 44–5
Patton, C. and Sawicki, D. 110, 111, 118
Pendleton Act 47

performance   66, 84, 87, 91–2, 96–7,
    101, 229, 232, 240–1, 245–7,
    251, 259–65, 268–9, 263–4, 333
  appraisal   91–2, 229, 245, 263–4,
    333
  budgets   250–1, 259–62, 271–2
  indicators   88, 91, 96–7, 101, 251,
    263–5, 268–9
  management   84, 87, 91–2, 96–7,
    229, 245–6, 251, 263–5, 268–9;
    in managerial model   85–7,
    91–2, 96–7, 245–6, 251, 263–5,
    268–9; in traditional model   66,
    232
  measurement   66, 84–8, 232,
    263–5, 268–9
  pay   240–1, 246–7
personality in administration   2, 44–5,
    49–50
personnel management   6, 63–6, 84–5,
    92, 101, 229–33, 240–9 263
  change in expectation   247–8
  employment conditions   6, 229–30,
    241–5
  reform   84–5, 92, 101, 229–30,
    240–5
  reform problems   245–9
  retirement schemes   63, 229, 231
  traditional model   64, 66, 231–3,
    248–9, 263
  transition to human resource
    management   229–30, 240–5
Peters, B.   61, 99, 203, 245, 277
Peters, B. and Pierre, J.   133
Peters, T. and Waterman, R.   81
phases of government intervention
    32–8
Pierre, J. and Peters, B.   16, 124–5,
    127, 129, 131, 139–40
pluralism   180, 182–3
policy analysis   103–22
  empirical methods   105–9, 112,
    118–19
  inductive social science   112
  limitations   117–21
  see also public policy
policy communities   171–5
policy instruments   24–8
policy process models   109–11

political control   60–1, 72
political nature of public service   60,
    97–8
political public policy   104, 113–15
politicization   97–8
politics/administration dichotomy
    5–6, 54, 186, 195–7
politics separated from administration
    5–6, 53–4, 59–61, 93, 186,
    195–7, 319
  a myth   6, 60–1, 186, 197
Pollitt, C.   4, 57, 79–80, 88–9, 94–7,
    140, 247, 317, 329, 333
Pollitt, C. *et al.*   243
Pollitt C. and Bouckaert, G.   97, 202,
    204, 245, 267, 316–9, 326, 331,
    334, 336–7
Popper, K.   112
Porter, M.   210
'POSDCORB'   58–9, 238–9
position of the official   50–2
post-bureaucratic paradigm   81
pressure groups   *see* interest groups
principal–agent theory   13, 84, 131–2,
    187–9
Private Finance Initiative   155
private management   7–9, 67–8, 75–6,
    78, 84–6, 162–3, 187–90
  accountability   162–3, 187–90
private sector   7–9, 14, 19–22, 70,
    84–5, 95–6, 145, 162–3, 273,
    278–83
  and corporate failure   20
  and public sector   7–9, 19–22, 70,
    84–5, 95–6, 145
  and technology   273, 278–80, 283
  need for public sector   22, 145,
    162–3
privatization   10, 14, 20, 41, 74, 92,
    144–5, 153–4, 157, 160–4, 302,
    311
  and accountability   163–4
  economic arguments for   160–1
  ideological arguments for   163
  in developing countries   302, 311
  in UK   160, 163
  management arguments for   162–3
procurement   283
production   24–5

programme budgeting   101, 258–60,
   266–7
   advantages   259–60
   criticisms   266–7
promotion by seniority   64, 66, 67,
   92, 232, 240
Pross, P.   171, 173–5
provision   24–5
public administration   1–6, 15–17,
   43–73, 76–7, 80, 84, 102–7,
   128–9, 166–70, 228–33, 237–8,
   256–7, 318–20, 333–7
   and authority   128–9
   and leadership   2, 66, 228–30
   and practitioners   16–17, 333–5
   and public management   3–4, 66
   and public policy   103–7
   and scientific management   55–9
   and strategy   76–7
   as a field of study   15–17, 333–5
   as a paradigm   43–4, 318–20
   definition   3–4, 59
   employment conditions   6, 49
   external constituencies   93, 166–7,
      169–70
   financial management   256–7
   focus on process not results   4, 61,
      73–6, 84, 90–1, 199–200, 228–9,
      233, 237–8, 245–6, 262, 337
   Golden Age   58–9, 65, 247
   impersonal system   2, 49–50, 68,
      230
   input-dominated   65–6, 256
   obsolete   62–4, 72–3, 168, 335–7
   outstanding success   43–4, 72
   performance management   66, 232
   problems of   59–73
   replaced   3, 62, 73, 102, 335–6
   separation from politics   5–6,
      53–4, 59–61, 93, 185–6, 195–7,
      319
   theoretical basis   43, 72
   verities of   4–6, 80
   see also traditional model
public choice theory   12, 61, 69–73,
   84
public enterprise   10, 25, 34, 41, 74,
   92, 144–5, 157–64, 300–2, 311
   control and accountability   163–4

definition   158
developing countries   300–2, 311
kinds of   158–60
management efficiency   162–3
management problems   164
privatization   10, 14, 20, 41, 74,
   92, 144–5, 153–4, 157, 160–4,
   302, 311
reasons for establishing   157–8
public goods   23, 28–9, 70
public interest, the   5, 12, 82–3, 151
public management   1–9, 19–21, 61,
   74–102, 128–9, 197–202, 205–7,
   228–40, 245–6, 262, 315–37
   accountability   90, 93, 98, 101,
      197–202, 205–7
   an international movement   331–3
   and authority   128–9
   and democracy   101, 330–1
   and economics   3, 75, 82–4, 95
   and e-government   287–9
   and leadership   66, 233–40
   and new contractualism   92–3
   personal responsibility for results
      4, 61, 73–6, 84, 90–2, 200–1,
      228–30, 233, 237–8, 245–6, 262,
      337
   and private management   4, 7–9,
      19–21, 75–6, 84–5, 95–6
   and strategy   208–9
   as a discipline   9, 15–17, 75, 333–5
   as paradigm   75–6, 83, 315–37
   beginnings of   78–83
   client focus   90, 93, 139, 172,
      199–202, 282
   compared with traditional model
      74, 82–3, 101–2
   criticisms   2–3, 75, 94–102
   definition   3–4
   different from New Public
      Management   327
   direct accountability in   186,
      198–202, 205–7
   ethical problems   75, 99–100
   external constituencies   166–80
   flexibility   85, 92, 248
   ideological basis   20, 40, 315,
      329
   in developing countries   295–314

public management (*cont.*)
  morale problems   100–1, 244–5,
    247–8
  performance measurement   66,
    84–8, 232, 263–5, 268–9
  political commitment by managers
    93
  politicization   97–8
  problems of model   2–3, 75,
    94–102
  productivity   89–90
  programme budgeting   101,
    258–60
  theoretical basis   7, 83–5
  see also managerialism
public policy   3–4, 15–16, 103–22,
    137
  and decisions   108–9, 117, 121
  and networks   137
  and public management   106–7,
    115
  and political science   106–7
  and public administration   103–7,
    117, 121–2
  as paradigm   105
  as political process   113–5
  as separate discipline   119–21
  definition   3–4, 104–7
  economics and   103–5, 107,
    111–13, 121–2
  empirical methods   105–6, 108–9,
    112, 118–9
  evidence-based   104, 116–17
  inductive social science   112,
    118–19
  limitations   111, 117–21
  output of government   16, 106
  process models   109–11
public–private partnerships (PPPs)
    145, 154–7, 163
public sector   7–9, 19–42, 70, 84–96,
    127–8, 145, 304–9
  and private sector   7–9, 19–22, 70,
    84–5, 95–6, 145
  change imperatives   9–15
  coercive basis   7–8, 22, 127–8
  definition   21–2
  reform   6–9, 89–94, 304–9
  role   19–42

  size and scope   38–41
  uniqueness   95–6
public service anonymity and neutrality
    53–4, 64, 84, 84, 97, 172
public utilities   *see* natural monopoly
public value   176, 186, 221–3
purchasing offices   44–5
purchaser and provider   *see* 'steering
    not rowing'
Pusey, M.   11, 35
Putt, A. and Springer, J.   105, 108,
    112, 118

Quade, E.   105–6

Rainey, H.   121
Ranson, S. and Stewart, J.   10
rationality   35, 69, 113, 118–9
rational/legal authority   48, 69, 304,
    319
Reagan government in USA   10, 20,
    35–6, 72, 329
Rees, R.   157–8
regulation   23, 25–7, 30, 144–51,
    164–5, 183–4
  and deregulation   151
  defined   25–6, 145–6
  economic   26, 145–51
  enforcement of contracts   146–7
  environmental   23, 149–50
  financial   147–8
  property rights   146–7
  responsive   150–1
  social   26, 145–6
regulation of competition   *see*
    competition policy
Rehfuss, J.   153
re-inventing government   81–2
responsibility   *see* accountability
responsiveness   172
results focus   4, 61, 73–6, 84, 90–2,
    200–1, 228–30, 233, 237–8,
    245–6, 262, 337
Rhodes, R.   81, 124, 127, 133, 136–7,
    141, 176, 324
Rhodes, R. and Wanna, J.   222–3
Richardson, J. and Jordan, A.   173–4
Right, the   20, 32, 37, 41, 72, 80,
    183–4, 329
Ritter, G.   34

role of government   19–42, 149–50,
     297–8, 304–7
  collective goods and services   23
  duties of the sovereign   32–3
  economic infrastructure   23
  in developing countries   297–8,
     304–7
  maintenance of competition   23
  natural resource protection   23, 30,
     149–50
  stabilization of the economy   24
Romzek, B.   45, 192–4, 205
Rose, R. and Peters, B.   38
Rose-Ackerman, S.   312
Rosenau, J.   123–4, 127, 130–1
Rosenbloom, D.   15
Rubin, I. and Kelly, J.   334
Rugge, F.   89, 328

Salamon, L.   26, 176–7
Sarbanes–Oxley Act   26, 132, 147
Savas, E.   74, 133, 151, 162
Schachter, H.   56–8
Schedler, K. *et al.*   326, 335
Schelling, T.   210
Schick, A.   322
scientific management   5, 54–8, 61,
     297, 319
  a continuing debate   57–8
  government and   55–6
  reinterpretation   57–8
Scott, G.   81, 321–2, 334–5
secrecy   62–3, 292
Self, P.   12
Seneviratne, S.   277
Senior Executive Service   79
seniority   64, 66–7, 92, 232, 240
separation of politics and
     administration   5–6, 53–4,
     59–61, 93, 186, 195–7, 319
service delivery   68, 72, 101, 168,
     240–1, 243
service orientation   *see* client focus
Simon, H.   115, 118
Singapore   281
size of government   38–41
Skelcher, C.   154, 156
Smith, Adam   22, 32–3, 35, 70
Smith, B.   298–300

Smith, S.   151
socialism   20, 34, 158, 295, 298
Spain   10
Spann, R.   4
Sparrow, M.   120–1, 150–1
spoils system   45–7, 60
stabilization of economy   254
stakeholders   93, 98, 166–84
Stark, A.   323
statistics   108
'steering not rowing'   74, 133–4, 151
Stigler, G.   11, 31, 182–3
Stiglitz, J.   22, 147, 161, 307
Stillman, R.   56, 58
Stokey, E. and Zeckhauser, R.
     109–10
strategic management   91, 208–27
  difference from planning   212–13,
     219–21
  implementation   218, 220–1
  stakeholders   220–1
strategic planning models   91, 101,
     211–12, 214–19
  defined   214–15
  limitations   212, 218–19
strategy   76–7, 91–2, 209–10, 221–3
  and public value   221–3
strategy in private sector   210–13
strategy in public sector   208–27
  criticisms   223–6
  environmental scan   216–17
  in managerial model   219–27
  in traditional mode   208–9
  not a panacea   226–7
subsidy   25
Sweden   10, 38–40
Szymanski, S.   153

Talbot, C.   264
Tanzania   298, 300
Tarschys, D.   141–2
Taylor, F.   5, 54–9, 61, 96–7, 138,
     141, 297, 318
technological change   14–15
Terry, L.   330
Thaler, R. and Sunstein, C.   70, 94
Thatcher government in UK   10, 20,
     27, 35–6, 72, 79, 81, 160, 163,
     198, 329

third party government   177
Thompson, F.   262
time-and-motion studies   55–6
Toft, G.   212–3, 221
tools of government   26
traditional model of administration
        1–9, 43–73, 105, 167–70, 192–7,
        228–34, 256, 296–303, 315–20,
        335–7
    accountability   60–1, 192–7, 205
    and leadership   2, 66, 228–30,
        233–4
    and public policy   105
    and scientific management   54–9
    and technology   275–8
    as paradigm   43–4, 318–20
    external constituencies   167–70
    financial management   256–7
    in developing countries   296–303
    input focus   65–6, 256
    obsolescence   1–3, 62–4, 72–3,
        168, 335–7
    outstanding success   44, 72
    performance management   66,
        232
    personnel management   63–4, 66,
        84–5, 228, 230–3
    problems of   59–74
    reform movement   43, 46–8
    replacement   2–3, 72, 76, 80, 315,
        335–7
    theoretical basis   43, 72
    see also public administration
transaction costs   13–14, 84, 98,
        152
Truman, D.   182
trust   201–2
Turner, M. and Hulme, D.   298,
        301–4, 313

Uhrig, J.   158
United Kingdom   6, 10, 20, 27, 29,
        33–4, 36, 38, 41, 46–8, 54, 72,
        79, 81–2, 86–7, 99, 104, 116,
        132, 141, 153, 155–8, 160, 194,
        198, 232, 240, 244, 251, 255,
        263–4, 270, 280, 297, 301,
        329
    accountability   54

Blair government   36
Cameron government   36, 41,
        141
FMI   251, 263–4
Fulton Report   79, 198, 240
Next Steps   99, 104
Northcote-Trevelyan Report   46–7,
        54, 244
Thatcher government   10, 20, 27,
        35–6, 72, 79, 81, 160, 163, 198,
        329
United States   6, 10, 20, 25–7, 29,
        34–41, 45–7, 60, 72, 79, 81–2,
        97–8, 132, 147, 149, 159, 169,
        181, 194–5, 197–9, 232–3,
        240–1, 255–6, 258, 280, 329
    accountability   60, 194–5, 197–9
    budgeting   38–40, 255–6, 258
    civil service   232–3
    Civil Service Reform Act   79,
        240–1
    political appointees   46
    Reagan government   10, 20, 35–6,
        72, 329
    Sarbanes–Oxley   26, 132, 147
    spoils system   45–7, 60

Van Dooren, W., Bouckaert, G. and
        Halligan, J.   265, 269–70
Van Thiel, S., Pollitt, C. and Homburg,
        V.   324–5
Vecchio, R.   66
Vickers, J. and Yarrow, G.   13, 189
Volberda, H.   66

Walsh, K.   11–12, 31, 84
Weber, M.   1–2, 5, 43–73, 196,
        230–1, 233, 235–6, 244, 276–7,
        295, 297, 299, 302, 304, 318
    and scientific management   55
Weberian bureaucracy   1, 43–73, 84,
        230
Weimer, D. and Vining, A.   113
welfare state   33–5
White, L.   45
Wildavsky, A.   252, 266, 271
Wilenski, P.   256
Willamson, O.   13–14, 98, 125,
        152

Wilson, G.   167–8, 172, 175, 182
Wilson, Woodrow   5, 47–8, 53–4,
   59–61, 186, 318–19
World Bank   10, 22, 82, 125, 129–30,
   290, 296–7, 304–8, 310–12

Yeager, T.   306
Yong, J.   284

Zambia   301
Zifcak, S.   232, 251

Printed and bound by CPI Group (UK) Ltd, Croydon, CR0 4YY